HARDPRESS.NET
HOME OF HARD-TO-FIND BOOKS

Novels and Tales
by Johann Wolfgang von Goethe

Address:
HardPress
8345 NW 66TH ST #2561
MIAMI FL 33166-2626
USA
Email: info@hardpress.net

BOHN'S STANDARD LIBRARY.

NOVELS AND TALES,

BY

GÖETHE.

NOVELS AND TALES,

BY

GÖETHE.

ELECTIVE AFFINITIES;

THE SORROWS OF WERTHER; GERMAN

EMIGRANTS; THE 'GOOD WOMEN;

AND A NOUVELETTE,

TRANSLATED CHIEFLY BY R. D. BOYLAN, ESQ.

LONDON:
HENRY G. BOHN, YORK STREET, COVENT GARDEN.
1854.

PRINTED BY HARRISON AND SONS,
LONDON GAZETTE OFFICE, ST. MARTIN'S LANE.

PREFACE.

———•———

THE works of Goethe, comprised in the present volume, are entirely new translations, made expressly for the series of German Classical Works, which find their place from time to time in the "Standard Library." The "Elective Affinities" has been executed by a gentleman well known in the literary world, who does not wish his name to appear. It is possible that exceptions may be taken to some of the statements contained in this production of Goethe. But to use the language of Carlyle, "Fidelity is all the merit a translator need aim at, to convey the author's sentiments as he himself expressed them, and to follow the original in all its variations. In many points, it were to be wished that Goethe had not so written; but to alter anything is not in the translator's commission. The literary and moral persuasions of a man like Goethe, are objects of a rational curiosity, and the duty of a translator is simple and distinct." The same observations will apply with equal force to many of the sentiments which pervade the second tale in this volume, the "Sorrows of Werther."

It is somewhat remarkable that the "Sorrows of Werther," notwithstanding its great popularity, has never before been translated directly from the German into the English language. The translation by which the work has become familiarized in this country, was made from the French, a medium wholly incapable of maintaining the vigorous strength of the original. Well may it be styled "a faint and garbled version," by a competent authority, who farther observes: "That the German Werther is a very different person from his English namesake. His sorrows in the original are recorded in a tone of strength and sarcastic emphasis, of which the other offers no vestige, and intermingled with touches of painful thought, glimpses of a philosophy deep as it is bitter, which our sagacious translator has seen proper wholly to omit." The story of Werther is known to be the narration of an actual fact which happened within the knowledge of the author; and though it has been sometimes affirmed that Goethe subsequently smiled at this performance of his youth, yet he has left on record an account of his own state of mind during its composition, which is well worthy of perusal. "The resolution," says Goethe, "to preserve my internal nature according to its peculiarities, and to let external nature influence me according to its qualities, impelled me to the strange element in which "Werther" is designed and written. I sought to free myself internally from all that was foreign to me, to regard the external with love, and to allow all beings, from man downwards, as long as they were comprehensible, to act upon me, each after its own kind. Thus arose a wonderful affinity with the single objects of nature, and a hearty concord, a harmony with the whole, so that every change, whether of place and region, or of the day and year, or whatever else could happen, affected me in the deepest manner. The glance of the painter associated itself to that of the poet, the beautiful rural landscape, animated by the pleasant river, increased my love of solitude, and favoured my silent observations as they extended on all sides."

The tales with which the volume concludes, are in point of date almost contemporaneous with "Werther," and though slight in their structure, bear "indubitable traces of the greatest genius of modern times."

The entire volume, excepting the "Affinities," has been translated by R. D. Boylan, Esq., who is favourably known to the readers of the "Standard Library," by his version of Schiller's "Don Carlos."

H. G. B.

CONTENTS.

———◆———

ELECTIVE AFFINITIES.

PART I.

———•———

CHAPTER I.

EDWARD—so we shall call a wealthy nobleman in the prime of life—had been spending several hours of a fine April morning in his nursery-garden, budding the stems of some young trees with cuttings which had been recently sent to him. He had finished what he was about, and having laid his tools together in their box, was complacently surveying his work, when the gardener came up and complimented his master on his industry.

"Have you seen my wife anywhere?" inquired Edward, as he moved to go away.

"My lady is alone yonder in the new grounds," said the man; "the summer-house which she has been making on the rock over against the castle is finished to-day, and really it is beautiful. It cannot fail to please your grace. The view from it is perfect:—the village at your feet; a little to your right the church, with its tower, which you can just see over; and directly opposite you, the castle and the garden."

"Quite true," replied Edward; "I can see the people at work a few steps from where I am standing."

"And then, to the right of the church again," continued the gardener, "is the opening of the valley; and you look along over a range of wood and meadow far into the distance. The steps up the rock, too, are excellently arranged. My gracious lady understands these things; it is a pleasure to work under her."

B

"Go to her," said Edward, "and desire her to be so good as to wait for me there. Tell her I wish to see this new creation of hers, and enjoy it with her."

The gardener went rapidly off, and Edward soon followed. Descending the terrace, and stopping as he passed to look into the hot-houses and the forcing-pits, he came presently to the stream, and thence, over a narrow bridge, to a place where the walk leading to the summer-house branched off in two directions. One path led across the churchyard, immediately up the face of the rock. The other, into which he struck, wound away to the left, with a more gradual ascent, through a pretty shrubbery. Where the two paths joined again, a seat had been made, where he stopped a few moments to rest; and then, following the now single road, he found himself, after scrambling along among steps and slopes of all sorts and kinds, conducted at last through a narrow more or less steep outlet to the summer-house.

Charlotte was standing at the door to receive her husband. She made him sit down where, without moving, he could command a view of the different landscapes through the door and window—these serving as frames, in which they were set like pictures. Spring was coming on; a rich, beautiful life would soon everywhere be bursting; and Edward spoke of it with delight.

"There is only one thing which I should observe," he added, "the summer-house itself is rather small."

"It is large enough for you and me, at any rate," answered Charlotte.

"Certainly," said Edward; "there is room for a third, too, easily."

"Of course; and for a fourth also," replied Charlotte. "For larger parties we can contrive other places."

"Now that we are here by ourselves, with no one to disturb us, and in such a pleasant mood," said Edward, "it is a good opportunity for me to tell you that I have for some time had something on my mind, about which I have wished to speak to you, but have never been able to muster up my courage."

"I have observed that there has been something of the sort," said Charlotte.

"And even now," Edward went on, "if it were not for a

letter which the post brought me this morning, and which obliges me to come to some resolution to-day, I should very likely have still kept it to myself."

"What is it, then?" asked Charlotte, turning affectionately towards him.

"It concerns our friend the Captain," answered Edward; "you know the unfortunate position in which he, like many others, is placed. It is through no fault of his own; but you may imagine how painful it must be for a person with his knowledge and talents and accomplishments, to find himself without employment. I—I will not hesitate any longer with what I am wishing for him. I should like to have him here with us for a time."

"We must think about that," replied Charlotte; "it should be considered on more sides than one."

"I am quite ready to tell you what I have in view," returned Edward. "Through his last letters there is a prevailing tone of despondency; not that he is really in any want. He knows thoroughly well how to limit his expenses; and I have taken care for everything absolutely necessary. It is no distress to him to accept obligations from me; all our lives we have been in the habit of borrowing from and lending to each other; and we could not tell, if we would, how our debtor and creditor account stands. It is being without occupation which is really fretting him. The many accomplishments which he has cultivated in himself, it is his only pleasure—indeed, it is his passion—to be daily and hourly exercising for the benefit of others. And now, to sit still, with his arms folded; or to go on studying, acquiring, and acquiring, when he can make no use of what he already possesses;—my dear creature, it is a painful situation; and alone as he is, he feels it doubly and trebly."

"But I thought," said Charlotte, "that he had had offers from many different quarters. I myself wrote to numbers of my own friends, male and female, for him; and, as I have reason to believe, not without effect."

"It is true," replied Edward; "but these very offers—these various proposals—have only caused him fresh embarrassment. Not one of them is at all suitable to such a person as he is. He would have nothing to do; he would have to sacrifice himself, his time, his purposes, his whole method of life; and to that he cannot bring himself. The more I think of it all, the more I feel about it, and the more anxious I am to see him here with us."

" It is very beautiful and amiable in you," answered Charlotte, "to enter with so much sympathy into your friend's position; only you must allow me to ask you to think of yourself and of me, as well."

" I have done that," replied Edward. "For ourselves, we can have nothing to expect from his presence with us, except pleasure and advantage. I will say nothing of the expense. In any case, if he came to us, it would be but small; and you know he will be of no inconvenience to us at all. He can have his own rooms in the right wing of the castle, and everything else can be arranged as simply as possible. What shall we not be thus doing for him! and how agreeable and how profitable may not his society prove to us! I have long been wishing for a plan of the property and the grounds. He will see to it, and get it made. You intend yourself to take the management of the estate, as soon as our present steward's term is expired; and that, you know, is a serious thing. His various information will be of immense benefit to us; I feel only too acutely how much I require a person of this kind. The country people have knowledge enough, but their way of imparting it is confused, and not always honest. The students from the towns and universities are sufficiently clever and orderly, but they are deficient in personal experience. From my friend, I can promise myself both knowledge and method, and hundreds of other circumstances I can easily conceive arising, affecting you as well as me, and from which I can foresee innumerable advantages. Thank you for so patiently listening to me. Now, do you say what you think, and say it out freely and fully; I will not interrupt you."

" Very well," replied Charlotte; " I will begin at once with a general observation. Men think most of the immediate—the present; and rightly, their calling being to do and to work. Women, on the other hand, more of how things hang together in life; and that rightly too, because their destiny—the destiny of their families—is bound up in this interdependence, and it is exactly this which it is their mission to promote. So now let us cast a glance at our present and our past life; and you will acknowledge that the invitation of the Captain does not fall in so entirely with our purposes, our plans, and our arrangements. I will go back to those happy days of our earliest intercourse. We loved each other, young as we then were, with all our hearts. We were parted: you from me—your father, from an insatiable desire of wealth, choosing to marry you to an elderly and rich lady; I from you, having to give my hand, without any especial motive, to an excellent man, whom I respected, if I did not love. We became again free—you first, your poor mother at the same time leaving you in possession of your large fortune; I later, just at the time when you returned from abroad. So we met once more. We spoke of the past; we could enjoy and love the recollection of it; we might have been contented, in each other's society, to leave things as they were. You were urgent for our marriage. I at first hesitated. We were about the same age; but I as a woman had grown older than you as a man. At last I could not refuse you what you seemed to think the one thing you cared for. All the discomfort which you had ever experienced, at court, in the army, or in travelling, you were to recover from at my side; you would settle down and enjoy life; but only with me for your companion. I settled my daughter at a school, where she could be more completely educated than would be possible in the retirement of the country; and I placed my niece Ottilie there with her as well, who, perhaps, would have grown up better at home with me, under my own care. This was done with your consent, merely that we might have our own lives to ourselves—merely that we might enjoy undisturbed our so-long-wished-for, so-long-delayed happiness. We came here and settled ourselves. I undertook the domestic part of the ménage, you the out-of-doors, and the general control. My own principle has been to meet your wishes in everything, to live only for you. At least, let us give ourselves a fair trial how far in this way we can be enough for one another.''

" Since the interdependence of things, as you call it, is your especial element," replied Edward, " one should either never listen to any of your trains of reasoning, or make up one's mind to allow you to be in the right; and, indeed, you have been in the right up to the present day. The foundation which we have hitherto been laying for ourselves, is of the true, sound sort; only, are we to build nothing upon it? is nothing to be developed out of it? All the work we have done—I in the garden, you in the park—is it all only for a pair of hermits?"

"Well, well," replied Charlotte, "very well. What we have to look to is, that we introduce no alien element, nothing which shall cross or obstruct us. Remember, our plans, even those which only concern our amusements, depend mainly on our being together. You were to read to me, in consecutive order, the journal which you made when you were abroad. You were to take the opportunity of arranging it, putting all the loose matter connected with it in its place; and with me to work with you and help you, out of these invaluable but chaotic leaves and sheets to put together a complete thing, which should give pleasure to ourselves and to others. I promised to assist you in transcribing; and we thought it would be so pleasant, so delightful, so charming, to travel over in recollection the world which we were unable to see together. The beginning is already made. Then, in the evenings, you have taken up your flute again, accompanying me on the piano, while of visits backwards and forwards among the neighbourhood, there is abundance. For my part, I have been promising myself out of all this the first really happy summer I have ever thought to spend in my life."

"Only I cannot see," replied Edward, rubbing his forehead, "how, through every bit of this which you have been so sweetly and so sensibly laying before me, the Captain's presence can be any interruption; I should rather have thought it would give it all fresh zest and life. He was my companion during a part of my travels. He made many observations from a different point of view from mine. We can put it all together, and so make a charmingly complete work of it."

"Well, then, I will acknowledge openly," answered Charlotte, with some impatience, "my feeling is against this plan. I have an instinct which tells me no good will come of it."

"You women are invincible in this way," replied Edward. "You are so sensible, that there is no answering you, then so affectionate, that one is glad to give way to you; full of feelings, which one cannot wound, and full of forebodings, which terrify one."

" I am not superstitious," said Charlotte; " and I care nothing for these dim sensations, merely as such; but in general they are the result of unconscious recollections of happy or unhappy consequences, which we have experienced as following on our own or others' actions. Nothing is of greater moment, in any state of things, than the intervention of a third person. I have seen friends, brothers and sisters, lovers, husbands and wives, whose relation to each other, through the accidental or intentional introduction of a third person, has been altogether changed—whose whole moral condition has been inverted by it."

" That may very well be," replied Edward, " with people who live on without looking where they are going; but not, surely, with persons whom experience has taught to understand themselves."

" That understanding ourselves, my dearest husband," insisted Charlotte, " is no such certain weapon. It is very often a most dangerous one for the person who bears it. And out of all this, at least so much seems to arise, that we should not be in too great a hurry. Let me have a few days to think; don't decide."

" As the matter stands," returned Edward, " wait as many days as we will, we shall still be in too great a hurry. The arguments for and against are all before us; all we want is the conclusion, and as things are, I think the best thing we can do is to draw lots."

" I know," said Charlotte, " that in doubtful cases it is your way to leave them to chance. To me, in such a serious matter, this seems almost a crime."

" Then what am I to write to the Captain?" cried Edward; " for write I must at once."

" Write him a kind, sensible, sympathising letter," answered Charlotte.

" That is as good as none at all," replied Edward.

" And there are many cases," answered she, " in which we are obliged, and in which it is the real kindness, rather to write nothing than not to write."

CHAPTER II.

EDWARD was alone in his room.   The repetition of the
incidents of his life from Charlotte's lips; the representation
of their mutual situation, their mutual purposes; had worked
him, sensitive as he was, into a very pleasant state of mind.
While close to her—while in her presence—he had felt so
happy, that he had thought out a warm, kind, but quiet and
indefinite epistle which he would send to the Captain.
When, however, he had settled himself at his writing-table,
and taken up his friend's letter to read it over once more, the
sad condition of this excellent man rose again vividly before
him.   The feelings which had been all day distressing him
again awoke, and it appeared impossible to him to leave one
whom he called his friend in such painful embarrassment.

Edward was unaccustomed to deny himself anything.   The
only child, and consequently the spoilt child, of wealthy
parents, who had persuaded him into a singular, but highly
advantageous marriage with a lady far older than himself;
and again by her petted and indulged in every possible way,
she seeking to reward his kindness to her by the utmost
liberality; after her early death his own master, travelling
independently of every one, equal to all contingencies and all
changes, with desires never excessive, but multiple and
various—free-hearted, generous, brave, at times even noble—
what was there in the world to cross or thwart him?

Hitherto, everything had gone as he desired!   Charlotte
had become his; he had won her at last, with an obstinate, a
romantic fidelity; and now he felt himself, for the first time,
contradicted, crossed in his wishes, when those wishes were
to invite to his home the friend of his youth—just as he was
longing, as it were, to throw open his whole heart to him.
He felt annoyed, impatient; he took up his pen again and
again, and as often threw it down again, because he could not
make up his mind what to write.   Against his wife's wishes
he would not go; against her expressed desire he could not.
Ill at ease as he was, it would have been impossible for him,
even if he had wished, to write a quiet, easy letter.   The
most natural thing to do, was to put it off.   In a few words,
he begged his friend to forgive him for having left his letter

unanswered; that day he was unable to write circumstantially; but shortly, he hoped to be able to tell him what he felt at greater length.

The next day, as they were walking to the same spot, Charlotte took the opportunity of bringing back the conversation to the subject, perhaps because she knew that there is no surer way of rooting out any plan or purpose, than by often talking it over.

It was what Edward was wishing. He expressed himself in his own way, kindly and sweetly. For although, sensitive as he was, he flamed up readily—although the vehemence with which he desired anything made him pressing, and his obstinacy made him impatient—his words were so softened by his wish to spare the feelings of those to whom he was speaking, that it was impossible not to be charmed, even when one most disagreed, with him.

This morning, he first contrived to bring Charlotte into the happiest humour, and then so disarmed her with the graceful turn which he gave to the conversation, that she cried out at last:

"You are determined that what I refused to the husband you will make me grant to the lover. At least, my dearest," she continued, "I will acknowledge that your wishes, and the warmth and sweetness with which you express them, have not left me untouched, have not left me unmoved. You drive me to make a confession;—till now, I too have had a concealment from you; I am in exactly the same position with you, and I have hitherto been putting the same restraint on my inclination which I have been exhorting you to put on yours."

"Glad am I to hear that," said Edward. "In the married state, a difference of opinion now and then, I see, is no bad thing; we learn something of one another by it."

"You are to learn at present, then," said Charlotte, "that it is with me about Ottilie as it is with you about the Captain. The dear child is most uncomfortable at the school, and I am thoroughly uneasy about her. Luciana, my daughter, born as she is for the world, is there training hourly for the world; languages, history, everything that is taught there, she acquires with so much ease that, as it were, she learns them off at sight. She has quick natural gifts, and an excellent memory; one may almost say she forgets everything, and in

a moment calls it all back again.   She distinguishes herself
above every one at the school with the freedom of her carriage, the grace of her movement, and the elegance of her
address, and with the inborn royalty of nature makes herself the queen of the little circle there.   The superior of
the establishment regards her as a little divinity, who,
under her hands, is shaping into excellence, and who will
do her honour, gain her reputation, and bring her a large
increase of pupils ; the first pages of this good lady's letters,
and her monthly notices of progress, are for ever hymns about
the excellence of such a child, which I have to translate into
my own prose ; while her concluding sentences about Ottilie
are nothing but excuse after excuse—attempts at explaining
how it can be that a girl in other respects growing up so
lovely seems coming to nothing, and shows neither capacity
nor accomplishment.   This, and the little she has to say
besides, is no riddle to me, because I can see in this dear
child the same character as that of her mother, who was my
own dearest friend ; who grew up with myself, and whose
daughter, I am certain, if I had the care of her education,
would form into an exquisite creature.

" This, however, has not fallen in with our plan, and as one
ought not to be picking and pulling, or for ever introducing
new elements among the conditions of our life, I think it
better to bear, and to conquer as I can, even the unpleasant
impression that my daughter, who knows very well that
poor Ottilie is entirely dependent upon us, does not refrain
from flourishing her own successes in her face, and so, to a
certain extent, destroys the little good which we have done
for her.   Who are well trained enough never to wound
others by a parade of their own advantages ? and who stands
so high as not at times to suffer under such a slight ?   In
trials like these, Ottilie's character is growing in strength,
but since I have clearly known the painfulness of her situation, I have been thinking over all possible ways to make some
other arrangement.   Every hour I am expecting an answer
to my own last letter, and then I do not mean to hesitate any
more.   So, my dear Edward, it is with me.   We have both,
you see, the same sorrows to bear, touching both our hearts
in the same point.   Let us bear them together, since we
neither of us can press our own against the other."

"We are strange creatures," said Edward, smiling. "If we can only put out of sight anything which troubles us, we fancy at once we have got rid of it. We can give up much in the large and general; but to make sacrifices in little things is a demand to which we are rarely equal. So it was with my mother,—as long as I lived with her, while a boy and a young man, she could not bear to let me be a moment out of her sight. If I was out later than usual in my ride, some misfortune must have happened to me. If I got wet through in a shower, a fever was inevitable. I travelled; I was absent from her altogether; and, at once, I scarcely seemed to belong to her. If we look at it closer," he continued, "we are both acting very foolishly, very culpably. Two very noble natures, both of which have the closest claims on our affection, we are leaving exposed to pain and distress, merely to avoid exposing ourselves to a chance of danger. If this is not to be called selfish, what is? You take Ottilie. Let me have the Captain; and, for a short period, at least, let the trial be made."

"We might venture it," said Charlotte, thoughtfully, "if the danger were only to ourselves. But do you think it prudent to bring Ottilie and the Captain into a situation where they must necessarily be so closely intimate; the Captain, a man no older than yourself, of an age (I am not saying this to flatter you) when a man becomes first capable of love and first deserving of it, and a girl of Ottilie's attractiveness?"

"I cannot conceive how you can rate Ottilie so high," replied Edward. "I can only explain it to myself by supposing her to have inherited your affection for her mother. Pretty she is, no doubt. I remember the Captain observing it to me, when we came back last year, and met her at your aunt's. Attractive she is,—she has particularly pretty eyes; but I do not know that she made the slightest impression upon me."

"That was quite proper in you," said Charlotte, "seeing that I was there; and, although she is much younger than I, the presence of your old friend had so many charms for you, that you overlooked the promise of the opening beauty. It is one of your ways; and that is one reason why it is so pleasant to live with you."

Charlotte, openly as she appeared to be speaking, was

keeping back something, nevertheless; which was that at the time when Edward came first back from abroad, she had purposely thrown Ottilie in his way, to secure, if possible, so desirable a match for her protégée. For of herself, at that time, in connection with Edward, she never thought at all. The Captain, also, had a hint given to him to draw Edward's attention to her; but the latter, who was clinging determinately to his early affection for Charlotte, looked neither right nor left, and was only happy in the feeling that it was at last within his power to obtain for himself the one happiness which he so earnestly desired; and which a series of incidents had appeared to have placed for ever beyond his reach.

They were on the point of descending the new grounds, in order to return to the castle, when a servant came hastily to meet them, and, with a laugh on his face, called up from below, " Will your grace be pleased to come quickly to the castle? The Herr Mittler has just galloped into the court. He shouted to us, to go all of us in search of you, and we were to ask whether there was need, ' whether there is need,' he cried after us, ' do you hear? but be quick, be quick.' "

" The odd fellow," exclaimed Edward.   " But has he not come at the right time, Charlotte? Tell him, there is need, —grievous need. He must alight. See his horse taken care of. Take him into the saloon, and let him have some luncheon. We shall be with him immediately."

" Let us take the nearest way," he said to his wife, and struck into the path across the churchyard, which he usually avoided.   He was not a little surprised to find here, too, traces of Charlotte's delicate hand. Sparing, as far as possible, the old monuments, she had contrived to level it, and lay it carefully out, so as to make it appear a pleasant spot on which the eye and the imagination could equally repose with pleasure. The oldest stones had each their special honour assigned them. They were ranged according to their dates along the wall, either leaning against it, or let into it, or however it could be contrived; and the string-course of the church was thus variously ornamented.

Edward was singularly affected as he came in upon it through the little wicket; he pressed Charlotte's hand, and tears started into his eyes. But these were very soon put to flight, by the appearance of their singular visitor. This gentleman had declined sitting down in the castle; he had ridden straight through the village to the churchyard gate; and then, halting, he called out to his friends, "Are you not making a fool of me? Is there need, really? If there is, I can stay till mid-day. But don't keep me. I have a great deal to do before night."

"Since you have taken the trouble to come so far," cried Edward to him, in answer, "you had better come through the gate. We meet at a solemn spot. Come and see the variety which Charlotte has thrown over its sadness."

"Inside there," called out the rider, "come I neither on horseback, nor in carriage, nor on foot. These here rest in peace: with them I have nothing to do. One day I shall be carried in feet foremost. I must bear that as I can.—Is it serious, I want to know?"

"Indeed it is," cried Charlotte, "right serious. For the first time in our married lives, we are in a strait and difficulty, from which we do not know how to extricate ourselves."

"You do not look as if it were so," answered he. "But I will believe you. If you are deceiving me, for the future you shall help yourselves. Follow me quickly, my horse will be none the worse for a rest."

The three speedily found themselves in the saloon together. Luncheon was brought in, and Mittler told them what that day he had done, and was going to do. This eccentric person had in early life been a clergyman, and had distinguished himself in his office by the never-resting activity with which he contrived to make up and put an end to quarrels; quarrels in families, and quarrels between neighbours; first among the individuals immediately about him, and afterwards among whole congregations, and among the country gentlemen round. While he was in the ministry, no married couple were allowed to separate; and the district courts were untroubled with either cause or process. A knowledge of the law, he was well aware, was necessary to him. He gave himself with all his might to the study of it, and very soon felt himself a match for the best trained advocate. His circle of activity extended wonderfully, and people were on the point of inducing him to move to the

Residence, where he would find opportunities of exercising in the higher circles what he had begun in the lowest, when he won a considerable sum of money in a lottery. With this, he bought himself a small property. He let the ground to a tenant, and made it the centre of his operations, with the fixed determination, or rather in accordance with his old customs and inclinations, never to enter a house when there was no dispute to make up, and no help to be given. People who were superstitious about names, and about what they imported, maintained that it was his being called Mittler which drove him to take upon himself this strange employment.

Luncheon was laid on the table, and the stranger then solemnly pressed his host not to wait any longer with the disclosure which he had to make. Immediately after refreshing himself he would be obliged to leave them.

Husband and wife made a circumstantial confession; but scarcely had he caught the substance of the matter, when he started angrily up from the table, rushed out of the saloon, and ordered his horse to be saddled instantly.

" Either you do not know me, you do not understand me," he cried, " or you are sorely mischievous. Do you call this a quarrel? Is there any want of help here? Do you suppose that I am in the world to give *advice*? Of all occupations which man can pursue, that is the most foolish. Every man must be his own counsellor, and do what he cannot let alone. If all go well, let him be happy, let him enjoy his wisdom and his fortune; if it go ill, I am at hand to do what I can for him. The man who desires to be rid of an evil knows what he wants; but the man who desires something better than he has got is stone blind. Yes, yes, laugh as you will, he is playing blindman's-buff; perhaps he gets hold of something, but the question is what he has got hold of. Do as you will, it is all one. Invite your friends to you, or let them be, it is all the same. The most prudent plans I have seen miscarry, and the most foolish succeed. Don't split your brains about it; and if, one way or the other, evil comes of what you settle, don't fret; send for me, and you shall be helped. Till which time, I am your humble servant."

So saying, he sprang on his horse, without waiting the arrival of the coffee.

" Here you see," said Charlotte, " the small service a third person can be, when things are off their balance between two persons closely connected; we are left, if possible, more confused and more uncertain than we were."

They would both, probably, have continued hesitating some time longer, had not a letter arrived from the Captain, in reply to Edward's last. He had made up his mind to accept one of the situations which had been offered him, although it was not in the least up to his mark. He was to share the ennui of certain wealthy persons of rank, who depended on his ability to dissipate it.

Edward's keen glance saw into the whole thing, and he pictured it out in just, sharp lines.

"Can we endure to think of our friend in such a position?" he cried; "you cannot be so cruel, Charlotte."

"That strange Mittler is right after all," replied Charlotte; "all such undertakings are ventures; what will come of them it is impossible to foresee. New elements introduced among us may be fruitful in fortune or in misfortune, without our having to take credit to ourselves for one or the other. I do not feel myself firm enough to oppose you further. Let us make the experiment; only one thing I will entreat of you—that it be only for a short time. You must allow me to exert myself more than ever, to use all my influence among all my connections, to find him some position which will satisfy him in his own way."

Edward poured out the warmest expressions of gratitude. He hastened, with a light, happy heart, to write off his proposals to his friend. Charlotte, in a postscript, was to signify her approbation with her own hand, and unite her own kind entreaties with his. She wrote, with a rapid pen, pleasantly and affectionately, but yet with a sort of haste which was not usual with her; and, most unlike herself, she disfigured the paper at last with a blot of ink, which put her out of temper, and which she only made worse with her attempts to wipe it away.

Edward laughed at her about it, and, as there was still room, added a second postscript, that his friend was to see from this symptom the impatience with which he was expected, and measure the speed at which he came to them by the haste in which the letter was written.

The messenger was gone; and Edward thought he could

not give a more convincing evidence of his gratitude, than by
insisting again and again that Charlotte should at once send
for Ottilie from the school.   She said she would think about
it; and, for that evening, induced Edward to join with her
in the enjoyment of a little music.   Charlotte played exceedingly well on the piano, Edward not quite so well on the
flute.   He had taken a great deal of pains with it at times;
but he was without the patience, without the perseverance,
which are requisite for the completely successful cultivation
of such a talent; consequently, his part was done unequally,
some pieces well, only perhaps too quickly—while with
others he hesitated, not being quite familiar with them; so
that, for any one else, it would have been difficult to have
gone through a duet with him.   But Charlotte knew how to
manage it.   She held in, or let herself be run away with,
and fulfilled in this way the double part of a skilful conductor
and a prudent housewife, who are able always to keep right
on the whole, although particular passages will now and then
fall out of order.

CHAPTER III.

THE Captain came, having previously written a most
sensible letter, which had entirely quieted Charlotte's apprehensions.   So much clearness about himself, so just an
understanding of his own position and the position of his
friends, promised everything which was best and happiest.

The conversation of the first few hours, as is generally the
case with friends who have not met for a long time, was
eager, lively, almost exhausting.   Towards evening, Charlotte
proposed a walk to the new grounds.   The Captain was
delighted with the spot, and observed every beauty which
had been first brought into sight and made enjoyable by the
new walks.   He had a practised eye, and at the same time
one easily satisfied; and although he knew very well what
was really valuable, he never, as so many persons do, made
people who were showing him things of their own uncomfortable, by requiring more than the circumstances admitted

of, or by mentioning anything more perfect, which he remembered having seen elsewhere.

When they arrived at the summer-house, they found it dressed out for a holiday, only, indeed, with artificial flowers and evergreens, but with some pretty bunches of natural corn-ears among them, and other field and garden fruit, so as to do credit to the taste which had arranged them.

" Although my husband does not like in general to have his birthday or christening-day kept," Charlotte said, " he will not object to-day to these few ornaments being expended on a treble festival."

" Treble ?" cried Edward.

" Yes, indeed," she replied. " Our friend's arrival here we are bound to keep as a festival; and have you never thought, either of you, that this is the day on which you were both christened? Are you not both named Otto?"

The two friends shook hands across the little table.

" You bring back to my mind," Edward said, " this little link of our boyish affection. As children, we were both called so; but when we came to be at school together, it was the cause of much confusion, and I readily made over to him all my right to the pretty laconic name."

" Wherein you were not altogether so very high-minded," said the Captain; " for I well remember that the name of Edward had then begun to please you better, from its attractive sound when spoken by certain pretty lips."

They were now sitting all three round the same table where Charlotte had spoken so vehemently against their guest's coming to them. Edward, happy as he was, did not wish to remind his wife of that time; but he could not help saying,

" There is good room here for one more person."

At this moment the notes of a bugle were heard across from the castle. Full of happy thoughts and feelings as the friends all were together, the sound fell in among them with a strong force of answering harmony. They listened silently, each for the moment withdrawing into himself, and feeling doubly happy in the fair circle of which he formed a part. The pause was first broken by Edward, who started up and walked out in front of the summer-house.

" Our friend must not think," he said to Charlotte, " that this narrow little valley forms the whole of our domain and

c

possessions.   Let us take him up to the top of the hill, where
he can see farther and breathe more freely."

"For this once, then," answered Charlotte, "we must
climb up the old footpath, which is not too easy. By the next
time, I hope my walks and steps will have been carried right
up."

And so, among rocks, and shrubs, and bushes, they made
their way to the summit, where they found themselves, not
on a level flat, but on a sloping grassy terrace, running along
the ridge of the hill.   The village, with the castle behind it,
was out of sight.   At the bottom of the valley, sheets of
water were seen spreading out right and left, with wooded
hills rising immediately from their opposite margin, and, at
the end of the upper water, a wall of sharp, precipitous rocks
directly overhanging it, their huge forms reflected in its
level surface.   In the hollow of the ravine, where a considerable brook ran into the lake, lay a mill, half hidden among
the trees, a sweetly retired spot, most beautifully surrounded;
and through the entire semicircle over which the view
extended, ran an endless variety of hills and valleys, copse
and forest, the early green of which promised the near
approach of a luxuriant clothing of foliage.   In many places
particular groups of trees caught the eye; and especially a
cluster of planes and poplars directly at the spectator's feet,
close to the edge of the centre lake.   They were at their full
growth, and they stood there, spreading out their boughs all
around them, in fresh and luxuriant strength.

To these Edward called his friend's attention.

"I myself planted them," he cried, "when I was a boy.
They were small trees which I rescued when my father was
laying out the new part of the great castle garden, and in the
middle of one summer had rooted them out.   This year you
will no doubt see them show their gratitude in a fresh set of
shoots."

They returned to the castle in high spirits, and mutually
pleased with each other.   To the guest was allotted an agreeable and roomy set of apartments in the right wing of the
castle ; and here he rapidly got his books and papers and
instruments in order, to go on with his usual occupation.
But Edward, for the first few days, gave him no rest.   He
took him about everywhere, now on foot, now on horseback,

making him acquainted with the country and with the estate; and he embraced the opportunity of imparting to him the wishes which he had been long entertaining, of getting at some better acquaintance with it, and learning to manage it more profitably.

"The first thing we have to do," said the Captain, "is to make a magnetic survey of the property. That is a pleasant and easy matter; and if it does not admit of entire exactness, it will be always useful, and will do, at any rate, for an agreeable beginning. It can be made, too, without any great staff of assistants, and one can be sure of getting it completed. If by-and-by you come to require anything more exact, it will be easy then to find some plan to have it made."

The Captain was exceedingly skilful at work of this kind. He had brought with him whatever instruments he required, and commenced immediately. Edward provided him with a number of foresters and peasants, who, with his instruction, were able to render him all necessary assistance. The weather was favourable. The evenings and the early mornings were devoted to the designing and drawing, and in a short time it was all filled in and coloured. Edward saw his possessions grow out like a new creation upon the paper; and it seemed as if now for the first time he knew what they were, as if they now first were properly his own.

Thus there came occasion to speak of the park, and of the ways of laying it out; a far better disposition of things being made possible after a survey of this kind, than could be arrived at by experimenting on nature, on partial and accidental impressions.

"We must make my wife understand this," said Edward.

"We must do nothing of the kind," replied the Captain, who did not like bringing his own notions in collision with those of others. He had learnt by experience that the motives and purposes by which men are influenced, are far too various to be made to coalesce upon a single point, even on the most solid representations. "We must not do it," he cried; "she will be only confused. With her, as with all people who employ themselves on such matters merely as amateurs, the important thing is, rather that she shall do something, than that something shall be done. Such persons feel their way with nature. They have fancies for this plan or that; they do not venture on removing obstacles. They are not bold enough to make a sacrifice. They do not know beforehand in what their work is to result. They try an experiment—it succeeds —it fails; they alter it; they alter, perhaps, what they ought to leave alone, and leave what they ought to alter; and so, at last, there always remains but a patchwork, which pleases and amuses, but never satisfies."

" Acknowledge candidly," said Edward, " that you do not like this new work of hers."

" The idea is excellent," he replied; " if the execution were equal to it, there would be no fault to find. But she has tormented herself to find her way up that rock; and she now torments every one, if you must have it, that she takes up after her. You cannot walk together—you cannot walk behind one another with any freedom. Every moment your step is interrupted one way or another. There is no end to the mistakes which she has made."

" Would it have been easy to have done it otherwise?" asked Edward.

" Perfectly," replied the Captain. " She had only to break away a corner of the rock, which is now but an unsightly object, made up as it is of little pieces, and she would at once have a sweep for her walk and stone in abundance for the rough masonry work, to widen it in the bad places, and make it smooth. But this I tell you in strictest confidence. Her it would only confuse and annoy. What is done must remain as it is. If any more money and labour is to be spent there, there is abundance to do above the summer-house on the hill, which we can settle our own way."

If the two friends found in their occupation abundance of present employment, there was no lack either of entertaining reminiscences of early times, in which Charlotte took her part as well. They determined, moreover, that as soon as their immediate labours were finished, they would go to work upon the journal, and in this way, too, reproduce the past.

For the rest, when Edward and Charlotte were alone, there were fewer matters of private interest between them than formerly. This was especially the case since the fault-finding about the grounds, which Edward thought so just, and which he felt to the quick. He held his tongue about what the

Captain had said for a long time; but at last, when he saw his wife again preparing to go to work above the summer-house, with her paths and steps, he could not contain himself any longer, but, after a few circumlocutions, came out with his new views.

Charlotte was thoroughly disturbed. She was sensible enough to perceive at once that they were right, but there was the difficulty with what was already done,—and what was made was made. She had liked it; even what was wrong had become dear to her in its details. She fought against her convictions; she defended her little creations; she railed at men who were for ever going to the broad and the great. They could not let a pastime, they could not let an amusement alone, she said, but they must go and make a work out of it, never thinking of the expense which their larger plans involved. She was provoked, annoyed, and angry. Her old plans she could not give up, the new she would not quite throw from her; but, divided as she was, for the present she put a stop to the work, and gave herself time to think the thing over, and let it ripen by itself.

At the same time that she lost this source of active amuse-ment, the others were more and more together over their own business. They took to occupying themselves, moreover, with the flower-garden and the hot-houses; and as they filled up the intervals with the ordinary gentlemen's amusements, hunting, riding, buying, selling, breaking horses, and such matters, she was every day left more and more to herself. She devoted herself more assiduously than ever to her corre-spondence on account of the Captain; and yet she had many lonely hours; so that the information which she now received from the school became of more agreeable interest.

To a long-drawn letter of the superior of the establishment, filled with the usual expressions of delight at her daughter's progress, a brief postcript was attached, with a second from the hand of a gentleman in employment there as an assistant, both of which we here communicate.

POSTSCRIPT OF THE SUPERIOR.

" Of Ottilie, I can only repeat to your ladyship what I have already stated in my former letters. I do not know how to find fault with her, yet I cannot say that I am satis-

fied. She is always unassuming, always ready to oblige
others; but it is not pleasing to see her so timid, so almost
servile.

" Your ladyship lately sent her some money, with several
little matters for her wardrobe. The money she has never
touched, the dresses lay unworn in their place. She keeps
her things very nice and very clean; but this is all she seems
to care about. Again, I cannot praise her excessive abstemiousness in eating and drinking. There is no extravagance
at our table, but there is nothing that I like better than to
see the children eat enough of good, wholesome food. What
is carefully provided and set before them ought to be taken ;
and to this I never can succeed in bringing Ottilie. She is
always making herself some occupation or other, always
finding something which she must do, something which the
servants have neglected, to escape the second course or the
dessert; and now it has to be considered (which I cannot
help connecting with all this) that she frequently suffers, I
have lately learnt, from pain in the left side of her head. It is
only at times, but it is distressing, and may be of importance.
So much upon this otherwise sweet and lovely girl."

SECOND POSTSCRIPT, BY THE ASSISTANT.

" Our excellent superior commonly permits me to read the
letters in which she communicates her observations upon her
pupils to their parents and friends. Such of them as are
addressed to your ladyship I ever read with twofold attention
and pleasure. We have to congratulate you upon a daughter who unites in herself every brilliant quality with which
people distinguish themselves in the world; and I at least
think you no less fortunate in having had bestowed upon you,
in your step-daughter, a child who has been born for the
good and happiness of others, and assuredly also for her own.
Ottilie is almost our only pupil about whom there is a difference of opinion between myself and our reverend superior.
I do not complain of the very natural desire in that good lady
to see outward and definite fruits arising from her labours.
But there are also fruits which are not outward, which are
of the true germinal sort, and which develop themselves
sooner or later in a beautiful life. And this I am certain is
the case with your protégée. So long as she has been under

my care, I have watched her moving with an even step,
slowly, steadily forward—never back.   As with a child it
is necessary to begin everything at the beginning, so it is
with her.   She can comprehend nothing which does not
follow from what precedes it; let a thing be as simple and
easy as possible, she can make nothing of it if it is not in
a recognizable connection; but find the intermediate links,
and make them clear to her, and then nothing is too difficult
for her.

" Progressing with such slow steps, she remains behind her
companions, who, with capacities of quite a different kind,
hurry on and on, learn everything readily, connected or
unconnected, recollect it with ease, and apply it with correct-
ness.   And again, some of the lessons here are given by
excellent, but somewhat hasty and impatient teachers, who
pass from result to result, cutting short the process by which
they are arrived at; and these are not of the slightest service
to her; she learns nothing from them.   There is a complaint
of her handwriting.   They say she will not, or cannot, understand how to form her letters.   I have examined closely into
this.   It is true she writes slowly, stiffly, if you like; but the
hand is neither timid nor without character.   The French
language is not my department, but I have taught her something of it, in the step-by-step fashion; and this she understands easily.   Indeed, it is singular that she knows a great
deal, and knows it well, too; and yet when she is asked a
question, it seems as if she knew nothing.

"To conclude generally, I should say she learns nothing
like a person who is being educated, but she learns like one
who is to educate—not like a pupil, but like a future teacher.
Your ladyship may think it strange that I, as an educator
and a teacher, can find no higher praise to give to any one
than by a comparison with myself.   I may leave it to your
own good sense, to your deep knowledge of the world and of
mankind, to make the best of my most inadequate, but well-
intended expressions.   You may satisfy yourself that you
have much happiness to promise yourself from this child.   I
commend myself to your ladyship, and I beseech you to permit me to write to you again as soon as I see reason to
believe that I have anything important or agreeable to communicate."

This letter gave Charlotte great pleasure. The contents of it coincided very closely with the notions which she had herself conceived of Ottilie. At the same time, she could not help smiling at the excessive interest of the assistant, which seemed greater than the insight into a pupil's excellence usually calls forth. In her quiet, unprejudiced way of looking at things, this relation, among others, she was contented to permit to lie before her as a possibility : she could value the interest of so sensible a man in Ottilie, having learnt, among the lessons of her life, to see how highly true regard is to be prized, in a world where indifference or dislike are the common natural residents.

CHAPTER IV.

THE topographical chart of the property and its environs was completed. It was executed on a considerable scale ; the character of the particular localities was made intelligible by various colours ; and by means of a trigonometrical survey, the Captain had been able to arrive at a very fair exactness of measurement. He had been rapid in his work. There was scarcely ever any one who could do with less sleep than this most laborious man ; and, as his day was always devoted to an immediate purpose, every evening something had been done.

"Let us now," he said to his friend, " go on to what remains for us, to the statistics of the estate. We shall have a good deal of work to get through at the beginning, and afterwards we shall come to the farm estimates, and much else which will naturally arise out of them. Only we must have one thing distinctly settled and adhered to. Everything which is properly *business* we must keep carefully separate from *life*. Business requires earnestness and method ; life must have a freer handling. Business demands the utmost stringency and sequence ; in life, inconsecutiveness is frequently necessary, indeed, is charming and graceful. If you are firm in the first, you can afford yourself more liberty in the second ; while if you mix them, you will find the free interfering with and breaking in upon the fixed."

In these sentiments Edward felt a slight reflection upon himself. Though not naturally disorderly, he could never bring himself to arrange his papers in their proper places. What he had to do in connection with others, was not kept separate from what only depended on himself. Business got mixed up with amusement, and serious work with recreation. Now, however, it was easy for him, with the help of a friend, who would take the trouble upon himself; and a second "I" worked out the separation, to which the single "I" was always unequal.

In the Captain's wing, they contrived a depositary for what concerned the present, and an archive for the past. Here they brought all the documents, papers, and notes from their various hiding-places, rooms, drawers, and boxes, with the utmost speed. Harmony and order were introduced into the wilderness, and the different packets were marked and registered in their several pigeon-holes. They found all they wanted in greater completeness even than they had expected; and here an old clerk was found of no slight service, who for the whole day and part of the night never left his desk, and with whom, till then, Edward had been always dissatisfied.

"I should not know him again," he said to his friend, "the man is so handy and useful."

"That," replied the Captain, "is because we give him nothing fresh to do till he has finished, at his convenience, what he has already; and so, as you perceive, he gets through a great deal. If you disturb him, he becomes useless at once."

Spending their days together in this way, in the evenings they never neglected their regular visits to Charlotte. If there was no party from the neighbourhood, as was often the case, they read and talked, principally on subjects connected with the improvement of the condition and comfort of social life.

Charlotte, always accustomed to make the most of opportunities, not only saw her husband pleased, but found personal advantages for herself. Various domestic arrangements, which she had long wished to make, but which she did not know exactly how to set about, were managed for her through the contrivance of the Captain. Her domestic medicine-chest, hitherto but poorly furnished, was enlarged and enriched, and Charlotte herself, with the help of good books and personal instruction, was put in the way of being able to exercise her disposition to be of practical assistance more frequently and more efficiently than before.

In providing against accidents, which, though common, yet only too often find us unprepared, they thought it especially necessary to have at hand whatever is required for the recovery of drowning men—accidents of this kind, from the number of canals, reservoirs, and waterworks in the neighbourhood, being of frequent occcurrence. This department the Captain took expressly into his own hands; and the observation escaped Edward, that a case of this kind had made a very singular epoch in the life of his friend. The latter made no reply, but seemed to be trying to escape from a painful recollection. Edward immediately stopped; and Charlotte, who, as well as he, had a general knowledge of the story, took no notice of the expression.

"These preparations are all exceedingly valuable," said the Captain, one evening. "Now, however, we have not got the one thing which is most essential—a sensible man who understands how to manage it all. I know an army surgeon, whom I could exactly recommend for the place. You might get him at this moment, on easy terms. He is highly distinguished in his profession, and has frequently done more for me, in the treatment even of violent inward disorders, than celebrated physicians. Help upon the spot, is the thing you often most want in the country."

He was written for at once; and Edward and Charlotte were rejoiced to have found so good and necessary an object, on which to expend so much of the money which they set apart for such accidental demands upon them.

Thus Charlotte, too, found means of making use, for her purposes, of the Captain's knowledge and practical skill; and she began to be quite reconciled to his presence, and to feel easy about any consequences which might ensue. She commonly prepared questions to ask him; among other things, it was one of her anxieties to provide against whatever was prejudicial to health and comfort, against poisons and such like. The lead-glazing on the china, the verdigris which formed about her copper and bronze vessels, &c., had long been a trouble to her. She got him to tell her about these, and, naturally, they often had to fall back on the first elements of medicine and chemistry.

An accidental, but welcome occasion for entertainment of this kind, was given by an inclination of Edward to read aloud. · He had a particularly clear, deep voice, and earlier in life had earned himself a pleasant reputation for his feeling and lively recitations of works of poetry and oratory. At this time he was occupied with other subjects, and the books which, for some time past, he had been reading, were either chemical, or on some other branch of natural or technical science.

One of his especial peculiarities—which, by-the-by, he very likely shares with a number of his fellow-creatures—was, that he could not bear to have any one looking over him when he was reading. In early life, when he used to read poems, plays, or stories, this had been the natural consequence of the desire which the reader feels, like the poet, or the actor, or the story-teller, to make surprises, to pause, to excite expectation; and this sort of effect was naturally defeated when a third person's eyes could run on before him, and see what was coming. On such occasions, therefore, he was accustomed to place himself in such a position that no one could get behind him. With a party of only three, this was unnecessary; and as with the present subject there was no opportunity for exciting feelings or giving the imagination a surprise, he did not take any particular pains to protect himself.

One evening he had placed himself carelessly, and Charlotte happened by accident to cast her eyes upon the page. His old impatience was aroused; he turned to her, and said, almost unkindly,

" I do wish, once for all, you would leave off doing a thing so out of taste and so disagreeable. When I read aloud to a person, is it not the same as if I was telling him something by word of mouth? The written, the printed word, is in the place of my own thoughts, of my own heart. If a window were broken into my brain or into my heart, and if the man to whom I am counting out my thoughts, or delivering my sentiments, one by one, knew already beforehand exactly what was to come out of me, should I take the trouble to put them into words? When anybody looks over my book, I always feel as if I were being torn in two."

Charlotte's tact, in whatever circle she might be, large or small, was remarkable, and she was able to set aside disagreeable or excited expressions without appearing to notice them. When a conversation grew tedious, she knew how to interrupt it; when it halted, she could set it going. And this time her good gift did not forsake her.

"I am sure you will forgive me my fault," she said, "when I tell you what it was this moment which came over me. I heard you reading something about Affinities, and I thought directly of some relations of mine, two of whom are just now occupying me a great deal. Then my attention went back to the book. I found it was not about living things at all, and I looked over to get the thread of it right again."

"It was the comparison which led you wrong and confused you," said Edward. "The subject is nothing but earths and minerals. But man is a true Narcissus; he delights to see his own image everywhere; and he spreads himself underneath the universe, like the amalgam behind the glass."

"Quite true," continued the Captain. "That is the way in which he treats everything external to himself. His wisdom and his folly, his will and his caprice, he attributes alike to the animal, the plant, the elements, and the gods."

"Would you," said Charlotte, "if it is not taking you away too much from the immediate subject, tell me briefly what is meant here by Affinities?"

"I shall be very glad indeed," replied the Captain, to whom Charlotte had addressed herself. "That is, I will tell you as well as I can. My ideas on the subject date ten years back; whether the scientific world continues to think the same about it, I cannot tell."

"It is most disagreeable," cried Edward, "that one cannot now-a-days learn a thing once for all, and have done with it. Our forefathers could keep to what they were taught when they were young; but we have, every five years, to make revolutions with them, if we do not wish to drop altogether out of fashion."

"We women need not be so particular," said Charlotte; "and, to speak the truth, I only want to know the meaning of the word. There is nothing more ridiculous in society than to misuse a strange technical word; and I only wish you to tell me in what sense the expression is made use of in connection with these things. What its scientific application is, I am quite contented to leave to the learned; who, by-the-by, as far as I have been able to observe, do not find it easy to agree among themselves."

" Whereabouts shall we begin," said Edward, after a pause, to the Captain, " to come most quickly to the point ?"

The latter, after thinking a little while, replied shortly,

" You must let me make what will seem a wide sweep; we shall be on our subject almost immediately."

Charlotte settled her work at her side, promising the fullest attention.

The Captain began :

" In all natural objects with which we are acquainted, we observe immediately that they have a certain relation to themselves. It may sound ridiculous to be asserting what is obvious to every one; but it is only by coming to a clear understanding together about what we know, that we can advance to what we do not know."

" I think," interrupted Edward, " we can make the thing more clear to her, and to ourselves, with examples; conceive water, or oil, or quicksilver; among these you will see a certain oneness, a certain connection of their parts; and this oneness is never lost, except through force or some other determining cause. Let the cause cease to operate, and at once the parts unite again."

" Unquestionably," said Charlotte, " that is plain; rain-drops readily unite and form streams; and when we were children, it was our delight to play with quicksilver, and wonder at the little globules splitting and parting and running into one another."

" And here," said the Captain, " let me just cursorily mention one remarkable thing, I mean, that the full, complete correlation of parts which the fluid state makes possible, shows itself distinctly and universally in the globular form. The falling water-drop is round; you yourself spoke of the globules of quicksilver; and a drop of melted lead let fall, if it has time to harden before it reaches the ground, is found at the bottom in the shape of a ball."

" Let me try and see," said Charlotte, " whether I can understand where you are bringing me. As everything has a reference to itself, so it must have some relation to others."

"And that," interrupted Edward, "will be different according to the natural differences of the things themselves. Sometimes they will meet like friends and old acquaintances; they will come rapidly together, and unite without either having to alter itself at all—as wine mixes with water. Others, again, will remain as strangers side by side, and no amount of mechanical mixing or forcing will succeed in combining them. Oil and water may be shaken up together, and the next moment they are separate again, each by itself."

"One can almost fancy," said Charlotte, "that in these simple forms one sees people that one is acquainted with; one has met with just such things in the societies amongst which one has lived; and the strangest likenesses of all with these soulless creatures, are in the masses in which men stand divided one against the other, in their classes and professions; the nobility and the third estate, for instance, or soldiers and civilians."

"Then again," replied Edward, "as these are united together under common laws and customs, so there are intermediate members in our chemical world, which will combine elements that are mutually repulsive."

"Oil, for instance," said the Captain, "we make combine with water with the help of alkalis———"

"Do not go on too fast with your lesson," said Charlotte. "Let me see that I keep step with you. Are we not here arrived among the affinities?"

"Exactly," replied the Captain; "we are on the point of apprehending them in all their power and distinctness; such natures as, when they come in contact, at once lay hold of each other, and mutually affect one another, we speak of as having an affinity one for the other. With the alkalis and acids, for instance, the affinities are strikingly marked. They are of opposite natures; very likely their being of opposite natures is the secret of their effect on one another—they seek one another eagerly out, lay hold of each other, modify each other's character, and form in connection an entirely new substance. There is lime, you remember, which shows the strongest inclination for all sorts of acids—a distinct desire of combining with them. As soon as our chemical chest arrives, we can show you a number of entertaining experiments, which will give you a clearer idea than words, and names, and technical expressions."

"It appears to me," said Charlotte, "that if you choose to call these strange creatures of yours related, the relationship is not so much a relationship of blood, as of soul or of spirit. It is the way in which we see all really deep friendships arise among men ; opposite peculiarities of disposition being what best makes internal union possible. But I will wait to see what you can really show me of these mysterious proceedings; and for the present," she added, turning to Edward, "I will promise not to disturb you any more in your reading. You have taught me enough of what it is about to enable me to attend to it."

"No, no," replied Edward, "now that you have once stirred the thing, you shall not get off so easily. It is just the most complicated cases which are the most interesting. In these you come first to see the degrees of the affinities, to watch them as their power of attraction is weaker or stronger, nearer or more remote. Affinities only begin really to interest when they bring about separations."

"What!" cried Charlotte, "is that miserable word, which unhappily we hear so often now-a-days in the world; is that to be found in nature's lessons too?"

"Most certainly," answered Edward; "the title with which chemists were supposed to be most honourably distinguished was, artists of separation."

"It is not so any more," replied Charlotte; "and it is well that it is not. It is a higher art, and it is a higher merit, to unite. An artist of union, is what we should welcome in every province of the universe. However, as we are on the subject again, give me an instance or two of what you mean."

"We had better keep," said the Captain, "to the same instances of which we have already been speaking. Thus, what we call limestone is a more or less pure calcareous earth in combination with a delicate acid, which is familiar to us in the form of a gas. Now, if we place a piece of this stone in diluted sulphuric acid, this will take possession of the lime, and appear with it in the form of gypsum, the gaseous acid

at the same time going off in vapour. Here is a case of
separation; a combination arises, and we believe ourselves
now justified in applying to it the words 'Elective Affinity;'
it really looks as if one relation had been deliberately chosen
in preference to another.

"Forgive me," said Charlotte, "as I forgive the natural
philosopher. I cannot see any choice in this; I see a natural
necessity rather, and scarcely that. After all, it is perhaps
merely a case of opportunity. Opportunity makes relations as
it makes thieves; and as long as the talk is only of natural
substances, the choice to me appears to be altogether in the
hands of the chemist who brings the creatures together.
Once, however, let them be brought together, and then God
have mercy on them. In the present case, I cannot help
being sorry for the poor acid gas, which is driven out up and
down infinity again."

"The acid's business," answered the Captain, "is now to
get connected with water, and so serve as a mineral fountain
for the refreshing of sound or disordered mankind."

"That is very well for the gypsum to say," said Charlotte.
"The gypsum is all right, is a body, is provided for. The
other poor, desolate creature may have trouble enough to go
through before it can find a second home for itself."

"I am much mistaken," said Edward, smiling, "if there
be not some little *arrière pensée* behind this. Confess your
wickedness! You mean me by your lime; the lime is laid
hold of by the Captain, in the form of sulphuric acid, torn
away from your agreeable society, and metamorphosed into a
refractory gypsum."

"If your conscience prompts you to make such a reflection," replied Charlotte, "I certainly need not distress myself.
These comparisons are pleasant and entertaining; and who is
there that does not like playing with analogies? But man is
raised very many steps above these elements; and if he has
been somewhat liberal with such fine words as Election and
Elective Affinities, he will do well to turn back again into
himself, and take the opportunity of considering carefully the
value and meaning of such expressions. Unhappily, we
know cases enough where a connection apparently indissoluble
between two persons, has, by the accidental introduction
of a third, been utterly destroyed, and one or the other o-

the once happily united pair been driven out into the wilderness."

" Then you see how much more gallant the chemists are," said Edward. " They at once add a fourth, that neither may go away empty."

" Quite so," replied the Captain. " And those are the cases which are really most important and remarkable—cases where this attraction, this affinity, this separating and combining, can be exhibited, the two pairs severally crossing each other ; where four creatures, connected previously, as two and two, are brought into contact, and at once forsake their first combination to form into a second. In this forsaking and embracing, this seeking and flying, we believe that we are indeed observing the effects of some higher determination ; we attribute a sort of will and choice to such creatures, and feel really justified in using technical words, and speaking of ' Elective Affinities.' "

" Give me an instance of this," said Charlotte.

" One should not spoil such things with words," replied the Captain. " As I said before, as soon as I can show you the experiment, I can make it all intelligible and pleasant for you. For the present, I can give you nothing but horrible scientific expresssions, which at the same time will give you no idea about the matter. You ought yourself to see these creatures, which seem so dead, and which are yet so full of inward energy and force, at work before your eyes. You should observe them with a real personal interest. Now they seek each other out, attract each other, seize, crush, devour, destroy each other, and then suddenly reappear again out of their combinations, and come forward in fresh, renovated, unexpected form ; thus you will comprehend how we attribute to them a sort of immortality—how we speak of them as having sense and understanding ; because we feel our own senses to be insufficient to observe them adequately, and our reason too weak to follow them."

" I quite agree," said Edward, " that the strange scientific nomenclature, to persons who have not been reconciled to it by a direct acquaintance with or understanding of its object, must seem unpleasant, even ridiculous ; but we can easily, just for once, contrive with symbols to illustrate what we are speaking of."

"If you do not think it looks pedantic," answered the Captain, "I can put my meaning together with letters. Suppose an A connected so closely with a B, that all sorts of means, even violence, have been made use of to separate them, without effect. Then suppose a C in exactly the same position with respect to D. Bring the two pairs into contact ; A will fling himself on D, C on B, without its being possible to say which had first left its first connection, or made the first move towards the second."

"Now then," interposed Edward, "till we see all this with our eyes, we will look upon the formula as an analogy, out of which we can devise a lesson for immediate use. You stand for A, Charlotte, and I am your B ; really and truly I cling to you, I depend on you, and follow you, just as B does with A. C is obviously the Captain, who at present is in some degree withdrawing me from you. So now it is only just that if you are not to be left to solitude, a D should be found for you, and that is unquestionably the amiable little lady, Ottilie. You will not hesitate any longer to send and fetch her."

"Good," replied Charlotte; "although the example does not, in my opinion, exactly fit our case. However, we have been fortunate, at any rate, in to-day for once having met all together: and these natural or elective affinities have served to unite us more intimately. I will tell you, that since this afternoon I have made up my mind to send for Ottilie. My faithful housekeeper, on whom I have hitherto depended for everything, is going to leave me shortly, to be married. (It was done at my own suggestion, I believe, to please me.) What it is which has decided me about Ottilie, you shall read to me. I will not look over the pages again. Indeed, the contents of them are already known to me. Only read, read !"

With these words, she produced a letter, and handed it to Edward.

CHAPTER V.

LETTER OF THE LADY SUPERIOR.

" Your ladyship will forgive the brevity of my present letter. The public examinations are but just concluded, and I have to communicate to all the parents and guardians the progress which our pupils have made during the past year. To you I may well be brief, having to say much in few words. Your ladyship's daughter has proved herself first in every sense of the word. The testimonials which I inclose, and her own letter, in which she will detail to you the prizes which she has won, and the happiness which she feels in her success, will surely please, and I hope delight you. For myself, it is the less necessary that I should say much, because I see that there will soon be no more occasion to keep with us a young lady so far advanced. I send my respects to your ladyship, and in a short time I shall take the liberty of offering you my opinion as to what in future may be of most advantage to her.

" My good assistant will tell you about Ottilie."

LETTER OF THE ASSISTANT.

" Our reverend superior leaves it to me to write to you of Ottilie, partly because, with her ways of thinking about it, it would be painful to her to say what has to be said ; partly, because she herself requires some excusing, which she would rather have done for her by me.

" Knowing, as I did too well, how little able the good Ottilie was to show out what lies in her, and what she is capable of, I was all along afraid of this public examination. I was the more uneasy, as it was to be of a kind which does not admit of any especial preparation ; and even if it had been conducted as usual, Ottilie never can be prepared to make a display. The result has only too entirely justified my anxiety. She has gained no prize ; she is not even amongst those whose names have been mentioned with approbation. I need not go into details. In writing, the letters of the other girls were not so well formed, but their strokes were far more free. In arithmetic, they were all quicker than she ;

and in the more difficult problems, which she does the best, there was no examination. In French, she was outshone and out-talked by many; and in history she was not ready with her names and dates. In geography, there was a want of attention to the political divisions; and for what she could do in music there was neither time nor quiet enough for her few modest melodies to gain attention. In drawing she certainly would have gained the prize; her outlines were clear, and the execution most careful and full of spirit; unhappily, she had chosen too large a subject, and it was incomplete.

"After the pupils were dismissed, the examiners consulted together, and we teachers were partially admitted into the council. I very soon observed that of Ottilie either nothing would be said at all, or if her name was mentioned, it would be with indifference, if not absolute disapproval. I hoped to obtain some favour for her by a candid description of what she was, and I ventured it with the greater earnestness, partly because I was only speaking my real convictions, and partly because I remembered in my own younger years finding myself in the same unfortunate case. I was listened to with attention, but as soon as I had ended, the presiding examiner said to me very kindly but laconically, 'We presume capabilities: they are to be converted into accomplishments. This is the aim of all education. It is what is distinctly intended by all who have the care of children, and silently and indistinctly by the children themselves. This also is the object of examinations, where teachers and pupils are alike standing their trial. From what we learn of you, we may entertain good hopes of the young lady, and it is to your own credit also that you have paid so much attention to your pupil's capabilities. If in the coming year you can develop these into accomplishments, neither yourself nor your pupil shall fail to receive your due praise.'

"I had made up my mind to what must follow upon all this; but there was something worse that I had not anticipated, which had soon to be added to it. Our good Superior, who like a trusty shepherdess could not bear to have one of her flock lost, or, as was the case here, to see it undistinguished, after the examiners were gone could not contain her displeasure, and said to Ottilie, who was standing quite quietly by the window, while the others were exulting over their prizes. 'Tell me, for heaven's sake, how can a person look so stupid if she is not so?' Ottilie replied, quite calmly, 'Forgive me, my dear mother, I have my headache again to-day, and it is very painful.' Kind and sympathizing as she generally is, the Superior this time answered, 'No one can believe that,' and turned angrily away.

"Now it is true,—no one can believe it,—for Ottilie never alters the expression of her countenance. I have never even seen her move her hand to her head when she has been asleep.

"Nor was this all. Your ladyship's daughter, who is at all times sufficiently lively and impetuous, after her triumph to-day was overflowing with the violence of her spirits. She ran from room to room with her prizes and testimonials, and shook them in Ottilie's face. 'You have come badly off this morning,' she cried. Ottilie replied in her calm, quiet way, 'This is not the last day of trial.'—'But you will always remain the last,' cried the other, and ran away.

"No one except myself saw that Ottilie was disturbed. She has a way when she experiences any sharp unpleasant emotion which she wishes to resist, of showing it in the unequal colour of her face; the left cheek becomes for a moment flushed, while the right turns pale. I perceived this symptom, and I could not prevent myself from saying something. I took our Superior aside, and spoke seriously to her about it. The excellent lady acknowledged that she had been wrong. We considered the whole affair; we talked it over at great length together, and not to weary your ladyship, I will tell you at once the desire with which we concluded, namely, that you will for a while have Ottilie with yourself. Our reasons you will yourself readily perceive. If you consent, I will say more to you on the manner in which I think she should be treated. The young lady your daughter we may expect will soon leave us, and we shall then with pleasure welcome Ottilie back to us.

"One thing more, which another time I might forget to mention: I have never seen Ottilie eager for anything, or at least ask pressingly for anything. But there have been occasions, however rare, when on the other hand she has wished to decline things which have been pressed upon her, and she does it with a gesture which to those who have caught its meaning is irresistible. She raises her hands, presses the palms together, and draws them against her breast, leaning her body a little forward at the same time, and turns such a look upon the person who is urging her, that he will be glad enough to cease to ask or wish for anything of her. If your ladyship ever sees this attitude, as with your treatment of her it is not likely that you will, think of me, and spare Ottilie."

Edward read these letters aloud, not without smiles and shakes of the head. Naturally, too, there were observations made on the persons and on the position of the affair.

"Enough!" Edward cried at last, "it is decided. She comes. You, my love, are provided for, and now we can get forward with our work. It is becoming highly necessary for me to move over to the right wing to the Captain; evenings and mornings are the time for us best to work together, and then you, on your side, will have admirable room for yourself and Ottilie."

Charlotte made no objection, and Edward sketched out the method in which they should live. Among other things, he cried, "It is really very polite in this niece to be subject to a slight pain on the left side of her head. I have it frequently on the right. If we happen to be afflicted together, and sit opposite one another,—I leaning on my right elbow, and she on her left, and our heads on the opposite sides, resting on our hands,—what a pretty pair of pictures we shall make."

The Captain thought that might be dangerous. "No, no!" cried out Edward. "Only do you, my dear friend, take care of the D, for what will become of B, if poor C is taken away from it?"

"That, I should have thought, would have been evident enough," replied Charlotte.

"And it is, indeed," cried Edward; "he would turn back to his A, to his Alpha and Omega;" and he sprung up and taking Charlotte in his arms, pressed her to his breast.

CHAPTER VI.

THE carriage which brought Ottilie drove up to the door. Charlotte went out to receive her. The dear girl ran to meet her, threw herself at her feet, and embraced her knees.

"Why such humility?" said Charlotte, a little embarrassed, and endeavouring to raise her from the ground.

"It is not meant for humility," Ottilie answered, without moving from the position in which she had placed herself; "I am only thinking of the time when I could not reach higher than to your knees, and when I had just learnt to know how you loved me."

She stood up, and Charlotte embraced her warmly. She was introduced to the gentlemen, and was at once treated with especial courtesy as a visitor. Beauty is a welcome guest everywhere. She appeared attentive to the conversation, without taking a part in it.

The next morning Edward said to Charlotte, "What an agreeable, entertaining girl she is!"

"Entertaining!" answered Charlotte, with a smile; "why, she has not opened her lips yet!"

"Indeed!" said Edward, as he seemed to bethink himself; "that is very strange."

Charlotte had to give the new-comer but a very few hints on the management of the household. Ottilie saw rapidly all the arrangements, and what was more, she felt them. She comprehended easily what was to be provided for the whole party, and what for each particular member of it. Everything was done with the utmost punctuality; she knew how to direct, without appearing to be giving orders, and when any one had left anything undone, she at once set it right herself.

As soon as she had found how much time she would have to spare, she begged Charlotte to divide her hours for her, and to these she adhered exactly. She worked at what was set before her in the way which the Assistant had described to Charlotte. They let her alone. It was but seldom that Charlotte interfered. Sometimes she changed her pens for others which had been written with, to teach her to make bolder strokes in her handwriting, but these, she found, would be soon cut sharp and fine again.

The ladies had agreed with one another when they were alone to speak nothing but French, and Charlotte persisted in it the more, as she found Ottilie more ready to talk in a foreign language, when she was told it was her duty to exercise herself in it. In this way she often said more than she seemed to intend. Charlotte was particularly pleased with a description, most complete, but at the same time most charming and amiable, which she gave her one day, by accident, of the school. She soon felt her to be a delightful companion, and before long she hoped to find in her an attached friend.

At the same time she looked over again the more early accounts which had been sent her of Ottilie, to refresh her recollection with the opinion which the Superior and the Assistant had formed about her, and compare them with her in her own person. For Charlotte was of opinion that we cannot too quickly become acquainted with the character of those with whom we have to live, that we may know what to expect of them; where we may hope to do anything in the way of improvement with them, and what we must make up our minds, once for all, to tolerate and let alone.

This examination led her to nothing new, indeed; but much which she already knew became of greater meaning and importance. Ottilie's moderation in eating and drinking, for instance, became a real distress to her.

The next thing on which the ladies were employed was Ottilie's toilet. Charlotte wished her to appear in clothes of a richer and more *recherché* sort, and at once the clever active girl herself cut out the stuff which had been previously sent to her, and with a very little assistance from others was able, in a short time, to dress herself out most tastefully. The new fashionable dresses set off her figure. An agreeable person, it is true, will show through all disguises; but we always fancy it looks fresher and more graceful when its peculiarities appear under some new drapery. And thus, from the moment of her first appearance, she became more and more a delight to the eyes of all who beheld her. As the emerald refreshes the sight with its beautiful hues, and exerts it is said, a beneficent influence on that noble sense, so does human beauty work with far larger potency on the outward and on the inward sense; whoever looks upon it is charmed against the breath of evil, and feels in harmony with himself and with the world.

In many ways, therefore, the party had gained by Ottilie's arrival. The Captain and Edward kept regularly to the hours, even to the minutes, for their general meeting together. They never kept the others waiting for them, either for dinner or tea, or for their walks; and they were in less haste, especially in the evenings, to leave the table. This did not escape Charlotte's observation; she watched them both, to see whether one more than the other was the occasion of it. But she could not perceive any difference. They had both become more companionable. In their conversation they seemed to consider what was best adapted to interest Ottilie; what was most on a level with her capacities and her general knowledge. If she left the room when they were reading or telling stories, they would wait till she returned. They had grown softer and altogether more united.

In return for this, Ottilie's anxiety to be of use increased every day; the more she came to understand the house, its inmates, and their circumstances, the more eagerly she entered into everything, caught every look and every motion; half a word, a sound, was enough for her. With her calm attentiveness, and her easy, unexcited activity, she was always the same. Sitting, rising up, going, coming, fetching, carrying, returning to her place again, it was all in the most perfect repose; a constant change, a constant agreeable movement; while, at the same time, she went about so lightly that her step was almost inaudible.

This cheerful obligingness in Ottilie gave Charlotte the greatest pleasure. There was one thing, however, which she did not exactly like, of which she had to speak to her. " It is very polite in you," she said one day to her, "when people let anything fall from their hand, to be so quick in stooping and picking it up for them; at the same time, it is a sort of confession that they have a right to require such attention, and in the world we are expected to be careful to whom we pay it. Towards women, I will not prescribe any rule as to how you should conduct yourself. You

are young. To those above you, and older than you, services of this sort are a duty; towards your equals they
are polite; to those younger than yourself and your inferiors
you may show yourself kind and good-natured by such
things,—only it is not becoming in a young lady to do them
for men."

"I will try to forget the habit," replied Ottilie; "I think,
however, you will in the mean time forgive me for my want
of manners, when I tell you how I came by it. We were
taught history at school; I have not gained as much out of it
as I ought, for I never knew what use I was to make of it; a
few little things, however, made a deep impression upon me,
among which was the following:—When Charles the First of
England was standing before his so-called judges, the gold
top came off the stick which he had in his hand, and fell
down. Accustomed as he had been on such occasions to
have everything done for him, he seemed to look round and
expect that this time too some one would do him this little
service. No one stirred, and he stooped down for it himself.
It struck me as so piteous, that from that moment I have
never been able to see any one let a thing fall, without myself
picking it up. But, of course, as it is not always proper, and
as I cannot," she continued, smiling, "tell my story every
time I do it, in future I will try and contain myself."

In the mean time the fine arrangements which the two
friends had been led to make for themselves, went uninterruptedly forward. Every day they found something new to
think about and undertake.

One day as they were walking together through the village, they had to remark with dissatisfaction how far behind-
hand it was in order and cleanliness, compared to villages
where the inhabitants were compelled by the expense of
building-ground to be careful about such things.

"You remember a wish we once expressed when we were
travelling in Switzerland together," said the Captain, "that
we might have the laying out some country park, and how
beautiful we would make it by introducing into some village
situated like this, not the Swiss style of building, but the
Swiss order and neatness which so much improve it."

"And how well it would answer here! The hill on which
the castle stands, slopes down to that projecting angle. The

village, you see, is built in a semicircle, regularly enough, just opposite to it. The brook runs between. It is liable to floods; and do observe the way the people set about protecting themselves from them; one with stones, another with stakes; the next puts up a boarding, and a fourth tries beams and planks; no one, of course, doing any good to another with his arrangement, but only hurting himself and the rest too. And then there is the road going along just in the clumsiest way possible,—up hill and down, through the water, and over the stones. If the people would only lay their hands to the business together, it would cost them nothing but a little labour to run a semicircular wall along here, take the road in behind it, raising it to the level of the houses, and so give themselves a fair open space in front, making the whole place clean, and getting rid, once for all, in one good general work, of all their little trifling ineffectual makeshifts."

"Let us try it," said the Captain, as he ran his eyes over the lay of the ground, and saw quickly what was to be done.

"I can undertake nothing in company with peasants and shopkeepers," replied Edward, "unless I may have unrestricted authority over them."

"You are not so wrong in that," returned the Captain; "I have experienced too much trouble myself in life in matters of that kind. How difficult it is to prevail on a man to venture boldly on making a sacrifice for an after-advantage! How hard to get him to desire an end, and not hesitate at the means! So many people confuse means with ends; they keep hanging over the first, without having the other before their eyes. Every evil is to be cured at the place where it comes to the surface, and they will not trouble themselves to look for the cause which produces it, or the remote effect which results from it. This is why it is so difficult to get advice listened to, especially among the many: they can see clearly enough from day to day, but their scope seldom reaches beyond the morrow; and if it comes to a point where with some general arrangement one person will gain while another will lose, there is no prevailing on them to strike a balance. Works of public advantage can only be carried through by an uncontrolled absolute authority."

While they were standing and talking, a man came up and begged of them. He looked more impudent than really in want, and Edward, who was annoyed at being interrupted, after two or three fruitless attempts to get rid of him by a gentler refusal, spoke sharply to him. The fellow began to grumble and mutter abusively; he went off with short steps, talking about the right of beggars. It was all very well to refuse them an alms, but that was no reason why they should be insulted. A beggar, and everybody else too, was as much under God's protection as a lord. It put Edward out of all patience.

The Captain, to pacify him, said, "Let us make use of this as an occasion for extending our rural police arrangements to such cases. We are bound to give away money, but we do better in not giving it in person, especially at home. We should be moderate and uniform in everything, in our charities as in all else; too great liberality attracts beggars instead of helping them on their way. At the same time there is no harm when one is on a journey, or passing through a strange place, in appearing to a poor man in the street in the form of a chance deity of fortune, and making him some present which shall surprise him. The position of the village and of the castle makes it easy for us to put our charities here on a proper footing. I have thought about it before. The public-house is at one end of the village, a respectable old couple live at the other. At each of these places deposit a small sum of money, and let every beggar, not as he comes in, but as he goes out, receive something. Both houses lie on the roads which lead to the castle, so that any one who goes there can be referred to one or the other.

"Come," said Edward, "we will settle that on the spot. The exact sum can be made up another time."

They went to the innkeeper, and to the old couple, and the thing was done.

"I know very well," Edward said, as they were walking up the hill to the castle together, "that everything in this world depends on distinctness of idea and firmness of purpose.

Your judgment of what my wife has been doing in the park was entirely right; and you have already given me a hint how it might be improved. I will not deny that I told her of it."

"So I have been led to suspect," replied the Captain; "and I could not approve of your having done so. You have perplexed her. She has left off doing anything; and on this one subject she is vexed with us. She avoids speaking of it. She has never since invited us to go with her to the summer-house, although at odd hours she goes up there with Ottilie."

"We must not allow ourselves to be deterred by that," answered Edward. "If I am once convinced about anything good, which could and should be done, I can never rest till I see it done. We are clever enough at other times in introducing what we want, into the general conversation; suppose we have out some descriptions of English parks, with copperplates, for our evening's amusement. Then we can follow with your plan. We will treat it first problematically, and as if we were only in jest. There will be no difficulty in passing into earnest."

The scheme was concerted, and the books were opened. In each group of designs they first saw a ground-plan of the spot, with the general character of the landscape, drawn in its rude, natural state. Then followed others, showing the changes which had been produced by art, to employ and set off the natural advantages of the locality. From these to their own property and their own grounds, the transition was easy.

Everybody was pleased. The chart which the Captain had sketched was brought and spread out. The only difficulty was, that they could not entirely free themselves of the plan in which Charlotte had begun. However, an easier way up the hill was found; a lodge was suggested to be built on the height at the edge of the cliff, which was to have an especial reference to the castle. It was to form a conspicuous object from the castle windows, and from it the spectator was to be able to overlook both the castle and the garden.

The Captain had thought it all carefully over, and taken his measurements; and now he brought up again the village road and the wall by the brook, and the ground which was to be raised behind it.

"Here you see," said he, "while I make this charming walk up the height, I gain exactly the quantity of stone which I require for that wall. Let one piece of work help the other, and both will be carried out most satisfactorily and most rapidly."

"But now," said Charlotte, "comes my side of the business. A certain definite outlay of money will have to be made. We ought to know how much will be wanted for such a purpose, and then we can apportion it out—so much work, and so much money, if not by weeks, at least by months. The cash-box is under my charge. I pay the bills, and I keep the accounts."

"You do not appear to have overmuch confidence in us," said Edward.

"I have not much in arbitrary matters," Charlotte answered. "Where it is a case of inclination, we women know better how to control ourselves than you."

It was settled; the dispositions were made, and the work was begun at once.

The Captain being always on the spot, Charlotte was almost daily a witness to the strength and clearness of his understanding. He, too, learnt to know her better; and it became easy for them both to work together, and thus bring something to completeness. It is with work as with dancing; persons who keep the same step must grow indispensable to one another. Out of this a mutual kindly feeling will necessarily arise; and that Charlotte had a real kind feeling towards the Captain, after she came to know him better, was sufficiently proved by her allowing him to destroy her pretty seat, which in her first plans she had taken such pains in ornamenting, because it was in the way of his own, without experiencing the slightest feeling about the matter.

CHAPTER VII.

Now that Charlotte was occupied with the Captain, it was a natural consequence that Edward should attach himself more to Ottilie. Independently of this, indeed, for some time past he had begun to feel a silent kind of attraction towards her. Obliging and attentive she was to every one, but his self-love whispered that towards him she was particularly so. She had observed his little fancies about his food. She knew exactly what things he liked, and the way in which he liked them to be prepared; the quantity of sugar which he liked in his tea; and so on. Moreover, she was particularly careful to prevent draughts, about which he was excessively sensitive, and, indeed, about which, with his wife, who could never have air enough, he was often at variance. So, too, she had come to know about fruit-gardens and flower-gardens; whatever he liked, it was her constant effort to procure for him, and to keep away whatever annoyed him; so that very soon she grew indispensable to him—she became like his guardian angel, and he felt it keenly whenever she was absent. Besides all this, too, she appeared to grow more open and conversible as soon as they were alone together.

Edward, as he advanced in life, had retained something childish about himself, which corresponded singularly well with the youthfulness of Ottilie. They liked talking of early times, when they had first seen each other; and these reminiscences led them up to the first epoch of Edward's affection for Charlotte. Ottilie declared that she remembered them both as the handsomest pair about the court; and when Edward would question the possibility of this, when she must have been so exceedingly young, she insisted that she recollected one particular incident as clearly as possible. He had come into the room where her aunt was, and she had hid her face in Charlotte's lap—not from fear, but from a childish surprise. She might have added, because he had made so strong an impression upon her—because she had liked him so much.

While they were occupied in this way, much of the business which the two friends had undertaken together had come to a standstill; so that they found it necessary to inspect how things were going on—to work up a few designs and get letters written. For this purpose, they betook themselves to their office, where they found their old copyist at his desk. They set themselves to their work, and soon gave the old man enough to do, without observing that they were laying many things on his shoulders which at other times they had always done for themselves. At the same time, the first design the Captain' tried would not answer, and Edward was as unsuccessful with his first letter. They fretted for a while, planning and erasing, till at last Edward, who was getting on the worst, asked what o'clock it was. And then it appeared that the Captain had forgotten, for the first time for many years, to wind up his chronometer; and they seemed, if not to feel, at least to have a dim perception, that time was beginning to be indifferent to them.

In the meanwhile, as the gentlemen were thus rather slackening in their energy, the activity of the ladies increased all the more. The every-day life of a family, which is composed of given persons, and is shaped out of necessary circumstances, may easily receive into itself an extraordinary affection, an incipient passion—may receive it into itself as into a vessel ; and a long time may elapse before the new ingredient produces a visible effervescence, and runs foaming over the edge.

With our friends, the feelings which were mutually arising had the most agreeable effects. Their dispositions opened out, and a general goodwill arose out of the several individual affections. Every member of the party was happy ; and they each shared their happiness with the rest.

Such a temper elevates the spirit, while it enlarges the heart, and everything which, under the influence of it, people do and undertake, has a tendency towards the illimitable. The friends could not remain any more shut up at home ; their walks extended themselves further and further. Edward would hurry on before with Ottilie, to choose the path or pioneer the way ; and the Captain and Charlotte would follow quietly on the track of their more hasty precursors, talking on some grave subject, or delighting themselves with some spot they had newly discovered, or some unexpected natural beauty.

One day their walk led them down from the gate at the right wing of the castle, in the direction of the hotel, and thence over the bridge towards the ponds, along the sides of which they proceeded as far as it was generally thought possible to follow the water; thickly wooded hills sloping directly up from the edge, and beyond these a wall of steep rocks, making further progress difficult, if not impossible. But Edward, whose hunting experience had made him thoroughly familiar with the spot, pushed forward along an overgrown path with Ottilie, knowing well that the old mill could not be far off, which was somewhere in the middle of the rocks there. The path was so little frequented, that they soon lost it; and for a short time they were wandering among mossy stones and thickets; it was not for long, however, the noise of the water-wheel speedily telling them that the place which they were looking for was close at hand. Stepping forward on a point of rock, they saw the strange old, dark wooden building in the hollow before them, quite shadowed over with precipitous crags and huge trees. They determined directly to climb down amidst the moss and the blocks of stone. Edward led the way; and when he looked back and saw Ottilie following, stepping lightly, without fear or nervousness, from stone to stone, so beautifully balancing herself, he fancied he was looking at some celestial creature floating above him; while if, as she often did, she caught the hand which in some difficult spot he would offer her, or if she supported herself on his shoulder, then he was left in no doubt that it was a very exquisite human creature who touched him. He almost wished that she might slip or stumble, that he might catch her in his arms and press her to his heart. This, however, he would under no circumstances have done, for more than one reason. He was afraid to wound her, and he was afraid to do her some bodily injury.

What the meaning of this could be, we shall immediately learn. When they had got down, and were seated opposite each other at a table under the trees, and when the miller's wife had gone for milk, and the miller, who had come out to them, was sent to meet Charlotte and the Captain, Edward, with a little embarrassment, began to speak:

" I have a request to make, dear Ottilie; you will forgive me for asking it, if you will not grant it. You make no secret (I am sure you need not make any), that you wear a miniature under your dress against your breast. It is the

E

picture of your noble father.   You could hardly have known
him; but in every sense he deserves a place by your heart.
Only, forgive me, the picture is exceedingly large, and the
metal frame and the glass, if you take up a child in your
arms, if you are carrying anything, if the carriage swings
violently, if we are pushing through bushes, or just now, as
we were coming down these rocks,—cause me a thousand
anxieties for you.   Any unforeseen blow, a fall, a touch,
may be fatally injurious to you; and I am terrified at the
possibility of it.   For my sake do this: put away the picture,
not out of your affections, not out of your room; let it have
the brightest, the holiest place which you can give it; only do
not wear upon your breast a thing, the presence of which seems
to me, perhaps from an extravagant anxiety, so dangerous."

Ottilie said nothing, and while he was speaking she kept
her eyes fixed straight before her; then, without hesitation
and without haste, with a look turned more towards heaven
than on Edward, she unclasped the chain, drew out the
picture, and pressed it against her forehead, and then reached
it over to her friend, with the words:

"Do you keep it for me till we come home; I cannot give
you a better proof how deeply I thank you for your affectionate care."

He did not venture to press the picture to his lips; but he
caught her hand and raised it to his eyes.   They were, perhaps, two of the most beautiful hands which had ever been
clasped together.   He felt as if a stone had fallen from his
heart, as if a partition-wall had been thrown down between
him and Ottilie.

Under the miller's guidance, Charlotte and the Captain
came down by an easier path, and now joined them.   There
was the meeting, and a happy talk, and then they took some
refreshments.   They would not return by the same way as
they came; and Edward struck into a rocky path on the other
side of the stream, from which the ponds were again to be
seen.   They made their way along it, with some effort, and
then had to cross a variety of wood and copse—getting
glimpses, on the land side, of a number of villages and
manor-houses, with their green lawns and fruit-gardens;
while very near them, and sweetly situated on a rising
ground, a farm lay in the middle of the wood.   From a

gentle ascent, they had a view, before and behind, which showed them the richness of the country to the greatest advantage; and then, entering a grove of trees, they found themselves, on again emerging from it, on the rock opposite the castle.

They came upon it rather unexpectedly, and were of course delighted. They had made the circuit of a little world; they were standing on the spot where the new building was to be erected, and were looking again at the windows of their own home.

They went down to the summer-house, and sat all four in it for the first time together; nothing was more natural than that with one voice it should be proposed to have the way they had been that day, and which, as it was, had taken them much time and trouble, properly laid out and gravelled, so that people might loiter along it at their leisure. They each said what they thought; and they reckoned up that the circuit, over which they had taken many hours, might be travelled easily with a good road all the way round to the castle, in a single one.

Already a plan was being suggested for making the distance shorter, and adding a fresh beauty to the landscape, by throwing a bridge across the stream, below the mill, where it ran into the lake; when Charlotte brought their inventive imagination somewhat to a stand-still, by putting them in mind of the expense which such an undertaking would involve.

" There are ways of meeting that too," replied Edward; " we have only to dispose of that farm in the forest which is so pleasantly situated, and which brings in so little in the way of rent: the sum which will be set free will more than cover what we shall require, and thus, having gained an invaluable walk, we shall receive the interest of well-expended capital in substantial enjoyment—instead of, as now, in the summing up at the end of the year, vexing and fretting ourselves over the pitiful little income which is returned for it."

Even Charlotte, with all her prudence, had little to urge against this. There had been, indeed, a previous intention of selling the farm. The Captain was ready immediately with a plan for breaking up the ground into small portions among the peasantry of the forest. Edward, however, had a simpler and shorter way of managing it. His present steward had

E 2

already proposed to take it off his hands—he was to pay for it by instalments—and so, gradually, as the money came in, they would get their work forward from point to point.

So reasonable and prudent a scheme was sure of universal approbation, and already, in prospect, they began to see their new walk winding along its way, and to imagine the many beautiful views and charming spots which they hoped to discover in its neighbourhood.

To bring it all before themselves with greater fulness of detail, in the evening they produced the new chart. With the help of this they went over again the way that they had come, and found various places where the walk might take a rather different direction with advantage. Their other scheme was now once more talked through, and connected with the fresh design. The site for the new house in the park, opposite the castle, was a second time examined into and approved, and fixed upon for the termination of the intended circuit.

Ottilie had said nothing all this time. At length Edward pushed the chart, which had hitherto been lying before Charlotte, across to her, begging her to give her opinion; she still hesitated for a moment. Edward in his gentlest way again pressed her to let them know what she thought—nothing had as yet been settled—it was all as yet in embryo.

"I would have the house built here," she said, as she pointed with her finger to the highest point of the slope on the hill. "It is true you cannot see the castle from thence, for it is hidden by the wood; but for that very reason you find yourself in another quite new world; you lose village and houses and all at the same time. The view of the ponds with the mill, and the hills and mountains in the distance, is singularly beautiful—I have often observed it when I have been there."

"She is right," Edward cried; "how could we have overlooked it. This is what you mean, Ottilie, is it not?" He took a lead pencil, and drew a great black rectangular figure on the summit of the hill.

It went through the Captain's soul to see his carefully and clearly-drawn chart disfigured in such a way. He collected himself, however, after a slight expression of his disapproval, and went into the idea. "Ottilie is right," he said; "we are ready enough to walk any distance to drink tea or eat fish, because they would not have tasted as well at home—we require change of scene and change of objects. Your ancestors showed their judgment in the spot which they chose for the castle ; for it is sheltered from the wind, with the conveniences of life close at hand. A place, on the contrary, which is more for pleasure parties than for a regular residence, may be very well yonder there, and in the fair time of year the most agreeable hours may be spent there."

The more they talked it over, the more conclusive was their judgment in favour of Ottilie ; and Edward could not conceal his triumph that the thought had been hers. He was as proud as if he had hit upon it himself.

CHAPTER VIII.

EARLY the following morning the Captain examined the spot : he first threw off a sketch of what should be done, and afterwards, when the thing had been more completely decided on, he made a complete design, with accurate calculations and measurements. It cost him a good deal of labour, and the business connected with the sale of the farm had to be gone into, so that both the gentlemen now found a fresh impulse to activity.

The Captain made Edward observe that it would be proper, indeed that it would be a kind of duty, to celebrate Charlotte's birthday with laying the foundation-stone. Not much was wanted to overcome Edward's disinclination for such festivities—for he quickly recollected that a little later Ottilie's birthday would follow, and that he could have a magnificent celebration for that.

Charlotte, to whom all this work and what it would involve was a subject for much serious and almost anxious thought, busied herself in carefully going through the time and outlay which it was calculated would be expended on it. During the day they rarely saw each other, so that the evening meeting was looked forward to with all the more anxiety.

Ottilie meantime was complete mistress of the household —and how could it be otherwise, with her quick methodical ways of working? Indeed, her whole mode of thought was suited better to home life than to the world, and to a more

free existence.   Edward soon observed that she only walked
about with them out of a desire to please; that when she
stayed out late with them in the evening it was because she
thought it a sort of social duty, and that she would often find
a pretext in some household matter for going in again—consequently he soon managed so to arrange the walks which they
took together, that they should be at home before sunset;
and he began again, what he had long left off, to read aloud
poetry—particularly such as had for its subject the expression
of a pure but passionate love.

They ordinarily sat in the evening in the same places round
a small table—Charlotte on the sofa, Ottilie on a chair opposite to her, and the gentlemen on each side.   Ottilie's place was
on Edward's right, the side where he put the candle when he
was reading—at such times she would draw her chair a little
nearer to look over him, for Ottilie also trusted her own eyes
better than another person's lips, and Edward would then
always make a move towards her, that it might be as easy as
possible for her—indeed he would frequently make longer
stops than necessary, that he might not turn over before she
had got to the bottom of the page.

Charlotte and the Captain observed this, and exchanged
many a quiet smile at it; but they were both taken by surprise at another symptom, in which Ottilie's latent feeling
accidentally displayed itself.

One evening, which had been partly spoilt for them by a
tedious visit, Edward proposed that they should not separate
so early—he felt inclined for music—he would take his flute,
which he had not done for many days past.   Charlotte looked
for the sonatas which they generally played together, and they
were not to be found.   Ottilie, with some hesitation, said that
they were in her room—she had taken them there to copy
them.

"And you can, you will, accompany me on the piano?"
cried Edward, his eyes sparkling with pleasure.   "I think
perhaps I can," Ottilie answered.   She brought the music and
sate down to the instrument.   The others listened, and were
sufficiently surprised to hear how perfectly Ottilie had taught
herself the piece—but far more surprised were they at the
way in which she contrived to adopt herself to Edward's style
of playing.   Adapt herself, is not the right expression—Char-

lotte's skill and power enabled her, in order to please her husband, to keep up with him when he went too fast, and hold in for him if he hesitated; but Ottilie, who had several times heard them play the sonata together, seemed to have learnt it according to the idea in which they accompanied each other—she had so completely made his defects her own, that a kind of living whole resulted from it, which did not move indeed according to exact rule, but the effect of which was in the highest degree pleasant and delightful. The composer himself would have been pleased to hear his work disfigured in a manner so charming.

Charlotte and the Captain watched this strange unexpected occurrence in silence, with the kind of feeling with which we often observe the actions of children—unable exactly to approve of them, from the serious consequences which may follow, and yet without being able to find fault, perhaps with a kind of envy. For, indeed, the regard of these two for one another was growing also, as well as that of the others—and it was perhaps only the more perilous because they were both stronger, more certain of themselves, and better able to restrain themselves.

The Captain had already begun to feel that a habit which he could not resist was threatening to bind him to Charlotte. He forced himself to stay away at the hour when she commonly used to be at the works; by getting up very early in the morning he contrived to finish there whatever he had to do, and went back to the castle to his work in his own room. The first day or two Charlotte thought it was an accident—she looked for him in every place where she thought he could possibly be. Then she thought she understood him—and admired him all the more.

Avoiding, as the Captain now did, being alone with Charlotte, the more industriously did he labour to hurry forward the preparations for keeping her rapidly-approaching birthday with all splendour. While he was bringing up the new road from below behind the village, he made the men, under pretence that he wanted stones, begin working at the top as well, and work down, to meet the others; and he had calculated his arrangements so that the two should exactly meet on the eve of the day. The excavations for the new house were already done; the rock was blown away with gunpowder; and a fair foundation-stone had been hewn, with a hollow chamber, and a flat slab adjusted to cover it.

This outward activity, these little mysterious purposes of friendship, prompted by feelings which more or less they were obliged to repress, rather prevented the little party when together from being as lively as usual. Edward, who felt that there was a sort of void, one evening called upon the Captain to fetch his violin—Charlotte should play the piano, and he should accompany her. The Captain was unable to refuse the general request, and they executed together one of the most difficult pieces of music with an ease, and freedom, and feeling, which could not but afford themselves, and the two who were listening to them, the greatest delight. They promised themselves a frequent repetition of it, as well as further practice together. "They do it better than we, Ottilie," said Edward; "we will admire them—but we can enjoy ourselves together too."

CHAPTER IX.

THE birthday was come, and everything was ready. The wall was all complete which protected the raised village road against the water, and so was the walk; passing the church, for short time it followed the path which had been laid out by Charlotte, and then winding upwards among the rocks, inclined first under the summer-house to the right, and then, after a wide sweep, passed back above it to the right again, and so by degrees out on to the summit.

A large party had assembled for the occasion. They went first to church, where they found the whole congregation collected together in their holiday dresses. After service, they filed out in order; first the boys, then the young men, then the old: after them came the party from the castle, with their visitors and retinue; and the village maidens, young girls, and women, brought up the rear.

At the turn of the walk, a raised stone seat had been contrived, where the Captain made Charlotte and the visitors stop and rest. From here they could see over the whole distance from the beginning to the end—the troops of men who had gone up before them, the file of women following, and now drawing up to where they were. It was lovely weather, and the whole effect was singularly beautiful. Charlotte was taken by surprise, she was touched, and she pressed the Captain's hand warmly.

They followed the crowd who had slowly ascended, and were now forming a circle round the spot where the future house was to stand. The lord of the castle, his family, and the principal strangers were now invited to descend into the vault, where the foundation-stone, supported on one side, lay ready to be let down. A well-dressed mason, a trowel in one hand and a hammer in the other, came forward, and with much grace spoke an address in verse, of which in prose we can give but an imperfect rendering.

"Three things," he began, "are to be looked to in a building—that it stand on the right spot; that it be securely founded; that it be successfully executed. The first is the business of the master of the house—his and his only. As in the city the prince and the council alone determine where a building shall be, so in the country it is the right of the lord of the soil that he shall say, 'Here my dwelling shall stand; here, and nowhere else.'"

Edward and Ottilie were standing opposite one another, as these words were spoken; but they did not venture to look up and exchange glances.

"To the third, the execution, there is neither art nor handicraft which must not in some way contribute. But the second, the founding, is the province of the mason; and, boldly to speak it out, it is the head and front of all the undertaking—a solemn thing it is—and our bidding you descend hither is full of meaning. You are celebrating your Festival in the deep of the earth. Here within this small hollow spot, you shew us the honour of appearing as witnesses of our mysterious craft. Presently we shall lower down this carefully-hewn stone into its place; and soon these earth-walls, now ornamented with fair and worthy persons, will be no more accessible—but will be closed in for ever!

"This foundation-stone, which with its angles typifies the just angles of the building, with the sharpness of its moulding, the regularity of it, and with the truth of its lines to the horizontal and perpendicular, the uprightness and equal height of all the walls, we might now without more ado let down—it would rest in its place with its own weight. But even here there shall not fail of lime and means to bind it. For as human beings who may be well inclined to each other by nature, yet hold more firmly together when the law cements them, so are stones also, whose forms may already fit together, united far better by these binding forces. It is not seemly to be idle among the working, and here you will not refuse to be our fellow-labourer,"—with these words he reached the trowel to Charlotte, who threw mortar with it under the stone— several of the others were then desired to do the same, and then it was at once let fall. Upon which the hammer was placed next in Charlotte's, and then in the others' hands, to strike three times with it, and conclude, in this expression, the wedlock of the stone with the earth.

"The work of the mason," went on the speaker, "now under the free sky as we are, if it be not done in concealment, yet must pass into concealment—the soil will be laid smoothly in, and thrown over this stone, and with the walls which we rear into the daylight we in the end are seldom remembered. The works of the stone-cutter and the carver remain under the eyes; but for us it is not to complain when the plasterer blots out the last trace of our hands, and appropriates our work to himself; when he overlays it, and smooths it, and colours it.

"Not from regard for the opinion of others, but from respect for himself, the mason will be faithful in his calling. There is none who has more need to feel in himself the consciousness of what he is. When the house is finished, when the soil is smoothed, and the surface plastered over, and the outside all overwrought with ornament, he can even see in yet through all disguises, and still recognize those exact and careful adjustments, to which the whole is indebted for its being and for its persistence.

"But as the man who commits some evil deed has to fear, that, notwithstanding all precautions, it will one day come to light—so too must he expect who has done some good thing in secret, that it also, in spite of himself, will appear in the day; and therefore we make this foundation-stone at the same time a stone of memorial. Here, in these various hollows which have been hewn into it, many things are now to be buried, as a witness to some far-off world—these metal cases hermetically sealed contain documents in writing; matters of various note are engraved on these plates; in these fair glass bottles we bury the best old wine, with a note of the year of its vintage. We have coins too of many kinds, from the mint of the current year. All this we have received through the liberality of him for whom we build. There is space yet remaining, if guest or spectator desires to offer anything to the after-world!"

After a slight pause the speaker looked round; but, as is commonly the case on such occasions, no one was prepared; they were all taken by surprise. At last, a merry-looking young officer set the example, and said, "If I am to contribute anything which as yet is not to be found in this treasure-chamber, it shall be a pair of buttons from my uniform—I don't see why they do not deserve to go down to posterity!" No sooner said than done, and then a number of persons found something of the same sort which they could do; the young ladies did not hesitate to throw in some of their side hair combs—smelling bottles and other trinkets were not spared. Only Ottilie hung back; till a kind word from Edward roused her from the abstraction in which she was watching the various things being heaped in. Then she unclasped from her neck the gold chain on which her father's picture had hung, and with a light gentle hand laid it down on the other jewels. Edward rather disarranged the proceedings, by at once, in some haste, having the cover let fall, and fastened down.

The young mason who had been most active through all this, again took his place as orator, and went on, "We lay down this stone for ever, for the establishing the present and the future possessors of this house. But in that we bury this treasure together with it, we do it in the remembrance—in this most enduring of works—of the perishableness of all human things. We remember that a time may come when this cover so fast sealed shall again be lifted: and that can only be when all shall again be destroyed which as yet we have not brought into being.

"But now—now that at once it may begin to be, back with our thoughts out of the future—back into the present. At once, after the feast which we have this day kept together, let us on with our labour; let no one of all those trades which are to work on our foundation, through us keep unwilling holiday. Let the building rise swiftly to its height, and out of the windows, which as yet have no existence, may the master of the house, with his family and with his guests, look forth with a glad heart over his broad lands. To him and to all here present herewith be health and happiness."

With these words he drained a richly cut tumbler at a draught, and flung it into the air, thereby to signify the excess of pleasure by destroying the vessel which had served for such a solemn occasion. This time, however, it fell out otherwise. The glass did not fall back to the earth, and indeed without a miracle.

In order to get forward with the buildings, they had already thrown out the whole of the soil at the opposite corner; indeed, they had begun to raise the wall, and for this purpose had reared a scaffold as high as was absolutely necessary. On the occasion of the festival, boards had been laid along the top of this, and a number of spectators were allowed to stand there. It had been meant principally for the advantage of the workmen themselves. The glass had flown up there, and had been caught by one of them, who took it as a sign of good luck for himself. He waved it round without letting it out of his hand, and the letters E and O were to be seen very richly cut upon it, running one into the other. It was one of the glasses which had been executed for Edward when he was a boy.

The scaffoldings were again deserted, and the most active among the party climbed up to look round them, and could not speak enough in praise of the beauty of the prospect on all sides. How many new discoveries does not a person make when on some high point he ascends but a single story higher. Inland many fresh villages came in sight. The line of the river could be traced like a thread of silver; indeed, one of the party thought that he distinguished the spires of the capital. On the other side, behind the wooded hill, the blue peaks of the far-off mountains were seen rising, and the country immediately about them was spread out like a map.

" If the three ponds," cried some one, " were but thrown

together to make a single sheet of water, there would be everything here which is noblest and most excellent."

"That might easily be effected," the Captain said. "In early times they must have formed all one lake among the hills here."

"Only I must beseech you to spare my clump of planes and poplars that stand so prettily by the centre pond," said Edward. "See,"—he turned to Ottilie, bringing her a few steps forward, and pointing down,—"those trees I planted myself."

"How long have they been standing there?" asked Ottilie.

"Just about as long as you have been in the world," replied Edward. "Yes, my dear child, I planted them when you were still lying in your cradle."

The party now betook themselves back to the castle. After dinner was over they were invited to walk through the village to take a glance at what had been done there as well. At a hint from the Captain, the inhabitants had collected in front of the houses. They were not standing in rows, but formed in natural family groups, partly occupied at their evening work, part out enjoying themselves on the new benches. They had determined, as an agreeable duty which they imposed upon themselves, to have everything in its present order and cleanliness, at least every Sunday and holiday.

A little party, held together by such feelings as had grown up among our friends, is always unpleasantly interrupted by a large concourse of people. All four were delighted to find themselves again alone in the large drawing-room, but this sense of home was a little disturbed by a letter which was brought to Edward, giving notice of fresh guests who were to arrive the following day.

"It is as we supposed," Edward cried to Charlotte. "The Count will not stay away; he is coming to-morrow."

"Then the Baroness, too, is not far off," answered Charlotte.

"Doubtless not," said Edward. "She is coming, too, to-morrow, from another place. They only beg to be allowed to stay for a night; the next day they will go on together."

"We must prepare for them in time, Ottilie," said Charlotte.

"What arrangement shall I desire to be made?" Ottilie asked.

Charlotte gave a general direction, and Ottilie left the room.

The Captain inquired into the relation in which these two persons stood towards one another, and with which he was only very generally acquainted. They had some time before, both being already married, fallen violently in love with one another; a double marriage was not to be interfered with without attracting attention. A divorce was proposed. On the Baroness's side it could be effected, on that of the Count it could not. They were obliged seemingly to separate, but their position towards one another remained unchanged, and though in the winter at the Residence they were unable to be together, they indemnified themselves in the summer, while making tours and staying at watering-places.

They were both slightly older than Edward and Charlotte, and had been intimate with them from early times at court. The connection had never been absolutely broken off, although it was impossible to approve of their proceedings. On the present occasion their coming was most unwelcome to Charlotte; and if she had looked closely into her reasons for feeling it so, she would have found it was on account of Ottilie. The poor innocent girl should not have been brought so early in contact with such an example.

"It would have been more convenient if they had not come till a couple of days later," Edward was saying, as Ottilie re-entered, "till we had finished with this business of the farm. The deed of sale is complete. One copy of it I have here, but we want a second, and our old clerk has fallen ill." The Captain offered his services, and so did Charlotte, but there was something or other to object to both of them.

"Give it to me," cried Ottilie, a little hastily.

"You will never be able to finish it," said Charlotte.

"And really I must have it early the day after to-morrow, and it is long," Edward added.

"It shall be ready," Ottilie cried; and the paper was already in her hands.

The next morning, as they were looking out from their highest windows for their visitors, whom they intended to go some way and meet, Edward said, "Who is that yonder, riding slowly along the road?"

The Captain described accurately the figure of the horseman.

"Then it is he," said Edward; "the particulars, which you can see better than I, agree very well with the general figure, which I can see too. It is Mittler; but what is he doing, coming riding at such a pace as that?"

The figure came nearer, and Mittler it veritably was. They received him with warm greetings as he came slowly up the steps.

"Why did you not come yesterday?" Edward cried, as he approached.

"I do not like your grand festivities," answered he; "but I am come to-day to keep my friend's birthday with you quietly."

"How are you able to find time enough?" asked Edward, with a laugh.

"My visit, if you can value it, you owe to an observation which I made yesterday. I was spending a right happy afternoon in a house where I had established peace, and then I heard that a birthday was being kept here. Now this is what I call selfish, after all, said I to myself: you will only enjoy yourself with those whose broken peace you have mended. Why cannot you for once go and be happy with friends who keep the peace for themselves? No sooner said than done. Here I am, as I determined with myself that I would be."

"Yesterday you would have met a large party here; to-day you will find but a small one," said Charlotte; "you will meet the Count and the Baroness, with whom you have had enough to do already, I believe."

Out of the middle of the party, who had all four come down to welcome him, the strange man dashed in the keenest disgust, seizing at the same time his hat and whip. "Some unlucky star is always over me," he cried, "directly I try to rest and enjoy myself. What business have I going out of my proper character? I ought never to have come, and now I am persecuted away. Under one roof with those two I will not remain, and you take care of yourselves. They bring nothing but mischief; their nature is like leaven, and propagates its own contagion."

They tried to pacify him, but it was in vain. "Whoever

strikes at marriage," he cried ;—" whoever, either by word or act, undermines this, the foundation of all moral society, that man has to settle with me, and if I cannot become his master, I take care to settle myself out of his way. Marriage is the beginning and the end of all culture. It makes the savage mild ; and the most cultivated has no better opportunity for displaying his gentleness. Indissoluble it must be, because it brings so much happiness that what small exceptional unhappiness it may bring counts for nothing in the balance. And what do men mean by talking of unhappiness ? Impatience it is which from time to time comes over them, and then they fancy themselves unhappy. Let them wait till the moment is gone by, and then they will bless their good fortune that what has stood so long continues standing. There never can be any adequate ground for separation. The condition of man is pitched so high, in its joys and in its sorrows, that the sum which two married people owe to one another defies calculation. It is an infinite debt, which can only be discharged through all eternity.

" Its annoyances marriage may often have; I can well believe that, and it is as it should be. We are all married to our consciences, and there are times when we should be glad to be divorced from them; mine gives me more annoyance than ever a man or a woman can give."

All this he poured out with the greatest vehemence : he would very likely have gone on speaking longer, had not the sound of the postilions' horns given notice of the arrival of the visitors, who, as if on a concerted arrangement, drove into the castle-court from opposite sides at the same moment. Mittler slipped away as their host hastened to receive them, and desiring that his horse might be brought out immediately, rode angrily off.

CHAPTER X.

THE visitors were welcomed and brought in. They were delighted to find themselves again in the same house and in the same rooms where in early times they had passed many happy days, but which they had not seen for a long time. Their friends too were very glad to see them. The Count and the Baroness had both those tall fine figures which please in middle life almost better than in youth. If something of the first bloom had faded off them, yet there was an air in their appearance which was always irresistibly attractive. Their manners too were thoroughly charming. Their free way of taking hold of life and dealing with it, their happy humour, and apparent easy unembarrassment, communicated itself at once to the rest; and a lighter atmosphere hung about the whole party, without their having observed it stealing on them.

The effect made itself felt immediately on the entrance of the new-comers. They were fresh from the fashionable world, as was to be seen at once, in their dress, in their equipment, and in everything about them; and they formed a contrast not a little striking with our friends, their country style, and the vehement feelings which were at work underneath among them. This, however, very soon disappeared in the stream of past recollection and present interests, and a rapid, lively conversation soon united them all. After a short time they again separated. The ladies withdrew to their own apartments, and there found amusement enough in the many things which they had to tell each other, and in setting to work at the same time to examine the new fashions, the spring dresses, bonnets, and such like; while the gentlemen were employing themselves looking at the new travelling chariots, trotting out the horses, and beginning at once to bargain and exchange.

They did not meet again till dinner; in the mean time they had changed their dress. And here, too, the newly-arrived pair showed to all advantage. Everything they wore was new, and in a style which their friends at the castle had never seen, and yet, being accustomed to it themselves, it appeared perfectly natural and graceful.

The conversation was brilliant and well sustained, as,

F

indeed, in the company of such persons everything and nothing appears to interest. They spoke in French that the attendants might not understand what they said, and swept in happiest humour over all that was passing in the great or the middle world. On one particular subject they remained, however, longer than was desirable. It was occasioned by Charlotte asking after one of her early friends, of whom she had to learn, with some distress, that she was on the point of being separated from her husband.

"It is a melancholy thing," Charlotte said, "when we fancy our absent friends are finally settled, when we believe persons very dear to us to be provided for for life, suddenly to hear that their fortunes are cast loose once more; that they have to strike into a fresh path of life, and very likely a most insecure one."

"Indeed, my dear friend," the Count answered, "it is our own fault if we allow ourselves to be surprised at such things. We please ourselves with imagining matters of this earth, and particularly matrimonial connections, as very enduring; and as concerns this last point, the plays which we see over and over again help to mislead us; being, as they are, so untrue to the course of the world. In a comedy we see a marriage as the last aim of a desire which is hindered and crossed through a number of acts, and at the instant when it is reached the curtain falls, and the momentary satisfaction continues to ring on in our ears. But in the world it is very different. The play goes on still behind the scenes, and when the curtain rises again we may see and hear, perhaps, little enough of the marriage."

"It cannot be so very bad, however," said Charlotte, smiling. "We see people who have gone off the boards of the theatre, ready enough to undertake a part upon them again."

"There is nothing to say against that," said the Count. "In a new character a man may readily venture on a second trial; and when we know the world we see clearly that it is only this positive eternal duration of marriage in a world where everything is in motion, which has anything unbecoming about it. A certain friend of mine, whose humour displays itself principally in suggestions for new laws, maintained that every marriage should be concluded only for five years.

Five, he said, was a sacred number—pretty and uneven. Such a period would be long enough for people to learn one another's character, bring a child or two into the world, quarrel, separate, and what was best, get reconciled again. He would often exclaim, ' How happily the first part of the time would pass away !' Two or three years, at least, would be perfect bliss. On one side or other there would not fail to be a wish to have the relation continue longer, and the amiability would increase the nearer they got to the parting time. The indifferent, even the dissatisfied party, would be softened and gained over by such behaviour; they would forget, as in pleasant company the hours pass always unobserved, how the time went by, and they would be delightfully surprised when, after the term had run out, they first observed that they had unknowingly prolonged it."

Charming and pleasant as all this sounded, and deep (Charlotte felt it to her soul) as was the moral significance which lay below it, expressions of this kind, on Ottilie's account, were most distasteful to her. She knew very well that nothing was more dangerous than the licentious conversation which treats culpable or semi-culpable actions as if they were common, ordinary, and even laudable, and of such undesirable kind assuredly were all which touched on the sacredness of marriage. She endeavoured, therefore, in her skilful way, to give the conversation another turn, and when she found that she could not, it vexed her that Ottilie had managed everything so well that there was no occasion for her to leave the table. In her quiet observant way a nod or a look was enough for her to signify to the head servant whatever was to be done, and everything went off perfectly, although there were a couple of strange men in livery in the way, who were rather a trouble than a convenience. And so the Count, without feeling Charlotte's hints, went on giving his opinions on the same subject. Generally, he was little enough apt to be tedious in conversation; but this was a thing which weighed so heavily on his heart, and the difficulties which he found in getting separated from his wife were so great that it had made him bitter against everything which concerned the marriage bond,—that very bond which, notwithstanding, he was so anxiously desiring between himself and the Baroness.

F 2

"The same friend," he went on, "has another law which he proposes. A marriage shall only be held indissoluble when either both parties, or at least one or the other, enter into it for the third time. Such persons must be supposed to acknowledge beyond a doubt that they find marriage indispensable for themselves; they have had opportunities of thoroughly knowing themselves; of knowing how they conducted themselves in their earlier unions; whether they have any peculiarities of temper, which are a more frequent cause of separation than bad dispositions. People would then observe one another more closely; they would pay as much attention to the married as to the unmarried, no one being able to tell how things may turn out."

"That would add no little to the interest of society," said Edward. "As things are now, when a man is married nobody cares any more either for his virtues or for his vices."

"Under this arrangement," the Baroness struck in, laughing, "our good hosts have passed successfully over their two steps, and may make themselves ready for their third."

"Things have gone happily with them," said the Count. "In their case death has done with a good will what in others the consistorial courts do with a very bad one.

"Let the dead rest," said Charlotte, with a half serious look.

"Why so," persevered the Count, "when we can remember them with honour? They were generous enough to content themselves with less than their number of years for the sake of the larger good which they could leave behind them."

"Alas! that in such cases," said the Baroness, with a suppressed sigh, "happiness is only bought with the sacrifice of our fairest years."

"Indeed, yes," answered the Count; "and it might drive us to despair, if it were not the same with everything in this world. Nothing goes as we hope. Children do not fulfil what they promise; young people very seldom;—and if they keep their word, the world does not keep its word with them."

Charlotte, who was delighted that the conversation had taken a turn at last, replied cheerfully,

"Well, then, we must content ourselves with enjoying what good we are to have in fragments and pieces, as we can get it; and the sooner we can accustom ourselves to this the better."

"Certainly," the Count answered, "you two have had the enjoyment of very happy times. When I look back upon the years when you and Edward were the loveliest couple at the court, I see nothing now to be compared with those brilliant times, and such magnificent figures. When you two used to dance together, all eyes were turned upon you, fastened upon you, while you saw nothing but each other."

"So much has changed since those days," said Charlotte, "that we can listen to such pretty things about ourselves without our modesty being shocked at them."

"I often privately found fault with Edward," said the Count, "for not being more firm. Those singular parents of his would certainly have given way at last; and ten fair years is no trifle to gain."

"I must take Edward's part," struck in the Baroness. "Charlotte was not altogether without fault—not altogether free from what we must call prudential considerations; and although she had a real, hearty love for Edward, and did in her secret soul intend to marry him, I can bear witness how sorely she often tried him; and it was through this that he was at last unluckily prevailed upon to leave her and go abroad, and try to forget her."

Edward bowed to the Baroness, and seemed grateful for her advocacy.

"And then I must add this," she continued, "in excuse for Charlotte. The man who was at that time suing for her, had for a long time given proofs of his constant attachment to her; and, when one came to know him well, was a far more loveable person than the rest of you may like to acknowledge."

"My dear friend," the Count replied, a little pointedly, "confess, now, that he was not altogether indifferent to yourself, and that Charlotte had more to fear from you than from any other rival. I find it one of the highest traits in women, that they continue so long in their regard for a man, and that absence of no duration will serve to disturb or remove it."

"This fine feature, men possess, perhaps, even more,"

answered the Baroness. "At any rate, I have observed with
you, my dear Count, that no one has more influence over you
than a lady to whom you were once attached. I have seen
you take more trouble to do things when a certain person has
asked you, than the friend of this moment would have
obtained of you, if she had tried."

"Such a charge as that one must bear the best way one
can," replied the Count. "But as to what concerns Charlotte's first husband, I could not endure him, because he
parted so sweet a pair from one another—a really pre-
destined pair, who, once brought together, have no reason
to fear the five years, or be thinking of a second or third
marriage."

"We must try," Charlotte said, "to make up for what we
then allowed to slip from us."

"Aye, and you must keep to that," said the Count; "your
first marriages," he continued, with some vehemence, "were
exactly marriages of the true detestable sort. And, unhappily, marriages generally, even the best, have (forgive me for
using a strong expression) something awkward about them.
They destroy the delicacy of the relation; everything is made
to rest on the broad certainty out of which one side or
other, at least, is too apt to make their own advantage. It is
all a matter of course; and they seem only to have got themselves tied together, that one or the other, or both, may go
their own way the more easily."

At this moment, Charlotte, who was determined once for
all that she would put an end to the conversation, made a
bold effort at turning it, and succeeded. It then became
more general. She and her husband and the Captain were
able to take a part in it. Even Ottilie had to give her
opinion; and the dessert was enjoyed in the happiest humour.
It was particularly beautiful, being composed almost entirely
of the rich summer fruits in elegant baskets, with epergnes
of lovely flowers arranged in exquisite taste.

The new laying-out of the park came to be spoken of; and
immediately after dinner they went to look at what was going
on. Ottilie withdrew, under pretence of having household
matters to look to; in reality, it was to set to work again at
the transcribing. The Count fell into conversation with the
Captain, and Charlotte afterwards joined them. When they

were at the summit of the height, the Captain good-naturedly ran back to fetch the plan, and in his absence the Count said to Charlotte,

"He is an exceedingly pleasing person. He is very well informed, and his knowledge is always ready. His practical power, too, seems methodical and vigorous. What he is doing here would be of great importance in some higher sphere."

Charlotte listened to the Captain's praises with an inward delight. She collected herself, however, and composedly and clearly confirmed what the Count had said. But she was not a little startled when he continued :

"This acquaintance falls most opportunely for me. I know of a situation for which he is perfectly suited, and I shall be doing the greatest favour to a friend of mine, a man of high rank, by recommending to him a person who is so exactly everything which he desires."

Charlotte felt as if a thunder-stroke had fallen on her. The Count did not observe it : women, being accustomed at all times to hold themselves in restraint, are always able, even in the most extraordinary cases, to maintain an apparent composure ; but she heard not a word more of what the Count said, though he went on speaking.

"When I have made up my mind upon a thing, " he added, " I am quick about it. I have put my letter together already in my head, and I shall write it immediately. You can find me some messenger, who can ride off with it this evening."

Charlotte was suffering agonies. Startled with the proposal, and shocked at herself, she was unable to utter a word. Happily, the Count continued talking of his plans for the Captain, the desirableness of which was only too apparent to Charlotte.

It was time that the Captain returned. He came up and unrolled his design before the Count. But with what changed eyes Charlotte now looked at the friend whom she was to lose. In her necessity, she bowed and turned away, and hurried down to the summer-house. Before she was half way there, the tears were streaming from her eyes, and she flung herself into the narrow room in the little hermitage, and gave herself up to an agony, a passion, a despair, of the possibility of which, but a few moments before, she had not had the slightest conception.

Edward had gone with the Baroness in the other direction towards the ponds. This ready-witted lady, who liked to be in the secret about everything, soon observed, in a few conversational feelers which she threw out, that Edward was very fluent and free-spoken in praise of Ottilie. She contrived in the most natural way to lead him out by degrees so completely, that at last she had not a doubt remaining that here was not merely an incipient fancy, but a veritable, full-grown passion.

Married women, if they have no particular love for one another, yet are silently in league together, especially against young girls. The consequences of such an inclination presented themselves only too quickly to her world-experienced spirit. Added to this, she had been already, in the course of the day, talking to Charlotte about Ottilie; she had disapproved of her remaining in the country, particularly being a girl of so retiring a character; and she had proposed to take Ottilie with her to the residence of a friend, who was just then bestowing great expense on the education of an only daughter, and who was only looking about to find some well-disposed companion for her,—to put her in the place of a second child, and let her share in every advantage. Charlotte had taken time to consider. But now this glimpse of the Baroness into Edward's heart changed what had been but a suggestion at once into a settled determination; and the more rapidly she made up her mind about it, the more she outwardly seemed to flatter Edward's wishes. Never was there any one more self-possessed than this lady; and to have mastered ourselves in extraordinary cases, disposes us to treat even a common case with dissimulation—it makes us inclined, as we have had to do so much violence to ourselves, to extend our control over others, and hold ourselves in a degree compensated in what we outwardly gain for what we inwardly have been obliged to sacrifice. To this feeling there is often joined a kind of secret, spiteful pleasure in the blind, unconscious ignorance with which the victim walks on into the snare. It is not the immediately doing as we please which we enjoy, but the thought of the surprise and exposure which is to follow. And thus was the Baroness malicious enough to invite Edward to come with Charlotte and pay her a visit at the grape-gathering; and, to his question whether they might bring Ottilie with them, to frame an answer which, if he pleased, he might interpret to his wishes.

Edward had already begun to pour out his delight at the beautiful scenery, the broad river, the hills, the rocks, the vineyard, the old castles, the water-parties, and the jubilee at the grape-gathering, the wine-pressing, etc., in all of which, in the innocence. of his heart, he was only exuberating in the anticipation of the impression which these scenes were to make on the fresh spirit of Ottilie. At this moment they saw her approaching, and the Baroness said quickly to Edward, that he had better say nothing to her of this intended autumn expedition—things which we set our hearts upon so long before, so often failing to come to pass. Edward gave his promise; but he obliged his companion to move more quickly to meet her; and at last, when they came very close, he ran on several steps in advance. A heartfelt happiness expressed itself in his whole being. He kissed her hand as he pressed into it a nosegay of wild flowers, which he had gathered on his way.

The Baroness felt bitter to her heart at the sight of it. At the same time that she was able to disapprove of what was really objectionable in this affection, she could not bear to see what was sweet and beautiful in it thrown away on such a poor paltry girl.

When they had collected again at the supper-table, an entirely different temper was spread over the party. The Count, who had in the meantime written his letter and dispatched a messenger with it, occupied himself with the Captain, whom he had been drawing out more and more—spending the whole evening at his side, talking of serious matters. The Baroness, who sat on the Count's right, found but small amusement in this; nor did Edward find any more. The latter, first because he was thirsty, and then because he was excited, did not spare the wine, and attached himself entirely to Ottilie, whom he had made sit by him. On the other side, next to the Captain, sat Charlotte; for her it was hard, it was almost impossible, to conceal the emotion under which she was suffering.

The Baroness had sufficient time to make her observations

at leisure. She perceived Charlotte's uneasiness, and occupied as she was with Edward's passion for Ottilie, she easily satisfied herself that her abstraction and distress were owing to her husband's behaviour; and she set herself to consider in what way she could best compass her ends.

Supper was over, and the party remained divided. The Count, whose object was to probe the Captain to the bottom, had to try many turns before he could arrive at what he wished with so quiet, so little vain, but so exceedingly laconic a person. They walked up and down together on one side of the saloon, while Edward, excited with wine and hope, was laughing with Ottilie at a window, and Charlotte and the Baroness were walking backwards and forwards, without speaking, on the other side. Their being so silent, and their standing about in this uneasy, listless way, had its effect at last in breaking up the rest of the party. The ladies withdrew to their rooms, the gentlemen to the other wing of the castle; and so this day appeared to be concluded.

CHAPTER XI.

EDWARD went with the Count to his room. They continued talking, and he was easily prevailed upon to stay a little time longer there. The Count lost himself in old times, spoke eagerly of Charlotte's beauty, which, as a critic, he dwelt upon with much warmth.

" A pretty foot is a great gift of nature," he said. " It is a grace which never perishes. I observed it to-day, as she was walking. I should almost have liked to have kissed her shoe, and repeat that somewhat barbarous but significant practice of the Sarmatians, who know no better way of showing reverence for any one they love or respect, than by using his shoe to drink his health out of."

The point of the foot did not remain the only subject of praise between two old acquaintances; they went from the person back upon old stories and adventures, and came on the hindrances which at that time people had thrown in the way of the lovers' meetings—what trouble they had taken, what arts they had been obliged to devise, only to be able to tell each other that they loved.

"Do you remember," continued the Count, "an adventure in which I most unselfishly stood your friend when their High Mightinesses were on a visit to your uncle, and were all together in that great, straggling castle. The day went in festivities and glitter of all sorts; and a part of the night at least in pleasant conversation."

"And you, in the meantime, had observed the back-way which led to the court ladies' quarter," said Edward, "and so managed to effect an interview for me with my beloved."

"And she," replied the Count, "thinking more of propriety than of my enjoyment, had kept a frightful old duenna with her. So that, while you two, between looks and words, got on extremely well together, my lot, in the meanwhile, was far from pleasant."

"It was only yesterday," answered Edward, "when we heard that you were coming, that I was talking over the story with my wife, and describing our adventure on returning. We missed the road, and got into the entrance-hall from the garden. Knowing our way from thence so well as we did, we supposed we could get along easily enough. But you remember our surprise on opening the door. The floor was covered over with mattresses, on which the giants lay in rows stretched out and sleeping. The single sentinel at his post looked wonderingly at us; but we, in the cool way young men do things, strode quietly on over the outstretched boots, without disturbing a single one of the snoring children of Anak."

"I had the strongest inclination to stumble," the Count said, "that there might be an alarm given. What a resurrection we should have witnessed."

At this moment the castle clock struck twelve.

"It is deep midnight," the Count added, laughing, "and just the proper time; I must ask you, my dear Baron, to show me a kindness. Do you guide me to-night, as I guided you then. I promised the Baroness that I would see her before going to bed. We have had no opportunity of any private talk together the whole day. We have not seen each other for a long time, and it is only natural that we should wish for a confidential hour. If you will show me the way there, I will manage to get back again; and in any case, there will be no boots for me to stumble over."

" I shall be very glad to show you such a piece of hospitality," answered Edward; " only the three ladies are together in the same wing. Who knows whether we shall not find them still with one another, or make some other mistake, which may have a strange appearance ?"

" Do not be afraid," said the Count; " the Baroness expects me. She is sure by this time to be in her own room, and alone."

" Well, then, the thing is easy enough," Edward answered.

He took a candle, and lighted the Count down a private staircase leading into a long gallery. At the end of this, he opened a small door. They mounted a winding flight of stairs, which brought them out upon a narrow landing-place; and then, putting the candle in the Count's hand, he pointed to a tapestried door on the right, which opened readily at the first trial, and admitted the Count, leaving Edward outside in the dark.

Another door on the left led into Charlotte's sleeping-room. He heard her voice, and listened. She was speaking to her maid. " Is Ottilie in bed ?" she asked. " No," was the answer; " she is sitting writing in the room below." " You may light the night-lamp," said Charlotte; " I shall not want you any more. It is late. I can put out the candle, and do whatever I may want else myself."

It was a delight to Edward to hear that Ottilie was writing still. She is working for me, he thought triumphantly. Through the darkness, he fancied he could see her sitting all alone at her desk. He thought he would go to her, and see her; and how she would turn to receive him. He felt a longing, which he could not resist, to be near her once more. But, from where he was, there was no way to the apartments which she occupied. He now found himself immediately at his wife's door. A singular change of feeling came over him. He tried the handle,. but the bolts were shot. He knocked gently. Charlotte did not hear him. She was walking rapidly up and down in the large dressing-room adjoining. She was repeating over and over what, since the Count's unexpected proposal, she had often enough had to say to herself. The Captain seemed to stand before her. At home, and everywhere, he had become her all in all. And now he was to go; and it was all to be desolate again. She repeated whatever wise things one can say to oneself; she even anticipated, as people so often do, the wretched comfort, that time would come at last to her relief; and then she cursed the time which would have to pass before it could lighten her sufferings—she cursed the dead, cold time when they would be lightened. At last she burst into tears; they were the more welcome, since tears with her were rare. She flung herself on the sofa, and gave herself up unreservedly to her sufferings. Edward, meanwhile, could not take himself from the door. He knocked again; and a third time rather louder; so that Charlotte, in the stillness of the night, distinctly heard it, and started up in fright. Her first thought was,—it can only be, it must be, the Captain; her second, that it was impossible. She thought she must have been deceived. But surely she had heard it; and she wished, and she feared to have heard it. She went into her sleeping-room, and walked lightly up to the bolted tapestry-door. She blamed herself for her fears. "Possibly it may be the Baroness wanting something," she said to herself; and she called out quietly and calmly, "Is anybody there?" A light voice answered, "It is I." "Who?" returned Charlotte, not being able to make out the voice. She thought she saw the Captain's figure standing at the door. In a rather louder tone, she heard the word "Edward!" She drew back the bolt, and her husband stood before her. He greeted her with some light jest. She was unable to reply in the same tone. He complicated the mysterious visit by his mysterious explanation of it.

"Well, then," he said at last, "I will confess, the real reason why I am come is, that I have made a vow to kiss your shoe this evening."

"It is long since you thought of such a thing as that," said Charlotte.

"So much the worse," he answered; "and so much the better."

She had thrown herself back in an armchair, to prevent him from seeing the slightness of her dress. He flung himself down before her, and she could not prevent him from giving her shoe a kiss. And when the shoe came off in his hand, he caught her foot and pressed it tenderly against his breast.

Charlotte was one of those women who, being of a naturally calm temperament, continue in marriage, without any purpose or any effort, the air and character of lovers. She was never expressive towards her husband; generally, indeed, she rather shrank from any warm demonstration on his part. It was not that she was cold, or at all hard and repulsive, but she remained always like a loving bride, who draws back with a kind of shyness even from what is permitted. And so Edward found her this evening, in a double sense. How sorely did she not long that her husband would go; the figure of his friend seemed to hover in the air and reproach her. But what should have had the effect of driving Edward away only attracted him the more. There were visible traces of emotion about her. She had been crying; and tears, which with weak persons detract from their graces, add immeasurably to the attractiveness of those whom we know commonly as strong and self-possessed.

Edward was so agreeable, so gentle, so pressing; he begged to be allowed to stay with her. He did not demand it, but half in fun, half in earnest, he tried to persuade her; he never thought of his rights. At last, as if in mischief, he blew out the candle.

In the dim lamplight, the inward affection, the imagination, maintained their rights over the real;—it was Ottilie that was resting in Edward's arms; and the Captain, now faintly, now clearly, hovered before Charlotte's soul. And so, strangely intermingled, the absent and the present flowed in a sweet enchantment one into the other.

And yet the present would not let itself be robbed of its own unlovely right. They spent a part of the night talking and laughing at all sorts of things, the more freely, as the heart had no part in it. But when Edward awoke in the morning, on his wife's breast, the day seemed to stare in with a sad, awful look, and the sun to be shining in upon a crime. He stole lightly from her side; and she found herself, with strange enough feelings, when she awoke, alone.

CHAPTER XII.

WHEN the party assembled again at breakfast, an attentive observer might have read in the behaviour of its various members the different things which were passing in their inner thoughts and feelings. The Count and the Baroness met with the air of happiness which a pair of lovers feel, who, after having been forced to endure a long separation, have mutually assured each other of their unaltered affection. On the other hand, Charlotte and Edward equally came into the presence of the Captain and Ottilie with a sense of shame and remorse. For such is the nature of love that it believes in no rights except its own, and all other rights vanish away before it. Ottilie was in child-like spirits. For her—she was almost what might be called open. The Captain appeared serious. His conversation with the Count, which had roused in him feelings that for some time past had been at rest and dormant, had made him only too keenly conscious that here he was not fulfilling his work, and at bottom was but squandering himself in a half-activity of idleness.

Hardly had their guests departed, when fresh visitors were announced—to Charlotte most welcomely, all she wished for being to be taken out of herself, and to have her attention dissipated. They annoyed Edward, who was longing to devote himself to Ottilie; and Ottilie did not like them either; the copy which had to be finished the next morning early being still incomplete. They staid a long time, and immediately that they were gone she hurried off to her room.

It was now evening. Edward, Charlotte, and the Captain had accompanied the strangers some little way on foot, before the latter got into their carriage, and previous to returning home they agreed to take a walk along the water-side.

A boat had come, which Edward had had fetched from a distance, at no little expense; and they decided that they would try whether it was easy to manage. It was made fast on the bank of the middle pond, not far from some old ash trees, on which they calculated to make an effect in their future improvements. There was to be a landing-place made there, and under the trees a seat was to be raised, with some wonderful architecture about it: it was to be the point for which people were to make when they went across the water.

"And where had we better have the landing-place on the other side?" said Edward. "I should think under my plane trees."

"They stand a little too far to the right," said the Captain. "You are nearer the castle if you land further down. However, we must think about it."

The Captain was already standing in the stern of the boat, and had taken up an oar. Charlotte got in, and Edward with her—he took the other oar; but as he was on the point of pushing off, he thought of Ottilie—he recollected that this water-party would keep him out late; who could tell when he would get back? He made up his mind shortly and promptly; sprang back to the bank, and reaching the other oar to the Captain, hurried home—making excuses to himself as he ran.

Arriving there he learnt that Ottilie had shut herself up— she was writing. In spite of the agreeable feeling that she was doing something for him, it was the keenest mortification to him not to be able to see her. His impatience increased every moment. He walked up and down the large drawing-room; he tried a thousand things, and could not fix his attention upon any. He was longing to see her alone, before Charlotte came back with the Captain. It was dark by this time, and the candles were lighted.

At last she came in beaming with loveliness: the sense that she had done something for her friend had lifted all her being above itself. She put down the original and her transcript on the table before Edward.

"Shall we collate them?" she said, with a smile.

Edward did not know what to answer. He looked at her —he looked at the transcript. The first few sheets were written with the greatest carefulness in a delicate woman's hand—then the strokes appeared to alter, to become more light and free—but who can describe his surprise as he ran his eyes over the concluding page? "For heaven's sake," he cried, "what is this? this is my hand!" He looked at Ottilie, and again at the paper; the conclusion, especially, was exactly as if he had written it himself. Ottilie said nothing, but she looked at him with her eyes full of the warmest delight. Edward stretched out his arms. "You love me!" he cried: "Ottilie, you love me!" They fell on each other's breast—which had been the first to catch the other it would have been impossible to distinguish.

From that moment the world was all changed for Edward. He was no longer what he had been, and the world was no longer what it had been. They parted—he held her hands; they gazed in each other's eyes. They were on the point of embracing each other again.

Charlotte entered with the Captain. Edward inwardly smiled at their excuses for having stayed out so long. Oh! how far too soon you have returned, he said to himself.

They sate down to supper. They talked about the people who had been there that day. Edward, full of love and ecstacy, spoke well of every one—always sparing, often approving. Charlotte, who was not altogether of his opinion, remarked this temper in him, and jested with him about it— he who had always the sharpest thing to say on departed visitors, was this evening so gentle and tolerant.

With fervour and heartfelt conviction, Edward cried, "One has only to love a single creature with all one's heart, and the whole world at once looks lovely!"

Ottilie dropped her eyes on the ground, and Charlotte looked straight before her.

The Captain took up the word, and said, "It is the same with deep feelings of respect and reverence: we first learn to recognize what there is that is to be valued in the world, when we find occasion to entertain such sentiments towards a particular object."

Charlotte made an excuse to retire early to her room, where she could give herself up to thinking over what had passed in the course of the evening between herself and the Captain.

When Edward sprang on shore, and, pushing off the boat, had himself committed his wife and his friend to the uncertain element, Charlotte found herself face to face with the man on whose account she had been already secretly suffering so bitterly, sitting in the twilight before her, and sweeping along the boat with the sculls in easy motion. She felt a depth of sadness, very rare with her, weighing on her spirits. The undulating movement of the boat, the splash of the oars, the faint breeze playing over the watery mirror, the

G

sighing of the reeds, the long flight of the birds, the fitful twinkling of the first stars—there was something spectral about it all in the universal stillness. She fancied her friend was bearing her away to set her on some far-off shore, and leave her there alone; strange emotions were passing through her, and she could not give way to them and weep.

The Captain was describing to her the manner in which, in his opinion, the improvements should be continued. He praised the construction of the boat; it was so convenient, he said, because one person could so easily manage it with a pair of oars. She should herself learn how to do this; there was often a delicious feeling in floating along alone upon the water, one's own ferryman and steersman.

The parting which was impending, sank on Charlotte's heart as he was speaking. Is he saying this on purpose? she thought to herself. Does he know it yet? Does he suspect it? or is it only accident; and is he unconsciously foretelling me my fate?

A weary, impatient heaviness took hold of her; she begged him to make for land as soon as possible, and return with her to the castle.

It was the first time that the Captain had been upon the water, and, though generally he had acquainted himself with its depth, he did not know accurately the particular spots. Dusk was coming on; he directed his course to a place where he thought it would be easy to get on shore, and from which he knew the footpath which led to the castle was not far distant. Charlotte, however, repeated her wish to get to land quickly, and the place which he thought of being at a short distance, he gave it up, and exerting himself as much as he possibly could, made straight for the bank. Unhappily the water was shallow, and he ran aground some way off from it. From the rate at which he was going the boat was fixed fast, and all his efforts to move it were in vain. What was to be done? There was no alternative but to get into the water and carry his companion ashore.

It was done without difficulty or danger. He was strong enough not to totter with her, or give her any cause for anxiety; but in her agitation she had thrown her arms about his neck. He held her fast, and pressed her to himself—and at last laid her down upon a grassy bank, not without emotion

and confusion . . . . she still lay upon his neck . . . he caught
her up once more in his arms, and pressed a warm kiss upon
her lips. The next moment he was at her feet: he took her
hand, and held it to his mouth, and cried,

" Charlotte, will you forgive me ?"

The kiss which he had ventured to give, and which she had
all but returned to him, brought Charlotte to herself again—
she pressed his hand—but she did not attempt to raise him
up. She bent down over him, and laid her hand upon his
shoulder, and said,

" We cannot now prevent this moment from forming an
epoch in our lives ; but it depends on us to bear ourselves in
a manner which shall be worthy of us. You must go away,
my dear friend ; and you are going. The Count has plans for
you, to give you better prospects—I am glad, and I am sorry.
I did not mean to speak of it till it was certain: but this
moment obliges me to tell you my secret . . . . . Since it
does not depend on ourselves to alter our feelings, I can only
forgive you, I can only forgive myself, if we have the courage
to alter our situation." She raised him up, took his arm to
support herself, and they walked back to the castle without
speaking.

But now she was standing in her own room, where she had
to feel and to know that she was Edward's wife. Her strength
and the various discipline in which through life she had
trained herself, came to her assistance in the conflict.
Accustomed as she had always been to look steadily into
herself and to control herself, she did not now find it difficult, with an earnest effort, to come to the resolution
which she desired. She could almost smile when she remembered the strange visit of the night before. Suddenly she
was seized with a wonderful instinctive feeling, a thrill of
fearful delight which changed into holy hope and longing.
She knelt earnestly down, and repeated the oath which she
had taken to Edward before the altar.

Friendship, affection, renunciation, floated in glad, happy
images before her. She felt restored to health and to herself.
A sweet weariness came over her. She lay down, and sunk
into a calm, quiet sleep.

CHAPTER XIII.

EDWARD, on his part, was in a very different temper. So
little he thought of sleeping that it did not once occur to him
even to undress himself. A thousand times he kissed the
transcript of the document, but it was the beginning of it, in
Ottilie's childish, timid hand; the end he scarcely dared to
kiss, for he thought it was his own hand which he saw.
Oh, that it were another document! he whispered to himself;
and, as it was, he felt it was the sweetest assurance that his
highest wish would be fulfilled. Thus it remained in his
hands, thus he continued to press it to his heart, although
disfigured by a third name subscribed to it. The waning
moon rose up over the wood. The warmth of the night drew
Edward out into the free air. He wandered this way and
that way; he was at once the most restless and the happiest
of mortals. He strayed through the gardens—they seemed
too narrow for him; he hurried out into the park, and it was
too wide. He was drawn back toward the castle; he stood
under Ottilie's window. He threw himself down on the
steps of the terrace below. 'Walls and bolts,' he said to
himself, 'may still divide us, but our hearts are not divided.
If she were here before me, into my arms she would fall, and
I into hers; and what can one desire but that sweet certainty!'   All was stillness round him; not a breath was
moving;—so still it was, that he could hear the unresting
creatures underground at their work, to whom day or night
are alike. He abandoned himself to his delicious dreams; at
last he fell asleep, and did not wake till the sun with his
royal beams was mounting up in the sky and scattering the
early mists.

He found himself the first person awake on his domain.
The labourers seemed to be staying away too long: they came;
he thought they were too few, and the work set out for the
day too slight for his desires. He inquired for more workmen; they were promised, and in the course of the day they
came.   But these, too, were not enough for him to carry
his plans out as rapidly as he wished. To do the work gave
him no pleasure any longer; it should all be done. And
for whom? The paths should be gravelled that Ottilie might

walk pleasantly upon them; seats should be made at every spot and corner that Ottilie might rest on them. The new park house was hurried forward. It should be finished for Ottilie's birthday. In all he thought and all he did, there was no more moderation. The sense of loving and of being loved, urged him out into the unlimited. How changed was now to him the look of all the rooms, their furniture, and their decorations! He did not feel as if he was in his own house any more. Ottilie's presence absorbed everything. He was utterly lost in her; no other thought ever rose before him; no conscience disturbed him; every restraint which had been laid upon his nature burst loose. His whole being centred upon Ottilie. This impetuosity of passion did not escape the Captain, who longed, if he could, to prevent its evil consequences. All those plans which were now being hurried on with this immoderate speed, had been drawn out and calculated for a long, quiet, easy execution. The sale of the farm had been completed; the first instalment had been paid. Charlotte, according to the arrangement, had taken possession of it. But the very first week after, she found it more than usually necessary to exercise patience and resolution, and to keep her eye on what was being done. In the present hasty style of proceeding, the money which had been set apart for the purpose would not go far.

Much had been begun, and much yet remained to be done. How could the Captain leave Charlotte in such a situation? They consulted together, and agreed that it would be better that they themselves should hurry on the works, and for this purpose employ money which could be made good again at the period fixed for the discharge of the second instalment of what was to be paid for the farm. It could be done almost without loss. They would have a freer hand. Everything would progress simultaneously. There were labourers enough at hand, and they could get more accomplished at once, and arrive swiftly and surely at their aim. Edward gladly gave his consent to a plan which so entirely coincided with his own views.

During this time Charlotte persisted with all her heart in what she had determined for herself, and her friend stood by her with a like purpose, manfully. This very circumstance, however, produced a greater intimacy between them. They spoke openly to one another of Edward's passion, and consulted what had better be done. Charlotte kept Ottilie more about herself, watching her narrowly; and the more she understood her own heart, the deeper she was able to penetrate into the heart of the poor girl. She saw no help for it, except in sending her away.

It now appeared a happy thing to her that Luciana had gained such high honours at the school; for her great aunt, as soon as she heard of it, desired to take her entirely to herself, to keep her with her, and bring her out into the world. Ottilie could, therefore, return thither. The Captain would leave them well provided for, and everything would be as it had been a few months before; indeed, in many respects better. Her own position in Edward's affection, Charlotte thought she could soon recover; and she settled it all, and laid it all out before herself so sensibly that she only strengthened herself more completely in her delusion, as if it were possible for them to return within their old limits,—as if a bond which had been violently broken could again be joined together as before.

In the mean time Edward felt very deeply the hindrances which were thrown in his way. He soon observed that they were keeping him and Ottilie separate; that they made it difficult for him to speak with her alone, or even to approach her, except in the presence of others. And while he was angry about this, he was angry at many things besides. If he caught an opportunity for a few hasty words with Ottilie, it was not only to assure her of his love, but to complain of his wife and of the Captain. He never felt that with his own irrational haste he was on the way to exhaust the cash-box. He found bitter fault with them, because in the execution of the work they were not keeping to the first agreement, and yet he had been himself a consenting party to the second; indeed, it was he who had occasioned it and made it necessary.

Hatred is a partisan, but love is even more so. Ottilie also estranged herself from Charlotte and the Captain. As Edward was complaining one day to Ottilie of the latter, saying that he was not treating him like a friend, or, under the circumstances, acting quite uprightly, she answered unthinkingly, "I have once or twice had a painful feeling that he was not quite honest with you. I heard him say once to Charlotte, 'If Edward would but spare us that eternal flute of his! He can make nothing of it, and it is too disagreeable to listen to him.' You may imagine how it hurt me, when I like accompanying you so much."

She had scarcely uttered the words when her conscience whispered to her that she had much better have been silent. However, the thing was said. Edward's features worked violently. Never had anything stung him more. He was touched on his tenderest point. It was his amusement; he followed it like a child. He never made the slightest pretensions; what gave him pleasure should be treated with forbearance by his friends. He never thought how intolerable it is for a third person to have his ears lacerated by an unsuccessful talent. He was indignant; he was hurt in a way which he could not forgive. He felt himself discharged from all obligations.

The necessity of being with Ottilie, of seeing her, whispering to her, exchanging his confidence with her, increased with every day. He determined to write to her, and ask her to carry on a secret correspondence with him. The strip of paper on which he had, laconically enough, made his request, lay on his writing-table, and was swept off by a draught of wind as his valet entered to dress his hair. The latter was in the habit of trying the heat of the iron by picking up any scraps of paper which might be lying about. This time his hand fell on the billet; he twisted it up hastily, and it was burnt. Edward observing the mistake, snatched it out of his hand. After the man was gone, he sat himself down to write it over again. The second time it would not run so readily off his pen. It gave him a little uneasiness; he hesitated, but he got over it. He squeezed the paper into Ottilie's hand the first moment he was able to approach her. Ottilie answered him immediately. He put the note unread in his waistcoat pocket, which, being made short in the fashion of the time, was shallow, and did not hold it as it ought. It worked out, and fell without his observing it on the ground. Charlotte saw it, picked it up, and after giving a hasty glance at it, reached it to him.

"Here is something in your handwriting," she said, "which you may be sorry to lose."

He was confounded. Is she dissembling? he thought to himself. Does she know what is in the note, or is she deceived by the resemblance of the hand? He hoped, he believed the latter. He was warned—doubly warned; but those strange accidents, through which a higher intelligence seems to be speaking to us, his passion was not able to interpret. Rather, as he went further and further on, he felt the restraint under which his friend and his wife seemed to be holding him the more intolerable. His pleasure in their society was gone. His heart was closed against them, and though he was obliged to endure their society, he could not succeed in re-discovering or in re-animating within his heart anything of his old affection for them. The silent reproaches which he was forced to make to himself about it, were disagreeable to him. He tried to help himself with a kind of humour which, however, being without love, was also without its usual grace.

Over all such trials, Charlotte found assistance to rise in her own inward feelings. She knew her own determination. Her own affection, fair and noble as it was, she would utterly renounce.

And sorely she longed to go to the assistance of the other two. Separation, she knew well, would not alone suffice to heal so deep a wound. She resolved that she would speak openly about it to Ottilie herself. But she could not do it. The recollection of her own weakness stood in her way. She thought she could talk generally to her about the sort of thing. But general expressions about "the sort of thing," fitted her own case equally well, and she could not bear to touch it. Every hint which she would give Ottilie, recoiled back on her own heart. She would warn, and she was obliged to feel that she might herself still be in need of warning.

She contented herself, therefore, with silently keeping the lovers more apart, and by this gained nothing. The slight hints which frequently escaped her had no effect upon Ottilie; for Ottilie had been assured by Edward that Charlotte was devoted to the Captain, that Charlotte herself wished for a separation, and that he was at this moment considering the readiest means by which it could be brought about.

Ottilie, led by the sense of her own innocence along the road to the happiness for which she longed, only lived for

Edward. Strengthened by her love for him in all good, more light and happy in her work for his sake, and more frank and open towards others, she found herself in a heaven upon earth.

So all together, each in his or her own fashion, reflecting or unreflecting, they continued on the routine of their lives. All seemed to go its ordinary way, as, in monstrous cases, when everything is at stake, men will still live on, as if it were all nothing.

CHAPTER XIV.

In the mean time a letter came from the Count to the Captain—two, indeed—one which he might produce, holding out fair, excellent prospects in the distance; the other containing a distinct offer of an immediate situation, a place of high importance and responsibility at the Court, his rank as Major, a very considerable salary, and other advantages. A number of circumstances, however, made it desirable that for the moment he should not speak of it, and consequently he only informed his friends of his distant expectations, and concealed what was so nearly impending.

He went warmly on, at the same time, with his present occupation, and quietly made arrangements to secure the works being all continued without interruption after his departure. He was now himself desirous that as much as possible should be finished off at once, and was ready to hasten things forward to prepare for Ottilie's birthday. And so, though without having come to any express understanding, the two friends worked side by side together. Edward was now well pleased that the cash-box was filled by their having taken up money. The whole affair went forward at fullest speed.

The Captain had done his best to oppose the plan of throwing the three ponds together into a single sheet of water. The lower embankment would have to be made much stronger, the two intermediate embankments to be taken away, and altogether, in more than one sense, it seemed a very questionable proceeding. However, both these schemes had been already undertaken; the soil which was removed above, being carried at once down to where it was wanted. And here there came opportunely on the scene a young architect, an old pupil of the Captain, who partly by introducing workmen who understood work of this nature, and partly by himself, whenever it was possible, contracting for the work itself, advanced things not a little, while at the same time they could feel more confidence in their being securely and lastingly executed. In secret this was a great pleasure to the Captain. He could now be confident that his absence would not be so severely felt. It was one of the points on which he was most resolute with himself, never to leave anything which he had taken in hand uncompleted, unless he could see his place satisfactorily supplied. And he could not but hold in small respect, persons who introduce confusion around themselves only to make their absence felt, and are ready to disturb in wanton selfishness what they will not be at hand to restore.

So they laboured on, straining every nerve to make Ottilie's birthday splendid, without any open acknowledgment that this was what they were aiming at, or, indeed, without their directly acknowledging it to themselves. Charlotte, wholly free from jealousy as she was, could not think it right to keep it as a real festival. Ottilie's youth, the circumstances of her fortune, and her relationship to their family, were not at all such as made it fit that she should appear as the queen of the day; and Edward would not have it talked about, because everything was to spring out, as it were, of itself, with a natural and delightful surprise.

They, therefore, came all of them to a sort of tacit understanding that on this day, without further circumstance, the new house in the park was to be opened, and they might take the occasion to invite the neighbourhood and give a holiday to their own people. Edward's passion, however, knew no bounds. Longing as he did to give himself to Ottilie, his presents and his promises must be infinite. The birthday gifts which on the great occasion he was to offer to her seemed, as Charlotte had arranged them, far too insignificant. He spoke to his valet, who had the care of his wardrobe, and who consequently had extensive acquaintance among the tailors and mercers and fashionable milliners; and he, who not only understood himself what valuable presents were, but also the most graceful way in which they should be offered, immediately ordered an elegant box, covered with red morocco and studded with steel nails, to be filled with presents worthy of such a shell. Another thing, too, he suggested to Edward. Among the stores at the castle was a small show of fireworks which had never been let off. It would be easy to get some more, and have something really fine. Edward caught the idea, and his servant promised to see to its being executed. This matter was to remain a secret.

While this was going on, the Captain, as the day drew nearer, had been making arrangements for a body of police to be present—a precaution which he always thought desirable when large numbers of men are to be brought together. And, indeed, against beggars, and against all other inconveniences by which the pleasure of a festival can be disturbed, he had made effectual provision.

Edward and his confidant, on the contrary, were mainly occupied with their fireworks. They were to be let off on the side of the middle water in front of the great ash-tree. The party were to be collected on the opposite side, under the planes, that at a sufficient distance from the scene, in ease and safety, they might see them to the best effect, with the reflections on the water, the water-rockets, and floating-lights, and all the other designs.

Under some other pretext, Edward had the ground underneath the plane-trees cleared of bushes and grass and moss. And now first could be seen the beauty of their forms, together with their full height and spread, right up from the earth. He was delighted with them. It was just this very time of the year that he had planted them. How long ago could it have been? he said to himself. As soon as he got home, he turned over the old diary books, which his father, especially when in the country, was very careful in keeping. He might not find an entry of this particular planting, but another important domestic matter, which Edward well remembered, and which had occurred on the same day, would surely be mentioned. He turned over a few volumes. The circumstance he was looking for was there. How amazed, how overjoyed he was, when he discovered the stranestg coincidence! The day and the year on which he had planted those trees, was the very day, the very year, when Ottilie was born.

CHAPTER XV.

THE long-wished-for morning dawned at last on Edward; and very soon a number of guests arrived. They had sent out a large number of invitations, and many who had missed the laying of the foundation-stone, which was reported to have been so charming, were the more careful not to be absent on the second festivity.

Before dinner the carpenter's people appeared, with music, in the court of the castle. They bore an immense garland of flowers, composed of a number of single wreaths, winding in and out, one above the other; saluting the company, they made request, acording to custom, for silk handkerchiefs and ribands, at the hands of the fair sex, with which to dress themselves out. When the castle party went into the dining-hall, they marched off singing and shouting, and after amusing themselves a while in the village, and coaxing many a riband out of the women there, old and young, they came at last, with crowds behind them and crowds expecting them, out upon the height where the park-house was now standing. After dinner, Charlotte rather held back her guests. She did not wish that there should be any solemn or formal procession, and they found their way in little parties, broken up, as they pleased, without rule or order, to the scene of action. Charlotte staid behind with Ottilie, and did not improve matters by doing so. For Ottilie being really the last that appeared, it seemed as if the trumpets and the clarionets had only been waiting for her, and as if the gaieties had been ordered to commence directly on her arrival.

To take off the rough appearance of the house, it had been hung with green boughs and flowers. They had dressed it out in an architectural fashion, according to a design of the Captain's; only that, without his knowledge, Edward had desired the Architect to work in the date upon the cornice in flowers, and this was necessarily permitted to remain. The

Captain had only arrived on the scene in time to prevent Ottilie's name from figuring in splendour on the gable. The beginning, which had been made for this, he contrived to turn skilfully to some other use, and to get rid of such of the letters as had been already finished.

The garland was set up, and was to be seen far and wide about the country. The flags and the ribands fluttered gaily in the air; and a short oration was, the greater part of it, dispersed by the wind. The solemnity was at an end. There was now to be a dance on the smooth lawn in front of the building, which had been enclosed with boughs and branches. A gaily-dressed working mason took Edward up to a smart-looking girl of the village, and called himself upon Ottilie, who stood out with him. These two couples speedily found others to follow them, and Edward contrived pretty soon to change partners, catching Ottilie, and making the round with her. The younger part of the company joined merrily in the dance with the people, while the elder among them stood and looked on.

Then, before they broke up and walked about, an order was given that they should all collect again at sunset under the plane-trees. Edward was the first upon the spot, ordering everything, and making his arrangements with his valet, who was to be on the other side, in company with the firework-maker, managing his exhibition of the spectacle.

The Captain was far from satisfied at some of the preparations which he saw made; and he endeavoured to get a word with Edward about the crush of spectators which was to be expected. But the latter, somewhat hastily, begged that he might be allowed to manage this part of the day's amusements himself.

The upper end of the embankment having been recently raised, was still far from compact. It had been staked, but there was no grass upon it, and the earth was uneven and insecure. The crowd pressed on, however, in great numbers. The sun went down, and the castle party was served with refreshments under the plane-trees, to pass the time till it should have become sufficiently dark. The place was approved of beyond measure, and they looked forward to frequently enjoying the view over so lovely a sheet of water, on future occasions.

A calm evening, a perfect absence of wind, promised every thing in favour of the spectacle, when suddenly loud and violent shrieks were heard. Large masses of the earth had given way on the edge of the embankment, and a number of people were precipitated into the water. The pressure from the throng had gone on increasing till at last it had become more than the newly-laid soil would bear, and the bank had fallen in. Everybody wanted to obtain the best place, and now there was no getting either backwards or forwards.

People ran this and that way, more to see what was going on than to render assistance. What could be done when no one could reach the place?

The Captain, with a few determined persons, hurried down and drove the crowd off the embankment back upon the shore; in order that those who were really of service might have free room to move. One way or another they contrived to seize hold of such as were sinking; and with or without assistance all who had been in the water were got out safe upon the bank, with the exception of one boy, whose struggles in his fright, instead of bringing him nearer to the embankment, had only carried him further from it. His strength seemed to be failing—now only a hand was seen above the surface, and now a foot. By an unlucky chance the boat was on the opposite shore filled with fireworks—it was a long business to unload it, and help was slow in coming. The Captain's resolution was taken; he flung off his coat; all eyes were directed towards him, and his sturdy vigorous figure gave every one hope and confidence: but a cry of surprise rose out of the crowd as they saw him fling himself into the water— every eye watched him as the strong swimmer swiftly reached the boy, and bore him, although to appearance dead, to the embankment.

Now came up the boat. The Captain stepped in and examined whether there were any still missing, or whether they were all safe. The surgeon was speedily on the spot, and took charge of the inanimate boy. Charlotte joined them, and entreated the Captain to go now and take care of himself, to hurry back to the castle and change his clothes. He would not go, however, till persons on whose sense he could rely, who had been close to the spot at the time of the accident, and who had assisted in saving those who had fallen in, assured him that all were safe.

Charlotte saw him on his way to the house, and then she remembered that the wine and the tea, and everything else which he could want, had been locked up, for fear any of the servants should take advantage of the disorder of the holiday, as on such occasions they are too apt to do. She hurried through the scattered groups of her company, which were loitering about the plane-trees. Edward was there, talking to every one—beseeching every one to stay. He would give the signal directly, and the fireworks should begin. Charlotte went up to him, and entreated him to put off an amusement which was no longer in place, and which at the present moment no one could enjoy. She reminded him of what ought to be done for the boy who had been saved, and for his preserver.

"The surgeon will do whatever is right, no doubt," replied Edward. "He is provided with everything which he can want, and we should only be in the way if we crowded about him with our anxieties."

Charlotte persisted in her opinion, and made a sign to Ottilie, who at once prepared to retire with her. Edward seized her hand, and cried, "We will not end this day in a lazaretto. She is too good for a sister of mercy. Without us, I should think, the half-dead may wake, and the living dry themselves."

Charlotte did not answer, but went. Some followed her—others followed these: in the end, no one wished to be the last, and all followed. Edward and Ottilie found themselves alone under the plane-trees. He insisted that stay he would, earnestly, passionately, as she entreated him to go back with her to the castle. "No, Ottilie!" he cried; "the extraordinary is not brought to pass in the smooth common way—the wonderful accident of this evening brings us more speedily together. You are mine—I have often said it to you, and sworn it to you. We will not say it and swear it any more —we will make it BE."

The boat came over from the other side. The valet was in it—he asked, with some embarrassment, what his master wished to have done with the fireworks?

"Let them off!" Edward cried to him: "let them off!—It was only for you that they were provided, Ottilie, and you shall be the only one to see them! Let me sit beside you, and enjoy them with you." Tenderly, timidly, he sate down at her side, without touching her.

Rockets went hissing up—cannon thundered—Roman candles shot out their blazing balls—squibs flashed and darted—wheels spun round, first singly, then in pairs, then all at once, faster and faster, one after the other, and more and more together. Edward, whose bosom was on fire, watched the blazing spectacle with eyes gleaming with delight; but Ottilie, with her delicate and nervous feelings, in all this noise and fitful blazing and flashing, found more to distress her than to please. She leant shrinking against Edward, and he, as she drew to him and clung to him, felt the delightful sense that she belonged entirely to him.

The night had scarcely reassumed its rights, when the moon rose and lighted their path as they walked back. A figure, with his hat in his hand, stepped across their way, and begged an alms of them—in the general holiday he said that he had been forgotten. The moon shone upon his face, and Edward recognized the features of the importunate beggar; but, happy as he then was, it was impossible for him to be angry with any one. He could not recollect that, especially for that particular day, begging had been forbidden under the heaviest penalties—he thrust his hand into his pocket, took the first coin which he found, and gave the fellow a piece of gold. His own happiness was so unbounded that he would have liked to have shared it with every one.

In the mean time all had gone well at the castle. The skill of the surgeon, every thing which was required being ready at hand, Charlotte's assistance—all had worked together, and the boy was brought to life again. The guests dispersed, wishing to catch a glimpse or two of what was to be seen of the fireworks from the distance; and, after a scene of such confusion, were glad to get back to their own quiet homes.

The Captain also, after having rapidly changed his dress, had taken an active part in what required to be done. It was now all quiet again, and he found himself alone with Charlotte—gently and affectionately he now told her that his time for leaving them approached. She had gone through so much that evening, that this discovery made but a slight impression upon her—she had seen how her friend could sacrifice himself; how he had saved another, and had himself been saved. These strange incidents seemed to foretell an important future to her—but not an unhappy one.

Edward, who now entered with Ottilie, was informed at once of the impending departure of the Captain. He suspected that Charlotte had known longer how near it was; but he was far too much occupied with himself, and with his own plans, to take it amiss, or care about it.

On the contrary, he listened attentively, and with signs of pleasure, to the account of the excellent and honourable position in which the Captain was to be placed. The course of the future was hurried impetuously forward by his own secret wishes. Already he saw the Captain married to Charlotte, and himself married to Ottilie. It would have been the richest present which any one could have made him, on the occasion of the day's festival!

But how surprised was Ottilie, when, on going to her room, she found upon the table the beautiful box! Instantly she opened it; inside, all the things were so nicely packed and arranged, that she did not venture to take them out, she scarcely even ventured to lift them. There were muslin, cambric, silk, shawls and lace, all rivalling each other in delicacy, beauty, and costliness—nor were ornaments forgotten. The intention had been, as she saw well, to furnish her with more than one complete suit of clothes: but it was all so costly, so little like what she had been accustomed to, that she scarcely dared, even in thought, to believe it could be really for her.

CHAPTER XVI.

THE next morning the Captain had disappeared, having left a grateful, feeling letter addressed to his friends upon his table. He and Charlotte had already taken a half leave of each other the evening before—she felt that the parting was for ever, and she resigned herself to it; for in the Count's second letter, which the Captain had at last shown to her, there was a hint of a prospect of an advantageous marriage, and, although

H

he had paid no attention to it at all, she accepted it for as good as certain, and gave him up firmly and fully.

Now, therefore, she thought that she had a right to require of others the same control over themselves which she had exercised herself: it had not been impossible to her, and it ought not to be impossible to them. With this feeling she began the conversation with her husband; and she entered upon it the more openly and easily, from a sense that the question must now, once for all, be decisively set at rest.

"Our friend has left us," she said; "we are now once more together as we were—and it depends upon ourselves whether we choose to return altogether into our old position."

Edward, who heard nothing except what flattered his own passion, believed that Charlotte, in these words, was alluding to her previous widowed state, and, in a roundabout way, was making a suggestion for a separation; so that he answered, with a laugh, "Why not? all we want is to come to an understanding." But he found himself sorely enough undeceived, as Charlotte continued, "And we have now a choice of opportunities for placing Ottilie in another situation. Two openings have offered themselves for her, either of which will do very well. Either she can return to the school, as my daughter has left it and is with her great-aunt; or she can be received into a desirable family, where, as the companion of an only child, she will enjoy all the advantages of a solid education."

Edward, with a tolerably successful effort at commanding himself, replied, "Ottilie has been so much spoilt, by living so long with us here, that she will scarcely like to leave us now."

"We have all of us been too much spoilt," said Charlotte; "and yourself not least. This is an epoch which requires us seriously to bethink ourselves. It is a solemn warning to us to consider what is really for the good of all the members of our little circle—and we ourselves must not be afraid of making sacrifices."

"At any rate I cannot see that it is right that Ottilie should be made a sacrifice," replied Edward; "and that would be the case if we were now to allow her to be sent away among strangers. The Captain's good genius has sought him out here—we can feel easy, we can feel happy, at seeing him leave us; but who can tell what may be before Ottilie? There is no occasion for haste."

"What is before us is sufficiently clear," Charlotte answered, with some emotion; and as she was determined to have it all out at once, she went on: "You love Ottilie; every day you are becoming more attached to her. A reciprocal feeling is rising on her side as well, and feeding itself in the same way. Why should we not acknowledge in words what every hour makes obvious? and are we not to have the common prudence to ask ourselves in what it is to end?"

"We may not be able to find an answer on the moment," replied Edward, collecting himself; "but so much may be said, that if we cannot exactly tell what will come of it, we may resign ourselves to wait and see what the future may tell us about it."

"No great wisdom is required to prophesy here," answered Charlotte; "and, at any rate, we ought to feel that you and I are past the age when people may walk blindly where they should not or ought not to go. There is no one else to take care of us—we must be our own friends, our own managers. No one expects us to commit ourselves in an outrage upon decency: no one expects that we are going to expose ourselves to censure or to ridicule."

"How can you so mistake me?" said Edward, unable to reply to his wife's clear, open words. "Can you find it a fault in me, if I am anxious about Ottilie's happiness? I do not mean future happiness—no one can count on that—but what is present, palpable, and immediate. Consider, don't deceive yourself; consider frankly Ottilie's case, torn away from us, and sent to live among strangers. I, at least, am not cruel enough to propose such a change for her!"

Charlotte saw too clearly into her husband's intentions, through this disguise. For the first time she felt how far he had estranged himself from her. Her voice shook a little— "Will Ottilie be happy if she divides us?" she said. "If she deprives me of a husband, and his children of a father!"

"Our children, I should have thought, were sufficiently provided for," said Edward, with a cold smile; adding, rather more kindly, "but why at once expect the very worst?"

"The very worst is too sure to follow this passion of yours," returned Charlotte: "do not refuse good advice while there is yet time; do not throw away the means which I propose to save us.   In troubled cases those must work and help who see the clearest—this time it is I.   Dear, dearest Edward! listen to me—can you propose to me, that now at once I shall renounce my happiness! renounce my fairest rights! renounce you!"

"Who says that?" replied Edward, with some embarrassment.

"You, yourself," answered Charlotte; "in determining to keep Ottilie here, are you not acknowledging everything which must arise out of it? I will urge nothing on you—but if you cannot conquer yourself, at least you will not be able much longer to deceive yourself."

Edward felt how right she was.   It is fearful to hear spoken out, in words, what the heart has gone on long permitting to itself in secret.   To escape only for a moment, Edward answered, "It is not yet clear to me what you want."

"My intention," she replied, "was to talk over with you these two proposals—each of them has its advantages.   The school would be best suited to her, as she now is; but the other situation is larger, and wider, and promises more, when I think what she may become."   She then detailed to her husband circumstantially what would lie before Ottilie in each position, and concluded with the words, "For my own part I should prefer the lady's house to the school, for more reasons than one; but particularly because I should not like the affection, the love indeed, of the young man there, which Ottilie has gained, to increase."

Edward appeared to approve; but it was only to find some means of delay.   Charlotte, who desired to commit him to a definite step, seized the opportunity, as Edward made no immediate opposition, to settle Ottilie's departure, for which she had already privately made all preparations, for the next day.

Edward shuddered—he thought he was betrayed.   His wife's affectionate speech he fancied was an artfully contrived trick to separate him for ever from his happiness.   He appeared to leave the thing entirely to her; but in his heart his resolution was already taken.   To gain time to breathe, to put off the immediate intolerable misery of Ottilie's being sent away, he determined to leave his house.   He told Charlotte he was going; but he had blinded her to his real reason, by telling her that he would not be present at Ottilie's departure; indeed, that, from that moment, he would see her no more. Charlotte, who believed that she had gained her point, approved most cordially. He ordered his horse, gave his valet the necessary directions what to pack up, and where he should follow him; and then, on the point of departure, he sate down and wrote:

"EDWARD TO CHARLOTTE.

"The misfortune, my love, which has befallen us, may or may not admit of remedy; only this I feel, that if I am not at once to be driven to despair, I must find some means of delay for myself, and for all of us. In making myself the sacrifice, I have a right to make a request. I am leaving my home, and I only return to it under happier and more peaceful auspices. While I am away, you keep possession of it—*but with Ottilie.* I choose to know that she is with you, and not among strangers. Take care of her; treat her as you have treated her—only more lovingly, more kindly, more tenderly! I promise that I will not attempt any secret intercourse with her.—Leave me, as long a time as you please, without knowing anything about you. I will not allow myself to be anxious—nor need you be uneasy about me: only, with all my heart and soul, I beseech you, make no attempt to send Ottilie away, or to introduce her into any other situation. Beyond the circle of the castle and the park, placed in the hands of strangers, she belongs to me, and I will take possession of her! If you have any regard for my affection, for my wishes, for my sufferings, you will leave me alone to my madness: and if any hope of recovery from it should ever hereafter offer itself to me, I will not resist."

This last sentence ran off his pen—not out of his heart. Even when he saw it upon the paper, he began bitterly to weep. That he, under any circumstances, should renounce the happiness—even the wretchedness—of loving Ottilie! He only now began to feel what he was doing—he was going away without knowing what was to be the result. At any rate he was not to see her again *now*—with what certainty could he promise himself that he would ever see her again? But the letter was written—the horses were at the door; every moment he was afraid he might see Ottilie somewhere, and then his whole purpose would go to the winds. He collected himself—he remembered, that, at any rate, he would be able to return at any moment he pleased; and that, by his absence he would have advanced nearer to his wishes: on the other side, he pictured Ottilie to himself forced to leave the house if he stayed. He sealed the letter, ran down the steps, and sprang upon his horse.

As he rode past the hotel, he saw the beggar to whom he had given so much money the night before, sitting under the trees: the man was busy enjoying his dinner, and, as Edward passed, stood up, and made him the humblest obeisance. That figure had appeared to him yesterday, when Ottilie was on his arm; now it only served as a bitter reminiscence of the happiest hour of his life. His grief redoubled. The feeling of what he was leaving behind was intolerable. He looked again at the beggar. "Happy wretch!" he cried, " you can still feed upon the alms of yesterday—and I cannot any more on the happiness of yesterday!"

CHAPTER XVII.

OTTILIE heard some one ride away, and went to the window in time just to catch a sight of Edward's back. It was strange, she thought, that he should have left the house without seeing her, without having even wished her good morning. She grew uncomfortable, and her anxiety did not diminish when Charlotte took her out for a long walk, and talked of various other things; but not once, and apparently on purpose, mentioning her husband. When they returned she found the table laid only with two covers.

It is unpleasant to miss even the most trifling thing to which we have been accustomed. In serious things such a loss becomes miserably painful. Edward and the Captain were not there. The first time, for a long while, Charlotte sate at the head of the table herself—and it seemed to Ottilie as if she was deposed. The two ladies sate opposite each other; Charlotte talked, without the least embarrassment, of the Captain and his appointment, and of the little hope there was of seeing him again for a long time. The only comfort Ottilie could find for herself was in the idea that Edward had ridden after his friend, to accompany him a part of his journey.

On rising from table, however, they saw Edward's travelling carriage under the window. Charlotte, a little as if she was put out, asked who had had it brought round there. She was told it was the valet, who had some things there to pack up. It required all Ottilie's self-command to conceal her wonder and her distress.

The valet came in, and asked if they would be so good as to let him have a drinking cup of his master's, a pair of silver spoons, and a number of other things, which seemed to Ottilie to imply that he was gone some distance, and would be away for a long time.

Charlotte gave him a very cold dry answer. She did not know what he meant—he had everything belonging to his master under his own care. What the man wanted was to speak a word to Ottilie, and on some pretence or other to get her out of the room; he made some clever excuse, and persisted in his request so far that Ottilie asked if she should go to look for the things for him? But Charlotte quietly said that she had better not. The valet had to depart, and the carriage rolled away.

It was a dreadful moment for Ottilie. She understood nothing—comprehended nothing. She could only feel that Edward had been parted from her for a long time. Charlotte felt for her situation, and left her to herself.

We will not attempt to describe what she went through, or how she wept. She suffered infinitely. She prayed that God would help her only over this one day. The day passed, and the night, and when she came to herself again she felt herself a changed being.

She had not grown composed. She was not resigned, but after having lost what she had lost, she was still alive, and there was still something for her to fear. Her anxiety, after returning to consciousness, was at once lest, now that the gentlemen were gone, she might be sent away too. She never guessed at Edward's threats, which had secured her remaining with her aunt. Yet Charlotte's manner served partially to reassure her. The latter exerted herself to find employment for the poor girl, and hardly ever,—never, if she could help it,—left her out of her sight; and although she knew well how little words can do against the power of passion, yet she knew, too, the sure though slow influence of thought and reflection, and therefore missed no opportunity of inducing Ottilie to talk with her on every variety of subject.

It was no little comfort to Ottilie when one day Charlotte took an opportunity of making (she did it on purpose) the wise observation, "How keenly grateful people were to us when we were able by stilling and calming them to help them out of the entanglements of passion! Let us set cheerfully to work," she said, "at what the men have left incomplete: we shall be preparing the most charming surprise for them when they return to us, and our temperate proceedings will have carried through and executed what their impatient natures would have spoilt."

"Speaking of temperance, my dear aunt, I cannot help saying how I am struck with the intemperance of men, particularly in respect of wine. It has often pained and distressed me, when I have observed how, for hours together, clearness of understanding, judgment, considerateness, and whatever is most amiable about them, will be utterly gone, and instead of the good which they might have done if they had been themselves, most disagreeable things sometimes threaten. How often may not wrong, rash determinations have arisen entirely from that one cause!"

Charlotte assented, but she did not go on with the subject. She saw only too clearly that it was Edward of whom Ottilie was thinking. It was not exactly habitual with him, but he allowed himself much more frequently than was at all desirable to stimulate his enjoyment and his power of talking and acting by such indulgence. If what Charlotte had just said had set Ottilie thinking again about men, and particularly about Edward, she was all the more struck and startled when her aunt began to speak of the impending marriage of the Captain as of a thing quite settled and acknowledged. This gave a totally different aspect to affairs from what Edward had previously led her to entertain. It made her watch every expression of Charlotte's, every hint, every action, every step. Ottilie had become jealous, sharp-eyed, and suspicious, without knowing it.

Meanwhile, Charlotte with her clear glance looked through

the whole circumstances of their situation, and made arrangements which would provide, among other advantages, full employment for Ottilie. She contracted her household, not parsimoniously, but into narrower dimensions; and, indeed, in one point of view, these moral aberrations might be taken for a not unfortunate accident. For in the style in which they had been going on, they had fallen imperceptibly into extravagance; and from a want of seasonable reflection, from the rate at which they had been living, and from the variety of schemes into which they had been launching out, their fine fortune, which had been in excellent condition, had been shaken, if not seriously injured.

The improvements which were going on in the park she did not interfere with; she rather sought to advance whatever might form a basis for future operations. But here, too, she assigned herself a limit. Her husband on his return should still find abundance to amuse himself with.

In all this work she could not sufficiently value the assistance of the young architect. In a short time the lake lay stretched out under her eyes, its new shores turfed and planted with the most discriminating and excellent judgment. The rough work at the new house was all finished. Everything which was necessary to protect it from the weather she took care to see provided, and there for the present she allowed it to rest in a condition in which what remained to be done could hereafter be readily commenced again. Thus hour by hour she recovered her spirits and her cheerfulness. Ottilie only seemed to have done so. She was only for ever watching, in all that was said and done, for symptoms which might show her whether Edward would be soon returning: and this one thought was the only one in which she felt any interest.

It was, therefore, a very welcome proposal to her when it was suggested that they should get together the boys of the peasants, and employ them in keeping the park clean and neat. Edward had long entertained the idea. A pleasant-looking sort of uniform was made for them, which they were to put on in the evenings, after they had been properly cleaned and washed. The wardrobe was kept in the castle; the more sensible and ready of the boys themselves were entrusted with the management of it—the Architect acting as chief director. In a very short time, the children acquired a kind of character. It was found easy to mould them into what was desired; and they went through their work not without a sort of manœuvre. As they marched along, with their garden shears, their long-handled pruning knives, their rakes, their little spades and hoes, and sweeping brooms; others following after these with baskets to carry off the stones and rubbish; and others, last of all, trailing along the heavy iron roller—it was a thoroughly pretty, delightful procession. The Architect observed in it a beautiful series of situations and occupations to ornament the frieze of a garden house. Ottilie, on the other hand, could see nothing in it but a kind of parade, to salute the master of the house on his near return.

And this stimulated her, and made her wish to begin something of the sort herself. They had before endeavoured to encourage the girls of the village in knitting, and sewing, and spinning, and whatever else women could do; and since what had been done for the improvement of the village itself, there had been a perceptible advance in these descriptions of industry. Ottilie had given what assistance was in her power, but she had given it at random, as opportunity or inclination prompted her; now she thought she would go to work more satisfactorily and methodically. But a company is not to be formed out of a number of girls, as easily as out of a number of boys. She followed her own good sense, and, without being exactly conscious of it, her efforts were solely directed towards connecting every girl as closely as possible each with her own home, her own parents, brothers and sisters: and she succeeded with many of them. One lively little creature only was incessantly complained of as shewing no capacity for work, and as never likely to do any thing if she were left at home.

Ottilie could not be angry with the girl, for to herself the little thing was especially attached—she clung to her, went after her, and ran about with her, whenever she was permitted —and then she would be active and cheerful and never tire. It appeared to be a necessity of the child's nature to hang about a beautiful mistress. At first, Ottilie allowed her to be her companion; then she herself began to feel a sort of affection for her; and, at last, they never parted at all, and Nanny attended her mistress wherever she went.

The latter's footsteps were often bent towards the garden,

where she liked to watch the beautiful show of fruit. It was just the end of the raspberry and cherry season, the few remains of which were no little delight to Nanny. On the other trees there was a promise of a magnificent bearing for the autumn, and the gardener talked of nothing but his master; and how he wished that he might be at home to enjoy it. Ottilie could listen to the good old man for ever! He thoroughly understood his business; and Edward—Edward—Edward—was for ever the theme of his praise!

Ottilie observed, how well all the grafts which had been budded in the spring had taken. "I only wish," the gardener answered, "my good master may come to enjoy them. If he were here this autumn, he would see what beautiful sorts there are in the old castle garden, which the late lord, his honoured father, put there. I think the fruit gardeners that are now don't succeed as well as the Carthusians used to do. We find many fine names in the catalogue, and then we bud from them, and bring up the shoots, and, at last, when they come to bear, it is not worth while to have such trees standing in our garden."

Over and over again, whenever the faithful old servant saw Ottilie, he asked when his master might be expected home; and when Ottilie had nothing to tell him, he would look vexed, and let her see in his manner that he thought she did not care to tell him: the sense of uncertainty which was thus forced upon her became painful beyond measure, and yet she could never be absent from these beds and borders. What she and Edward had sown and planted together were now in full flower, requiring no further care from her, except that Nanny should be at hand with the watering-pot; and who shall say with what sensations she watched the later flowers, which were just beginning to show, and which were to be in the bloom of their beauty on Edward's birthday, the holiday to which she had looked forward with such eagerness, when these flowers were to have expressed her affection and her gratitude to him!—but the hopes which she had formed of that festival were dead now, and doubt and anxiety never ceased to haunt the soul of the poor girl.

Into real open, hearty understanding with Charlotte, there was no more a chance of her being able to return; for, indeed, the position of these two ladies was very different.

If things could remain in their old state—if it were possible that they could return again into the smooth, even way of calm ordered life, Charlotte gained everything; she gained happiness for the present, and a happy future opened before her. On the other hand, for Ottilie all was lost—one may say, all; for she had first found in Edward what life and happiness meant; and, in her present position, she felt an infinite and dreary chasm of which before she could have formed no conception. A heart which seeks, feels well that it wants something; a heart which has lost, feels that something is gone—its yearning and its longing changes into uneasy impatience—and a woman's spirit, which is accustomed to waiting and to enduring, must now pass out from its proper sphere; become active, and attempt and do something to make its own happiness.

Ottilie had not given up Edward—how could she?—although Charlotte, wisely enough, in spite of her conviction to the contrary, assumed it as a thing of course, and resolutely took it as decided that a quiet rational regard was possible between her husband and Ottilie. How often, however, did not Ottilie remain at nights, after bolting herself into her room, on her knees before the open box, gazing at the birthday presents, of which as yet she had not touched a single thing—not cut out or made up a single dress! How often with the sunrise did the poor girl hurry out of the house, in which she once had found all her happiness, away into the free air, into the country which then had had no charms for her.—Even on the solid earth she could not bear to stay; she would spring into the boat, and row out into the middle of the lake, and there, drawing out some book of travels, lie rocked by the motion of the waves, reading and dreaming that she was far away, where she would never fail to find her friend—she remaining ever nearest to his heart, and he to hers.

CHAPTER XVIII.

IT may easily be supposed that the strange, busy gentleman, whose acquaintance we have already made—Mittler—as soon as he received information of the disorder which had broken out among his friends, felt desirous, though neither side had as yet called on him for assistance, to fulfil a friend's part towards them, and do what he could to help them in their misfortune. He thought it advisable, however, to wait first a little while; knowing too well, as he did, that it was more difficult to come to the aid of cultivated persons in their moral perplexities, than of the uncultivated. He left them, therefore, for some time to themselves; but at last he could withhold no longer, and he hastened to seek out Edward, on whose traces he had already lighted. His road led him to a pleasant, pretty valley, with a range of green, sweetly-wooded meadows, down the centre of which ran a never-failing stream, sometimes winding slowly along, then tumbling and rushing among rocks and stones. The hills sloped gently up on either side, covered with rich corn-fields and well-kept orchards. The villages were at proper distances from each other. The whole had a peaceful character about it, and the detached scenes seemed designed expressly, if not for painting, at least for life.

At last a neatly-kept farm, with a clean, modest dwelling-house, situated in the middle of a garden, fell under his eye. He conjectured that this was Edward's present abode; and he was not mistaken.

Of this our friend in his solitude we have only thus much to say—that in his seclusion he was resigning himself utterly to the feeling of his passion, thinking out plan after plan, and feeding himself with innumerable hopes. He could not deny that he longed to see Ottilie there; that he would like to carry her off there, to tempt her there; and whatever else (putting, as he now did, no check upon his thoughts) pleased to suggest itself, whether permitted or unpermitted. Then his imagination wandered up and down, picturing every sort of possibility. If he could not have her there, if he could not lawfully possess her, he would secure to her the possession of the property for her own. There she should live.

for herself, silently, independently; she should be happy in that spot—sometimes his self-torturing mood would lead him further—be happy in it, perhaps, with another.

So days flowed away in increasing oscillation between hope and suffering, between tears and happiness—between purposes, preparations, and despair. The sight of Mittler did not surprise him; he had long expected that he would come; and now that he did, he was partly welcome to him. He believed that he had been sent by Charlotte. He had prepared himself with all manner of excuses and delays; and if these would not serve, with decided refusals; or else, perhaps, he might hope to learn something of Ottilie,—and then he would be dear to him as a messenger from heaven.

Not a little vexed and annoyed was Edward, therefore, when he understood that Mittler had not come from the castle at all, but of his own free accord. His heart closed up, and at first the conversation would not open itself. Mittler, however, knew very well that a heart that is occupied with love has an urgent necessity to express itself—to pour out to a friend what is passing within it; and he allowed himself, therefore, after a few speeches backwards and forwards, for this once to go out of his character, and play the confidant in place of the mediator. He had calculated justly. He had been finding fault in a good-natured way with Edward, for burying himself in that lonely place, upon which Edward replied:

"I do not know how I could spend my time more agreeably. I am always occupied with her; I am always close to her. I have the inestimable comfort of being able to think where Ottilie is at each moment—where she is going, where she is standing, where she is reposing. I see her moving and acting before me as usual; ever doing or designing something which is to give me pleasure. But this will not always answer; for how can I be happy away from her? And then my fancy begins to work; I think what Ottilie should do to come to me; I write sweet, loving letters in her name to myself, and then I answer them, and keep the sheets together. I have promised that I will take no steps to seek her; and that promise I will keep. But what binds her, that she should make no advances to me? Has Charlotte had the barbarity to exact a promise, to exact an oath from her, not to write to me, not to send me a word, a hint, about herself? Very likely she has. It is only natural; and yet to me it is monstrous, it is horrible. If she loves me—as I think, as I know that she does—why does she not resolve, why does she not venture to fly to me, and throw herself into my arms? I often think she ought to do it; and she could do it. If I ever hear a noise in the hall, I look towards the door. It must be her—she is coming—I look up to see her. Alas! because the possible is impossible, I let myself imagine that the impossible must become possible. At night, when I lie awake, and the lamp flings an uncertain light about the room, her form, her spirit, a sense of her presence, sweeps over me, approaches me, seizes me. It is but for a moment; it is that I may have an assurance that she is thinking of me, that she is mine. Only one pleasure remains to me. When I was with her I never dreamt of her; now when I am far away, and, oddly enough, since I have made the acquaintance of other attractive persons in this neighbourhood, for the first time, her figure appears to me in my dreams, as if she would say to me, ' Look on them, and on me. You will find none more beautiful, more lovely than I.' And so she is present in every dream I have. In whatever happens to me with her, we are woven in and in together. Now we are subscribing a contract together. There is her hand, and there is mine; there is her name, and there is mine; and they move one into the other, and seem to devour each other. Sometimes she does something which injures the pure idea which I have of her; and then I feel how intensely I love her, by the indescribable anguish which it causes me. Again, unlike herself, she will rally and vex me; and then at once the figure changes—her sweet, round, heavenly face draws out; it is not her, it is another; but I lie vexed, dissatisfied and wretched. Laugh not, dear Mittler, or laugh on as you will. I am not ashamed of this attachment, of this—if you please to call it so—foolish, frantic passion. No, I never loved before. It is only 'now that I know what to love means. Till now, what I have called life was nothing but its prelude—amusement, sport to kill the time with. I never lived till I knew her, till I loved her—entirely and only loved her. People have often said of me, not to my face, but behind my back, that in most things I was but a botcher and a bungler. It may be so ; for I had not then found in what I could show myself a master. I should like to see the man who outdoes me in the talent of love. A miserable life it is, full of anguish and tears ; but it is so natural, so dear to me, that I could hardly change it for another."

Edward had relieved himself slightly by this violent un-loading of his heart. But in doing so every feature of his strange condition had been brought out so clearly before his eyes, that, overpowered by the pain of the struggle, he burst into tears, which flowed all the more freely as his heart had been made weak by telling it all.

Mittler, who was the less disposed to put a check on his inexorable good sense and strong, vigorous feeling, because by this violent outbreak of passion on Edward's part he saw himself driven far from the purpose of his coming, showed sufficiently decided marks of his disapprobation. Edward should act as a man, he said ; he should remember what he owed to himself as a man. He should not forget that the highest honour was to command ourselves in misfortune ; to bear pain, if it must be so, with equanimity and self-collectedness. That was what we should do, if we wished to be valued and looked up to as examples of what was right.

Stirred and penetrated as Edward was with the bitterest feelings, words like these could but have a hollow, worthless sound.

" It is well," he cried, " for the man who is happy, who has all that he desires, to talk ; but he would be ashamed of it if he could see how intolerable it was to the sufferer. Nothing short of an infinite endurance would be enough, and easy and contented as he was, what could he know of an infinite agony? There are cases," he continued, " yes, there are, where comfort is a lie, and despair is a duty. Go, heap your scorn upon the noble Greek, who well knows how to delineate heroes, when in their anguish he lets those heroes weep. He has even a proverb, ' Men who can weep are good.' Leave me, all you with dry heart and dry eye. Curses on the happy, to whom the wretched serve but for a spectacle. When body and soul are torn in pieces with agony, they are to bear it—yes, to be noble and bear it, if they are to be allowed to go off the scene with applause. Like the gladiators, they must die gracefully before the eyes of the multitude. My dear Mittler, I thank you for your visit; but really you would oblige me much, if you would go out and look about you in the garden. We will meet again. I will try to compose myself, and become more like you."

Mittler was unwilling to let a conversation drop which it might be difficult to begin again, and still persevered. Edward, too, was quite ready to go on with it; besides that of itself, it was tending towards the issue which he desired.

"Indeed," said the latter, "this thinking and arguing backwards and forwards leads to nothing. In this very conversation I myself have first come to understand myself; I have first felt decided as to what I must make up my mind to do. My present and my future life I see before me; I have to choose only between misery and happiness. Do you, my best friend, bring about the separation which must take place, which, in fact, is already made; gain Charlotte's consent for me. I will not enter upon the reasons why I believe there will be the less difficulty in prevailing upon her. You, my dear friend, must go. Go, and give us all peace; make us all happy."

Mittler hesitated. Edward continued:

"My fate and Ottilie's cannot be divided, and shall not be shipwrecked. Look at this glass; our initials are engraved upon it. A gay reveller flung it into the air, that no one should drink of it more. It was to fall on the rock and be dashed to pieces; but it did not fall; it was caught. At a high price I bought it back, and now I drink out of it daily—to convince myself that the connection between us cannot be broken; that destiny has decided."

"Alas, alas!" cried Mittler, "what must I not endure with my friends? Here comes superstition, which of all things I hate the worst—the most mischievous and accursed of all the plagues of mankind. We trifle with prophecies, with forebodings, and dreams, and give a seriousness to our every-day life with them; but when the seriousness of life itself begins to show, when everything around us is heaving and rolling, then come in these spectres to make the storm more terrible."

"In this uncertainty of life," cried Edward, "poised as it is

I

between hope and fear, leave the poor heart its guiding-star. It may gaze towards it, if it cannot steer towards it."

" Yes, I might leave it ; and it would be very well," replied Mittler, " if there were but one consequence to expect ; but I have always found that nobody will attend to symptoms of warning. Man cares for nothing except what flatters him and promises him fair ; and his faith is alive exclusively for the sunny side."

Mittler, finding himself carried off into the shadowy regions, in which the longer he remained in them, the more uncomfortable he always felt, was the more ready to assent to Edward's eager wish that he should go to Charlotte. Indeed, if he stayed, what was there further which at that moment he could urge on Edward ? To gain time, to inquire in what state things were with the ladies, was the best thing which even he himself could suggest as at present possible.

He hastened to Charlotte, whom he found as usual, calm and in good spirits. She told him readily of everything which had occurred ; for from what Edward had said he had only been able to gather the effects. On his own side, he felt his way with the utmost caution. He could not prevail upon himself even cursorily to mention the word separation. It was a surprise, indeed, to him, but from his point of view an unspeakably delightful one, when Charlotte, at the end of a number of unpleasant things, finished with saying :

" I must believe, I must hope, that things will all work round again, and that Edward will return to me. How can it be otherwise, as soon as I become a mother ?"

" Do I understand you right ?" returned Mittler.

" Perfectly," Charlotte answered.

" A thousand times blessed be this news !" he cried, clasping his hands together. " I know the strength of this argument on the mind of a man. Many a marriage have I seen first cemented by it, and restored again when broken. Such a good hope as this is worth more than a thousand words. Now indeed it is the best hope which we can have. For myself, though," he continued, " I have all reason to be vexed about it. In this case I can see clearly no self-love of mine will be flattered. I shall earn no thanks from you by my services ; I am in the same case as a certain medical friend of mine, who succeeds in all cures which he undertakes with the poor for the love of God; but can seldom do anything for the rich who will pay him. Here, thank God, the thing cures itself, after all my talking and trying had proved fruitless."

Charlotte now asked him if he would carry the news to Edward: if he would take a letter to him from her, and then see what should be done. But he declined undertaking this. " All is done," he cried; " do you write your letter—any messenger will do as well as I—I will come back to wish you joy. I will come to the christening!"

For this refusal she was vexed with him—as she frequently was. His eager impetuous character brought about much good; but his over-haste was the occasion of many a failure. No one was more dependent than he on the impressions which he formed on the moment.

Charlotte's messenger came to Edward, who received him half in terror. The letter was to decide his fate, and it might as well contain No as Yes. He did not venture, for a long time, to open it. At last he tore off the cover, and stood petrified at the following passage, with which it concluded:

" Remember the night-adventure when you visited your wife as a lover—how you drew her to you, and clasped her as a well-beloved bride in your arms. In this strange accident let us revere the providence of heaven, which has woven a new link to bind us, at the moment when the happiness of our lives was threatening to fall asunder and to vanish."

What passed from that moment in Edward's soul it would be difficult to describe! Under the weight of such a stroke, old habits and fancies come out again to assist to kill the time and fill up the chasms of life. Hunting and fighting are an ever-ready resource of this kind for a nobleman; Edward longed for some outward peril, as a counterbalance to the storm within him. He craved for death, because the burden of life threatened to become too heavy for him to bear. It comforted him to think that he would soon cease to be, and so would make those whom he loved happy by his departure.

No one made any difficulty in his doing what he purposed —because he kept his intention a secret. He made his will with all due formalities. It gave him a very sweet feeling to secure Ottilie's fortune—provision was made for Charlotte, for the unborn child, for the Captain, and for the servants. The war, which had again broken out, favoured his wishes : he had disliked exceedingly the half-soldiering which had fallen to him in his youth, and that was the reason why he had left the service. Now it gave him a fine exhilarating feeling to be able to rejoin it, under a commander of whom it could be said, that under his conduct death was likely, and victory was sure.

Ottilie, when Charlotte's secret was made known to her, bewildered by it, like Edward, and more than he, retired into herself—she had nothing further to say : hope she could not, and wish she dared not. A glimpse into what was passing in her we can gather from her Diary, some passages of which we think to communicate.

PART II.

———•———

CHAPTER I.

THERE often happens to us in common life what, in an epic poem, we are accustomed to praise as a stroke of art in the poet; namely, that when the chief figures go off the scene, conceal themselves or retire into inactivity, some other or others, whom hitherto we have scarcely observed, come forward and fill their places. And these putting out all their force, at once fix our attention and sympathy on themselves, and earn our praise and admiration.

Thus, after the Captain and Edward were gone, the Architect, of whom we have spoken, appeared every day a more important person. The ordering and executing of a number of undertakings depended entirely upon him, and he proved himself thoroughly understanding and businesslike in the style in which he went to work; while in a number of other ways he was able also to make himself of assistance to the ladies, and find amusement for their weary hours. His outward air and appearance were of the kind which win confidence and awake affection. A youth in the full sense of the word, well-formed, tall, perhaps a little too stout; modest without being timid, and easy without being obtrusive, there was no work and no trouble which he was not delighted to take upon himself; and as he could keep accounts with great facility, the whole economy of the household soon was no secret to him, and everywhere his salutary influence made itself felt. Any stranger who came he was commonly set to entertain, and he was skilful either at declining unexpected visits, or at least so far preparing the ladies for them as to spare them any disagreeableness.

Among others, he had one day no little trouble with a young lawyer, who had been sent by a neighbouring noble-

man to speak about a matter which, although of no particular
moment, yet touched Charlotte to the quick. We have to
mention this incident because it gave occasion for a number
of things which otherwise might perhaps have remained long
untouched.

We remember certain alterations which Charlotte had
made in the churchyard. The entire body of the monuments
had been removed from their places, and had been ranged
along the walls of the church, leaning against the string-
course. The remaining space had been levelled, except a
broad walk which led up to the church, and past it to the
opposite gate; and it had been all sown with various kinds
of trefoil, which had shot up and flowered most beautifully.

The new graves were to follow one after another in a
regular order from the end, but the spot on each occasion
was to be carefully smoothed over and again sown. No one
could deny that on sundays and holidays when the people
went to church the change had given it a most cheerful and
pleasant appearance. At the same time the clergyman, an
old man and clinging to old customs, who at first had not
been especially pleased with the alteration, had become
thoroughly delighted with it, all the more because when he
sat out like Philemon with his Baucis under the old linden
trees at his back door, instead of the humps and mounds he
had a beautiful clean lawn to look out upon; and which,
moreover, Charlotte having secured the use of the spot to the
Parsonage, was no little convenience to his household.

Notwithstanding this, however, many members of the
congregation had been displeased that the means of marking
the spots where their forefathers rested had been removed,
and all memorials of them thereby obliterated. However
well preserved the monuments might be, they could only shew
who had been buried, but not where he had been buried, and
the *where*, as many maintained, was everything.

Of this opinion was a family in the neighbourhood, who
for many years had been in possession of a considerable vault
for a general resting-place of themselves and their relations,
and in consequence had settled a small annual sum for the
use of the church. And now this young lawyer had been
sent to cancel this settlement, and to show that his client did
not intend to pay it any more, because the condition under

which it had been hitherto made had not been observed by the other party, and no regard had been paid to objection and remonstrance. Charlotte, who was the originator of the alteration herself, chose to speak to the young man, who in a decided though not a violent manner, laid down the grounds on which his client proceeded, and gave occasion in what he said for much serious reflection.

"You see," he said, after a slight introduction, in which he sought to justify his peremptoriness; "you see, it is right for the lowest as well as for the highest to mark the spot which holds those who are dearest to him. The poorest peasant, who buries a child, finds it some consolation to plant a light wooden cross upon the grave, and hang a garland upon it, to keep alive the memorial, at least as long as the sorrow remains; although such a mark, like the mourning, will pass away with time. Those better off change the cross of wood into iron, and fix it down and guard it in various ways; and here we have endurance for many years. But because this too will sink at last, and become invisible, those who are able to bear the expense see nothing fitter than to raise a stone which shall promise to endure for generations, and which can be restored and made fresh again by posterity. Yet this stone it is not which attracts us; it is that which is contained beneath it, which is entrusted, where it stands, to the earth. It is not the memorial so much of which we speak, as of the person himself; not of what once was, but of what is. Far better, far more closely, can I embrace some dear departed one in the mound which rises over his bed, than in a monumental writing which only tells us that once he was. In itself, indeed, it is but little; but around it, as around a central mark, the wife, the husband, the kinsman, the friend, after their departure, shall gather in again; and the living shall have the right to keep far off all strangers and evil-wishers from the side of the dear one who is sleeping there.

"And, therefore, I hold it quite fair and fitting that my principal shall withdraw his grant to you. It is, indeed, but too reasonable that he should do it, for the members of his family are injured in a way for which no compensation could be even proposed. They are deprived of the sad sweet feelings of laying offerings on the remains of their dead, and of the one comfort in their sorrow of one day lying down at their side."

"The matter is not of that importance," Charlotte answered, "that we should disquiet ourselves about it with the vexation of a law-suit. I regret so little what I have done, that I will gladly myself indemnify the church for what it loses through you. Only I must confess candidly to you, your arguments have not convinced me; the pure feeling of an universal equality at last, after death, seems to me more composing than this hard determined persistence in our personalities and in the conditions and circumstances of our lives. What do you say to it?" she added, turning to the Architect.

"It is not for me," replied he, "either to argue, or to attempt to judge in such a case. Let me venture, however, to say what my own art and my own habits of thinking suggest to me. Since we are no longer so happy as to be able to press to our breasts the the in-urned remains of those we have loved, since we are neither wealthy enough, nor of cheerful heart enough to preserve them undecayed in large elaborate sarcophagi; since, indeed, we cannot even find place any more for ourselves and ours in the churches, and are banished out into the open air, we all, I think, ought to approve the method which you, my gracious lady, have introduced. If the members of a common congregation are laid out side by side, they are resting by the side of, and among their kindred; and, if the earth be once to receive us all, I can find nothing more natural or more desirable than that the mounds, which, if they are thrown up, are sure to sink slowly in again together, should be smoothed off at once, and the covering, which all bear alike, will press lighter upon each."

"And is it all, is it all to pass away," said Ottilie, "without one token of remembrance, without anything to call back the past?"

"By no means," continued the Architect; "it is not from remembrance, it is from *place* that men should be set free. The architect, the sculptor, are highly interested that men should look to their art—to their hand, for a continuance of their being; and, therefore, I should wish to see well-designed, well-executed monuments; not sown up and down by themselves at random, but erected all in a single spot, where they can promise themselves endurance. Inasmuch as even the good and the great are contented to surrender the privilege of resting in person in the churches, *we* may, at least, erect there or in some fair hall near the burying place, either monuments or monumental writings. A thousand forms might be suggested for them, and a thousand ornaments with which they might be decorated."

"If the artists are so rich," replied Charlotte, "then tell me how it is that they are never able to escape from little obelisks, dwarf pillars, and urns for ashes? Instead of your thousand forms of which you boast, I have never seen anything but a thousand repetitions."

"It is very generally so with us," returned the Architect, "but it is not universal; and very likely the right taste and the proper application of it may be a peculiar art. In this case especially we have this great difficulty, that the monument must be something cheerful and yet commemorate a solemn subject; while its matter is melancholy, it must not itself be melancholy. As regards designs for monuments of all kinds, I have collected numbers of them, and I will take some opportunity of showing them to you; but at all times the fairest memorial of a man remains some likeness of himself. This, better than anything else, will give a notion of what he was; it is the best text for many or for few notes, only it ought to be made when he is at his best age, and that is generally neglected; no one thinks of preserving forms while they are alive, and if it is done at all, it is done carelessly and incompletely: and then comes death; a cast is taken swiftly off the face; this mask is set upon a block of stone, and that is what is called a bust. How seldom is the artist in a position to put any real life into such things as these!"

"You have contrived," said Charlotte, "without perhaps knowing it or wishing it, to lead the conversation altogether in my favour. The likeness of a man is quite independent; everywhere that it stands, it stands for itself, and we do not require it to mark the site of a particular grave. But I must acknowledge to you to having a strange feeling; even to likenesses I have a kind of disinclination. Whenever I see them they seem to be silently reproaching me. They point to something far away from us,—gone from us; and they remind me how difficult it is to pay right honour to the present. If we think how many people we have seen and known, and consider how little we have been to them and how little they have been to us, it is no very pleasant

reflection. We have met a man of genius without having
enjoyed much with him,—a learned man without having
learnt from him,—a traveller without having been instructed,
—a man to love without having shown him any kindness.

" And, unhappily, this is not the case only with accidental
meetings. Societies and families behave in the same way
towards their dearest members, towns towards their worthiest
citizens, people towards their most admirable princes, nations
towards their most distinguished men.

" I have heard it asked why we heard nothing but good
spoken of the dead, while of the living it is never without
some exception. It should be answered, because from the
former we have nothing any more to fear, while the latter
may still, here or there, fall in our way. So unreal is our
anxiety to preserve the memory of others,—generally no
more than a mere selfish amusement; and the real, holy,
earnest feeling, would be what should prompt us to be more
diligent and assiduous in our attentions toward those who
still are left to us."

CHAPTER II.

UNDER the stimulus of this accident, and of the conversations which arose out of it, they went the following day to
look over the burying-place, for the ornamenting of which
and relieving it in some degree of its sombre look, the
architect made many a happy proposal. His interest too
had to extend itself to the church as well; a building which
had caught his attention from the moment of his arrival.

It had been standing for many centuries, built in old
German style, the proportions good, the decorating elaborate and excellent; and one might easily gather that the
architect of the neighbouring monastery had left the stamp
of his art and of his love on this smaller building also; it
worked on the beholder with a solemnity and a sweetness,
although the change in its internal arrangements for the
Protestant service, had taken from it something of its repose
and majesty.

The Architect found no great difficulty in prevailing on Charlotte to give him a considerable sum of money to restore it externally and internally, in the original spirit, and thus, as he thought, to bring it into harmony with the resurrection-field which lay in front of it. He had himself much practical skill, and a few labourers who were still busy at the lodge, might easily be kept together, until this pious work too should be completed.

The building itself, therefore, with all its environs, and whatever was attached to it, was now carefully and thoroughly examined; and then showed itself, to the greatest surprise and delight of the architect, a little side chapel, which nobody had thought of, beautifully and delicately proportioned, and displaying still greater care and pains in its decoration. It contained at the same time many remnants, carved and painted, of the implements used in the old services, when the different festivals were distinguished by a variety of pictures and ceremonies, and each was celebrated in its own peculiar style.

It was impossible for him not at once to take this chapel into his plan; and he determined to bestow especial pains on the restoring of this little spot, as a memorial of old times, and of their taste. He saw exactly how he would like to have the vacant surfaces of the walls ornamented, and delighted himself with the prospect, of exercising his talent for painting upon them; but of this, at first, he made a secret to the rest of the party.

Before doing anything else, he fulfilled his promise of showing the ladies the various imitations of, and designs from, old monuments, vases, and other such things which he had made; and when they came to speak of the simple barrow-sepulchres of the northern nations, he brought a collection of weapons and implements which had been found in them. He had got them exceedingly nicely and conveniently arranged in drawers and compartments, laid on boards cut to fit them, and covered over with cloth; so that these solemn old things, in the way he treated them, had a smart dressy appearance, and it was like looking into the box of a trinket merchant.

Having once begun to show his curiosities, and finding them prove serviceable to entertain our friends in their loneliness; every evening he would produce one or other of his treasures.

They were most of them of German origin—pieces of metal, old coins, seals, and such like. All these things directed the imagination back upon old times; and when at last they came to amuse themselves with the first specimens of printing, woodcuts, and the earliest copper-plate engraving, and when the church, in the same spirit, was growing out, every day, more and more in form and colour like the past, they had almost to ask themselves whether they really were living in a modern time, whether it were not a dream, that manners, customs, modes of life, and convictions were all really so changed.

After such preparation, a great portfolio, which at last he produced, had the best possible effect. It contained indeed principally only outlines and figures, but as these had been traced upon original pictures, they retained perfectly their ancient character, and most captivating indeed this character was to the spectators. All the figures breathed only the purest feeling; every one, if not noble, at any rate was good; cheerful composure, ready recognition of One above us, to whom all reverence is due; silent devotion, in love and tranquil expectation, was expressed on every face, on every gesture. The old bald-headed man, the curly-pated boy, the light-hearted youth, the earnest man, the glorified saint, the angel hovering in the air, all seemed happy in an innocent, satisfied, pious expectation. The commonest object had a trait of celestial life; and every nature seemed adapted to the service of God, and to be, in some way or other, employed upon it.

Towards such a region most of them gazed as towards a vanished golden age, or on some lost paradise; only perhaps Ottilie had a chance of finding herself among beings of her own nature. Who could offer any opposition when the Architect asked to be allowed to paint the spaces between the arches and the walls of the chapel in the style of these old pictures; and thereby leave his own distinct memorial at a place where life had gone so pleasantly with him?

He spoke of it with some sadness, for he could see, in the state in which things were, that his sojourn in such delightful society could not last for ever; indeed, that perhaps it would now soon be ended.

For the rest, these days were not rich in incidents; yet full of occasion for serious entertainment. We therefore take the opportunity of communicating something of the remarks which Ottilie noted down among her manuscripts, to which we cannot find a fitter transition than through a simile which suggested itself to us on contemplating her exquisite pages.

There is, we are told, a curious contrivance in the service of the English marine. The ropes in use in the royal navy, from the largest to the smallest, are so twisted that a red thread runs through them from end to end, which cannot be extracted without undoing the whole; and by which the smallest pieces may be recognized as belonging to the crown.

Just so is there drawn through Ottilie's diary, a thread of attachment and affection which connects it all together, and characterizes the whole. And thus these remarks, these observations, these extracted sentences, and whatever else it may contain, were, to the writer, of peculiar meaning. Even the few separate pieces which we select and transcribe will sufficiently explain our meaning.

FROM OTTILIE'S DIARY.

" To rest hereafter at the side of those whom we love is the most delightful thought which man can have when once he looks out beyond the boundary of life. What a sweet expression is that—' He was gathered to his fathers!' "

" Of the various memorials and tokens which bring nearer to us the distant and the separated—none is so satisfactory as a picture. To sit and talk to a beloved picture, even though it be unlike, has a charm in it, like the charm which there sometimes is in quarrelling with a friend. We feel, in a strange sweet way, that we are divided and yet cannot separate."

" We entertain ourselves often with a present person as with a picture. He need not speak to us, he need not look at us, or take any notice of us; we look at him, we feel the relation in which we stand to him; such relation can even grow without his doing anything towards it, without his having any feeling of it: he is to us exactly as a picture."

" One is never satisfied with a portrait of a person that one knows. I have always felt for the portrait-painter on this account. One so seldom requires of people what is impossible, and of them we do really require what is impossible ; they must gather up into their picture the relation of every body to its subject, all their likings and all dislikings ; they must not only paint a man as they see him, but as every one else sees him. It does not surprise me if such artists become by degrees stunted, indifferent, and of but one idea ; and indeed it would not matter what came of it, if it were not that in consequence we have to go without the pictures of so many persons near and dear to us."

"It is too true, the Architect's collection of weapons and old implements, which were found with the bodies of their owners, covered in with great hills of earth and rock, proves to us how useless is man's so great anxiety to preserve his personality after he is dead ; and so inconsistent people are ! the Architect confesses to have himself opened these barrows of his forefathers, and yet goes on occupying himself with memorials for posterity."

"But after all why should we take it so much to heart ? is all that we do, done for eternity ? Do we not put on our dress in the morning, to throw it off again at night ? Do we not go abroad to return home again ? And why should we not wish to rest by the side of our friends, though it were but for a century ?"

" When we see the many grave-stones which have fallen in, which have been defaced by the footsteps of the congregation, which lie buried under the ruins of the churches, that have themselves crumbled together over them, we may fancy the life after death to be as a second life, into which a man enters in the figure, or the picture, or the inscription, and lives longer there than when he was really alive. But this figure also, this second existence, dies out too, sooner or later. Time will not allow himself to be cheated of his rights with the monuments of men or with themselves."

CHAPTER III.

IT causes us so agreeable a sensation to occupy ourselves with what we can only half do, that no person ought to find fault with the dilettante, when he is spending his time over an art which he can never learn; nor blame the artist if he chooses to pass out over the border of his own art, and amuse himself in some neighbouring field. With such complacency of feeling we regard the preparation of the Architect for the painting the chapel. The colours were got ready, the measurements taken; the cartoons designed. He had made no attempt at originality, but kept close to his outlines; his only care was to make a proper distribution of the sitting and floating figures, so as tastefully to ornament his space with them.

The scaffoldings were erected. The work went forward; and as soon as anything had been done on which the eye could rest, he could have no objection to Charlotte and Ottilie coming to see how he was getting on.

The life-like faces of the angels, their robes waving against the blue sky-ground, delighted the eye, while their still and holy air calmed and composed the spirit, and produced the most delicate effect.

The ladies ascended the scaffolding to him, and Ottilie had scarcely observed how easily and regularly the work was being done, than the power which had been fostered in her by her early education at once appeared to develope. She took a brush, and with a few words of direction, painted a richly folding robe, with as much delicacy as skill.

Charlotte, who was always glad when Ottilie would occupy or amuse herself with anything, left them both in the chapel, and went to follow the train of her own thoughts, and work her way for herself through her cares and anxieties which she was unable to communicate to a creature.

When ordinary men allow themselves to be worked up by common every-day difficulties into fever-fits of passion, we can give them nothing but a compassionate smile. But we look with a kind of awe on a spirit in which the seed of a great destiny has been sown, which must abide the unfolding of the germ, and neither dare nor can do anything to precipitate either the good or the ill, either the happiness or the misery, which is to arise out of it.

Edward had sent an answer by Charlotte's messenger, who had come to him in his solitude. It was written with kindness and interest, but it was rather composed and serious than warm and affectionate. He had vanished almost immediately after, and Charlotte could learn no news about him; till at last she accidentally found his name in the newspaper, where he was mentioned with honour among those who had most distinguished themselves in a late important engagement. She now understood the method which he had taken; she perceived that he had escaped from great danger; only she was convinced at the same time that he would seek out greater; and it was all too clear to her that in every sense he would hardly be withheld from any extremity.

She had to bear about this perpetual anxiety in her thoughts, and turn which way she would, there was no light in which she could look at it that would give her comfort.

Ottilie, never dreaming of anything of this, had taken to the work in the chapel with the greatest interest, and she had easily obtained Charlotte's permission to go on with it regularly. So now all went swiftly forward, and the azure heaven was soon peopled with worthy inhabitants. By continual practice both Ottilie and the architect had gained more freedom with the last figures; they became perceptibly better. The faces, too, which had been all left to the architect to paint, showed by degrees a very singular peculiarity. They began all of them to resemble Ottilie. The neighbourhood of the beautiful girl had made so strong an impression on the soul of the young man, who had no variety of faces preconceived in his mind, that by degrees, on the way from the eye to the hand, nothing was lost, and both worked in exact harmony together. Enough; one of the last faces succeeded perfectly; so that it seemed as if Ottilie herself was looking down out of the spaces of the sky.

They had finished with the arching of the ceiling. The walls they proposed to leave plain, and only to cover them over with a bright brown colour. The delicate pillars and the quaintly-moulded ornaments were to be distinguished from them by a dark shade. But as in such things one thing ever leads on to another, they determined at least on having festoons of flowers and fruit, which should as it were unite together heaven and earth. Here Ottilie was in her element. The gardens provided the most perfect patterns; and although the wreaths were as rich as they could make them, it was all finished sooner than they had supposed possible.

It was still looking rough and disorderly. The scaffolding poles had been run together, the planks thrown one on the top of the other; the uneven pavement was yet more disfigured by the particoloured stains of the paint which had been spilt over it.

The Architect begged that the ladies would give him a week to himself, and during that time would not enter the chapel; at the end of it, one fine evening, he came to them, and begged them both to go and see it. He did not wish to accompany them, he said, and at once took his leave.

"Whatever surprise he may have designed for us," said Charlotte, as soon as he was gone, "I cannot myself just now go down there. You can go by yourself, and tell me all about it. No doubt he has been doing something which we shall like. I will enjoy it first in your description, and afterwards it will be the more charming in the reality."

Ottilie, who knew well that in many cases Charlotte took care to avoid everything which could produce emotion, and particularly disliked to be surprised, set off down the walk by herself, and looked round involuntarily for the Architect, who however was nowhere to be seen, and must have concealed himself somewhere. She walked into the church, which she found open. This had been finished before; it had been cleaned up, and service had been performed in it. She went on to the chapel door; its heavy mass, all overlaid with iron, yielded easily to her touch, and she found an unexpected sight in a familiar spot.

A solemn beautiful light streamed in through the one tall window. It was filled with stained glass, gracefully put together. The entire chapel had thus received a strange tone, and a peculiar genius was thrown over it. The beauty of the vaulted ceiling and the walls was set off by the elegance of the pavement, which was composed of peculiarly shaped tiles, fastened together with gypsum, and forming exquisite patterns as they lay. This and the coloured glass for the windows the

K

Architect had prepared without their knowledge, and a short time was sufficient to have it put in its place.

Seats had been provided as well. Among the relics of the old church some finely carved chancel chairs had been discovered, which now were standing about at convenient places along the walls.

The parts which she knew so well now meeting her as an unfamiliar whole, delighted Ottile. She stood still, walked up and down, looked and looked again; at last she seated herself in one of the chairs, and it seemed, as she gazed up and down, as if she was, and yet was not—as if she felt and did not feel—as if all this would vanish from before her, and she would vanish from herself; and it was only when the sun left the window, on which before it had been shining full, that she awoke to possession of herself, and hastened back to the castle.

She did not hide from herself the strange epoch at which this surprise had occurred to her. It was the evening of Edward's birthday. Very differently she had hoped to keep it. How was not everything to be dressed out for this festival? and now all the splendour of the autumn flowers remained ungathered. Those sunflowers still turned their faces to the sky; those asters still looked out with quiet, modest eye; and whatever of them all had been wound into wreaths had served as patterns for the decorating a spot which, if it was not to remain a mere artist's fancy, was only adapted as a general mausoleum.

And then she had to remember the impetuous eagerness with which Edward had kept her birthday-feast. She thought of the newly-erected lodge, under the roof of which they had promised themselves so much enjoyment. The fireworks flashed and hissed again before her eyes and ears; the more lonely she was, the more keenly her imagination brought it all before her. But she felt herself only the more alone. She no longer leant upon his arm, and she had no hope ever any more to rest herself upon it.

FROM OTTILIE'S DIARY.

"I have been struck with an observation of the young architect.

"In the case of the creative artist, as in that of the artizan, it is clear that man is least permitted to appropriate to himself what is most entirely his own. His works forsake him as the birds forsake the nest in which they were hatched.

"The fate of the Architect is the strangest of all in this way. How often he expends his whole soul, his whole heart and passion, to produce buildings into which he himself may never enter. The halls of kings owe their magnificence to him; but he has no enjoyment of them in their splendour. In the temple he draws a partition line between himself and the Holy of Holies; he may never more set his foot upon the steps which he has laid down for the heart-thrilling ceremonial; as the goldsmith may only adore from far off the *monstrance* whose enamel and whose jewels he has himself set together. The builder surrenders to the rich man, with the key of his palace, all pleasure and all right there, and never shares with him in the enjoyment of it. And must not art in this way, step by step, draw off from the artist, when the work, like a child who is provided for, has no more to fall back upon its father? And what a power there must be in art itself, for its own self-advancing, when it has been obliged to shape itself almost solely out of what was open to all, only out of what was the property of every one, and therefore also of the artist!"

"There is a conception among old nations which is awful, and may almost seem terrible. They pictured their fore-fathers to themselves sitting round on thrones, in enormous caverns, in silent converse; when a new comer entered, if he were worthy enough, they rose up, and inclined their heads to welcome him. Yesterday, as I was sitting in the chapel, and other carved chairs stood round like that in which I was, the thought of this came over me with a soft, pleasant feeling. Why cannot you stay sitting here? I said to myself; stay here sitting meditating with yourself long, long, long, till at last your friends come, and you rise up to them, and with a gentle inclination direct them to their places. The coloured window panes convert the day into a solemn twilight; and some one should set up for us an ever-burning lamp, that the night might not be utter darkness."

"We may imagine ourselves in what situation we please, we always conceive ourselves as *seeing*. I believe men only dream that they may not cease to see. Some day, perhaps,

K 2

the inner light will come out from within us, and we shall
not any more require another.

" The year dies away, the wind sweeps over the stubble, and
there is nothing left to stir under its touch But the red
berries on yonder tall tree seem as if they would still remind
us of brighter things; and the stroke of the thrasher's flail
awakes the thought how much of nourishment and life lies
buried in the sickled ear."

CHAPTER IV.

How strangely, after all this, with the sense so vividly
impressed on her of mutability and perishableness, must
Ottilie have been affected by the news which could not any
longer be kept concealed from her, that Edward had exposed
himself to the uncertain chances of war!   Unhappily, none
of the observations which she had occasion to make upon it
escaped her.   But it is well for us that man can only endure
a certain degree of unhappiness; what is beyond that, either
annihilates him, or passes by him, and leaves him apathetic.
There are situations in which hope and fear run together, in
which they mutually destroy one another, and lose themselves
in a dull indifference.   If it were not so, how could we bear
to know of those who are most dear to us being in hourly
peril, and yet go on as usual with our ordinary everyday life ?

It was therefore as if some good genius was caring for Ottilie,
that, all at once, this stillness, in which she seemed to be
sinking from loneliness and want of occupation, was suddenly
invaded by a wild army, which, while it gave her externally
abundance of employment, and so took her out of herself, at
the same time awoke in her the consciousness of her own
power.

Charlotte's daughter, Luciana, had scarcely left the school
and gone out into the great world; scarcely had she found
herself at her aunt's house in the midst of a large society, than
her anxiety to please produced its effect in really pleasing;
and a young, very wealthy man, soon experienced a passionate desire to make her his own.   His large property gave
him a right to have the best of everything for his use, and
nothing seemed to be wanting to him except a perfect wife,

for whom, as for the rest of his good fortune, he should be the envy of the world.

This incident in her family had been for some time occupying . Charlotte. It had engaged all her attention, and taken up her whole correspondence, except so far as this was directed to the obtaining news of Edward; so that latterly Ottilie had been left more than was usual to herself. She knew, indeed, of an intended visit from Luciana. She had been making various changes and arrangements in the house in preparation for it; but she had no notion that it was so near. Letters, she supposed, would first have to pass, settling the time, and then unsettling it; and then a final fixing: when the storm broke suddenly over the castle and over herself.

Up drove, first, lady's maids and men-servants, their carriage loaded with trunks and boxes. The household was already swelled to double or to treble its size, and then appeared the visitors themselves. There was the great aunt, with Luciana and some of her friends; and then the bridegroom with some of his friends. The entrance-hall was full of things—bags, portmanteaus, and leather articles of every sort. The boxes had to be got out of their covers, and that was infinite trouble; and of luggage and of rummage there was no end. At intervals, moreover, there were violent showers, giving rise to much inconvenience. Ottilie encountered all this confusion with the easiest equanimity, and her happy talent showed in its fairest light. In a very little time she had brought things to order, and disposed of them. Every one found his room,—every one had his things exactly as they wished, and all thought themselves well attended to, because they were not prevented from attending on themselves.

The journey had been long and fatiguing, and they would all have been glad of a little rest after it. The bridegroom would have liked to pay his respects to his mother-in-law, express his pleasure, his gratitude, and so on. But Luciana could not rest. She had now arrived at the happiness of being able to mount a horse. The bridegroom had beautiful horses, and mount they must on the spot. Clouds and wind, rain and storm, they were nothing to Luciana, and now it was as if they only lived to get wet through, and to dry themselves again. If she took a fancy to go out walking, she never thought what sort of dress she had on, or what her shoes were

like, she must go and see the grounds of which she had heard
so much; what could not be done on horseback, she ran
through on foot. In a little while she had seen everything,
and given her opinion about everything; and with such rapidity
of character it was not easy to contradict or oppose her. The
whole household had much to suffer, but most particularly the
lady's maids, who were at work from morning to night, wash-
ing, and ironing, and stitching.

As soon as she had exhausted the house and the park, she
thought it was her duty to pay visits all round the neighbourhood. As they rode and drove very fast, all round the neighbourhood was a considerable distance. The castle was flooded
with return visits, and that they might not miss one another,
it soon came to days being fixed for them.

Charlotte, in the mean time, with her aunt, and the man
of business of the bridegroom, were occupied in determining
about the settlements, and it was left to Ottilie, with those
under her, to take care that all this crowd of people were
properly provided for. Gamekeepers and gardeners, fishermen
and shopdealers, were set in motion, Luciana always showing herself like the blazing nucleus of a comet with its long
tail trailing behind it. The ordinary amusements of the parties soon became too insipid for her taste. Hardly would she
leave the old people in peace at the card-table. Whoever
could by any means be set moving (and who could resist the
charm of being pressed by her into service?) must up, if not
to dance, then to play at forfeits, or some other game, where
they were to be victimized and tormented. Notwithstanding
all that, however, and although afterwards the redemption of
the forfeits had to be settled with herself, yet of those who
played with her, never any one, especially never any man, let
him be of what sort he would, went quite empty-handed away.
Indeed, some old people of rank who were there she succeeded
in completely winning over to herself, by having contrived to
find out their birthdays or christening days, and marking them
with some particular celebration. In all this she showed a
skill not a little remarkable. Every one saw himself favoured,
and each considered himself to be the one most favoured, a
weakness of which the oldest person of the party was the
most notably guilty.

It seemed to be a sort of pride with her, that men who had
anything remarkable about them—rank, character, or fame—

she must and would gain for herself. Gravity and seriousness she made give way to her, and, wild strange creature as she was, she found favour even with discretion itself. Not that the young were at all cut short in consequence. Everybody had his share, his day, his hour, in which she contrived to charm and to enchain him. It was therefore natural enough that before long she should have had the Architect in her eye, looking out so unconsciously as he did from under his long black hair, and standing so calm and quiet in the back-ground. To all her questions she received short sensible answers; but he did not seem inclined to allow himself to be carried away further, and at last, half provoked, half in malice, she resolved that she would make him the hero of a day, and so gain him for her court.

It was not for nothing that she had brought that quantity of luggage with her. Much, indeed, had followed her afterwards. She had provided herself with an endless variety of dresses. When it took her fancy she would change her dress three or four times a day, usually wearing something of an ordinary kind, but making her appearance suddenly at intervals in a thorough masquerade dress, as a peasant girl or a fish maiden, as a fairy or a flower-girl; and this would go on from morning till night. Sometimes she would even disguise herself as an old woman, that her young face might peep out the fresher from under the cap; and so utterly in this way did she confuse and mix together the actual and the fantastic, that people thought they were living with a sort of drawing-room witch.

But the principal use which she had for these disguises were pantomimic tableaux and dances, in which she was skilful in expressing a variety of character. A cavalier in her suite had taught himself to accompany her action on the piano with the little music which was required; they needed only to exchange a few words and they at once understood one another.

One day, in a pause of a brilliant ball, they were called upon suddenly to extemporize (it was on a private hint from themselves) one of these exhibitions. Luciana seemed embarrassed, taken by surprise, and contrary to her custom let herself be asked more than once. She could not decide upon her character, desired the party to choose, and asked, like an improvisatore, for a subject. At last her piano-playing com-

panion, with whom it had been all previously arranged, sat
down at the instrument, and began to play a mourning march,
calling on her to give them the Artemisia which she had been
studying so admirably. She consented; and after a short
absence reappeared, to the sad tender music of the dead march,
in the form of the royal widow, with measured step, carrying
an urn of ashes before her. A large black tablet was borne
in after her, and a carefully cut piece of chalk in a gold pencil
case.

One of her adorers and adjutants, into whose ear she whispered something, went directly to call the Architect, to desire
him, and if he would not come to drag him up, as master-
builder, to draw the grave for the mausoleum, and to tell him
at the same time that he was not to play the statist, but
enter earnestly into his part as one of the performers.

Embarrassed as the Architect outwardly appeared (for in
his black, closefitting, modern civilian's dress, he formed a
wonderful contrast with the gauze crape fringes, tinsel tassels,
and crown), he very soon composed himself internally, and
the scene became all the more strange. With the greatest
gravity he placed himself in front of the tablet, which
was supported by a couple of pages, and drew carefully an
elaborate tomb, which indeed would have suited better a
Lombard than a Carian prince; but it was in such beautiful
proportions, so solemn in its parts, so full of genius in its
decoration, that the spectators watched it growing with
delight, and wondered at it when it was finished.

All this time he had not once turned towards the queen,
but had given his whole attention to what he was doing.
At last he inclined his head before her, and signified that he
believed he had now fulfilled her commands. She held the
urn out to him, expressing her desire to see it represented on
the top of the monument. He complied, although unwillingly, as it would not suit the character of the rest of his
design. Luciana was now at last released from her impatience. Her intention had been by no means to get a
scientific drawing out of him. If he had only made a few
strokes, sketched out something which should have looked
like a monument, and devoted the rest of his time to her, it
would have been far more what she had wished, and would
have pleased her a great deal better. His manner of proceeding had thrown her into the greatest embarrassment. For

although in her sorrow, in her directions, in her gestures, in her approbation of the work as it slowly rose before her, she had tried to manage some sort of change of expression, and although she had hung about close to him, only to place herself into some sort of relation to him, yet he had kept himself throughout too stiff, so that too often she had been driven to take refuge with her urn; she had to press it to her heart and look up to heaven, and at last, a situation of that kind having a necessary tendency to intensify, she made herself more like a widow of Ephesus than a Queen of Caria. The representation had to lengthen itself out and became tedious. The pianoforte player, who had usually patience enough, did not know into what tune he could escape. He thanked God when he saw the urn standing on the pyramid, and fell involuntarily as the queen was going to express her gratitude, into a merry air; by which the whole thing lost its character, the company however being throughly cheered up by it, who forthwith divided, some going up to express their delight and admiration of the lady for her excellent performance, and some praising the Architect for his most artistlike and beautiful drawing.

The bridegroom especially paid marked attention to the Architect. "I am vexed," he said, "that the drawing should be so perishable; you will permit me however to have it taken to my room, where I should much like to talk to you about it."

"If it would give you any pleasure," said the Architect, "I can lay before you a number of highly finished designs for buildings and monuments of this kind, of which this is but a mere hasty sketch."

Ottilie was standing at no great distance, and went up to them. "Do not forget," she said to the Architect, "to take an opportunity of letting the Baron see your collection. He is a friend of art and of antiquity. I should like you to become better acquainted."

Luciana was passing at the moment. "What are they speaking of?" she asked.

"Of a collection of works of art," replied the Baron, "which this gentleman possesses, and which he is good enough to say that he will show us."

"Oh, let him bring them immediately," cried Luciana,

" you will bring them, will you not?" she added, in a soft and sweet tone, taking both his hands in hers.

"The present is scarcely a fitting time," the Architect answered.

"What!" Luciana cried, in a tone of authority; "you will not obey the command of your queen!" and then she begged him again with some piece of absurdity.

"Do not be obstinate," said Ottilie, in a scarcely audible voice.

The Architect left them with a bow, which said neither yes nor no.

He was hardly gone, when Luciana was flying up and down the saloon with a greyhound. "Alas!" she exclaimed, as she ran accidentally against her mother, "am I not an unfortunate creature? I have not brought my monkey with me. They told me I had better not; but I am sure it was nothing but the laziness of my people, and it is such a delight to me. But I will have it brought after me; somebody shall go and fetch it. If I could only see a picture of the dear creature, it would be a comfort to me; I certainly will have his picture taken, and it shall never be out of my sight."

"Perhaps I can comfort you," replied Charlotte. "There is a whole volume full of the most wonderful ape faces in the library, which you can have fetched if you like."

Luciana shrieked for joy. The great folio was produced instantly. The sight of these hideous creatures, so like to men, and with the resemblance even more caricatured by the artist, gave Luciana the greatest delight. Her amusement with each of the animals, was to find some one of her acquaintance whom it resembled. "Is that not like my uncle?" she remorselessly exclaimed; "and here, look, here is my milliner M., and here is Parson S., and here the image of that creature ———— bodily! After all, these monkeys are the real *incroyables*, and it is inconceivable why they are not admitted into the best society."

It was in the best society that she said this, and yet no one took it ill of her. People had become accustomed to allow her so many liberties in her prettinesses, that at last they came to allow them in what was unpretty.

During this time, Ottilie was talking to the bridegroom; she was looking anxiously for the return of the Architect, whose serious and tasteful collection was to deliver the party from the apes; and in the expectation of it, she had made it the subject of her conversation with the Baron, and directed his attention on various things which he was to see. But the Architect stayed away, and when at last he made his appearance, he lost himself in the crowd, without having brought anything with him, and without seeming as if he had been asked for anything.

For a moment Ottilie became—what shall we call it? —annoyed, put out, perplexed. She had been saying so much about him—she had promised the bridegroom an hour of enjoyment after his own heart; and with all the depth of his love for Luciana, he was evidently suffering from her present behaviour.

The monkeys had to give place to a collation. Round games followed, and then more dancing; at last, a general uneasy vacancy, with fruitless attempts at resuscitating exhausted amusements, which lasted this time, as indeed they usually did, far beyond midnight. It had already become a habit with Luciana to be never able to get out of bed in the morning or into it at night.

About this time, the incidents noticed in Ottilie's diary become more rare, while we find a larger number of maxims and sentences drawn from life and relating to life. It is not conceivable that the larger proportion of these could have arisen from her own reflection, and most likely some one had shown her varieties of them, and she had written out what took her fancy. Many, however, with an internal bearing, can be easily recognized by the red thread.

FROM OTTILIE'S DIARY.

"We like to look into the future, because the undetermined in it, which may be affected this or that way, we feel as if we could guide by our silent wishes in our own favour."

"We seldom find ourselves in a large party without thinking; the accident which brings so many here together, should bring our friends to us as well."

"Let us live in as small a circle as we will, we are

either debtors or creditors before we have had time to look round."

———

" If we meet a person who is under an obligation to us, we remember it immediately. But how often may we meet people to whom we are ourselves under obligation, without its even occurring to us !" .

———

" It is nature to communicate one's-self; it is culture to receive what is communicated as it is given."

———

" No one would talk much in society, if he only knew how often he misunderstands others."

———

" One alters so much what one has heard from others in repeating it, only because one has not understood it."

———

" Whoever indulges long in monologue in the presence of others, without flattering his listeners, provokes ill-will."

———

" Every word a man utters provokes the opposite opinion."

———

" Argument and flattery are but poor elements out of which to form a conversation."

———

" The pleasantest society is when the members of it have an easy and natural respect for one another."

———

" There is nothing in which people more betray their character than in what they find to laugh at."

———

" The ridiculous arises out of a moral contrast, in which two things are brought together before the mind in an innocent way."

———

" The foolish man often laughs where there is nothing to laugh at. Whatever touches him, his inner nature comes to the surface."

———

" The man of understanding finds almost everything ridiculous; the man of thought scarcely anything."

———

" Some one found fault with an elderly man for continuing to pay attention to young ladies. ' It is the only means,' he replied, ' of keeping one's-self young, and everybody likes to do that.' "

" People will allow their faults to be shown them; they will let themselves be punished for them; they will patiently endure many things because of them; they only become impatient when they have to lay them aside."

" Certain defects are necessary for the existence of individuality. We should not be pleased, if old friends were to lay aside certain peculiarities."

" There is a saying, ' He will die soon,' when a man acts unlike himself."

" What kind of defects may we bear with and even cultivate in ourselves? Such as rather give pleasure to others than injure them."

" The passions are defects or excellencies only in excess."

" Our passions are true phœnixes: as the old burn out, the new straight rise up out of the ashes."

" Violent passions are incurable diseases; the means which will cure them are what first make them thoroughly dangerous."

" Passion is both raised and softened by confession. In nothing, perhaps, were the middle way more desirable than in knowing what to say and what not to say to those we love."

CHAPTER V.

So swept on Luciana in the social whirlpool, driving the rush of life along before her. Her court multiplied daily, partly because her impetuosity roused and attracted so many, partly because she knew how to attach the rest to her by kindness and attention. Generous she was in the highest degree ; her aunt's affection for her, and her bridegroom's love, had heaped her with beautiful and costly presents, but she seemed as if nothing which she had was her own, and as if she did not know the value of the things which had streamed in upon her.   One day she saw a young lady looking rather poorly dressed by the side of the rest of the party, and she did not hesitate a moment to take off a rich shawl which she was wearing and hang it over her,—doing it, at the same time, in such a humorous, graceful way that no one could refuse such a present so given.   One of her courtiers always carried about a purse, with orders, whatever place they passed through, to inquire there for the most aged and most helpless persons, and give them relief, at least for the moment.   In this way she gained for herself all round the country a reputation for charitableness which caused her not a little inconvenience, attracting about her far too many troublesome sufferers.

Nothing, however, so much added to her popularity as her steady and consistent kindness towards an unhappy young man, who shrank from society because, while otherwise handsome and well-formed, he had lost his right hand, although with high honour, in action.   This mutilation weighed so heavily upon his spirits, it was so annoying to him that every new acquaintance he made had to be told the story of his misfortune, that he chose rather to shut himself up altogether, devoting himself to reading and other studious pursuits, and once for all would have nothing more to do with society.

She heard of the state of this young man.   At once she contrived to prevail him upon to come to her, first to small parties, then to greater, and then out into the world with her.   She showed more attention to him than to any other person ; particularly she endeavoured, by the services which she pressed upon him, to make him sensible of what he had lost in labouring herself to supply it.   At dinner, she would make him sit next to her ; she cut up his food for him, that he might only have to use his fork.   If people older or of higher rank prevented her from being close to him, she would stretch her attention across the entire table, and the servants were hurried off to make up to him what distance threatened to deprive him of.   At last she encouraged him to write with his left hand.   All his attempts he was to address to her, and thus, whether far or near, she always kept herself in correspondence with him. The young man did not know what had happened to him, and from that moment a new life opened out before him.

One may perhaps suppose that such behaviour must have caused some uneasiness to her bridegroom. But, in fact, it was quite the reverse. He admired her exceedingly for her exertions, and he had the more reason for feeling entirely satisfied about her, as she had certain features in her character almost in excess, which kept anything in the slightest degree dangerous utterly at a distance. She would run about with any body, just as she fancied; no one was free from danger of a push or a pull, or of being made the object of some sort of freak. But no person ever ventured to do the same to her; no person dared to touch her, or return, in the remotest degree, any liberty which she had taken herself. She kept every one within the strictest barriers of propriety in their behaviour to herself, while she, in her own behaviour, was every moment overleaping them.

On the whole, one might have supposed it had been a maxim with her to expose herself indifferently to praise or blame, to regard or to dislike. If in many ways she took pains to gain people, she commonly herself spoiled all the good she had done, by an ill tongue, which spared no one. Not a visit was ever paid in the neighbourhood, not a single piece of hospitality was ever shown to herself and her party among the surrounding castles or mansions, but what on her return her excessive recklessness let it appear that all men and all human things she was only inclined to see on the ridiculous side.

There were three brothers who, purely out of compliment to each other, which should marry first, had been overtaken by old age before they had got the question settled; here was a little young wife with a great old husband; there, on the other hand, was a dapper little man and an unwieldy giantess. In one house, every step one took one stumbled over a child; another, however many people were crammed into it, never would seem full, because there were no children there at all. Old husbands (supposing the estate was not entailed) should get themselves buried as quickly as possible, that such a thing as a laugh might be heard again in the house. Young married people should travel: housekeeping did not sit well upon them. And as she treated the persons, so she treated what belonged to them; their houses, their furniture, their dinner-services—everything. The ornaments of the walls of the rooms most particularly provoked her saucy remarks. From the oldest tapestry to the most modern printed paper; from the noblest family pictures to the most frivolous new copper-plate: one as well as the other had to suffer—one as well as the other had to be pulled in pieces by her satirical tongue, so that, indeed, one had to wonder how, for twenty miles round, anything continued to exist.

It was not, perhaps, exactly malice which produced all this destructiveness; wilfulness and selfishness were what ordinarily set her off upon it: but a genuine bitterness grew up in her feelings towards Ottilie.

She looked down with disdain on the calm, uninterrupted activity of the sweet girl, which every one had observed and admired, and when something was said of the care which Ottilie took of the garden and of the hot-houses, she not only spoke scornfully of it, in affecting to be surprised, if it were so, at there being neither flowers nor fruit to be seen, not caring to consider that they were living in the depth of winter, but every faintest scrap of green, every leaf, every bud which showed, she chose to have picked every day and squandered on ornamenting the rooms and tables, and Ottilie and the gardener were not a little distressed to see their hopes for the next year, and perhaps for a longer time, destroyed in this wanton recklessness.

As little would she be content to leave Ottilie to her quiet work at home, in which she could live with so much comfort. Ottilie must go with them on their pleasure-parties and sledging-parties; she must be at the balls which were being got up all about the neighbourhood. She was not to mind the snow, or the cold, or the night-air, or the storm; other people did not die of such things, and why should she? The delicate girl suffered not a little from it all, but Luciana gained nothing. For although Ottilie went about very simply dressed, she was always, at least so the men thought, the most beautiful person present. A soft attractiveness gathered them all about her; no matter whereabouts in the great rooms she was, first or last, it was always the same. Even

Luciana's bridegroom was constantly occupied with her; the more so, indeed, because he desired her advice and assistance in a matter with which he was just then engaged.

He had cultivated the acquaintance of the Architect. On seeing his collection of works of art, he had taken occasion to talk much with him on history and on other matters, and especially from seeing the chapel had learnt to appreciate his talent. The Baron was young and wealthy. He was a collector; he wished to build. His love for the arts was keen, his knowledge small. In the Architect he thought that he had found the man he wanted; that with his assistance there was more than one aim at which he could arrive at once. He had spoken to his bride of what he wished. She praised him for it, and was infinitely delighted with the proposal. But it was more, perhaps, that she might carry off this young man from Ottilie (for whom she fancied she saw in him a kind of inclination), than because she thought of applying his talents to any purpose. He had shown himself, indeed, very ready to help at any of her extemporized festivities, and had suggested various resources for this thing and that. But she always thought she understood better than he what should be done, and as her inventive genius was usually somewhat common, her designs could be as well executed with the help of a tolerably handy domestic as with that of the most finished artist. Further than to an altar on which something was to be offered, or to a crowning, whether of a living head or of one of plaster of Paris, the force of her imagination could not ascend, when a birthday, or other such occasion, made her wish to pay some one an especial compliment.

Ottilie was able to give the Baron the most satisfactory answer to his inquiries as to the relation of the Architect with their family. Charlotte had already, as she was aware, been exerting herself to find some situation for him; had it not been indeed for the arrival of the party, the young man would have left them immediately on the completion of the chapel, the winter having brought all building operations to a standstill; and it was, therefore, most fortunate if a new patron could be found to assist him, and to make use of his talents.

Ottilie's own personal position with the Architect was as

L

pure and unconscious as possible. His agreeable presence,
and his industrious nature, had charmed and entertained her,
as the presence of an elder brother might. Her feelings for
him remained at the calm unimpassioned level of blood relationship. For in her heart there was no room for more;
it was filled to overflowing with love for Edward; only God,
who interpenetrates all things, could share with him the
possession of that heart.

Meantime the winter sank deeper; the weather grew
wilder, the roads more impracticable, and therefore it
seemed all the pleasanter to spend the waning days in agreeable society. With short intervals of ebb, the crowd from
time to time flooded up over the house. Officers found their
way there from distant garrison towns; the cultivated among
them being a most welcome addition, the ruder the inconvenience of every one. Of civilians too there was no lack;
and one day the Count and the Baroness quite unexpectedly
came driving up together.

Their presence gave the castle the air of a thorough court.
The men of rank and character formed a circle about the
Baron, and the ladies yielded precedence to the Baroness.
The surprise at seeing both together, and in such high spirits
was not allowed to be of long continuance. It came out that
the Count's wife was dead, and the new marriage was to take
place as soon as ever decency would allow it.

Well did Ottilie remember their first visit, and every word
which was then uttered about marriage and separation, binding and dividing, hope, expectation, disappointment, renunciation. Here were these two persons, at that time without
prospect for the future, now standing before her, so near their
wished-for happiness, and an involuntary sigh escaped out of
her heart.

No sooner did Luciana hear that the Count was an ama-
teur of music, than at once she must get up something of a
concert. She herself would sing and accompany herself on
the guitar. It was done. The instrument she did not play
without skill; her voice was agreeable: as for the words one
understood about as little of them as one commonly does
when a German beauty sings to the guitar. However, every
one assured her that she had sung with exquisite expression,
and she found quite enough approbation to satisfy her. A

singular misfortune befell her, however, on this occasion. Among the party there happened to be a poet, whom she hoped particularly to attach to herself, wishing to induce him to write a song or two, and address them to her. This evening, therefore, she produced scarcely anything except songs of his composing. Like the rest of the party he was perfectly courteous to her, but she had looked for more. She spoke to him several times, going as near the subject as she dared, but nothing further could she get. At last, unable to bear it any longer, she sent one of her train to him, to sound him and find out whether he had not been delighted to hear his beautiful poems so beautifully executed.

" My poems?" he replied, with amazement; " pray excuse me, my dear sir," he added, " I heard nothing but the vowels, and not all of those; however, I am in duty bound to express all gratitude for so amiable an intention." The dandy said nothing and kept his secret; the other endeavoured to get himself out of the scrape by a few well-timed compliments. She did not conceal her desire to have something of his which should be written for herself.

If it would not have been too ill-natured, he might have handed her the alphabet, to imagine for herself, out of that, such laudatory poem as would please her, and set it to the first melody that came to hand; but she was not to escape out of this business without mortification. A short time after, she had to learn that the very same evening he had written, at the foot of one of Ottilie's favourite melodies, a most lovely poem, which was something more than complimentary.

Luciana, like all persons of her sort, who never can distinguish between where they show to advantage and where to disadvantage, now determined to try her fortune in reciting. Her memory was good, but, if the truth must be told, her execution was spiritless, and she was vehement without being . passionate. She recited ballad stories, and whatever else is usually delivered in declamation. At the same time she had contracted an unhappy habit of accompanying what she delivered with gestures, by which, in a disagreeable way, what is purely epic and lyric is more confused than connected with the dramatic.

The Count, a keensighted man, soon saw through the party, their inclinations, dispositions, wishes, and capabilities, and by some means or other contrived to bring Luciana to a new kind of exhibition, which was perfectly suited to her.

" I see here," he said, " a number of persons with fine figures, who would surely be able to imitate pictorial emotions and postures. Suppose they were to try, if the thing is new to them, to represent some real and well-known picture. An imitation of this kind, if it requires some labour in arrangement, has an inconceivably charming effect."

Luciana was quick enough in perceiving that here she was on her own ground entirely. Her fine shape, her well-rounded form, the regularity and yet expressiveness of her features, her light-brown braided hair, her long neck—she ran them all over in her mind, and calculated on their pictorial effects, and if she had only known that her beauty showed to more advantage when she was still than when she was in motion, because in the last case certain ungracefulnesses continually escaped her, she would have entered even more eagerly than she did into this natural picture-making.

They looked out the engravings of celebrated pictures, and the first which they chose was Van Dyk's Belisarius. A large well-proportioned man, somewhat advanced in years, was to represent the seated, blind general. The Architect was to be the affectionate soldier standing sorrowing before him, there really being some resemblance between them. Luciana, half from modesty, had chosen the part of the young woman in the background, counting out some large alms into the palm of his hand, while an old woman beside her is trying to prevent her, and representing that she is giving too much. Another woman who is in the act of giving him something, was not forgotten. Into this and other pictures they threw themselves with all earnestness. The Count gave the Architect a few hints as to the best style of arrangement, and he at once set up a kind of theatre, all necessary pains being taken for the proper lighting of it. They were already deep in the midst of their preparations, before they observed how large an outlay what they were undertaking would require, and that in the country, in the middle of winter, many things which they required it would be difficult to procure; consequently, to prevent a stoppage, Luciana had nearly her whole wardrobe cut in pieces, to supply the various costumes which the original artist had arbitrarily selected.

The appointed evening came, and the exhibition was carried out in the presence of a large assemblage, and to the universal satisfaction. They had some good music to excite expectation, and the performance opened with the Belisarius. The figures were so successful, the colours were so happily distributed, and the lighting managed so skilfully, that they might really have fancied themselves in another world, only that the presence of the real instead of the apparent, produced a kind of uncomfortable sensation.

The curtain fell, and was more than once raised again by general desire. A musical interlude kept the assembly amused while preparation was going forward, to surprise them with a picture of a higher stamp; it was the well-known design of Poussin, Ahasuerus and Esther. This time Luciana had done better for herself. As the fainting, sinking queen she had put out all her charms, and for the attendant maidens who were supporting her, she had cunningly selected pretty well-shaped figures, not one among whom, however, had the slightest pretension to be compared with herself. From this picture, as from all the rest, Ottilie remained excluded. To sit on the golden throne and represent the Zeus-like monarch, Luciana had picked out the finest and handsomest man of the party, so that this picture was really of inimitable perfection.

For a third they had taken the so-called " Father's Admonition" of Terburg, and who does not know Wille's admirable engraving of this picture? One foot thrown over the other, sits a noble knightly-looking father; his daughter stands before him, to whose conscience he seems to be addressing himself. She, a fine striking figure, in a folding drapery of white satin, is only to be seen from behind, but her whole bearing appears to signify that she is collecting herself. That the admonition is not too severe, that she is not being utterly put to shame, is to be gathered from the air and attitude of the father, while the mother seems as if she were trying to conceal some slight embarrassment—she is looking into a glass of wine, which she is on the point of drinking.

Here was an opportunity for Luciana to appear in her highest splendour. Her back hair, the form of her head, neck, and shoulders, were beyond all conception beautiful; and the waist, which in the modern antique of the ordinary dresses of young ladies is hardly visible, showed to the greatest advantage in all its graceful slender elegance in the really old costume. The Architect had contrived to dispose the rich folds of the white satin with the most exquisite nature, and, without any question whatever, this living imitation far exceeded the original picture, and produced universal delight.

The spectators could never be satisfied with demanding a repetition of the performance, and the very natural wish to see the face and front of so lovely a creature, when they had done looking at her from behind, at last became so decided, that a merry impatient young wit, cried out aloud the words one is accustomed to write at the bottom of a page, "Tournez, s'il vous plait," which was echoed all round the room.

The performers, however, understood their advantage too well, and had mastered too completely the idea of these works of art to yield to the most general clamour. The daughter remained standing in her shame, without favouring the spectators with the expression of her face. The father continued to sit in his attitude of admonition, and the mother did not lift nose or eyes out of the transparent glass, in which, although she seemed to be drinking, the wine did not diminish.

We need not describe the number of smaller after-pieces; for which had been chosen Flemish public-house scenes and fair and market days.

The Count and the Baroness departed, promising to return in the first happy weeks of their approaching union. And Charlotte now had hopes, after having endured two weary months of it, of ridding herself of the rest of the party at the same time. She was assured of her daughter's happiness, as soon as the first tumult of youth and betrothal should have subsided in her; for the bridegroom considered himself the most fortunate person in the world. His income was large, his disposition moderate and rational, and now he found himself further wonderfully favoured in the happiness of becoming the possessor of a young lady with whom all the world must be charmed. He had so peculiar a way of referring everything to her, and only to himself through her, that it gave him an unpleasant feeling when any newly-arrived person did not devote himself heart and soul to her, and was far from flattered if, as occasionally happened, particularly with elderly men, he neglected her for a closrintimacy with himself. Everything was settled about the Architect. On New-year's day he was to follow him, and spend the Carnival at his house in the city, where Luciana was promising herself infinite happiness from a repetition of her charmingly successful pictures, as well as from a hundred other things ; all the more as her aunt and her bridegroom seemed to make so light of the expense which was required for her amusements.

And now they were to break up. But this could not be managed in an ordinary way. They were one day making fun of Charlotte aloud, declaring that they would soon have eaten out her winter stores, when the nobleman who had represented Belisarius, being fortunately a man of some wealth, carried away by Luciana's charms, to which he had been so long devoting himself, cried out unthinkingly, "Why not manage then in the Polish fashion? you come now and eat up me, and then we will go on round the circle." No. sooner said than done. Luciana willed that it should be so. The next day they all packed up and the swarm alighted on a new property. There indeed they found room enough, but few conveniences and no preparations to receive them. Out of this arose many *contretemps*, which entirely enchanted Luciana; their life became ever wilder and wilder. Huge hunting-parties were set on foot in the deep snow, attended with every sort of disagreeableness ; women were not allowed to excuse themselves any more than men, and so they trooped on, hunting and riding, sledging and shouting, from one place to another till at last they approached the residence, and there the news of the day and the scandals and what else forms the amusement of people at courts and cities gave the imagination another direction, and Luciana with her train of attendants (her aunt had gone on some time before) swept at once into a new sphere of life.

FROM OTTILIE'S DIARY.

"We accept every person in the world as that for which he gives himself out, only he must give himself out for something. We can put up with the unpleasant more easily than we can endure the insignificant.

"We venture upon anything in society except only what involves a consequence.

" We never learn to know people when they come to us :
we must go to them to find out how things stand with
them.

" I find it almost natural that we should see many faults
in visitors, and that directly they are gone we should judge
them not in the most amiable manner. For we have, so to
say, a right to measure them by our own standard. Even
cautious, sensible men can scarcely keep themselves in such
cases from being sharp censors.

" When, on the contrary, we are staying at the houses of
others, when we have seen them in the midst of all their
habits and environments among those necessary conditions
from which they cannot escape, when we have seen how they
affect those about them, and how they adapt themselves to
their circumstances, it is ignorance, it is worse, it is ill-will,
to find ridiculous what in more than one sense has a claim on
our respect.

" That which we call politeness and good breeding effects
what otherwise can only be obtained by violence, or not even
by that.

" Intercourse with women is the element of good manners.

" How can the character, the individuality of a man co-
exist with polish of manner ?

" The individuality can only be properly made prominent
through good manners. Every one likes what has something
in it, only it must not be a disagreeable something.

" In life generally, and in society no one has such high
advantages as a well-cultivated soldier.

" The rudest fighting people at least do not go out of their
character, and generally behind the roughness there is a
certain latent good humour, so that in difficulties it is possible to get on even with them.

" No one is more intolerable than an underbred civilian.
From him one has a right to look for a delicacy, as he has no
rough work to do.

" When we are living with people who have a delicate
sense of propriety, we are in misery on their account when
anything unbecoming is committed. So I always feel for and
with Charlotte, when a person is tipping his chair. She cannot endure it.

" No one would ever come into a mixed party with spectacles on his nose, if he did but know that at once we women

lose all pleasure in looking at him or listening to what he has to say.

"Free-and-easiness, where there ought to be respect, is always ridiculous. No one would put his hat down when he had scarcely paid the ordinary compliments if he knew how comical it looks.

"There is no outward sign of courtesy that does not rest on a deep moral foundation. The proper education would be that which communicated the sign and the foundation of it at the same time.

"Behaviour is a mirror in which every one displays his own image.

"There is a courtesy of the heart. It is akin to love. Out of it arises the purest courtesy in the outward behaviour.

"A freely offered homage is the most beautiful of all relations. And how were that possible without love?

"We are never further from our wishes than when we imagine that we possess what we have desired.

"No one is more a slave than the man who thinks himself free while he is not.

"A man has only to declare that he is free, and the next moment he feels the conditions to which he is subject. Let him venture to declare that he is under conditions, and then he will feel that he is free.

"Against great advantages in another, there are no means of defending ourselves except love.

"There is something terrible in the sight of a highly-gifted man lying under obligations to a fool.

"'No man is a hero to his valet,' the proverb says. But that is only because it requires a hero to recognize a hero. The valet will probably know how to value the valet-hero.

"Mediocrity has no greater consolation than in the thought that genius is not immortal.

"The greatest men are connected with their own century always through some weakness.

"One is apt to regard people as more dangerous than they are.

"Fools and modest people are alike innocuous. It is only your half-fools and your half-wise who are really and truly dangerous.

"There is no better deliverance from the world than

through art; and a man can form no surer bond with it than through art.

"Alike in the moment of our highest fortune and our deepest necessity, we require the artist.

"The business of art is with the difficult and the good.

"To see the difficult easily handled, gives us the feeling of the impossible.

"Difficulties increase the nearer we are to our end.

"Sowing is not so difficult as reaping."

CHAPTER VI.

THE very serious discomfort which this visit had caused to Charlotte was in some way compensated to her through the fuller insight which it had enabled her to gain into her daughter's character. In this, her knowledge of the world was of no slight service to her. It was not the first time that so singular a character had come across her, although she had never seen any in which the unusual features were so largely developed; and she had had experience enough to show her that such persons after having felt the discipline of life, after having gone through something of it, and been in intercourse with older people, may come out at last really charming and amiable; the selfishness may soften and eager restless activity find a definite direction for itself. And therefore, as a mother, Charlotte was able to endure the appearance of symptoms which for others might perhaps have been unpleasing, from a sense that where strangers only desire to enjoy, or at least not to have their taste offended, the business of parents is rather to hope.

After her daughter's departure, however, she had to be pained in a singular and unlooked-for manner, in finding that, not so much through what there really was objectionable in her behaviour, as through what was good and praiseworthy in it, she had left an ill report of herself behind her. Luciana seemed to have prescribed it as a rule to herself not only to be merry with the merry, but miserable with the miserable; and in order to give full swing to the spirit of contradiction in her, often to make the happy, uncomfortable, and the sad, cheerful. In every family among whom she came, she inquired after such members of it as were ill or infirm, and unable to appear in society. She would go to see them in their rooms, enact the physician, and insist on prescribing powerful doses for them out of her own travelling medicine-chest, which she constantly took with her in her carriage; her attempted cures, as may be supposed, either succeeding or failing as chance happened to direct.

In this sort of benevolence she was thoroughly cruel, and would listen to nothing that was said to her, because she was convinced that she was managing admirably. One of these attempts of hers on the moral side failed very disastrously, and this it was which gave Charlotte so much trouble, inasmuch as it involved consequences and every one was talking about it. She never had heard of the story till Luciana was gone; Ottilie, who had made one of the party present at the time, had to give her a circumstantial account of it.

One of several daughters of a family of rank had the misfortune to have caused the death of one of her younger sisters; it had destroyed her peace of mind, and she had never been properly herself since. She lived in her own room, occupying herself and keeping quiet; and she could only bear to see the members of her own family when they came one by one. If there were several together, she suspected at once that they were making reflections upon her, and upon her condition. To each of them singly she would speak rationally enough, and talk freely for an hour at a time.

Luciana had heard of this, and had secretly determined with herself, as soon as she got into the house, that she would forthwith work a miracle, and restore the young lady to society. She conducted herself in the matter more prudently than usual, managed to introduce herself alone to the poor sick-souled girl, and, as far as people could understand, had wound her way into her confidence through music. At last came her fatal mistake; wishing to make a scene, and fancying that she had sufficiently prepared her for it, one evening she suddenly introduced the beautiful pale creature into the midst of the brilliant glittering assembly; and perhaps, even then, the attempt might not have so utterly failed. had not the crowd themselves, between curiosity and apprehension, conducted themselves so unwisely, first gathering about the invalid, and then shrinking from her again; and with their whispers, and shaking their heads together, confusing and agitating her. Her delicate sensibility could not endure it. With a dreadful shriek, which expressed, as it seemed, a horror at some monster that was rushing upon her, she fainted. The crowd fell back in terror on every side, and Ottilie had been one of those who had carried back the sufferer utterly insensible to her room.

Luciana meanwhile, just like herself, had been reading an angry lecture to the rest of the party, without reflecting for a moment that she herself was entirely to blame, and without letting herself be deterred by this and other failures, from going on with her experimentalizing.

The state of the invalid herself had since that time become more and more serious; indeed, the disorder had increased to such a degree, that the poor thing's parents were unable to keep her any longer at home, and had been forced to confide her to the care of a public institution. Nothing remained for Charlotte, except, by the delicacy of her own attention to the family, in some degree to alleviate the pain which had been occasioned by her daughter. On Ottilie, the thing had made a deep impression. She felt the more for the unhappy girl, as she was convinced, she did not attempt to deny it to Charlotte, that by a careful treatment the disorder might have been unquestionably removed.

So there came, too, as it often happens that we dwell more on past disagreeables than on past agreeables, a slight misunderstanding to be spoken of, which had led Ottilie to a wrong judgment of the Architect, when he did not choose to produce his collection that evening, although she had so eagerly begged him to produce it. His practical refusal had remained, ever since, hanging about her heart, she herself could not tell why. Her feelings about the matter were undoubtedly just; what a young lady like Ottilie could desire, a young man like the Architect ought not to have refused. The latter, however, when she took occasion to give him a gentle reproof for it, had a very valid excuse to offer for himself.

" If you knew," he said, " how roughly even cultivated

people allow themselves to handle the most valuable works of art, you would forgive me for not producing mine among the crowd. No one will take the trouble to hold a medal by the rim. They will finger the most beautiful impressions, and the smoothest surfaces; they will take the rarest coins between the thumb and forefinger, and rub them up and down, as if they were testing the execution with the touch. Without remembering that a large sheet of paper ought to be held in two hands, they will lay hold, with one, of an invaluable proof-engraving of some drawing which cannot be replaced, like a conceited politician laying hold of a newspaper, and passing judgment by anticipation, as he is cutting the pages, on the occurrences of the world. Nobody cares to recollect that if twenty people, one after the other, treat a work of art in this way, the one-and-twentieth will not find much to see there."

" Have not I often vexed you in this way?" asked Ottilie. " Have not I, through my carelessness, many times injured your treasures?"

" Never once," answered the Architect, " never. For you it would be impossible. In you the right thing is innate."

" In any case," replied Ottilie, " it would not be a bad plan, if in the next edition of the book of good manners, after the chapters which tell us how we ought to eat and drink in company, a good circumstantial chapter were inserted, how to behave among works of art and in museums."

" Undoubtedly," said the Architect; " and then curiosity-collectors and amateurs would be better contented to show their valuable treasures to the world."

Ottilie had long, long forgiven him; but as he seemed to have taken her reproof sorely to heart, and assured her again and again that he would gladly produce everything— that he was delighted to do anything for his friends—she felt that she had wounded his feelings, and that she owed him some compensation. It was not easy for her, therefore, to give an absolute refusal to a request which he made her in the conclusion of this conversation, although when she called her heart into counsel about it, she did not see how she could allow herself to do what he wished.

The circumstances of the matter were these: Ottilie's exclusion from the picture-exhibition by Luciana's jealousy, had irritated him in the highest degree; and at the same time he had observed with regret, that at this, the most brilliant part of all the amusements at the castle, ill health had prevented Charlotte from being more than rarely present; and now he did not wish to go away, without some additional proof of his gratitude, and, for the honour of one and the entertainment of the other, preparing a far more beautiful exhibition than any of those which had preceded it. Perhaps, too, unknown to himself, another secret motive was working on him. It was so hard for him to leave the house, and to leave the family. It seemed impossible to him to go away from Ottilie's eyes, under the calm, sweet, gentle glance of which the latter part of the time he had been living almost entirely alone.

The Christmas holidays were approaching; and it became at once clear to him that the very thing which he wanted was a representation with real figures of one of those pictures of the scene in the stable,—a sacred exhibition such as at this holy season good Christians delight to offer to the divine Mother and her Child, of the manner in which she, in her seeming lowliness, was honoured first by the shepherds and afterwards by kings.

He had thoroughly brought before himself how such a picture should be contrived. A fair, lovely child was found, and there would be no lack of shepherds and shepherdesses. But without Ottilie the thing could not be done. The young man had exalted her in his design to be the mother of God, and if she refused, there was no question but the undertaking must fall to the ground. Ottilie, half embarrassed at the proposal, referred him and his request to Charlotte. The latter gladly gave her permission, and lent her assistance in overcoming and overpersuading Ottilie's hesitation in assuming so sacred a personality. The Architect worked day and night, that by Christmas-eve everything might be ready.

Day and night, indeed, in the literal sense. At all times he was a man who had but few necessities; and Ottilie's presence seemed to be to him in the place of all delicacies. When he was working for her, it was as if he required no sleep; when he was busy about her, as if he could do without food. Accordingly by the hour of the evening solemnity, all was completed. He had found the means of collecting some

well-toned wind instruments to form an introduction, and produce the desired temper of thought and feeling.   But when the
curtain rose, Charlotte was taken completely by surprise.   The
picture which presented itself to her had been repeated so often
in the world, that one could scarcely have expected any new
impression to be produced.   But here, the reality as representing the picture had its especial advantages.   The whole
space was the colour rather of night than of twilight, and
there was nothing even of the details of the scene which was
obscure.   The inimitable idea that all the light should proceed from the child, the artist had contrived to carry out by
an ingenious method of illumination which was concealed by
the figures in the foreground, who were all in shadow.
Bright looking boys and girls were standing round, their fresh
faces sharply lighted from below; and there were angels too,
whose own brilliancy grew pale before the divine, whose
ethereal bodies showed dim and dense, and needing other
light in the presence of the body of the divine humanity.
By good fortune the infant had fallen asleep in the loveliest
attitude, so that nothing disturbed the contemplation when
the eye rested on the seeming mother, who with infinite grace
had lifted off a veil to reveal her hidden treasure.   At this
moment the picture seemed to have been caught, and there
to have remained fixed.   Physically dazzled, mentally surprised, the people round appeared to have just moved to
turn away their half-blinded eyes, to be glancing again towards
the child with curious delight, and to be showing more wonder
and pleasure than awe and reverence,—although these emotions
were not forgotten, and were to be traced upon the features
of some of the older spectators.

But Ottilie's figure, expression, attitude, glance, excelled
all which any painter has ever represented.   A man who
had true knowledge of art, and had seen this spectacle,
would have been in fear lest any portion of it should move;
he would have doubted whether anything could ever so much
please him again.   Unluckily, there was no one present who
could comprehend the whole of this effect.   The Architect
alone, who, as a tall, slender shepherd, was looking in from
the side over those who were kneeling, enjoyed, although he
was not in the best position for seeing, the fullest pleasure.
And who can describe the mien of the new-made queen of

heaven? The purest humility, the most exquisite feeling of modesty, at the great honour which had undeservedly been bestowed upon her, with indescribable and immeasurable happiness, was displayed upon her features, expressing as much her own personal emotion as that of the character which she was endeavouring to represent.

Charlotte was delighted with the beautiful figures; but what had most effect on her was the child. Her eyes filled with tears, and her imagination presented to her in the liveliest colours that she might soon hope to have such another darling creature on her own lap.

They had let down the curtain, partly to give the exhibitors some little rest, partly to make an alteration in the exhibition. The artist had proposed to himself to transmute the first scene of night and lowliness into a picture of splendour and glory; and for this purpose had prepared a blaze of light to fall in from every side, which this interval was required to kindle.

Ottilie, in the semi-theatrical position in which she found herself, had hitherto felt perfectly at her ease, because, with the exception of Charlotte and a few members of the household, no one had witnessed this devout piece of artistic display. She was, therefore, in some degree annoyed when in the interval she learnt that a stranger had come into the saloon, and had been warmly received by Charlotte. Who it was no one was able to tell her. She therefore made up her mind not to produce a disturbance, and to go on with her character. Candles and lamps blazed out, and she was surrounded by splendour perfectly infinite. The curtain rose. It was a sight to startle the spectators. The whole picture was one blaze of light; and instead of the full depth of shadow, there now were only the colours left remaining, which, from the skill with which they had been selected, produced a gentle softening of tone. Looking out under her long eyelashes, Ottilie perceived the figure of a man sitting by Charlotte. She did not recognize him; but the voice she fancied was that of the assistant at the school. A singular emotion came over her. How many things had happened since she last heard the voice of that her kind instructor! Like a flash of forked lightning the stream of her joys and her sorrow rushed swiftly before her soul, and the question rose in her heart. Dare you confess, dare you acknowledge it all to him? If not, how little can you deserve to appear before him under this sainted form; and how strange must it not seem to him who has only known you as your natural self to see you now under this disguise? In an instant, swift as thought, feeling and reflection began to clash and gain within her. Her eyes filled with tears, while she forced herself to continue to appear as a motionless figure, and it was a relief, indeed, to her when the child began to stir,—and the artist saw himself compelled to give the sign that the curtain should fall again.

If the painful feeling of being unable to meet a valued friend had, during the last few moments, been distressing Ottilie in addition to her other emotions, she was now in still greater embarrassment. Was she to present herself to him in this strange disguise? or had she better change her dress? She did not hesitate—she did the last; and in the interval she endeavoured to collect and to compose herself; nor did she properly recover her self-possession until at last, in her ordinary costume, she had welcomed the new visitor.

CHAPTER VII.

In so far as the Architect desired the happiness of his kind patronesses, it was a' pleasure to him, now that at last he was obliged to go, to know that he was leaving them in good society with the estimable Assistant. At the same time, however, when he thought of their goodness in its relation to himself, he could not help feeling it a little painful to see his place so soon, and as it seemed to his modesty, so well, so completely supplied. He had lingered and lingered, but now he forced himself away; what, after he was gone, he must endure as he could, at least he could not stay to witness with his own eyes.

To the great relief of this half-melancholy feeling, the ladies at his departure made him a present of a waistcoat, upon which he had watched them both for some time past at work, with a silent envy of the fortunate unknown, to whom

M

it was by-and-bye to belong. Such a present is the most agreeable which a true-hearted man can receive; for while he thinks of the unwearied play of the beautiful fingers at the making of it, he cannot help flattering himself that in so long-sustained a labour the feeling could not have remained utterly without an interest in its accomplishment.

The ladies had now a new visitor to entertain, for whom they felt a real regard, and whose stay with them it would be their endeavour to make as agreeable as they could. There is in all women a peculiar circle of inward interests, which remain always the same, and from which nothing in the world can divorce them. In outward social intercourse, on the other hand, they will gladly and easily allow themselves to take their tone from the person with whom at the moment they are occupied; and thus by a mixture of impassiveness and susceptibility, by persisting and by yielding, they continue to keep the government to themselves, and no man in the cultivated world can ever take it from them.

The Architect, following at the same time his own fancy and his own inclination, had been exerting himself and putting out his talents for their gratification, and for the purposes of his friends; and business and amusement, while he was with them, had been conducted in this spirit, and directed to the ends which most suited his taste. But now in a short time, through the presence of the Assistant, quite another sort of life was commenced. His great gift was to talk well, and to treat in his conversation of men and human relations, particularly in reference to the cultivation of young people. Thus arose a very perceptible contrast to the life which had been going on hitherto, all the more as the Assistant could not entirely approve of their having interested themselves in such subjects so exclusively.

Of the impersonated picture which received him on his arrival, he never said a single word. On the other hand, when they took him to see the church and the chapel with their new decorations, expecting to please him as much as they were pleased themselves, he did not hesitate to express a very contrary opinion about it.

"This mixing up of the holy with the sensuous," he said, "is anything but pleasing to my taste; I cannot like men to set apart certain especial places, consecrate them, and deck them out, that by so doing they may nourish in themselves a temper of piety. No ornaments, not even the very simplest, should disturb in us that sense of the Divine Being which accompanies us wherever we are, and can consecrate every spot into a temple. What pleases me is to see a home-service of God held in the saloon where people come together to eat, where they have their parties, and amuse themselves with games and dances. The highest, the most excellent in men, has no form; and one should be cautious how one gives it any form except noble action."

Charlotte, who was already generally acquainted with his mode of thinking, and in the short time he had been at the castle, had already probed it more deeply, found something also which he might do for her in his own department; and she had her garden children, whom the Architect had reviewed shortly before his departure, marshalled up into the great saloon. In their bright, clean uniforms, with their regular orderly movement, and their own natural vivacity, they looked exceedingly well. The Assistant examined them in his own way, and by a variety of questions, and by the turns which he gave them, soon brought to light the capacities and dispositions of the children; and without its seeming so, in the space of less than one hour he had really given them important instruction and assistance.

"How did you manage that?" said Charlotte, as the children marched away. "I listened with all my attention. Nothing was brought forward except things which were quite familiar, and yet I cannot tell the least how I should begin, to bring them to be discussed in so short a time so methodically, with all this questioning and answering."

"Perhaps," replied the Assistant, "we ought to make a secret of the tricks of our own handicraft. However, I will not hide from you one very simple maxim, with the help of which you may do this, and a great deal more than this. Take any subject, a substance, an idea, whatever you like; keep fast hold of it; make yourself thoroughly acquainted with it in all its parts, and then it will be easy for you, in conversation, to find out, with a mass of children, how much about it has already developed itself in them; what requires to be stimulated, what to be directly communicated. The

M 2

answers to your questions may be as unsatisfactory as they
will, they may wander wide of the mark; if you only take
care that your counter-question shall draw their thoughts and
senses inwards again; if you do not allow yourself to be
driven from your own position—the children will at last
reflect, comprehend, learn only what the teacher desires them
to learn, and the subject will be presented to them in the
light in which he wishes them to see it.   The greatest mistake which he can make is to allow himself to be run away
with from the subject; not to know how to keep fast to the
point with which he is engaged.   Do you try this on your
own account the next time the children come; you will find
you will be greatly entertained by it yourself."

"That is very good," said Charlotte.   "The right method
of teaching is the reverse, I see, of what we must do in life.
In society we must keep the attention long upon nothing,
and in instruction the first commandment is to permit no
dissipation of it."

"Variety, without dissipation, were the best motto for
both teaching and life, if this desirable equipoise were easy
to be preserved," said the Assistant, and he was going on
further with the subject, when Charlotte called out to him to
look again at the children, whose merry troop were at the
moment moving across the court.   He expressed his satisfaction at seeing them wearing a uniform.   "Men," he said,
"should wear a uniform from their childhood upwards.
They have to accustom themselves to work together; to lose
themselves among their equals; to obey in masses, and to
work on a large scale.   Every kind of uniform, moreover,
generates a military habit of thought, and a smart, straight-
forward carriage.   All boys are born soldiers, whatever you
do with them.   You have only to watch them at their mock
fights and games, their storming parties and scaling parties."

"On the other hand, you will not blame me," replied
Ottilie, "if I do not insist with my girls on such unity of
costume.   When I introduce them to you, I hope to gratify
you by a party-coloured mixture."

"I approve of that, entirely," replied the other.   "Women should go about in every sort of variety of dress; each
following her own style and her own likings, that each may

learn to feel what sits well upon her and becomes her. And for a more weighty reason as well—because it is appointed for them to stand alone all their lives, and work alone."

"That seems to me to be a paradox," answered Charlotte. "Are we then to be never anything for ourselves?"

"O, yes!" replied the Assistant. "In respect of other women assuredly. But observe a young lady as a lover, as a bride, as a housewife, as a mother. She always stands isolated. She is always alone, and will be alone. Even the most empty-headed woman is in the same case. Each one of them excludes all others. It is her nature to do so; because of each one of them is required everything which the entire sex have to do. With a man it is altogether different. He would make a second man if there were none. But a woman might live to an eternity, without even so much as thinking of producing a duplicate of herself."

"One has only to say the truth in a strange way," said Charlotte, "and at last the strangest thing will seem to be true. We will accept what is good for us out of your observations, and yet as women we will hold together with women, and do common work with them too; not to give the other sex too great an advantage over us. Indeed, you must not take it ill of us, if in future we come to feel a little malicious satisfaction when our lords and masters do not get on in the very best way together."

With much care, this wise, sensible person went on to examine more closely how Ottilie proceeded with her little pupils, and expressed his marked approbation of it. "You are entirely right," he said, "in directing these children only to what they can immediately and usefully put in practice. Cleanliness, for instance, will accustom them to wear their clothes with pleasure to themselves; and everything is gained if they can be induced to enter into what they do with cheerfulness and self-reflection."

In other ways he found, to his great satisfaction, that nothing had been done for outward display; but all was inward, and designed to supply what was indispensably necessary. "In how few words," he cried, "might the whole business of education be summed up, if people had but ears to hear!"

"Will you try whether I have any ears?" said Ottilie, smiling.

"Indeed I will," answered he, "only you must not betray me. Educate the boys to be servants, and the girls to be mothers, and everything is as it should be."

"To be mothers?" replied Ottilie. "Women would scarcely think that sufficient. They have to look forward, without being mothers, to going out into service. And, indeed, our young men think themselves a great deal too good for servants. One can see easily, in every one of them, that he holds himself far fitter to be a master."

"And for that reason we should say nothing about it to them," said the Assistant. "We flatter ourselves on into life; but life flatters not us. How many men would like to acknowledge at the outset, what at the end they must acknowledge whether they like it or not? But let us leave these considerations, which do not concern us here.

"I consider you very fortunate in having been able to go so methodically to work with your pupils. If your very little ones run about with their dolls, and stitch together a few petticoats for them; if the elder sisters will then take care of the younger, and the whole household know how to supply its own wants, and one member of it help the others, the further step into life will not then be great, and such a girl will find in her husband what she has lost in her parents.

"But among the higher ranks the problem is a sorely intricate one. We have to provide for higher, finer, more delicate relations; especially for such as arise out of society. We are, therefore, obliged to give our pupils an outward cultivation. It is indispensable, it is necessary, and it may be really valuable, if we do not overstep the proper measure in it. Only it is so easy, while one is proposing to cultivate the children for a wider circle, to drive them out into the indefinite, without keeping before our eyes the real requisites of the inner nature. Here lies the problem which more or less must be either solved or blundered over by all educators.

"Many things, with which we furnish our scholars at the school, do not please me; because experience tells me of how little service they are likely to be in after-life. How much is not at once stripped off; how much is not at once committed to oblivion, as soon as the young lady finds herself in the position of a housewife or a mother!

"In the meantime, since I have devoted myself to this occupation, I cannot but entertain a devout hope that one day, with the companionship of some faithful helpmate, I may succeed in cultivating purely in my pupils that, and that only, which they will require when they pass out into the field of independent activity and self-reliance; that I may be able to say to myself, in this sense is their education completed. Another education there is indeed which will again speedily recommence, and work on well nigh through all the years of our life—the education which circumstances will give us, if we do not give it to ourselves."

How true Ottilie felt were these words! What had not a passion, little dreamed of before, done to educate her in the past year! What trials did she not see hovering before her if she looked forward only to the next—to the very next, which was now so near!

It was not without a purpose that the young man had spoken of a helpmate—of a wife; for with all his diffidence, he could not refrain from thus remotely hinting at his own wishes. A number of circumstances and accidents, indeed, combined to induce him on this visit to approach a few steps towards his aim.

The Lady Superior of the school was advanced in years. She had been already for some time looking about among her fellow-labourers, male and female, for some person whom she could take into partnership with herself, and at last had made proposals to the Assistant, in whom she had the highest ground for feeling confidence. He was to conduct the business of the school with herself. He was to work with her in it, as if it was his own; and after her death, as her heir, to enter upon it as sole proprietor.

The principal thing now seemed to be, that he should find a wife who would co-operate with him. Ottilie was secretly before his eyes and before his heart. A number of difficulties suggested themselves, and yet again there were favourable circumstances on the other side to counterbalance them. Luciana had left the school; Ottilie could therefore return with the less difficulty. Of the affair with Edward, some little had transpired. It passed, however, as many such things do, as a matter of indifference, and this very circumstance might make it desirable that she should leave the castle. And yet, perhaps, no decision would have been arrived at, no step would have been taken, had not an unexpected visit given a special impulse to his hesitation. The appearance of remarkable people, in any and every circle, can never be without its effects.

The Count and the Baroness, who often found themselves asked for their opinion, almost every one being in difficulty about the education of their children, as to the value of the various schools, had found it desirable to make themselves particularly acquainted with this one, which was generally so well spoken of; and under their present circumstances, they were more easily able to carry on these inquiries in company.

The Baroness, however, had something else in view as well. While she was last at the castle, she had talked over with Charlotte the whole affair of Edward and Ottilie. She had insisted again and again that Ottilie must be sent away. She tried every means to encourage Charlotte to do it, and to keep her from being frightened by Edward's threats. Several modes of escape from the difficulty were suggested. Accidentally the school was mentioned, and the Assistant and his incipient passion, which made the Baroness more resolved than ever to pay her intended visit there.

She went; she made acquaintance with the Assistant; looked over the establishment, and spoke of Ottilie. The Count also spoke with much interest of her, having in his recent visit learnt to know her better. She had been drawn towards him; indeed, she had felt attracted by him; believing that she could see, that she could perceive in his solid, substantial conversation, something to which hitherto she had been an entire stranger. In her intercourse with Edward, the world had been utterly forgotten; in the presence of the Count, the world appeared first worth regarding. The attraction was mutual. The Count conceived a liking for Ottilie; he would have been glad to have had her for a daughter. Thus a second time, and worse than the first time, she was in the way of the Baroness. Who knows what, in times when passions ran hotter than they do now-a-days, this lady might not have devised against her? As things were, it was enough if she could get her married, and render her more innocuous for the future to the peace of mind of married women. She therefore artfully urged the Assistant, in a delicate, but effective manner, to set out on a little excursion to the castle; where his plans and his wishes, of which he made no secret to the lady, he might forthwith take steps to realize.

With the fullest consent of the Superior he started off on his expedition, and in his heart he nourished good hopes of success. He knew that Ottilie was not ill-disposed towards him; and although it was true there was some disproportion of rank between them, yet distinctions of this kind were fast disappearing in the temper of the time. Moreover, the Baroness had made him perceive clearly that Ottilie must always remain a poor portionless maiden. To be related to a wealthy family, it was said, could be of service to nobody. For even with the largest property, men have a feeling that it is not right to deprive of any considerable sum, those who, as standing in a nearer degree of relationship, appear to have a fuller right to possession; and really it is a strange thing, that the immense privilege which a man has of disposing of his property after his death, he so very seldom uses for the benefit of those whom he loves, out of regard to established usage only appearing to consider those who would inherit his estate from him supposing he made no will at all.

Thus, while on his journey, he grew to feel himself entirely on a level with Ottilie. A favourable reception raised his hopes. He found Ottilie indeed not altogether so open with him as usual, but she was considerably matured, more developed, and, if you please, generally more conversible than he had known her. She was ready to give him the fullest insight into many things which were in any way connected with his profession; but when he attempted to approach his proper object, a certain inward shyness always held him back.

Once, however, Charlotte gave him an opportunity for saying something. In Ottilie's presence she said to him, " Well now, you have looked closely enough into everything which is going forward in my circle. How do you find Ottilie? you had better say while she is here."

Hereupon the Assistant signified, with a clear perception and composed expression, how that, in respect of a freer car-

riage, of an easier manner in speaking, of a higher insight
into the things of the world, which showed itself more in
actions than in words, he found Ottilie altered much for the
better; but that he still believed it might be of serious advantage to her if she would go back for some little time to the
school, in order methodically and thoroughly to make her own
for ever what the world was only imparting to her in fragments and pieces, rather perplexing her than satisfying her,
and often too late to be of service. He did not wish to be
prolix about it. Ottilie herself knew best how much method
and connection there was in the style of instruction out of
which, in that case, she would be taken.

Ottilie had nothing to say against this; she could not
acknowledge what it was which these words made her feel,
because she was hardly able to explain it to herself. It
seemed to her as if nothing in the world was disconnected so
long as she thought of the one person whom she loved: and
she could not conceive how, without him, anything could be
connected at all.

Charlotte replied to the proposal with a wise kindness.
She said that she herself, as well as Ottilie, had long desired
her return to the school. At that time, however, the presence of so dear a companion and helper had become indispensable to herself; still she would offer no obstacle at some
future period, if Ottilie continued to wish it, to her going
back there for such a time as would enable her to complete
what she had begun, and to make entirely her own what had
been interrupted.

The Assistant listened with delight to this qualified assent.
Ottilie did not venture to say anything against it, although the
very thought made her shudder. Charlotte, on her side,
thought only how to gain time. She hoped that Edward
would soon come back and find himself a happy father, then
she was convinced all would go right; and one way or another
they would be able to settle something for Ottilie.

After an important conversation which has furnished matter
for after-reflection to all who have taken part in it, there commonly follows a sort of pause, which in appearance is like a
general embarrassment. They walked up and down the saloon.
The Assistant turned over the leaves of various books, and
came at last on the folio of engravings which had remained

lying there since Luciana's time. As soon as he saw that it contained nothing but apes, he shut it up again.

It may have been this, however, which gave occasion to a conversation of which we find traces in Ottilie's diary.

FROM OTTILIE'S DIARY.

" It is strange how men can have the heart to take such pains with the pictures of those hideous monkeys. One lowers one's-self sufficiently when one looks at them merely as animals, but it is really wicked to give way to the inclination to look for people whom we know behind such masks."

" It is a sure mark of a certain obliquity, to take pleasure in caricatures and monstrous faces, and pigmies. I have to thank our kind Assistant that I have never been vexed with natural history; I could never make myself at home with worms and beetles."

" Just now he acknowledged to me, that it was the same with him. ' Of nature,' he said, ' we ought to know nothing except what is actually alive immediately around us. With the trees which blossom and put out leaves and bear fruit in our own neighbourhood, with every shrub which we pass by, with every blade of grass on which we tread, we stand in a real relation. They are our genuine compatriots. The birds which hop up and down among our branches, which sing among our leaves, belong to us; they speak to us from our childhood upwards, and we learn to understand their language. But let a man ask himself whether or not every strange creature, torn out of its natural environment, does not at first sight make a sort of painful impression upon him, which is only deadened by custom. It is a mark of a motley, dissipated sort of life, to be able to endure monkeys, and parrots, and black people, about one's-self."

" Many times when a certain longing curiosity about these strange objects has come over me, I have envied the traveller who sees such marvels in living, every-day connection with other marvels. But he, too, must have become another man. Palm-trees will not allow a man to wander among them with impunity; and doubtless his tone of thinking becomes very different in a land where elephants and tigers are at home.''

"The only inquirers into nature whom we care to respect, are such as know how to describe and to represent to us the strange wonderful things which they have seen in their proper locality, each in its own especial element. How I should enjoy once hearing Humboldt talk!''

"A cabinet of natural curiosities we may regard like an Egyptian burying-place, where the various plant gods and animal gods stand about embalmed. It may be well enough for a priest-caste to busy itself with such things in a twilight of mystery. But in general instruction, they have no place or business; and we must beware of them all the more, because what is nearer to us, and more valuable, may be so easily thrust aside by them.''

"A teacher who can arouse a feeling for one single good action, for one single good poem, accomplishes more than he who fills our memory with rows on rows of natural objects, classified with name and form. For what is the result of all these, except what we know as well without them, that the human figure pre-eminently and peculiarly is made in the image and likeness of God?''

"Individuals may be left to occupy themselves with whatever amuses them, with whatever gives them pleasure, whatever they think useful; but the proper study of mankind is man.''

CHAPTER VIII.

THERE are but few men who care to occupy themselves with the immediate past. Either we are forcibly bound up in the present, or we lose ourselves in the long gone-by, and seek back for what is utterly lost, as if it were possible to summon it up again, and rehabilitate it. Even in great and wealthy families who are under large obligations to their ancestors, we commonly find men thinking more of their grandfathers than their fathers.

Such reflections as these suggested themselves to our Assistant, as, on one of those beautiful days in which the departing winter is accustomed to imitate the spring, he had been walking up and down the great old castle garden, and admiring the tall avenues of the lindens, and the formal walks and flower-beds which had been laid out by Edward's father. The trees had thriven admirably, according to the design of him who had planted them, and now when they ought to have begun to be valued and enjoyed, no one ever spoke of them. Hardly any one even went near them, and the interest and the outlay was now directed to the other side, out into the free and the open.

He remarked upon it to Charlotte on his return; she did not take it unkindly. "While life is sweeping us forwards," she replied, "we fancy that we are acting out our own impulses; we believe that we choose ourselves what we will do, and what we will enjoy. But in fact, if we look at it closely, our actions are no more than the plans, and the desires of the time which we are compelled to carry out."

"No doubt," said the Assistant. "And who is strong enough to withstand the stream of what is round him? Time passes on, and in it, opinions, thoughts, prejudices, and interests. If the youth of the son falls in the era of revolution, we may feel assured that he will have nothing in common with his father. If the father lived at a time when the desire was to accumulate property, to secure the possession of it, to narrow and to gather one's-self in, and to base one's enjoyment in separation from the world, the son will at once seek to extend himself, to communicate himself to others, to spread himself over a wide surface, and open out his closed stores."

"Entire periods," replied Charlotte, "resemble this father and son whom you have been describing. Of the state of things when every little town was obliged to have its walls and moats, when the castle of the nobleman was built in a swamp, and the smallest manor-houses were only accessible by a draw-bridge, we are scarcely able to form a conception. In our days, the largest cities take down their walls, the moats of the princes' castles are filled in; cities are no more than great *places*, and when one travels and sees all this, one

might fancy that universal peace was just established, and
the golden age was before the door.   No one feels himself
easy in a garden which does not look like the open country.
There must be nothing to remind him of form and constraint;
we choose to be entirely free, and to draw our breath without
sense of confinement.   Do you conceive it possible, my friend,
that we can ever return again out of this into another, into
our former condition?"

"Why should we not?" replied the Assistant.   "Every
condition has its own burden along with it, the most relaxed as
well as the most constrained.   The first presupposes abundance, and leads to extravagance.   Let want re-appear, and
the spirit of moderation is at once with us again.   Men who
are obliged to make use of their space and their soil, will
speedily enough raise walls up round their gardens to be sure
of their crops and plants.   Out of this will arise by degrees a
new phase of things: the useful will again gain the upper
hand; and even the man of large possessions will feel at last
that he must make the most of all which belongs to him.
Believe me, it is quite possible that your son may become
indifferent to all which you have been doing in the park,
and draw in again behind the solemn walls and the tall
lindens of his grandfather."

The secret pleasure which it gave Charlotte to have a son
foretold to her, made her forgive the Assistant his somewhat
unfriendly prophecy of how it might one day fare with her
lovely, beautiful park.   She therefore answered without any
discomposure: "You and I are not old enough yet to have
lived through very much of these contradictions; and yet when
I look back into my own early youth, when I remember the
style of complaints which I used then to hear from older
people, and when I think at the same time of what the country
and the town then were, I have nothing to advance against
what you say.   But is there nothing which one can do to
remedy this natural course of things?   Are father and son,
parents and children, to be always thus unable to understand
each other?   You have been so kind as to prophesy a boy to
me.   Is it necessary that he must stand in contradiction to
his father?   Must he destroy what his parents have erected,
instead of completing it, instead of following on upon the
same idea, and elevating it?

"There is a rational remedy for it," replied the Assistant. "But it is one which will be but seldom put in practice by men. The father should raise his son to a joint ownership with himself. He should permit him to plant and to build; and allow him the same innocent liberty which he allows to himself. One form of activity may be woven into another, but it cannot be pieced on to it. A young shoot may be readily and easily grafted with an old stem, to which no grown branch admits of being fastened."

The Assistant was glad to have had the opportunity, at the moment when he saw himself obliged to take his leave, of saying something agreeable to Charlotte, and thus making himself a new link to secure her favour. He had been already too long absent from home, and yet he could not make up his mind to return there, until after a full conviction that he must allow the approaching epoch of Charlotte's confinement first to pass by, before he could look for any decision from her in respect to Ottilie. He therefore accommodated himself to the circumstances, and returned with these prospects and hopes to the Superior.

Charlotte's confinement was now approaching; she kept more in her own room. The ladies who had gathered about her were her closest companions. Ottilie managed all domestic matters, hardly able, however, the while, to think what she was doing. She had indeed utterly resigned herself; she desired to continue to exert herself to the extent of her power for Charlotte, for the child, for Edward. But she could not see how it would be possible for her. Nothing could save her from utter distraction, except patiently to do the duty which each day brought with it.

A son was brought happily into the world, and the ladies declared, with one voice, it was the very image of its father. Only Ottilie, as she wished the new mother joy, and kissed the child with all her heart, was unable to see the likeness. Once already Charlotte had felt most painfully the absence of her husband, when she had to make preparations for her daughter's marriage. And now the father could not be present at the birth of his son. He could not have the choosing of the name by which the child was hereafter to be called.

The first among all Charlotte's friends who came to wish her joy was Mittler. He had placed expresses ready to

bring him news the instant the event took place.   He was
admitted to see her, and, scarcely able to conceal his triumph
even before Ottilie, when alone with Charlotte he broke
fairly out with it ; and was at once ready with means to
remove all anxieties, and set aside all immediate difficulties.
The baptism should not be delayed a day longer than necessary.   The old clergyman, who had one foot already in the
grave, should leave his blessing, to bind together the past
and the future.   The child should be called Otto ; what name
would he bear so fitly as that of his father and of his father's
friend ?

It required the peremptory resolution of this man to set aside
the innumerable considerations, arguments, hesitations, difficulties ; what this person knew, and that person knew better ;
the opinions, up and down, and backwards and forwards,
which every friend volunteered.   It always happens on such
occasions that when one inconvenience is removed, a fresh
inconvenience seems to arise ; and in wishing to spare all
sides, we inevitably go wrong on one side or the other.

The letters to friends and relations were all undertaken by
Mittler, and they were to be written and sent off at once.
It was highly necessary, he thought, that the good fortune
which he considered so important for the family, should be
known as widely as possible through the ill-natured and
misinterpreting world.   For indeed these late entanglements
and perplexities had got abroad among the public, which at
all times has a conviction that whatever happens, happens
only in order that it may have something to talk about.

The ceremony of the baptism was be observed with all due
honour, but it was to be as brief and as private as possible.
The people came together ; Ottilie and Mittler were to hold
the child as sponsors.   The old pastor, supported by the
servants of the church, came in with slow steps ; the prayers
were offered.   The child lay in Ottilie's arms, and as she
was looking affectionately down at it, it opened its eyes and
she was not a little startled when she seemed to see her own
eyes looking at her.   The likeness would have surprised
any one.   Mittler, who next had to receive the child, started
as well ; he fancying he saw in the little features a most
striking likeness to the Captain.   He had never seen a
resemblance so marked.

The infirmity of the good old clergyman had not permitted him to accompany the ceremony with more than the usual liturgy.

Mittler, however, who was full of his subject, recollected his old performances when he had been in the ministry, and indeed it was one of his peculiarities that on every sort of occasion, he always thought what he would like to say, and how he would express himself about it.

At this time he was the less able to contain himself, as he was now in the midst of a circle consisting entirely of well known friends. He began therefore towards the conclusion of the service, to put himself quietly into the place of the clergyman; to make cheerful speeches aloud, expressive of his duty and his hopes as godfather, and to dwell all the longer on the subject, as he thought he saw in Charlotte's gratified manner that she was pleased with his doing so.

It altogether escaped the eagerness of the orator, that the good old man would gladly have sat down; still less did he think that he was on the way to occasion a more serious evil. After he had described with all his power of impressiveness the relation in which every person present stood toward the child, thereby putting Ottilie's composure sorely to the proof, he turned at last to the old man with the words, "And you, my worthy father, you may now well say with Simeon, 'Lord, now lettest thou thy servant depart in peace, for mine eyes have seen the saviour of this house.' "

He was now in full swing towards a brilliant peroration, when he perceived the old man to whom he held out the child, first appear a little to incline towards it, and immediately after to totter and sink backwards. Hardly prevented from falling, he was lifted to a seat; but, notwithstanding the instant assistance which was rendered, he was found to be dead.

To see thus side by side birth and death, the coffin and the cradle, to see them and to realise them, to comprehend, not with the eye of imagination, but with the bodily eye, at one moment these fearful opposites, was a hard trial to the spectators; the harder, the more utterly it had taken them by surprise. Ottilie alone stood contemplating the slumberer, whose features still retained their gentle sweet expression, with a kind of envy. The life of her soul was killed;

N

why should the bodily life any longer drag on in weariness ?

But though Ottilie was frequently led by melancholy incidents which occurred in the day, to thoughts of the past, of separation and of loss, at night she had strange visions given her to comfort her, which assured her of the existence of her beloved, and thus strengthened her, and gave her life for her own. When she laid herself down at night to rest, and was floating among sweet sensations between sleep and waking, she seemed to be looking into a clear but softly illuminated space. In this she would see Edward with the greatest distinctness, and not in the dress in which she had been accustomed to see him, but in military uniform; never in the same position, but always in a natural one, and not the least with anything fantastic about him, either standing or walking, or lying down or riding. The figure, which was painted with the utmost minuteness, moved readily before her without any effort of hers, without her willing it or exerting her imagination to produce it. Frequently she saw him surrounded with something in motion, which was darker than the bright ground; but the figures were shadowy, and she could scarcely distinguish them—sometimes they were like men, sometimes they were like horses, or like trees, or like mountains. She usually went to sleep in the midst of the apparition, and when, after a quiet night, she woke again in the morning, she felt refreshed and comforted; she could say to herself, Edward still lives, and she herself was still remaining in the closest relation towards him.

CHAPTER IX.

THE spring was come; it was late, but it therefore burst out more rapidly and more exhilaratingly than usual. Ottilie now found in the garden the fruits of her carefulness. Everything shot up and came out in leaf and flower at its proper time. A number of plants which she had been training up under glass frames and in hotbeds, now burst forward at once to meet, at last, the advances of nature; and whatever there was to do, and to take care of, it did not remain the mere labour of hope which it had been, but brought its reward in immediate and substantial enjoyment.

There was many a chasm however among the finest shoots produced by Luciana's wild ways, for which she had to console the gardener, and the symmetry of many a leafy coronet was destroyed. She tried to encourage him to hope that it would all be soon restored again, but he had too deep a feeling, and too pure an idea of the nature of his business, for such grounds of comfort to be of much service with him. Little as the gardener allowed himself to have his attention dissipated by other tastes and inclinations, he could the less bear to have the peaceful course interrupted which the plant follows towards its enduring or its transient perfection. A plant is like a self-willed man, out of whom we can obtain all which we desire, if we will only treat him his own way. A calm eye, a silent method, in all seasons of the year, and at every hour, to do exactly what has then to be done, is required of no one perhaps more than of a gardener. These qualities the good man possessed in an eminent degree, and it was on that account that Ottilie liked so well to work with him; but for some time past he had not found himself able to exercise his peculiar talent with any pleasure to himself. Whatever concerned the fruit-gardening or kitchen-gardening, as well as whatever had in time past been required in the ornamental gardens, he understood perfectly. One man succeeds in one thing, another in another; he succeeded in these. In his management of the orangery, of the bulbous flowers, in budding shoots and growing cuttings from the carnations and auriculas, he might challenge nature herself. But the new ornamental shrubs and fashionable flowers remained in a measure strange to him. He had a kind of shyness of the endless field of botany, which had been lately opening itself, and the strange names humming about his ears made him cross and ill-tempered. The orders for flowers which had been made by his lord and lady in the course of the past year, he considered so much useless waste and extravagance. All the more, as he saw many valuable plants disappear; and as he had ceased to stand on the best possible terms with the nursery gardeners, who he fancied had not been serving him honestly.

Consequently, after a number of attempts, he had formed a sort of a plan, in which Ottilie encouraged him the more readily, because its first essential condition was the return of Edward, whose absence in this, as in many other matters, every day had to be felt more and more seriously.

Now that the plants were ever striking new roots, and putting out their shoots, Ottilie felt herself even more fettered to this spot. It was just a year since she had come there as a stranger, as a mere insignificant creature. How much had she not gained for herself since that time! but, alas! how much had she not also since that time lost again! Never had she been so rich, and never so poor. The feelings of her loss and of her gain alternated momentarily one with another, chasing each other through her heart; and she could find no other means to help herself, except always to set to work again at what lay nearest to her, with such interest and eagerness as she could command.

That everything which she knew to be dear to Edward received especial care from her may be supposed. And why should she not hope that he himself would now soon come back again; and that when present, he would show himself grateful for all the care and pains which she had taken for him in his absence?

But there was also a far different employment which she took upon herself in his service; she had undertaken the principal charge of the child, whose immediate attendant it was all the easier for her to be, as they had determined not to put it into the hands of a nurse, but to bring it up themselves by hand with milk and water. In the beautiful season it was much out of doors, enjoying the free air, and Ottilie liked best to take it out herself, to carry the unconscious sleeping infant among the flowers and blossoms which should one day smile so brightly on its childhood,—among the young shrubs and plants, which, by their youth, seemed designed to grow up with the young lord to their after stature. When she looked about her, she did not hide from herself to what a high position that child was born: far and wide, wherever the eye could see, all would one day belong to him. How desirable, how necessary it must therefore be, that it should grow up under the eyes of its father and its mother, and renew and strengthen the union between them!

Ottilie saw all this so clearly, that she represented it to herself as conclusively decided, and for herself, as concerned with it, she never felt at all. Under this fair heaven, by this bright sunshine, at once it became clear to her, that her love if it would perfect itself, must become altogether unselfish; and there were many moments in which she believed it was an elevation which she had already attained. She only desired the well-being of her friend. She fancied herself able to resign him, and never to see him any more, if she could only know that he was happy. The one only determination which she formed for herself was never to belong to another.

They had taken care that the autumn should be no less brilliant than the spring. Sun-flowers were there, and all the other plants which are never tired of blossoming in autumn, and continue boldly on into the cold; asters especially were sown in the greatest abundance, and scattered about in all directions, to form a starry heaven upon the earth.

FROM OTTILIE'S DIARY.

"Any good thought which we have read, anything striking which we have heard, we commonly enter in our diary; but if we would take the trouble, at the same time, to copy out of our friends' letters the remarkable observations, the original ideas, the hasty words so pregnant in meaning, which we might find in them, we should then be rich indeed. We lay aside letters never to read them again, and at last we destroy them out of discretion, and so disappears the most beautiful, the most immediate breath of life, irrecoverably for ourselves and for others. I intend to make amends in future for such neglect."

"So, then, once more the old story of the year is being repeated over again. We are come now, thank God, again to its most charming chapter. The violets and the may-flowers are as its superscriptions and its vignettes. It always makes a pleasant impression on us when we open again at these pages in the book of life."

"We find fault with the poor, particularly with the little ones among them, when they loiter about the streets and beg.

Do we not observe, that they begin to work again, as soon as ever there is anything for them to do? Hardly has nature unfolded her smiling treasures, than the children are at once upon her track to open out a calling for themselves. None of them beg any more; they have each a nosegay to offer you; they were out and gathering it before you had awakened out of your sleep, and the supplicating face looks as sweetly at you as the present which the hand is holding out. No person ever looks miserable who feels that he has a right to make a demand upon you."

———

"How is it that the year sometimes seems so short, and sometimes is so long? How is it that it is so short when it is passing, and so long as we look back over it? When I think of the past (and it never comes so powerfully over me as in the garden), I feel how the perishing and the enduring work one upon the other, and there is nothing whose endurance is so brief as not to leave behind it some trace of itself, something in its own likeness."

———

"We are able to tolerate the winter. We fancy that we can extend ourselves more freely when the trees are so spectral, so transparent. They are nothing, but they conceal nothing; but when once the germs and buds begin to show, then we become impatient for the full foliage to come out, for the landscape to put on its body, and the tree to stand before us as a form."

———

"Everything which is perfect in its kind, must pass out beyond and transcend its kind. It must be an inimitable something of another and a higher nature. In many of its tones the nightingale is only a bird; then it rises up above its class, and seems as if it would teach every feathered creature what singing really is."

———

"A life without love, without the presence of the beloved, is but poor *comédie à tiroir*. We draw out slide after slide, swiftly tiring of each, and pushing it back to make haste to the next. Even what we know to be good and important, hangs but wearily together; every step is an end, and every step is a fresh beginning."

———

CHAPTER X.

CHARLOTTE meanwhile was well and in good spirits. She was happy in her beautiful boy, whose fair promising little form every hour was a delight to both her eyes and heart. In him she found a new link to connect her with the world and with her property. Her old activity began anew to stir in her again.

Look which way she would, she saw how much had been done in the year that was past, and it was a pleasure to her to contemplate it. Enlivened by the strength of these feelings, she climbed up to the summer-house with Ottilie and the child, and as she laid the latter down on the little table, as on the altar of her house, and saw the two seats still vacant, she thought of gone-by times, and fresh hopes rose out before her for herself and for Ottilie.

Young ladies, perhaps, look timidly round them at this or that young man, carrying on a silent examination, whether they would like to have him for a husband; but whoever has a daughter or a female ward to care for, takes a wider circle in her survey. And so it fared at this moment with Charlotte, to whom, as she thought of how they had once sat side by side in that summer-house, a union did not seem impossible between the Captain and Ottilie. It had not remained unknown to her, that the plans for the advantageous marriage, which had been proposed to the Captain, had come to nothing.

Charlotte went on up the cliff, and Ottilie carried the child. A number of reflections crowded upon the former. Even on the firm land there are frequent enough shipwrecks, and the true wise conduct is to recover ourselves, and refit our vessel as fast as possible. Is life to be calculated only by its gains and losses? Who has not made arrangement on arrangement, and has not seen them broken in pieces? How often does not a man strike into a road and lose it again! How often are we not turned aside from one point which we had sharply before our eye, but only to reach some higher stage! The traveller, to his greatest annoyance, breaks a wheel upon his journey, and through this unpleasant accident makes some charming acquaintance, and forms some new connection, which has an influence on all his life. Destiny grants us our wishes, but in its own way, in order to give us something beyond our wishes.

Among these and similar reflections they reached the new building on the hill, where they intended to establish themselves for the summer. The view all round them was far more beautiful than could have been supposed; every little obstruction had been removed; all the loveliness of the landscape, whatever nature, whatever the season of the year had done for it, came out in its beauty before the eye; and already the young plantations, which had been made to fill up a few openings, were beginning to look green, and to form an agreeable connecting link between parts which before stood separate.

The house itself was nearly habitable; the views, particularly from the upper rooms, were of the richest variety. The longer you looked round you, the more beauties you discovered. What magnificent effects would not be produced here at the different hours of day—by sunlight and by moonlight? Nothing could be more delightful than to come and live there, and now that she found all the rough work finished, Charlotte longed to be busy again. An upholsterer, a tapestry-hanger, a painter, who could lay on the colours with patterns, and a little gilding, were all which were required, and these were soon found, and in a short time the building was completed. Kitchen and cellar stores were quickly laid in; being so far from the castle, it was necessary to have all essentials provided; and the two ladies with the child went up and settled there. From this residence, as from a new centre point, unknown walks opened out to them; and in these high regions the free fresh air and the beautiful weather were thoroughly delightful.

Ottilie's favourite walk, sometimes alone, sometimes with the child, was down below, towards the plane-trees; along a pleasant footpath, leading directly to the point where one of the boats was kept chained in which people used to go across the water. She often indulged herself in an expedition on the water, only without the child, as Charlotte was a little uneasy about it. She never missed, however, paying a daily visit to the castle garden and the gardener, and going to look with him at his show of greenhouse plants, which were all out now, enjoying the free air.

At this beautiful season, Charlotte was much pleased to receive a visit from an English nobleman, who had made acquaintance with Edward abroad, having met him more than once, and who was now curious to see the laying out of his park, which he had heard so much admired. He brought with him a letter of introduction from the Count, and introduced at the same time a quiet but most agreeable man as his travelling companion. He went about seeing everything, sometimes with Charlotte and Ottilie, sometimes with the gardeners and the foresters, often with his friend, and now and then alone; and they could perceive clearly from his observations that he took an interest in such matters, and understood them well; indeed, that he.had himself probably executed many such.

Although he was now advanced in life, he entered warmly into everything which could serve for an ornament to life, or contribute anything to its importance.

In his presence, the ladies came first properly to enjoy what was round them. His practised eye received every effect in its freshness, and he found all the more pleasure in what was before him, as he had not previously known the place, and was scarcely able to distinguish what man had done there from what nature had presented to him ready made.

We may even say that through his remarks the park grew and enriched itself; he was able to anticipate in their fulfilment the promises of the growing plantations. There was not a spot where there was any effect which could be either heightened or produced, but what he observed it.

In one place he pointed to a fountain which, if it was cleaned out, promised to be the most beautiful spot for a pic-nic party. In another, to a cave which had only to be enlarged and swept clear of rubbish to form a desirable seat. A few trees might be cut down, and a view would be opened from it of some grand masses of rock, towering magnificently against the sky. He wished the owners joy that so much was still remaining for them to do, and he besought them not to be in a hurry about it, but to keep for themselves for years to come the pleasures of shaping and improving.

At the hours which the ladies usually spent alone he was never in the way, for he was occupied the greatest part of the day in catching such views in the park as would make good paintings, in a portable camera obscura, and drawing from them, in order to secure some desirable fruits from his travels for himself and others. For many years past he had been in the habit of doing this in all remarkable places which he visited, and had provided himself by it with a most charming and interesting collection. He showed the ladies a large portfolio which he had brought with him, and entertained them with the pictures and with descriptions. And it was a real delight to them, here in their solitude, to travel so pleasantly over the world, and see sweep past them, shores and havens, mountains, lakes, and rivers, cities, castles, and a hundred other localities which have a name in history.

Each of the two ladies had an especial interest in it —Charlotte the more general interest in whatever was historically remarkable; Ottilie dwelling in preference on the scenes of which Edward used most to talk,—where he liked best to stay, and which he would most often revisit. Every man has somewhere, far or near, his peculiar localities which attract him; scenes which, according to his character, either from first impressions, or from particular associations, or from habit, have a charm for him beyond all others.

She, therefore, asked the Earl which, of all these places, pleased him best, where he would like to settle, and live for himself, if he might choose. There was more than one lovely spot which he pointed out, with what had happened to him there to make him love and value it; and the peculiar accentuated French in which he spoke, made it most pleasant to listen to him.

To the further question, which was his ordinary residence, which he properly considered his home; he replied, without any hesitation, in a manner quite unexpected by the ladies.

"I have accustomed myself by this time to be at home everywhere, and I find, after all, that it is much more agreeable to allow others to plant, and build, and keep house for me. I have no desire to return to my own possessions, partly on political grounds, but principally because my son, for whose sake alone it was any pleasure to me to remain and work there,—who will, by-and-bye, inherit it, and with whom I hoped to enjoy it,—took no interest in the place at all, but has gone out to India, where, like many other foolish fellows, he fancies he can make a higher use of his life. He is more likely to squander it.

" Assuredly we spend far too much labour and outlay in preparation for life. Instead of beginning at once to make ourselves happy in a moderate condition, we spread ourselves out wider and wider, only to make ourselves more and more uncomfortable. Who is there now to enjoy my mansion, my park, my gardens? Not I, nor any of mine,—strangers, visitors, or curious, restless travellers.

" Even with large means, we are ever but half and half at home, especially in the country, where we miss many things to which we have become accustomed in town. The book for which we are most anxious is not to be had, and just the thing which we most wanted is forgotten. We take to being domestic, only again to go out of ourselves; if we do not go astray of our own will and caprice, circumstances, passions, accidents, necessity, and one does not know what besides, manage it for us.''

Little did the Earl imagine how deeply his friend would be touched by these random observations. It is a danger to which we are all of us exposed when we venture on general remarks in a society the circumstances of which we might have supposed were well enough known to us. Such casual wounds, even from well-meaning, kindly-disposed people, were nothing new to Charlotte. She so clearly, so thoroughly knew and understood the world, that it gave her no particular pain if it did happen that through somebody's thoughtlessness or imprudence she had her attention forced into this or that unpleasant direction. But it was very different with Ottilie. At her half-conscious age, at which she rather felt than saw, and at which she was disposed, indeed was obliged, to turn her eyes away from what she should not or would not see, Ottilie was thrown by this melancholy conversation into the most pitiable state. It rudely tore away the pleasant veil from before her eyes, and it seemed to her as if everything which had been done all this time for house and court, for park and garden, for all their wide environs, were utterly in vain, because he to whom it all belonged could not enjoy it; because he,

like their present visitor, had been driven out to wander up and
down in the world—and, indeed, in the most perilous paths
of it—by those who were nearest and dearest to him.   She
was accustomed to listen in silence, but on this occasion she
sate on in the most painful condition; which, indeed, was
made rather worse than better by what the stranger went on
to say, as he continued with his peculiar, humorous gravity :

" I think I am now on the right way.   I look upon myself
steadily as a traveller, who renounces many things in order
to enjoy more.   I am accustomed to change; it has become,
indeed, a necessity to me ; just as in the opera, people are
always looking out for new and new decorations, because
there have already been so many.   I know very well what
I am to expect from the best hotels, and what from the
worst.   It may be as good or it may be as bad as it will, but
I nowhere find anything to which I am accustomed, and in
the end it comes to much the same thing whether we depend
for our enjoyment entirely on the regular order of custom, or
entirely on the caprices of accident.   I have never to vex
myself now, because this thing is mislaid, or that thing is
lost ; because the room in which I live is uninhabitable, and
I must have it repaired ; because somebody has broken my
favourite cup, and for a long time nothing tastes well out of
any other.   All this I am happily raised above.   If the house
catches fire about my ears, my people quietly pack my things
up, and we pass away out of the town in search of other
quarters.   And considering all these advantages, when I
reckon carefully, I calculate that, by the end of the year, I
have not sacrificed more than it would have cost me to be at
home."

In this description Ottilie saw nothing but Edward before
her ; how he too was now amidst discomfort and hardship,
marching along untrodden roads, lying out in the fields in
danger and want, and in all this insecurity and hazard
growing accustomed to be homeless and friendless, learning
to fling away everything that he might have nothing to lose.
Fortunately, the party separated for a short time.   Ottilie
escaped to her room, where she could give way to her tears.
No weight of sorrow had ever pressed so heavily upon her as
this clear perception (which she tried, as people usually do, to
make still clearer to herself), that men love to dally with and

exaggerate the evils which circumstances have once begun to inflict upon them.

The state in which Edward was, came before her in a light so piteous, so miserable, that she made up her mind, let it cost her what it would, that she would do everything in her power to unite him again with Charlotte, and she herself would go and hide her sorrow and her love in some silent scene, and beguile the time with such employment as she could find.

Meanwhile the Earl's companion, a quiet, sensible man and a keen observer, had remarked the mistake in the conversation, and spoke to his friend about it. The latter knew nothing of the circumstances of the family; but the other being one of those persons whose principal interest in travelling lay in gathering up the strange occurrences which arose out of the natural or artificial relations of society, which were produced by the conflict of the restraint of law with the violence of the will, of the understanding with the reason, of passion with prejudice—had some time before made himself acquainted with the outline of the story, and since he had been in the family he had learnt exactly all that had taken place, and the present position in which things were standing.

The Earl, of course, was very sorry, but it was not a thing to make him uneasy. A man must hold his tongue altogether in society if he is never to find himself in such a position; for not only remarks with meaning in them, but the most trivial expressions, may happen to clash in an inharmonious key with the interest of somebody present.

"We will set things right this evening," said he, "and escape from any general conversation; you shall let them hear one of the many charming anecdotes with which your portfolio and your memory have enriched themselves while we have been abroad."

However, with the best intentions, the strangers did not, on this next occasion, succeed any better in gratifying their friends with unalloyed entertainment. The Earl's friend told a number of singular stories—some serious, some amusing, some touching, some terrible—with which he had roused their attention and strained their interest to the highest tension, and he thought to conclude with a strange but softer incident, little dreaming how nearly it would touch his listeners.

THE TWO STRANGE CHILDREN

"Two children of neighbouring families, a boy and a girl, of an age which would suit well for them at some future time to marry, were brought up together with this agreeable prospect, and the parents on both sides, who were people of some position in the world, looked forward with pleasure to their future union.

"It was too soon observed, however, that the purpose seemed likely to fail; the dispositions of both children promised everything which was good, but there was an unaccountable antipathy between them. Perhaps they were too much like each other. Both were thoughtful, clear in their wills, and firm in their purposes. Each separately was beloved and respected by his or her companions, but whenever they were together they were always antagonists. Forming separate plans for themselves, they only met mutually to cross and thwart one another; never emulating each other in pursuit of one aim, but always fighting for a single object. Good-natured and amiable everywhere else, they were spiteful and even malicious whenever they came in contact.

"This singular relation first showed itself in their childish games, and it continued with their advancing years. The boys used to play at soldiers. divide into parties, and give each other battle, and the fierce haughty young lady set herself at once at the head of one of the armies, and fought against the other with such animosity and bitterness that the latter would have been put to a shameful flight, except for the desperate bravery of her own particular rival, who at last disarmed his antagonist and took her prisoner; and even then she defended herself with so much fury that to save his eyes from being torn out, and at the same time not to injure his enemy, he had been obliged to take off his silk handkerchief and tie her hands with it behind her back.

"This she never forgave him : she made so many attempts, she laid so many plans to injure him, that the parents, who had been long watching these singular passions, came to an understanding together and resolved to separate these two hostile creatures, and sacrifice their favourite hopes.

"The boy shot rapidly forward in the new situation in which he was placed. He mastered every subject which he was taught. His friends and his own inclination chose the army for his profession, and everywhere, let him be where he would, he was looked up to and beloved. His disposition seemed formed to labour for the well-being and the pleasure of others; and he himself, without being clearly conscious of it, was in himself happy at having got rid of the only antagonist which nature had assigned to him.

"The girl, on the other hand, became at once an altered creature. Her growing age, the progress of her education, above all, her own inward feelings, drew her away from the boisterous games with boys in which she had hitherto delighted. Altogether she seemed to want something; there was nothing anywhere about her which could deserve to excite her hatred, and she had never found any one whom she could think worthy of her love.

"A young man, somewhat older than her previous neighbour-antagonist, of rank, property, and consequence, beloved in society, and much sought after by women, bestowed his affections upon her. It was the first time that friend, lover, or servant had displayed any interest in her. The preference which he showed for her above others who were older, more cultivated, and of more brilliant pretensions than herself, was naturally gratifying; the constancy of his attention, which was never obtrusive, his standing by her faithfully through a number of unpleasant incidents, his quiet suit, which was declared indeed to her parents, but which as she was still very young he did not press, only asking to be allowed to hope; all this engaged him to her, and custom and the assumption in the world that the thing was already settled, carried her along with it. She had so often been called his bride that at last she began to consider herself so, and neither she nor any one else ever thought any further trial could be necessary before she exchanged rings with the person who for so long a time had passed for her bridegroom.

"The peaceful course which the affair had all along followed was not at all precipitated by the betrothal. Things were allowed to go on both sides just as they were; they were happy in being together, and they could enjoy to the end the fair season of the year as the spring of their future more serious life.

"The absent youth had meanwhile grown up into everything which was most admirable. He had obtained a well-deserved rank in his profession, and came home on leave to visit his family. Towards his fair neighbour he found himself again in a natural but singular position. For some time past she had been nourishing in herself such affectionate family feelings as suited her position as a bride; she was in harmony with everything about her; she believed that she was happy, and in a certain sense she was so. Now first for a long time something again stood in her way. It was not to be hated—she had become incapable of hatred. Indeed the childish hatred, which had in fact been nothing more than an obscure recognition of inward worth, expressed itself now in a happy astonishment, in pleasure at meeting, in ready acknowledgments, in a half willing, half unwilling, and yet irresistible attraction; and all this was mutual. Their long separation gave occasion for longer conversations; even their old childish foolishness served, now that they had grown wiser, to amuse them as they looked back; and they felt as if at least they were bound to make good their petulant hatred by friendliness and attention to each other—as if their first violent injustice to each other ought not to be left without open acknowledgment.

On his side it all remained in a sensible, desirable moderation. His position, his circumstances, his efforts, his ambition, found him so abundant an occupation, that the friendliness of this pretty bride he received as a very thankworthy present; but without, therefore, even so much as thinking of her in connection with himself, or entertaining the slightest jealousy of the bridegroom, with whom he stood on the best possible terms.

With her, however, it was altogether different. She seemed to herself as if she had awakened out of a dream. Her fightings with her young neighbour had been the beginnings of an affection; and this violent antagonism was no more than an equally violent innate passion for him, first showing under the form of opposition. She could remember nothing else than that she had always loved him. She laughed over her martial encounter with him with weapons in her hand; she dwelt upon the delight of her feelings when he disarmed her. She imagined that it had given her the greatest happiness when he bound her; and whatever she had done afterwards to injure him, or to vex him, presented itself to her as only an innocent means of attracting his attention. She cursed their separation. She bewailed the sleepy state into which she had fallen. She execrated the insidious lazy routine which had betrayed her into accepting so insignificant a bridegroom. She was transformed—doubly transformed, forwards or backwards, which ever way we like to take it.

"She kept her feelings entirely to herself; but if any one could have divined them and shared them with her, he could not have blamed her : for indeed the bridegroom could not sustain a comparison with the other as soon as they were seen together. If a sort of regard to the one could not be refused, the other excited the fullest trust and confidence. If one made an agreeable acquaintance, the other we should desire for a companion; and in extraordinary cases, where higher demands might have to be made on them, the bridegroom was a person to be utterly despaired of, while the other would give the feeling of perfect security.

"There is a peculiar innate tact in women which discovers to them differences of this kind; and they have cause as well as occasion to cultivate it.

"The more the fair bride was nourishing all these feelings in secret, the less opportunity there was for any one to speak a word which could tell in favour of her bridegroom, to remind her of what her duty and their relative position advised and commanded—indeed; what an unalterable necessity seemed now irrevocably to require ; the poor heart gave itself up entirely to its passion.

"On one side she was bound inextricably to the bridegroom by the world, by her family, and by her own promise; on the other, the ambitious young man made no secret of what he was thinking and planning for himself, conducting himself towards her no more than a kind but not at all a tender brother, and speaking of his departure as immediately impending; and now it seemed as if her early childish spirit woke up again in her with all its spleen and violence,

O

and was preparing itself in its distemper, on this higher stage of life, to work more effectively and destructively. She determined that she would die to punish the once hated, and now so passionately loved, youth for his want of interest in her; and as she could not possess himself, at least she would wed herself for ever to his imagination and to his repentance. Her dead image should cling to him, and he should never be free from it. He should never cease to reproach himself for not having understood, not examined, not valued her feelings toward him.

"This singular insanity accompanied her wherever she went. She kept it concealed under all sorts of forms; and although people thought her very odd, no one was observant enough or clever enough to discover the real inward reason.

"In the mean time, friends, relations, acquaintances had exhausted themselves in contrivances for pleasure parties. Scarcely a day passed, but something new and unexpected was set on foot. There was hardly a pretty spot in the country round which had not been decked out and prepared for the reception of some merry party. And now our young visitor before departing wished to do his part as well, and invited the young couple, with a small family circle, to an expedition on the water. They went on board a large beautiful vessel dressed out in all its colours,—one of the yachts which had a small saloon and a cabin or two besides, and are intended to carry with them upon the water the comfort and conveniences of land.

"They set out upon the broad river with music playing. The party had collected in the cabin, below deck, during the heat of the day, and were amusing themselves with games. Their young host, who could never remain without doing something, had taken charge of the helm, to relieve the old master of the vessel, and the latter had lain down and was fast asleep. It was a moment when the steerer required all his circumspectness, as the vessel was nearing a spot where two islands narrowed the channel of the river, while shallow banks of shingle stretching off, first on one side and then on the other, made the navigation difficult and dangerous. Prudent and sharp-sighted as he was, he thought for a moment that it would be better to wake the master; but he felt confident in himself, and he thought he would venture and make straight for the narrows. At this moment his fair enemy appeared upon deck with a wreath of flowers in her hair. 'Take this to remember me by,' she cried out. She took it off and threw it the steerer. 'Don't disturb me,' he answered quickly, as he caught the wreath; 'I require all my powers and all my attention now.' 'You will never be disturbed by me any more,' she cried; 'you will never see me again.' As she spoke, she rushed to the forward part of the vessel, and from thence she sprang into the water. Voice upon voice called out, 'Save her, save her, she is sinking!' He was in the most terrible difficulty. In the confusion the old ship-master woke, and tried to catch the rudder, which the young man bid him take. But there was no time to change hands. The vessel stranded; and at the same moment, flinging off the heaviest of his upper garments, he sprang into the water and swam towards his beautiful enemy. The water is a friendly element to a man who is at home in it, and who knows how to deal with it; it buoyed him up, and acknowledged the strong swimmer as its master. He soon overtook the beautiful girl, who had been swept away before him; he caught hold of her, raised her and supported her, and both of them were carried violently down by the current, till the shoals and islands were left far behind, and the river was again open and running smoothly. He now began to collect himself; they had past the first immediate danger, in which he had been obliged to act mechanically without time to think; he raised his head as high as he could to look about him; and then swam with all his might to a low bushy point, which ran out conveniently into the stream. There he brought his fair burden to dry land, but he could find no signs of life in her; he was in despair, when he caught sight of a trodden path leading among the bushes. Again he caught her up in his arms, hurried forward, and presently reached a solitary cottage. There he found kind, good people—a young married couple; the misfortunes and the dangers explained themselves instantly; every remedy he could think of was instantly applied; a bright fire blazed up: woollen blankets were spread on a bed, counterpane, cloaks, skins, whatever there was at hand which would serve for warmth, were heaped over her as fast as possible. The desire to save life overpowered, for the present, every other consideration.

Nothing was left undone to bring back to life the beautiful half-torpid, naked body. It succeeded; she opened her eyes! her friend was before her; she threw her heavenly arms about his neck. In this position she remained for a time; and then a stream of tears burst out and completed her recovery. 'Will you forsake me,' she cried, 'now when I find you again thus?' 'Never,' he answered, 'never:' hardly knowing what he said or did. 'Only consider yourself,' she added; 'take care of yourself, for your sake and for mine.'

"She now began to collect herself, and for the first time recollected the state in which she was; she could not be ashamed before her darling, before her preserver; but she gladly allowed him to go, that he might take care of himself; for the clothes which he still wore were wet and dripping."

"Their young hosts considered what could be done. The husband offered the young man, and the wife offered the fair lady, the dresses in which they had been married, which were hanging up in full perfection, and sufficient for a complete suit, inside and out, for two people. In a short time our pair of adventurers were not only equipped, but in full costume. They looked most charming, gazed at one another, when they met, with admiration, and then with infinite affection, half laughing at the same time at the quaintness of their appearance, they fell into each other's arms.

"The power of youth and the quickening spirit of love in a few moments completely restored them; and there was nothing wanted but music to have set them both off dancing.

"To have found themselves brought from the water on dry land, from death into life, from the circle of their families into a wilderness, from despair into rapture, from indifference to affection and to love, all in a moment: the head was not strong enough to bear it; it must either burst, or go distracted; or if so distressing an alternative were to be escaped, the heart must put out all its efforts.

"Lost wholly in each other, it was long before they recollected the alarm and anxiety of those who had been left behind; and they themselves, indeed, could not well think, without alarm and anxiety, how they were again to encounter them. 'Shall we run away? shall we hide ourselves?' said the young man. 'We will remain together,' she said, as she clung about his neck.

"The peasant having heard them say that a party was aground on the shoal, had hurried down, without stopping to ask another question, to the shore. When he arrived there, he saw the vessel coming safely down the stream. After much labour it had been got off; and they were now going on in uncertainty, hoping to find their lost ones again somewhere. The peasant shouted and made signs to them, and at last caught the attention of those on board; then he ran to a spot where there was a convenient place for landing, and went on signalling and shouting till the vessel's head was turned towards the shore; and what a scene there was for them when they landed. The parents of the two betrothed first pressed on the banks; the poor loving bridegroom had almost lost his senses. They had scarcely learnt that their dear children had been saved, when in their strange disguise the latter came forward out of the bushes to meet them. No one recognised them till they were come quite close. 'Who do I see?' cried the mothers. 'What do I see?' cried the fathers. The preserved ones flung themselves on the ground before them. 'Your children,' they called out; 'a pair.' 'Forgive us!' cried the maiden. 'Give us your blessing!' cried the young man. 'Give us your blessing!' they cried both, as all the world stood still in wonder. Your blessing! was repeated the third time; and who would have been able to refuse it?"

———

CHAPTER XI.

THE narrator made a pause, or rather he had already finished his story, before he observed the emotion into which Charlotte had been thrown by it. She got up, uttered some sort of an apology, and left the room. To her it was a well-known history. The principal incident in it had really taken place with the Captain and a neighbour of her own; not exactly, indeed, as the Englishman had related it. But the main features of it were the same. It had only been more finished off and elaborated in its details, as stories of that kind always are, when they have passed first through the lips of the multitude, and then through the fancy of a clever and imaginative narrator; the result of the process being usually to leave everything and nothing as it was.

Ottilie followed Charlotte, as the two friends begged her to do; and then it was the Earl's turn to remark, that perhaps they had made a second mistake, and that the subject of the story had been well known to or was in some way connected with the family. "We must take care," he added, "that we do no more mischief here; we seem to bring little good to our entertainers for all the kindness and hospitality which they have shown us; we will make some excuse for ourselves, and then take our leave."

"I must confess," answered his companion, "that there is something else which still holds me here, which I should be very sorry to leave the house without seeing cleared up or in some way explained. You were too busy yourself yesterday when we were in the park with the camera, in looking for spots where you could make your sketches, to have observed anything else which was passing. You left the broad walk, you remember, and went to a sequestered place on the side of the lake. There was a fine view of the opposite shore which you wished to take. Well, Ottilie, who was with us, got up to follow; and then proposed that she and I should find our way to you in the boat. I got in with her, and was delighted with the skill of my fair conductress. I assured her that never since I had been in Switzerland, where the young ladies so often fill the place of the boatmen, had I been so pleasantly ferried over the water. At the same time I could not help asking her why she had shown such an objection to going the way which you had gone, along the little bye-path. I had observed her shrink from it with a sort of painful uneasiness. She was not at all offended. 'If you will promise not to laugh at me,' she answered, 'I will tell you as much as I know about it; but to myself it is a mystery which I cannot explain. There is a particular spot in that path which I never pass without a strange shiver passing over me, which I do not remember ever feeling anywhere else, and which I cannot the least understand. But I shrink from exposing myself to the sensation, because it is followed immediately after by a pain on the left side of my head, from which at other times I suffer severely.' We landed. Ottilie was engaged with you, and I took the opportunity of examining the spot, which she pointed out to me as we went by on the water. I was not a little surprised to find there distinct traces of coal, in sufficient quantities to convince me that at a short distance below the surface there must be a considerable bed of it.

"Pardon me, my Lord; I see you smile; and I know very well that you have no faith in these things about which I am so eager, and that it is only your sense and your kindness which enable you to tolerate me. However, it is impossible for me to leave this place without trying on that beautiful creature an experiment with the pendulum."

The Earl, whenever these matters came to be spoken of, never failed to repeat the same objections to them over and over again; and his friend endured them all quietly and patiently, remaining firm, nevertheless, to his own opinion, and holding to his own wishes. He, too, again repeated, that there was no reason, because the experiment did not succeed with every one, that they should give them up, as if there was nothing in them but fancy. They should be examined into all the more earnestly and scrupulously; and there was no doubt that the result would be the discovery of a number of affinities of inorganic creatures for one another, and of organic creatures for them, and again for each other, which at present were unknown to us.

He had already spread out his apparatus of gold rings, markasites, and other metallic substances, a pretty little box of which he always carried about with himself; and he suspended a piece of metal by a string over another piece, which he placed upon the table. "Now, my Lord," he said, "you may take what pleasure you please (I can see in your face what you are feeling), at perceiving that nothing will set itself in motion with me, or for me. But my operation is no more than a pretence; when the ladies come back, they will be curious to know what strange work we are about."

The ladies returned. Charlotte understood at once what was going on. "I have heard much of these things," she said; "but I never saw the effect myself. You have everything ready there. Let me try whether I can succeed in producing anything."

She took the thread in her hand, and as she was perfectly

serious, she held it steady, and without any agitation. Not the slightest motion, however, could be detected. Ottilie was then called upon to try. She held the pendulum still more quietly and unconsciously over the plate on the table. But in a moment the swinging piece of metal began to stir with a distinct rotatory action, and turned as they moved the position of the plate, first to one side and then to the other; now in circles, now in ellipses; or else describing a series of straight lines; doing all the Earl's friend could expect, and far exceeding, indeed, all his expectations.

The Earl himself was a little staggered; but the other could never be satisfied, from delight and curiosity, and begged for the experiment again and again with all sorts of variations. Ottilie was good-natured enough to gratify him; till at last she was obliged to desire to be allowed to go, as her headache had come on again. In further admiration and even rapture, he assured her with enthusiasm that he would cure her for ever of her disorder, if she would only trust herself to his remedies. For a moment they did not know what he meant; but Charlotte, who comprehended immediately after, declined his well-meant offer, not liking to have introduced and practised about her a thing of which she had always had the strongest apprehensions.

The strangers were gone, and notwithstanding their having been the inadvertent cause of strange and painful emotions, left the wish behind them, that this meeting might not be the last. Charlotte now made use of the beautiful weather to return visits in the neighbourhood, which, indeed, gave her work enough to do, seeing that the whole country round, some from a real interest, some merely from custom, had been most attentive in calling to inquire after her. At home her delight was the sight of the child, and really it well deserved all love and interest. People saw in it a wonderful, indeed a miraculous child; the brightest, sunniest little face; a fine, well-proportioned body, strong and healthy; and what surprised them more, the double resemblance, which became more and more conspicuous. In figure and in the features of the face, it was like the Captain; the eyes every day it was less easy to distinguish from the eyes of Ottilie.

Ottilie herself, partly from this remarkable affinity, perhaps still more under the influence of that sweet woman's feeling which makes them regard with the most tender affection the offspring, even by another, of the man they love, was as good as a mother to the little creature as it grew, or rather, she was a second mother of another kind. If Charlotte was absent, Ottilie remained alone with the child and the nurse. Nanny had for some time past been jealous of the boy for monopolizing the entire affections of her mistress; she had left her in a fit of crossness, and gone back to her mother. Ottilie would carry the child about in the open air, and by degrees took longer and longer walks with it. She took her bottle of milk to give the child its food when it wanted any. Generally, too, she took a book with her; and so with the child in her arms, reading and wandering, she made a very pretty Penscrosa.

CHAPTER XII.

THE object of the campaign was attained, and Edward, with crosses and decorations, was honourably dismissed. He betook himself at once to the same little estate, where he found exact accounts of his family waiting for him, on whom all this time, without their having observed it or known of it, a sharp watch had been kept under his orders. His quiet residence looked most sweet and pleasant when he reached it. In accordance with his orders, various improvements had been made in his absence, and what was wanting to the establishment in extent, was compensated by its internal comforts and conveniences. Edward, accustomed by his more active habits of life, to take decided steps, determined to execute a project which he long had sufficient time to think over. First of all, he invited the Major to come to him. This pleasure in meeting again was very great to both of them. The friendships of boyhood, like relationship of blood, possess this important advantage, that mistakes and misunderstandings never produce irreparable injury; and the old regard after a time will always re-establish itself.

Edward began with inquiring about the situation of his

friend, and learnt that fortune had favoured him exactly as he most could have wished. He then half-seriously asked whether there was not something going forward about a marriage; to which he received a most decided and positive denial.

"I cannot and will not have any reserve with you," he proceeded. "I will tell you at once what my own feelings are, and what I intend to do. You know my passion for Ottilie; you must long have comprehended that it was this which drove me into the campaign. I do not deny that I desired to be rid of a life which, without her, would be of no further value to me. At the same time, however, I acknowledge that I could never bring myself utterly to despair. The prospect of happiness with her was so beautiful, so infinitely charming, that it was not possible for me entirely to renounce it. Feelings, too, which I cannot explain, and a number of happy omens, have combined to strengthen me in the belief, in the assurance, that Ottilie will one day be mine. The glass with our initials cut upon it, which was thrown into the air when the foundation-stone was laid, did not go to pieces; it was caught, and I have it again in my possession. After many miserable hours of uncertainty, spent in this place, I said to myself, 'I will put myself in the place of this glass, and it shall be an omen whether our union be possible or not. I will go; I will seek for death; not like a madman, but like a man who still hopes that he may live. Ottilie shall be the prize for which I fight. Ottilie shall be behind the ranks of the enemy; in every entrenchment, in every beleaguered fortress, I shall hope to find her, and to win her. I will do wonders, with the wish to survive them; with the hope to gain Ottilie, not to lose her.' These feelings have led me on; they have stood by me through all dangers; and now I find myself like one who has arrived at his goal, who has overcome every difficulty and who has nothing more left in his way. Ottilie is mine, and whatever lies between the thought and the execution of it, I can only regard as unimportant."

"With a few strokes you blot out," replied the Major, "all the objections that we can or ought to urge upon you, and yet they must be repeated. I must leave it to yourself to recall the full value of your relation with your wife; but you owe it to her, and you owe it to yourself, not to close your eyes to it. How can I so much as recollect that you have had a son given to you, without acknowledging at once that you two belong to one another for ever; that you are bound, for this little creature's sake, to live united, that united you may educate it, and provide for its future welfare?"

" It is no more than the blindness of parents," answered Edward, " when they imagine their existence to be of so much importance to their children. Whatever lives, finds nourishment and finds assistance; and if the son who has early lost his father does not spend so easy, so favoured a youth, he profits, perhaps, for that very reason, in being trained sooner for the world, and comes to a timely knowledge that he must accommodate himself to others, a thing which sooner or later we are all forced to learn Here, however, even these considerations are irrelevant; we are sufficiently well off to be able to provide for more children than one, and it is neither right nor kind to accumulate so large a property on a single head."

The Major attempted to say something of Charlotte's worth, and Edward's long-standing attachment to her; but the latter hastily interrupted him. " We committed ourselves to a foolish thing, that I see all too clearly. Whoever, in middle age, attempts to realize the wishes and hopes of his early youth, invariably deceives himself. Each ten years of a man's life has its own fortunes, its own hopes, its own desires. Woe to him who, either by circumstances or by his own infatuation, is induced to grasp at anything before him or behind him. We have done a foolish thing. Are we to abide by it all our lives? Are we, from some respect of prudence, to refuse to ourselves what the customs of the age do not forbid? In how many matters do men recall their intentions and their actions; and shall it not be allowed to them here, here, where the question is not of this thing or of that, but of everything; not of our single condition of life, but of the whole complex life itself?"

Again the Major powerfully and impressively urged on Edward to consider what he owed to his wife, what was due to his family, to the world, and to his own position; but he could not succeed in producing the slightest impression.

" All these questions, my friend," he returned, " I have
considered already again and again. They have passed before
me in the storm of battle, when the earth was shaking with
the thunder of the cannon, with the balls singing and whistling
round me, with my comrades falling right and left, my horse
shot under me, my hat pierced with bullets. They have
floated before me by the still watch-fire under the starry vault
of the sky. I have thought them all through, felt them all
through. I have weighed them, and I have satisfied myself
about them again and again, and now for ever. At such
moments why should I not acknowledge it to you? you too
were in my thoughts, you too belonged to my circle; as,
indeed, you and I have long belonged to one another. If I
have ever been in your debt I am now in a position to repay
it with interest; if you have been in mine you have now
the means to make it good to me. I know that you love
Charlotte, and she deserves it. I know that you are not
indifferent to her, and why should she not feel your worth?
Take her at my hand and give Ottilie to me, and we shall be
the happiest beings upon the earth."

" If you choose to assign me so high a character," replied
the Major, " it is the more reason for me to be firm and prudent. Whatever there may be in this proposal to make it
attractive to me, instead of simplifying the problem, it only
increases the difficulty of it. The question is now of me as
well as of you. The fortunes, the good name, the honour of
two men, hitherto unsullied with a breath, will be exposed to
hazard by so strange a proceeding, to call it by no harsher
name, and we shall appear before the world in a highly questionable light."

" Our very characters being what they are," replied
Edward, " give us a right to take this single liberty. A man
who has borne himself honourably through a whole life, makes
an action honourable which might appear ambiguous in others.
As concerns myself, after these last trials which I have taken
upon myself, after the difficult and dangerous actions which I
have accomplished for others, I feel entitled now to do something for myself. For you and Charlotte, that part of the
business may, if you like it, be given up; but neither you
nor any one shall keep me from doing what I have determined.
If I may look for help and furtherance, I shall be ready to

do everything which can be wished; but if I am to be left to myself, or if obstacles are to be thrown in my way, some extremity or other is sure to follow."

The Major thought it his duty to combat Edward's purposes as long as it was possible; and now he changed the mode of his attack and tried a diversion. He seemed to give way, and only spoke of the form of what they would have to do to bring about this separation, and these new unions; and so mentioned a number of ugly, undesirable matters, which threw Edward into the worst of tempers.

"I see plainly," he cried at last, "that what we desire can only be carried by storm, whether it be from our enemies or from our friends. I keep clearly before my own eyes what I demand, what, one way or another, I must have; and I will seize it promptly and surely. Connections like ours, I know very well, cannot be broken up and reconstructed again without much being thrown down which is standing, and much having to give way which would be glad enough to continue. We shall come to no conclusion by thinking about it. All rights are alike to the understanding, and it is always easy to throw extra weight into the ascending scale. Do you make up your mind, my friend, to act, and act promptly, for me and for yourself. Disentangle and untie the knots, and tie them up again. Do not be deterred from it by nice respects. We have already given the world something to say about us. It will talk about us once more; and when we have ceased to be a nine days' wonder, it will forget us as it forgets everything else, and allow us to follow our own way without further concern with us." The Major had nothing further to say, and was at last obliged to sit silent; while Edward treated the affair as now conclusively settled, talked through in detail all that had to be done, and pictured the future in every most cheerful colour, and then he went on again seriously and thoughtfully: "If we think to leave ourselves to the hope, to the expectation, that all will go right again of itself, that accident will lead us straight, and take care of us, it will be a most culpable self-deception. In such a way it would be impossible for us to save ourselves, or re-establish our peace again. I who have been the innocent cause of it all, how am I ever to console myself? By my own importunity I prevailed on Charlotte to write to you to stay with us; and Ottilie followed in consequence. We have had no more control over what ensued out of this, but we have the power to make it innocuous; to guide the new circumstances to our own happiness. Can you turn away your eyes from the fair and beautiful prospects which I open to us? Can you insist to me, can you insist to us all, on a wretched renunciation of them? Do you think it possible? Is it possible? Will there be no vexations, no bitterness, no inconvenience to overcome, if we resolve to fall back into our old state? and will any good, any happiness whatever, arise out of it? Will your own rank, will the high position which you have earned, be any pleasure to you, if you are to be prevented from visiting me, or from living with me? And after what has passed, it would not be anything but painful. Charlotte and I, with all our property, would only find ourselves in a melancholy state. And if, like other men of the world, you can persuade yourself that years and separation will eradicate our feelings, will obliterate impressions so deeply engraved; why, then the question is of these very years, which it would be better to spend in happiness and comfort than in pain and misery. But the last and most important point of all which I have to urge is this: supposing that we, our outward and inward condition being what it is, could nevertheless make up our minds to wait at all hazards, and bear what is laid upon us, what is to become of Ottilie? She must leave our family; she must go into society where we shall not be to care for her, and she will be driven wretchedly to and fro in a hard, cold world. Describe to me any situation in which Ottilie, without me, without us, could be happy, and you will then have employed an argument which will be stronger than every other; and if I will not promise to yield to it, if I will not undertake at once to give up all my own hopes, I will at least reconsider the question, and see how what you have said will affect it."

This problem was not so easy to solve; at least, no satisfactory answer to it suggested itself to his friend, and nothing was left to him except to insist again and again, how grave and serious, and in many senses how dangerous, the whole undertaking was; and at least that they ought maturely to consider how they had better enter upon it. Edward agreed to this, and consented to wait before he took any steps; but only under the condition that his friend should not leave him until they had come to a perfect understanding about it, and until the first measures had been taken.

CHAPTER XIII.

MEN who are complete strangers, and wholly indifferent to one another, if they live a long time together, are sure both of them to expose something of their inner nature, and thus a kind of intimacy will arise between them. All the more was it to be expected that there would soon be no secrets between our two friends, now that they were again under the same roof together, and in daily and hourly intercourse. They went over again the earlier stages of their history, and the Major confessed to Edward that Charlotte had intended Ottilie for him at the time at which he returned from abroad, and hoped that some time or other he might marry her. Edward was in ecstacies at this discovery, he spoke without reserve of the mutual affection of Charlotte and the Major, which, because it happened to fall in so conveniently with his own wishes, he painted in very lively colours.

Deny it altogether, the Major could not; at the same time, he could not altogether acknowledge it. But Edward only insisted on it the more. He had pictured the whole thing to himself not as possible, but as already concluded; all parties had only to resolve on what they all wished; there would be no difficulty in obtaining a separation; the marriages should follow as soon after as possible, and Edward could travel with Ottilie.

Of all the pleasant things which imagination pictures to us, perhaps there is none more charming than when lovers and young married people look forward to enjoying their new relation to each other in a fresh, new world, and test the endurance of the bond between them in so many changing circumstances. The Major and Charlotte were in the meantime to have unrestricted powers to settle all questions of money, property, and other such important worldly matters; and to do whatever was right and proper for the satisfaction of all parties. What Edward dwelt the most upon, however, what he seemed to promise himself the most advantage from was this:—as the child would have to remain with the mother, the Major would charge himself with the education of it; he would train the boy according to his own views, and develop what capacities there might be in him. It was not for nothing that he had received in his baptism the name of Otto, which belonged to them both.

Edward had so completely arranged everything for himself, that he could not wait another day to carry it into execution. On their way to the castle, they arrived at a small town, where Edward had a house, and where he was to stay to await the return of the Major. He could not, however, prevail upon himself to alight there at once, and accompanied his friend through the place. They were both on horseback, and falling into some interesting conversation, rode on further together.

On a sudden they saw, in the distance, the new house on the height, with its red tiles shining in the sun. An irresistible longing came over Edward; he would have it all settled that very evening; he would remain concealed in a village close by. The Major was to urge the business on Charlotte with all his power; he would take her prudence by surprise; and oblige her by the unexpectedness of his proposal to make a free acknowledgment of her feelings. Edward had transferred his own wishes to her; he felt certain that he was only meeting her half-way, and that her inclination were as decided as his own; and he looked for an immediate consent from her, because he himself could think of nothing else.

Joyfully he saw the prosperous issue before his eyes; and that it might be communicated to him as swiftly as possible, a few cannon shots were to be fired off, and if it was dark, a rocket or two sent up.

The Major rode to the castle. He did not find Charlotte there; he learnt that for the present she was staying at the new house; at that particular time, however, she was paying a visit in the neighbourhood, and she probably would not have returned till late that evening. He walked back to the hotel, to which he had previously sent his horse.

Edward, in the meantime, unable to sit still from restlessness and impatience, stole away out of his concealment along solitary paths only known to foresters and fishermen, into his park; and he found himself towards evening in the copse close to the lake, the broad mirror of which he now for the first time saw spread out in its perfectness before him.

Ottilie had gone out that afternoon for a walk along the shore. She had the child with her, and read as she usually did while she went along. She had gone as far as the oak-tree by the ferry. The boy had fallen asleep; she sat down; laid it on the ground at her side, and continued reading. The book was one of those which attract persons of delicate feeling, and afterwards will not let them go again. She forgot the time and the hours; she never thought what a long way round it was by land to the new house; but she sat lost in her book and in herself, so beautiful to look at, that the trees and the bushes round her ought to have been alive, and to have had eyes given them to gaze upon her and admire her. The sun was sinking; a ruddy streak of light fell upon her from behind, tinging with gold her cheek and shoulder. Edward, who had made his way to the lake without being seen, finding his park desolate, and no trace of human creature to be seen anywhere, went on and on. At last he broke through the copse behind the oak-tree, and saw her. At the same moment she saw him. He flew to her, and threw himself at her feet. After a long, silent pause, in which they both endeavoured to collect themselves, he explained in a few words why and how he had come there. He had sent the Major to Charlotte; and perhaps at that moment their common destiny was being decided. Never had he doubted her affection, and she assuredly had never doubted his. He begged for her consent; she hesitated; he implored her. He offered to resume his old privilege, and throw his arms around her, and embrace her; she pointed down to the child.

Edward looked at it, and was amazed. "Great God!" he cried; "if I had cause to doubt my wife and my friend, this face would witness fearfully against them. Is not this the very image of the Major? I never saw such a likeness."

"Indeed!" replied Ottilie; "all the world say it is like me."

"Is it possible?" Edward answered; and at the moment

F

the child opened its eyes—two large, black, piercing eyes,
deep and full of love; already the little face was full of
intelligence.   He seemed as if he knew both the figures
which he saw standing before him.   Edward threw himself
down beside the child, and then knelt a second time before
Ottilie. " It is you," he cried; " the eyes are yours! ah,
but let me look into yours; let me throw a veil over that
ill-starred hour which gave its being to this little creature.
Shall I shock your pure spirit with the fearful thought, that
man and wife who are estranged from each other, can yet
press each other to their heart, and profane the bonds by
which the law unites them by other eager wishes?   Oh yes!
As I have said so much; as my connection with Charlotte
must now be severed; as you will be mine, why should I
not speak out the words to you?   This child is the offspring
of a double adultery.   It should have been a tie between
my wife and myself; but it severs her from me, and me from
her.   Let it witness, then, against me.   Let these fair eyes
say to yours, that in the arms of another I belonged to you.
You must feel, Ottilie, oh! you must feel, that my fault, my
crime, I can only expiate in your arms."

  " Hark !" he called out, as he sprang up and listened.
He thought that he had heard a shot, and that it was the
sign which the Major was to give.   It was the gun of a
forester on the adjoining hill.   Nothing followed.   Edward
grew impatient.

  Ottilie now first observed that the sun was down behind
the mountains; its last rays were shining on the windows of
the house above. " Leave me, Edward," she cried; " go.
Long as we have been parted, much as we have borne,
yet remember what we both owe to Charlotte.   She must
decide our fate; do not let us anticipate her judgment.   I
am yours if she will permit it to be so.   If she will not, I
must renounce you.   As you think it is now so near an
issue, let us wait.   Go back to the village, where the Major
supposes you to be.   Is it likely that a rude cannon-shot will
inform you of the results of such an interview?   Perhaps
at this moment he is seeking for you.   He will not have
found Charlotte at home; of that I am certain.   He may
have gone to meet her; for they knew at the castle where
she was.   How many things may have happened!   Leave

me! she must be at home by this time; she is expecting me
with the baby above."

Ottilie spoke hurriedly; she called together all the possi-
bilities. It was too delightful to be with Edward; but she
felt that he must now leave her. "I beseech, I implore you,
my beloved," she cried out; "go back and wait for the Major."

"I obey your commands," cried Edward. He gazed at
her for a moment with rapturous love, and then caught her
close in his arms. She wound her own about him, and
pressed him tenderly to her breast. Hope streamed away,
like a star shooting in the sky, above their heads. They
thought then, they believed, that they did indeed belong to
one another. For the first time they exchanged free, genuine
kisses, and separated with pain and effort.

The sun had gone down. It was twilight, and a damp
mist was rising about the lake. Ottilie stood confused and
agitated. She looked across to the house on the hill, and
she thought she saw Charlotte's white dress on the balcony.
It was a long way round by the end of the lake; and she
knew how impatiently Charlotte would be waiting for the
child. She saw the plane-trees just opposite her, and only a
narrow interval of water divided her from the path which led
straight up to the house. Her nervousness about venturing
on the water with the child vanished in her present embarrassment. She hastened to the boat; she did not feel that
her heart was beating; that her feet were tottering; that
her senses were threatening to fail her.

She sprang in, seized the oar, and pushed off. She had to
use force; she pushed again. The boat shot off, and glided,
swaying and rocking into the open water. With the child in
her left arm, the book in her left hand, and the oar in her
right, she lost her footing, and fell over the seat; the oar
slipped from her on one side, and as she tried to recover
herself, the child and the book slipped on the other, all into
the water. She caught the floating dress, but lying entangled as she was herself, she was unable to rise. Her
right hand was free, but she could not reach round to help
herself up with it; at last she succeeded. She drew the
child out of the water; but its eyes were closed, and it had
ceased to breathe.

In a moment, she recovered all her self-possession; but so

much the greater was her agony; the boat was driving fast into the middle of the lake; the oar was swimming far away from her. She saw no one on the shore; and, indeed, if she had, it would have been of no service to her. Cut off from all assistance, she was floating on the faithless, unstable element.

She sought for help from herself; she had often heard of the recovery of the drowned; she had herself witnessed an instance of it on the evening of her birthday; she took off the child's clothes, and dried it with her muslin dress; she threw open her bosom, laying it bare for the first time to the free heaven. For the first time she pressed a living being to her pure, naked breast. Alas! and it was not a living being. The cold limbs of the ill-starred little creature chilled her to the heart. Streams of tears gushed from her eyes, and lent a show of life and warmth to the outside of the torpid limbs. She persevered with her efforts; she wrapped it in her shawl, she drew it close to herself, stroked it; breathed upon it, and with tears and kisses laboured to supply the help which, cut off as she was, she was unable to find.

It was all in vain; the child lay motionless in her arms; motionless the boat floated on the glassy water. But even here her beautiful spirit did not leave her forsaken. She turned to the Power above. She sank down upon her knees in the boat, and with both arms raised the unmoving child above her innocent breast, like marble in its whiteness; alas, too like marble, cold; with moist eyes she looked up and cried for help, where a tender heart hopes to find it in its fulness, when all other help has failed.

The stars were beginning one by one to glimmer down upon her; she turned to them and not in vain; a soft air stole over the surface, and wafted the boat under the plane trees.

CHAPTER XIV.

SHE hurried to the new house, and called the surgeon and gave the child into his hands. It was carried at once to Charlotte's sleeping-room. Cool and collected from a wide experience, he submitted the tender body to the usual process. Ottilie stood by him, through it all. She prepared everything, she fetched everything, but as if she were moving in another world; for the height of misfortune, like the height of happiness, alters the aspect of every object. And it was only when after every resource had been exhausted, the good man shook his head, and to her questions, whether there was hope, first was silent, and then answered with a gentle No! that she left the apartment, and had scarcely entered the sitting-room, when she fell fainting, with her face upon the carpet, unable to reach the sofa.

At that moment Charlotte was heard driving up. The surgeon implored the servants to keep back, and allow him to go to meet her and prepare her. But he was too late; while he was speaking she had entered the drawing-room. She found Ottilie on the ground, and one of the girls of the house came running and screaming to her open-mouthed. The surgeon entered at the same moment, and she was informed of everything. She could not at once, however, give up all hope. She was flying up stairs to the child, but the physician besought her to remain where she was. He went himself, to deceive her with a show of fresh exertions, and she sat down upon the sofa. Ottilie was still lying on the ground; Charlotte raised her, and supported her against herself, and her beautiful head sank down upon her knee. The kind medical man went backwards and forwards; he appeared to be busy about the child; his real care was for the ladies; and so came on midnight, and the stillness grew more and more deathly. Charlotte did not try to conceal from herself any longer that her child would never return to life again. She desired to see it now. It had been wrapped up in warm woollen coverings. And it was brought down as it was, lying in its cot, which was placed at her side on the sofa. The little face was uncovered; and there it lay in its calm sweet beauty.

The report of the accident soon spread through the village; every one was roused, and the story reached the hotel. The Major hurried up the well-known road; he went round and round the house; at last he met a servant who was going to one of the out-buildings to fetch something. He learnt from him in what state things were, and desired him to tell the surgeon that he was there. The latter came out, not a little surprised at the appearance of his old patron. He told him exactly what had happened, and undertook to prepare Charlotte to see him. He then went in, began some conversation to distract her attention, and led her imagination from one object to another, till at last he brought it to rest upon her friend, and the depth of feeling and of sympathy which would surely be called out in him. From the imaginative she was brought at once to the real. Enough! she was informed that he was at the door, that he knew everything and desired to be admitted.

The Major entered. Charlotte received him with a miserable smile. He stood before her; she lifted off the green silk covering under which the body was lying; and by the dim light of a taper, he saw before him, not without a secret shudder, the stiffened image of himself. Charlotte pointed to a chair, and there they sate opposite to one another, without speaking, through the night. Ottilie was still lying motionless on Charlotte's knee; she breathed softly, and slept or seemed to sleep.

The morning dawned, the lights went out; the two friends appeared to awake out of a heavy dream. Charlotte looked towards the Major, and said quietly: "Tell me through what circumstances you have been brought hither, to take part in this mourning scene."

"The present is not a time," the Major answered, in the same low tone as that in which Charlotte had spoken, for fear lest she might disturb Ottilie; "this is not a time, and this is not a place for reserve. The condition in which I find you is so fearful that even the earnest matter on which I am here, loses its importance by the side of it." He then informed her, quite calmly and simply, of the object of his mission, in so far as he was the ambassador of Edward: of the object of his coming, in so far as his own free will and his own interests were concerned in it. He laid both before her, delicately but uprightly; Charlotte listened quietly, and showed neither surprise nor unwillingness.

As soon as the Major had finished, she replied, in a voice so light that to catch her words he was obliged to draw his chair closer to her: "In such a case as this I have never before found myself; but in similar cases I have always said to myself, how will it be to-morrow? I feel very clearly that the fate of many persons is now in my hands, and what I have to do is soon said without scruple or hesitation. I consent to the separation; I ought to have made up my mind to it before; by my unwillingness and reluctance I have destroyed my child. There are certain things on which destiny obstinately insists. In vain may reason, may virtue, may duty, may all holy feelings place themselves in its way. Something shall be done which to it seems good, and which to us seems not good; and it forces its own way through at last, let us conduct ourselves as we will.

"And, indeed, what am I saying? It is but my own desire, my own purpose, against which I acted so unthinkingly, which destiny is again bringing in my way? Did I not long ago, in my thoughts, design Edward and Ottilie for one another? Did I not myself labour to bring them together? And you, my friend, you yourself were an accomplice in my plot. Why, why, could I not distinguish mere man's obstinacy from real love? Why did I accept his hand, when I could have made him happy as a friend, and when another could have made him happy as a wife? And now, look here on this unhappy slumberer. I tremble for the moment when she will recover out of this half death sleep into consciousness. How can she endure to live? How shall she ever console herself, if she may not hope to make good that to Edward, of which, as the instrument of the most wonderful destiny, she has deprived him? And she can make it all good again by the passion, by the devotion with which she loves him. If love be able to bear all things, it is able to do yet more; it can restore all things: of myself at such a moment I may not think.

"Do you go quietly away, my dear Major; say to Edward that I consent to the separation; that I leave it to him, to you, and to Mittler, to settle whatever is to be done. I have no anxiety for my own future condition; it may be what it will; it is nothing to me. I will subscribe whatever paper is submitted to me, only he must not require me to join actively. I cannot have to think about it, or give advice."

The Major rose to go. She stretched out her hand to him across Ottilie. He pressed it to his lips, and whispered gently: "And for myself, may I hope anything?"

"Do not ask me now!" replied Charlotte. "I will tell you another time. We have not deserved to be miserable; but neither can we say that we have deserved to be happy together."

The Major left her, and went, feeling for Charlotte to the

bottom of his heart, but not being able to be sorry for the fate of the poor child. Such an offering seemed necessary to him for their general happiness. He pictured Ottilie to himself with a child of her own in her arms, as the most perfect compensation for the one of which she had deprived Edward. He pictured himself with his own son on his knee, who should have better right to resemble him than the one which was departed.

With such flattering hopes and fancies passing through his mind, he returned to the hotel, and on his way back he met Edward, who had been waiting for him the whole night through in the open air, since neither rocket nor report of cannon would bring him news of the successful issue of his undertaking. He had already heard of the misfortune; and he too, instead of being sorry for the poor creature, regarded what had befallen it, without being exactly ready to confess it to himself, as a convenient accident, through which the only impediment in the way of his happiness was at once removed.

The Major at once informed him of his wife's resolution, and he therefore easily allowed himself to be prevailed upon to return again with him to the village, and from thence to go for a while to the little town, where they would consider what was next to be done, and make their arrangements.

After the Major had left her, Charlotte sate on, buried in her own reflections; but it was only for a few minutes. Ottilie suddenly raised herself from her lap, and looked full with her large eyes in her friend's face. Then she got up from off the ground, and stood upright before her.

"This is the second time," began the noble girl, with an irresistible solemnity of manner, "this is the second time that the same thing has happened to me. You once said to me that similar things often befall people more than once in their lives in a similar way, and if they do, it is always at important moments. I now find that what you said is true, and I have to make a confession to you. Shortly after my mother's death, when I was a very little child, I was sitting one day on a footstool close to you. You were on the sofa, as you are at this moment, and my head rested on your knees. I was not asleep, I was not awake: I was in a trance. I knew everything which was passing about me. I heard every word which was said with the greatest distinctness, and yet I could not stir, I could not speak; and if I had wished it, I could not have given a hint that I was conscious. On that occasion you were speaking about me to one of your friends; you were commiserating my fate, left as I was a poor orphan in the world. You described my dependent position, and how unfortunate a future was before me, unless some very happy star watched over me. I understood well what you said. I saw, perhaps too clearly, what you appeared to hope of me, and what you thought I ought to do. I made rules to myself, according to such limited insight as I had, and by these I have long lived; by these, at the time when you so kindly took charge of me, and had me with you in your house, I regulated whatever I did, and whatever I left undone.

"But I have wandered out of my course; I have broken my rules; I have lost the very power of feeling them. And now, after a dreadful occurrence, you have again made clear to me my situation, which is more pitiable than the first. While lying in a half torpor on your lap, I have again, as if out of another world, heard every syllable which you uttered. I know from you how all is with me. I shudder at the thought of myself; but again, as I did then, in my half sleep of death, I have marked out my new path for myself.

"I am determined, as I was before, and what I have determined I must tell you at once. I will never be Edward's wife. In a terrible manner God has opened my eyes to see the sin in which I was entangled. I will atone for it, and let no one think to move me from my purpose. It is by this, my dearest, kindest friend, that you must govern your own conduct. Send for the Major to come back to you. Write to him that no steps must be taken. It made me miserable that I could not stir or speak when he went;—I tried to rise,—I tried to cry out. Oh, why did you let him leave you with such unlawful hopes!"

Charlotte saw Ottilie's condition, and she felt for it; but she hoped that by time and persuasion she might be able to prevail upon her. On her uttering a few words, however, which pointed to a future,—to a time when her sufferings would be alleviated, and when there might be better room for hope, "No!" Ottilie cried, with vehemence, "do not endeavour to move me; do not seek to deceive me. At the moment at which I learn that you have consented to the separation, in that same lake I will expiate my errors and my crimes."

CHAPTER XV.

FRIENDS and relations, and all persons living in the same house together, are apt, when life is going smoothly and peacefully with them, to make what they are doing, or what they are going to do, even more than is right or necessary, a subject of constant conversation. They talk to each other of their plans and their occupations, and, without exactly taking one another's advice, consider and discuss together the entire progress of their lives. But this is far from being the case in serious moments ; just when it would seem men most require the assistance and support of others, they all draw singly within themselves every one to act for himself, every one to work in his own fashion ; they conceal from one another the particular means which they employ, and only the result, the object, the thing which they realize, is again made common property.

After so many strange and unfortunate incidents, a sort of silent seriousness had passed over the two ladies, which showed itself in a sweet mutual effort to spare each other's feelings. The child had been buried privately in the chapel. It rested there as the first offering to a destiny full of ominous foreshadowings.

Charlotte, as soon as ever she could, turned back to life and occupation, and here she first found Ottilie standing in need of her assistance. She occupied herself almost entirely with her, without letting it be observed. She knew how deeply the noble girl loved Edward. She had discovered by degrees the scene which had preceded the accident, and had gathered every circumstance of it, partly from Ottilie herself, partly from the letters of the Major.

Ottilie, on her side, made Charlotte's immediate life much more easy for her. She was open, and even talkative, but she never spoke of the present, or of what had lately past. She had been a close and thoughtful observer. She knew much, and now it all came to the surface. She entertained, she amused Charlotte, and the latter still nourished a hope in secret to see her married to Edward after all.

But something very different was passing in Ottilie. She

had disclosed the secret of the course of her life to her friend, and she showed no more of her previous restraint and submissiveness. By her repentance and her resolution she felt herself freed from the burden of her fault and her mis- fortune. She had no more violence to do to herself. In the bottom of her heart she had forgiven herself solely under condition of the fullest renunciation, and it was a condition which would remain binding for all time to come.

So passed away some time, and Charlotte now felt how deeply house and park, and lake and rocks and trees, served to keep alive in them all their most painful reminiscences. They wanted change of scene, both of them, it was plain enough; but how it was to be effected was not so easy to decide.

Were the two ladies to remain together? Edward's pre- viously-expressed will appeared to enjoin it,—his declarations and his threats appeared to make it necessary; only it could not be now mistaken that Charlotte and Ottilie, with all their goodwill, with all their sense, with all their efforts to conceal it, could not avoid finding themselves in a painful situation towards one another. In their conversation there was a constant endeavour to avoid doubtful subjects. They were often obliged only half to understand some allusion; more often, expressions were misinterpreted, if not by their under- standings, at any rate by their feelings. They were afraid to give pain to one another, and this very fear itself produced the evil which they were seeking to avoid.

If they were to try change of scene, and at the same time (at any rate for a while) to part, the old question came up again, where Ottilie was to go? There was the grand, rich family, who still wanted a desirable companion for their daughter, their attempts to find a person whom they could trust having hitherto proved ineffectual. The last time the Baroness had been at the castle, she had urged Charlotte to send Ottilie there, and she had been lately pressing it again and again in her letters. Charlotte now a second time proposed it; but Ottilie expressly declined going anywhere, where she would be thrown into what is called the great world.

" Do not think me foolish or self-willed, my dear aunt," she said; " I had better tell you what I feel, for fear you should judge hardly of me; although in any other case it would be my duty to be silent. A person who has fallen into uncommon misfortunes, however guiltless he may be, carries a frightful mark upon him. His presence, in every one who sees him and is aware of his history, excites a kind of horror. People see in him the terrible fate which has been laid upon him, and he is the object of a diseased and nervous curiosity. It is so with a house, it is so with a town, where any terrible action has been done; people enter them with awe; the light of day shines less brightly there, and the stars seem to lose their lustre.

"Perhaps we ought to excuse it, but how extreme is the indiscretion with which people behave towards such unfortunates, with their foolish importunities and awkward kindness! You must forgive me for speaking in this way, but that poor girl whom Luciana tempted out of her retirement, and with such mistaken good nature tried to force into society and amusement, has haunted me and made me miserable. The poor creature, when she was so frightened and tried to escape, and then sank and swooned away, and I caught her in my arms, and the party came all crowding round in terror and curiosity! little did I think, then, that the same fate was in store for me. But my feeling for her is as deep and warm and fresh as ever it was; and now I may direct my compassion upon myself, and secure myself from being the object of any similar exposure."

"But, my dear child," answered Charlotte, "you will never be able to withdraw yourself where no one can see you; we have no cloisters now : otherwise, there, with your present feelings, would be your resource."

"Solitude would not give me the resource for which I wish, my dear aunt," answered Ottilie. "The one true and valuable resource is to be looked for where we can be active and useful; all the self-denials and all the penances on earth will fail to deliver us from an evil-omened destiny, if it be determined to persecute us. Let me sit still in idleness and serve as a spectacle for the world, and it will overpower me and crush me. But find me some peaceful employment, where I can go steadily and unweariedly on doing my duty, and I shall be able to bear the eyes of men, when I need not shrink under the eyes of God."

"Unless I am much mistaken," replied Charlotte, "your inclination is to return to the school."

"Yes," Ottilie answered; "I do not deny it. I think it a happy destination to train up others in the beaten way, after having been trained in the strangest myself. And do we not see the same great fact in history? some moral calamity drives men out into the wilderness; but they are not allowed to remain as they had hoped in their concealment there. They are summoned back into the world, to lead the wanderers into the right way; and who are fitter for such a service, than those who have been initiated into the labyrinths of life? They are commanded to be the support of the unfortunate; and who can better fulfil that command than those who have no more misfortunes to fear upon earth?"

"You are selecting an uncommon profession for yourself," replied Charlotte. "I shall not oppose you, however. Let it be as you wish; only I hope it will be but for a short time."

"Most warmly I thank you," said Ottilie, "for giving me leave at least to try, to make the experiment. If I am not flattering myself too highly, I am sure I shall succeed: wherever I am, I shall remember the many trials which I went through myself, and how small, how infinitely small they were compared to those which I afterwards had to undergo. It will be my happiness to watch the embarrassments of the little creatures as they grow; to cheer them in their childish sorrows, and guide them back with a light hand out of their little aberrations. The fortunate is not the person to be of help to the fortunate; it is in the nature of man to require ever more and more of himself and others, the more he has received. The unfortunate who has himself recovered, knows best how to nourish, in himself and them, the feeling that every moderate good ought to be enjoyed with rapture."

"I have but one objection to make to what you propose," said Charlotte, after some thought, "although that one seems to me of great importance. I am not thinking of you, but of another person: you are aware of the feelings towards you of that good, right-minded, excellent assistant. In the way in which you desire to proceed, you will become every day more valuable and more indispensable to him. Already he himself believes that he can never live happily without you, and hereafter, when he has become accustomed to have you to work with him, he will be unable to carry on his business if he loses you; you will have assisted him at the beginning only to injure him in the end."

"Destiny has not dealt with me with too gentle a hand," replied Ottilie; "and whoever loves me has perhaps not much better to expect. Our friend is so good and so sensible, that I hope he will be able to reconcile himself to remaining in a simple relation with me; he will learn to see in me a consecrated person, lying under the shadow of an awful calamity, and only able to support herself and bear up against it by devoting herself to that Holy Being who is invisibly around us, and alone is able to shield us from the dark powers which threaten to overwhelm us."

All this, which the dear girl poured out so warmly, Charlotte privately reflected over; on many different occasions, although only in the gentlest manner, she had hinted at the possibility of Ottilie's being brought again in contact with Edward; but the slightest mention of it, the faintest hope, the least suspicion, seemed to wound Ottilie to the quick. One day when she could not evade it, she expressed herself to Charlotte clearly and peremptorily on the subject.

"If your resolution to renounce Edward," returned Charlotte, "is so firm and unalterable, then you had better avoid the danger of seeing him again. At a distance from the object of our love, the warmer our affection, the stronger is the control which we fancy that we can exercise on ourselves; because the whole force of the passion, diverted from its outward objects, turns inwards on ourselves. But how soon, how swiftly is our mistake made clear to us, when the thing which we thought that we could renounce, stands again before our eyes as indispensable to us! You must now do what you consider best suited to your circumstances. Look well into yourself; change, if you prefer it, the resolution which you have just expressed. But do it of yourself, with a free consenting heart. Do not allow yourself to be drawn in by an accident; do not let yourself be surprised into your former position. It will place you at issue with yourself and will be intolerable to you. As I said, before you take this step, before you remove from me, and enter upon a new life, which will lead you no one knows in what direction, consider once more whether really, indeed, you can renounce Edward for the whole time to come. If you have faithfully made up your mind that you will do this, then will you enter into an engagement with me, that you will never admit him into your presence; and if he seeks you out and forces himself upon you, that you will not exchange words with him?"

Ottilie did not hesitate a moment; she gave Charlotte the promise, which she had already made to herself.

Now, however, Charlotte began to be haunted with Edward's threat, that he would only consent to renounce Ottilie, as long as she was not parted from Charlotte. Since that time, indeed, circumstances were so altered, so many things had happened, that an engagement which was wrung from him in a moment of excitement might well be supposed to have been cancelled. She was unwilling, however, in the remotest sense to venture anything or to undertake anything which might displease him, and Mittler was therefore to find Edward, and inquire what, as things now were, he wished to be done.

Since the death of the child, Mittler had often been at the castle to see Charlotte, although only for a few moments at a time. The unhappy accident which had made her reconciliation with her husband in the highest degree improbable, had produced a most painful effect upon him. But ever, as his nature was, hoping and striving, he rejoiced secretly at the resolution of Ottilie. He trusted to the softening influence of passing time; he hoped that it might still be possible to keep the husband and the wife from separating; and he tried to regard these convulsions of passion only as trials of wedded love and fidelity.

Charlotte, at the very first, had informed the Major by letter of Ottilie's declaration. She had entreated him most earnestly to prevail on Edward to take no further steps for the present. They should keep quiet and wait, and see whether the poor girl's spirits would recover. She had let him know from time to time whatever was necessary of what had more lately fallen from her. And now Mittler had to undertake the really difficult commission of preparing Edward for an alteration in her situation. Mittler, however, well knowing that men can be brought more easily to submit to

what is already done, than to give their consent to what is yet
to be done, persuaded Charlotte that it would be better to
send Ottilie off at once to the school.

Consequently as soon as Mittler was gone, preparations
were at once made for the journey. Ottilie put her things
together; and Charlotte observed that neither the beautiful
box, nor anything out of it, was to go with her. Ottilie had
said nothing to her on the subject; and she took no notice, but
let her alone. The day of the departure came; Charlotte's
carriage was to take Ottilie the first day as far as a place where
they were well known, where she was to pass the night, and
on the second she would go on in it to the school. It was
settled that Nanny was to accompany her, and remain as her
attendant.

This capricious little creature had found her way back to
her mistress after the death of the child, and now hung about
her as warmly and passionately as ever; indeed she seemed,
with her loquacity and attentiveness, as if she wished to make
good her past neglect, and henceforth devote herself entirely to
Ottilie's service. She was quite beside herself now for joy at
the thought of travelling with her, and of seeing strange places,
when she had hitherto never been away from the scene of her
birth; and she ran from the castle to the village to carry the
news of her good fortune to her parents and her relations, and
to take leave. Unluckily for herself, she went among other
places into a room where a person was who had the measles,
and caught the infection, which came out upon her at once.
The journey could not be postponed. Ottilie herself was
urgent to go. She had travelled once already the same road.
She knew the people of the hotel where she was to sleep.
The coachman from the castle was going with her. There
could be nothing to fear.

Charlotte made no opposition. She, too, in thought, was
making haste to be clear of present embarrassments. The
rooms which Ottilie had occupied at the castle she would
have prepared for Edward as soon as possible, and restored
to the old state in which they had been before the arrival of
the Captain. The hope of bringing back old happy days
burns up again and again in us, as if it never could be
extinguished. And Charlotte was quite right; there was
nothing else for her except to hope as she did.

CHAPTER XVI.

WHEN Mittler was come to talk the matter over with Edward, he found him sitting by himself, with his head supported on his right hand, and his arm resting on the table. He appeared in great suffering.

"Is your headache troubling you again?" asked Mittler.

"It is troubling me," answered he; "and yet I cannot wish it were not so, for it reminds me of Ottilie. She too, I say to myself, is also suffering in the same way at this same moment, and suffering more perhaps than I; and why cannot I bear it as well as she? These pains are good for me. I might almost say that they were welcome; for they serve to bring out before me with the greater vividness her patience and all her other graces. It is only when we suffer ourselves, that we feel really the true nature of all the high qualities which are required to bear suffering."

Mittler, finding his friend so far resigned, did not hesitate to communicate the message with which he had been sent. He brought it out piecemeal, however; in order of time, as the idea had itself arisen between the ladies, and had gradually ripened into a purpose. Edward scarcely made an objection. From the little which he said, it appeared as if he was willing to leave everything to them; the pain which he was suffering at the moment making him indifferent to all besides.

Scarcely, however, was he again alone, than he got up, and walked rapidly up and down the room; he forgot his pain, his attention now turning to what was external to himself. Mittler's story had stirred the embers of his love, and awakened his imagination in all its vividness. He saw Ottilie by herself, or as good as by herself, travelling on a road which was well known to him—in a hotel with every room of which he was familiar. He thought, he considered, or rather he neither thought nor considered; he only wished—he only desired. He would see her; he would speak to her. Why, or for what good end that was to come of it, he did not care to ask himself; but he made up his mind at once. He must do it.

He summoned his valet into his council, and through him he made himself acquainted with the day and hour when

Q

Ottilie was to set out. The morning broke. Without taking any person with him, Edward mounted his horse, and rode off to the place where she was to pass the night. He was there too soon. The hostess was overjoyed at the sight of him; she was under heavy obligations to him for a service which he had been able to do for her. Her son had been in the army, where he had conducted himself with remarkable gallantry. He had performed one particular action of which no one had been a witness but Edward; and the latter had spoken of it to the commander-in-chief in terms of such high praise, that notwithstanding the opposition of various ill-wishers, he had obtained a decoration for him. The mother, therefore, could never do enough for Edward. She got ready her best room for him, which indeed was her own wardrobe and store-room, with all possible speed. He informed her, however, that a young lady was coming to pass the night there, and he ordered an apartment for her at the back, at the end of the gallery. It sounded a mysterious sort of affair; but the hostess was ready to do anything to please her patron, who appeared so interested and so busy about it. And he, what were his sensations as he watched through the long, weary hours till evening? He examined the room round and round in which he was to see her; with all its strangeness and homeliness it seemed to him to be an abode for angels. He thought over and over what he had better do; whether he should take her by surprise, or whether he should prepare her for meeting him. At last the second course seemed the preferable one. He sat down and wrote a letter, which she was to read:

EDWARD TO OTTILIE.

" While you read this letter, my best beloved, I am close to you. Do not agitate yourself; do not be alarmed; you have nothing to fear from me. I will not force myself upon you. I will see you or not, as you yourself shall choose.

" Consider, oh! consider your condition and mine. How must I not thank you, that you have taken no decisive step! But the step which you have taken is significant enough. Do not persist in it. Here, as it were, at a parting of the ways, reflect once again. Can you be mine?—will you be mine? Oh, you will be showing mercy on us all if you will; and on me, infinite mercy.

"Let me see you again!—happily, joyfully see you once more! Let me make my request to you with my own lips; and do you give me your answer your own beautiful self, on my breast, Ottilie! where you have so often rested, and which belongs to you for ever!"

As he was writing, the feeling rushed over him that what he was longing for was coming—was close—would be there almost immediately. By that door she would come in; she would read that letter; she in her own person would stand there before him as she used to stand; she for whose appearance he had thirsted so long. Would she be the same as she was?—was her form, were her feelings changed? He still held the pen in his hand; he was going to write as he thought, when the carriage rolled into the court. With a few hurried strokes he added: " I hear you coming. For a moment, farewell!"

He folded the letter, and directed it. He had no time for sealing. He darted into the room through which there was a second outlet into the gallery, when the next moment he recollected that he had left his watch and seals lying on the table. She must not see these first. He ran back and brought them away with him. At the same instant he heard the hostess in the antechamber showing Ottilie the way to her apartments. He sprang to the bedroom door. It was shut. In his haste, as he had come back for his watch, he had forgotten to take out the key, which had fallen out, and lay the other side. The door had closed with a spring, and he could not open it. He pushed at it with all his might, but it would not yield. Oh, how gladly would he have been a spirit, to escape through its cracks! In vain. He hid his face against the panels. Ottilie entered, and the hostess, seeing him, retired. From Ottilie herself, too, he could not remain concealed for a moment. He turned towards her; and there stood the lovers once more, in such strange fashion, in one another's presence. She looked at him calmly and earnestly, without advancing or retiring. He made a movement to approach her, and she withdrew a few steps towards the table. He stepped back again. "Ottilie!" he cried aloud, "Ottilie! let me break this frightful silence! Are we shadows, that we stand thus gazing at each other? Only listen to me; listen to this at least. It is an accident that you find me here thus. There is a letter on the table, at your side there, which was to have prepared you. Read it, I implore you—read it—and then determine as you will !"

She looked down at the letter; and after thinking a few seconds, she took it up, opened it, and read it : she finished it without a change of expression ; and she laid it lightly down ; then joining the palms of her hands together, turning them upwards, and drawing them against her breast, she leant her body a little forward, and regarded Edward with such a look, that, eager as he was, he was compelled to renounce everything he wished or desired of her. Such an attitude cut him to the heart ; he could not bear it. It seemed exactly as if she would fall upon her knees before him, if he persisted. He hurried in despair out of the room, and leaving her alone, sent the hostess in to her.

He walked up and down the antechamber. Night had come on, and there was no sound in the room. At last the hostess came out and drew the key out of the lock. The good woman was embarrassed and agitated, not knowing what it would be proper for her to do. At last as she turned to go, she offered the key to Edward, who refused it ; and putting down the candle, she went away.

In misery and wretchedness, Edward flung himself down on the threshold of the door which divided him from Ottilie, moistening it with his tears as he lay. A more unhappy night had been seldom passed by two lovers in such close neighbourhood!

Day came at last. The coachman brought round the carriage, and the hostess unlocked the door and went in. Ottilie was asleep in her clothes ; she went back and beckoned to Edward with a significant smile. They both entered and stood before her as she lay ; but the sight was too much for Edward. He could not bear it. She was sleeping so quietly that the hostess did not like to disturb her, but sat down opposite her, waiting till she woke. At last Ottilie opened her beautiful eyes, and raised herself on her feet. She declined taking any breakfast, and then Edward went in again and stood before her. He entreated her to speak but one word to him ; to tell him what she desired. He would do it, be it what it would, he swore to her ; but she remained silent. He asked her once more, passionately and tenderly, whether she would be his. With downcast eyes, and with the deepest tenderness of manner she shook her head to a gentle *No.* He asked if she still desired to go to the school. Without any show of feeling she declined. Would she then go back to Charlotte? She inclined her head in token of assent, with a look of comfort and relief. He went to the window to give directions to the coachman, and when his back was turned she darted like lightning out of the room, and was down the stairs and in the carriage in an instant. The coachman drove back along the road which he had come the day before, and Edward followed at some distance on horseback.

CHAPTER XVII.

It was with the utmost surprise that Charlotte saw the carriage drive up with Ottilie, and Edward at the same moment ride into the court-yard of the castle. She ran down to the hall. Ottilie alighted, and approached her and Edward. Violently and eagerly she caught the hands of the wife and husband, pressed them together, and hurried off to her own room. Edward threw himself on Charlotte's neck and burst into tears. He could not give her any explanation; he besought her to have patience with him, and to go at once to see Ottilie. Charlotte followed her to her room, and she could not enter it without a shudder. It had been all cleared out. There was nothing to be seen but the empty walls, which stood there looking cheerless, vacant, and miserable. Everything had been carried away except the little box, which from an uncertainty what was to be done with it, had been left in the middle of the room. Ottilie was lying stretched upon the ground, her arm and head leaning across the cover. Charlotte bent anxiously over her, and asked what had happened; but she received no answer.

Her maid had come with restoratives. Charlotte left her with Ottilie, and herself hastened back to Edward. She found him in the saloon, but he could tell her nothing. He threw himself down before her; he bathed her hands with tears; he flew to his own room, and she was going to follow him.

thither, when she met his valet. From this man she gathered as much as he was able to tell. The rest she put together in her own thoughts as well as she could, and then at once set herself resolutely to do what the exigencies of the moment required. Ottilie's room was put to rights again as quickly as possible ; Edward found his, to the last paper, exactly as he had left it.

The three appeared again to fall into some sort of relation with one another. But Ottilie persevered in her silence, and Edward could do nothing except entreat his wife to exert a patience which seemed wanting to himself. Charlotte sent messengers to Mittler and to the Major. The first was absent from home and could not be found. The latter came. To him Edward poured out all his heart, confessing every most trifling circumstance to him, and thus Charlotte learnt fully what had passed ; what it had been which had produced such violent excitement, and how so strange an alteration of their mutual position had been brought about.

She spoke with the utmost tenderness to her husband. She had nothing to ask of him, except that for the present he would leave the poor girl to herself. Edward was not insensible to the worth, the affection, the strong sense of his wife ; but his passion absorbed him exclusively. Charlotte tried to cheer him with hopes. She promised that she herself would make no difficulties about the separation ; but it had small effect with him. He was so much shaken that hope and faith alternately forsook him. A species of insanity appeared to have taken possession of him. He urged Charlotte to promise to give her hand to the Major. To satisfy him and to humour him, she did what he required. She engaged to become herself the wife of the Major, in the event of Ottilie consenting to the marriage with Edward ; with this express condition, however, that for the present the two gentlemen should go abroad together. The Major had a foreign appointment from the court, and it was settled that Edward should accompany him. They arranged it all together, and in doing so found a sort of comfort for themselves in the sense that at least something was being done.

In the meantime they had to remark that Ottilie took scarcely anything to eat or drink. She still persisted in refusing to speak. They at first used to talk to her, but it appeared to distress her, and they left it off. We are not, universally at least, so weak as to persist in torturing people for their good. Charlotte thought over what could possibly be done. At last she fancied it might be well to ask the Assistant of the school to come to them. He had much influence with Ottilie, and had been writing with much anxiety to inquire the cause of her not having arrived at the time he had been expecting her; but as yet she had not sent him any answer.

In order not to take Ottilie by surprise, they spoke of their intention of sending this invitation in her presence. It did not seem to please her; she thought for some little time; at last she appeared to have formed some resolution. She retired to her own room, and before the evening sent the following letter to the assembled party:

OTTILIE TO HER FRIENDS.

"Why need I express in words, my dear friends, what is in itself so plain? I have stepped out of my course, and I cannot recover it again. A malignant spirit which has gained power over me seems to hinder me from without, even if within I could again become at peace with myself.

"My purpose was entirely firm to renounce Edward, and to separate myself from him for ever. I had hoped that we might never meet again; it has turned out otherwise. Against his own will he stood before me. Too literally, perhaps, I have observed my promise never to admit him into conversation with me. My conscience and the feelings of the moment kept me silent towards him at the time, and now I have nothing more to say. I have taken upon myself, under the accidental impulse of the moment, a difficult vow, which if it had been formed deliberately, might perhaps be painful and distressing. Let me now persist in the observance of it so long as my heart shall enjoin it to me. Do not call in any one to mediate; do not insist upon my speaking; do not urge me to eat or to drink more than I absolutely must. Bear with me and let me alone, and so help me on through the time; I am young, and youth has many unexpected means of restoring itself. Endure my presence among you; cheer me with your love; make me wiser and better with what you say to one another: but leave me to my own inward self."

The two friends had made all preparation for their journey but their departure was still delayed by the formalities of the foreign appointment of the Major, a delay most welcome to Edward. Ottilie's letter had roused all his eagerness again; he had gathered hope and comfort from her words, and now felt himself encouraged and justified in remaining and waiting. He declared, therefore, that he would not go; it would be folly, indeed, he cried, of his own accord, to throw away, by over precipitateness, what was most valuable and most necessary to him, when although there was a danger of losing it, there was nevertheless a chance that it might be preserved. " What is the right name of conduct such as that?" he said. "It is only that we desire to show that we are able to will and to choose. I myself, under the influences of the same ridiculous folly, have torn myself away, days before there was any necessity for it, from my friends, merely that I might not be forced to go by the definite expiration of my term. This time I will stay: what reason is there for my going; is she not already removed far enough from me? I am not likely now to catch her hand or press her to my heart; I could not even think of it without a shudder. She has not separated herself from me; she has raised herself far above me."

And so he remained as he desired, as he was obliged; but he was never easy except when he found himself with Ottilie. She, too, had the same feeling with him; she could not tear herself away from the same happy necessity. On all sides they exerted an indescribable, almost magical power of attraction over one another. Living, as they were, under one roof, without even so much as thinking of each other, although they might be occupied with other things, or diverted this way or that way by the other members of the party, they always drew together. If they were in the same room, in a short time they were sure to be either standing or sitting near each other; they were only easy when as close together as they could be, but they were then completely easy. To be near was enough; there was no need for them either to look or to speak: they did not seek to touch one another, or make sign or gesture, but merely to be together. Then there were not two persons, there was but one person in unconscious and perfect content, at peace with itself and with the world. So it was that if either of them had been imprisoned at the further end of the house, the other would by degrees, without intending it, have moved towards its fellow till it found it; life to them was a riddle, the solution of which they could only find in union.

Ottilie was throughout so cheerful and quiet that they were able to feel perfectly easy about her; she was seldom absent from the society of her friends: all that she had desired was that she might be allowed to eat alone, with no one to attend upon her but Nanny.

What habitually befalls any person repeats itself more often than one is apt to suppose, because his own nature gives the immediate occasion for it. Character, individuality, inclination, tendency, locality, circumstance, and habits, form together a whole, in which every man moves as in an atmosphere, and where only he feels himself at ease in his proper element.

And so we find men, of whose changeableness so many complaints are made, after many years, to our surprise, unchanged, and in all their infinite tendencies, outward and inward, unchangeable.

Thus in the daily life of our friends, almost everything glided on again in its old smooth track. Ottilie still displayed by many silent attentions her obliging nature, and the others like her continued each themselves; and then the domestic circle exhibited an image of their former life, so like it, that they might be pardoned if at times they dreamt that it might all be again as it was.

The autumn days, which were of the same length with those old spring days, brought the party back into the house out of the air about the same hour. The gay fruits and flowers which belonged to the season, might have made them fancy it was now the autumn of that first spring, and the interval dropped out and forgotten; for the flowers which now were blowing, were the same as those which then they had sown, and the fruits which were now ripening on the trees, were those which at that time they had seen in blossom.

The Major went backwards and forwards, and Mittler came frequently. The evenings were generally spent in exactly the same way. Edward usually read aloud, with more life and feeling than before; much better, and even it may be said with more cheerfulness. It appeared as if he was endeavouring,

by light-heartedness as much as by devotion, to quicken
Ottilie's torpor into life, and dissolve her silence.   He seated
himself in the same position as he used to do, that she might
look over his book ; he was uneasy and distracted unless she
was doing so, unless he was sure that she was following his
words with her eyes.

Every trace had vanished of the unpleasant, ungracious
feelings of the intervening time.   No one had any secret
complaint against another; there were no cross purposes, no
bitterness.   The Major accompanied Charlotte's playing with
his violin, and Edward's flute sounded again, as formerly, in
harmony with Ottilie's piano.   Thus they were now approaching Edward's birthday, which the year before they had
missed celebrating.   This time they were to keep it without any outward festivities, in quiet enjoyment among themselves.   They had so settled it together, half expressly, half
from a tacit agreement.   As they approached nearer to this
epoch, however, an anxiety about it, which had hitherto
been more felt than observed, became more noticeable in
Ottilie's manner.   She was to be seen often in the garden
examining the flowers: she had signified to the gardener
that he was to save as many as he could of every sort, and
she had been especially occupied with the asters, which this
year were blowing in immense profusion.

CHAPTER XVIII.

THE most remarkable feature, however, which was observed
about Ottilie was that, for the first time, she had now un-
packed the box, and had selected a variety of things out of
it, which she had cut up, and which were intended evidently
to make one complete suit for her.   The rest, with Nanny's
assistance, she had endeavoured to replace again, and she
had been hardly able to get it done, the space being over full,
although a portion had been taken out.   The covetous little
Nanny could never satisfy herself with looking at all the
pretty things, especially as she found provision made there for

every article of dress which could be wanted, even the smallest. Numbers of shoes and stockings, garters with devices on them, gloves, and various other things were left, and she begged Ottilie just to give her one or two of them. Ottilie refused to do that, but opened a drawer in her wardrobe, and told the girl to take what she liked. The latter hastily and awkwardly dashed in her hand and seized what she could, running off at once with her booty, to show it off and display her good fortune among the rest of the servants.

At last Ottilie succeeded in packing everything carefully into its place. She then opened a secret compartment, which was contrived in the lid, where she kept a number of notes and letters from Edward, many dried flowers, the mementos of their early walks together, a lock of his hair, and various other little matters. She now added one more to them, her father's portrait, and then locked it all up, and hung the delicate key by a gold chain about her neck, against her heart.

In the mean time, her friends had now in their hearts begun to entertain the best hopes for her. Charlotte was convinced that she would one day begin to speak again. She had latterly seen signs about her which implied that she was engaged in secret about something; a look of cheerful self-satisfaction, a smile like that which hangs about the face of persons who have something pleasant and delightful, which they are keeping concealed from those whom they love. No one knew that she spent many hours in extreme exhaustion, and that only at rare intervals, when she appeared in public through the power of her will, she was able to rouse herself.

Mittler had latterly been a frequent visitor, and when he came he staid longer than he usually did at other times. This strong-willed, resolute person was only too well aware that there is a certain moment in which alone it will answer to smite the iron. Ottilie's silence and reserve he interpreted according to his own wishes; no steps had as yet been taken towards a separation of the husband and wife. He hoped to be able to determine the fortunes of the poor girl in some not undesirable way. He listened, he allowed himself to seem convinced; he was discreet and unobtrusive, and conducted himself in his own way with sufficient prudence. There was but one occasion on which he uniformly forgot himself—when he found an opportunity for giving his opinion upon subjects to which he attached a great importance. He lived much within himself, and when he was with others, his only relation to them generally was in active employment on their behalf; but if once, when among friends, his tongue broke fairly loose, as on more than one occasion we have already seen, he rolled out his words in utter recklessness, whether they wounded or whether they pleased, whether they did evil or whether they did good.

The evening before the birthday, the Major and Charlotte were sitting together expecting Edward, who had gone out for a ride; Mittler was walking up and down the saloon; Ottilie was in her own room, laying out the dress which she was to wear on the morrow, and making signs to her maid about a number of things, which the girl, who perfectly understood her silent language, arranged as she was ordered.

Mittler had fallen exactly on his favourite subject. One of the points on which he used most to insist was, that in the education of children, as well as in the conduct of nations, there was nothing more worthless and barbarous than laws and commandments forbidding this and that action. " Man is naturally active," he said, "wherever he is ; and if you know how to tell him what to do, he will do it immediately, and keep straight in the direction in which you set him. I myself, in my own circle, am far better pleased to endure faults and mistakes, till I know what the opposite virtue is that I am to enjoin, than to be rid of the faults and to have nothing good to put in their place. A man is really glad to do what is right and sensible, if he only knows how to get at it. It is no such great matter with him ; he does it because he must have something to do, and he thinks no more about it afterwards than he does of the silliest freaks which he engaged in out of the purest idleness. I cannot tell you how it annoys me to hear people going over and over those Ten Commandments in teaching children. The fifth is a thoroughly beautiful, rational, preceptive precept. ' Thou shalt honour thy father and thy mother.' If the children will inscribe that well upon their hearts, they have the whole day before them to put it in practice. But the sixth now ? What can we say to that ? ' Thou shalt do no murder;' as if

any man ever felt the slightest general inclination to strike another man dead. Men will hate sometimes; they will fly into passions and forget themselves; and as a consequence of this or other feelings, it may easily come now and then to a murder; but what a barbarous precaution it is to tell children that they are not to kill or murder! If the commandment ran, ' Have a regard for the life of another—put away whatever can do him hurt—save him though with peril to yourself—if you injure him, consider that you are injuring yourself;'—that is the form which should be in use among educated, reasonable people. And in our Catechism teaching we have only an awkward clumsy way of sliding into it, through a ' what do you mean by that?'

" And as for the seventh; that is utterly detestable. What! to stimulate the precocious curiosity of children to pry into dangerous mysteries; to obtrude violently upon their imaginations ideas and notions which beyond all things you should wish to keep from them! It were far better if such actions as that commandment speaks of were dealt with arbitrarily by some secret tribunal, than prated openly of before church and congregation——"

At this moment Ottilie entered the room.

" ' Thou shalt not commit adultery,' "—Mittler went on—" How coarse! how brutal! What a different sound it has, if you let it run, ' Thou shalt hold in reverence the bond of marriage. When thou seest a husband and a wife between whom there is true love, thou shalt rejoice in it, and their happiness shall gladden thee like the cheerful light of a beautiful day. If there arise anything to make division between them, thou shalt use thy best endeavour to clear it away. Thou shalt labour to pacify them, and to soothe them; to show each of them the excellencies of the other. Thou shalt not think of thyself, but purely and disinterestedly thou shalt seek to further the well-being of others, and make them feel what a happiness is that which arises out of all duty done; and especially out of that duty which holds man and wife indissolubly bound together.' "

Charlotte felt as if she was sitting on hot coals. The situation was the more distressing, as she was convinced that Mittler was not thinking the least where he was or what he was saying; and before she was able to interrupt him, she saw Ottilie, after changing colour painfully for a few seconds, rise and leave the room.

Charlotte constrained herself to seem unembarrassed: " You will leave us the eighth commandment," she said, with a faint smile.

" All the rest," replied Mittler, " if I may only insist first on the foundation of the whole of them."

At this moment Nanny rushed in, screaming and crying: " She is dying; the young lady is dying; come to her, come."

Ottilie had found her way back with extreme difficulty to her own room. The beautiful things which she was to wear the next day were laid out on a number of chairs; and the girl, who had been running from one to the other, staring at them and admiring them, called out in her ecstacy, " Look, dearest madam, only look! There is a bridal dress worthy of you."

Ottilie heard the word, and sank upon the sofa. Nanny saw her mistress turn pale, fall back, and faint. She ran for Charlotte, who came. The medical friend was on the spot in a moment. He thought it was nothing but exhaustion. He ordered some strong soup to be brought. Ottilie refused it with an expression of loathing: it almost threw her into convulsions, when they put the cup to her lips. A light seemed to break on the physician: he asked hastily and anxiously what Ottilie had taken that day. The little girl hesitated. He repeated his question, and she then acknowledged that Ottilie had taken nothing.

There was a nervousness of manner about Nanny which made him suspicious. He carried her with him into the adjoining room; Charlotte followed; and the girl threw herself on her knees, and confessed that for a long time past Ottilie had taken as good as nothing; at her mistress's urgent request, she had herself eaten the food which had been brought for her; she had said nothing about it, because Ottilie had by signs alternately begged her not to tell any one, and threatened her if she did; and, as she innocently added, " because it was so nice."

The Major and Mittler now came up as well. They found Charlotte busy with the physician. The pale, beautiful girl was sitting, apparently conscious, in the corner of the sofa.

They had begged her to lie down; she had declined to do this; but she made signs to have her box brought, and resting her feet upon it, placed herself in an easy, half recumbent position. She seemed to be wishing to take leave; and by her gestures, was expressing to all about her the tenderest affection, love, gratitude, entreaties for forgiveness, and the most heartfelt farewell.

Edward, on alighting from his horse, was informed of what had happened; he rushed to the room; threw himself down at her side; and seizing her hand, deluged it with silent tears. In this position he remained a long time. At last he called out: "And am I never more to hear your voice? Will you not turn back toward life, to give me one single word? Well, then, very well. I will follow you yonder, and there we will speak in another language."

She pressed his hand with all the strength she had; she gazed at him with a glance full of life and full of love; and drawing a long breath, and for a little while moving her lips inarticulately, with a tender effort of affection she called out, "Promise me to live;" and then fell back immediately.

" I promise, I promise!" he cried to her; but he cried only after her; she was already gone.

After a miserable night, the care of providing for the loved remains fell upon Charlotte. The Major and Mittler assisted her. Edward's condition was utterly pitiable. His first thought, when he was in any degree recovered from his despair, and able to collect himself, was, that Ottilie should not be carried out of the castle; she should be kept there, and attended upon as if she were alive: for she was not dead; it was impossible that she should be dead. They did what he desired; at least, so far as that they did not do what he had forbidden. He did not ask to see her.

There was now a second alarm, and a further cause for anxiety. Nanny, who had been spoken to sharply by the physician, had been compelled by threats to confess, and after her confession had been overwhelmed with reproaches, had now disappeared. After a long search she was found; but she appeared to be out of her mind. Her parents took her home; but the gentlest treatment had no effect upon her, and she had to be locked up for fear she should run away again.

They succeeded by degrees in recovering Edward from the extreme agony of despair; but only to make him more really wretched. He now saw clearly, he could not doubt now, that the happiness of his life was gone from him for ever. It was suggested to him that if Ottilie was placed in the chapel, she would still remain among the living, and it would be a calm, quiet, peaceful home for her. There was much difficulty in obtaining his consent; he would only give it under condition that she should be taken there in an open coffin; that the vault in which she was laid, if covered at all, should be only covered with glass, and a lamp should be kept always burning there. It was arranged that this should be done, and then he seemed resigned.

They clothed the delicate body in the festal dress, which she had herself prepared. A garland of asters was wreathed about her head, which shone sadly there like melancholy stars. To decorate the bier and the church and chapel, the gardens were robbed of their beauty; they lay desolate, as if a premature winter had blighted all their loveliness. In the earliest morning she was borne in an open coffin out of the castle, and the heavenly features were once more reddened with the rising sun. The mourners crowded about her as she was being taken along. None would go before; none would follow; every one would be where she was, every one would enjoy her presence for the last time. Men and women, and little boys, there was not one unmoved; least of all to be consoled were the girls, who felt most immediately what they had lost.

Nanny was not present; it had been thought better not to allow it, and they had kept secret from her the day and the hour of the funeral. She was at her parents' house, closely watched, in a room looking towards the garden. But when she heard the bells tolling, she knew too well what they meant; and her attendant having left her out of curiosity to see the funeral, she escaped out of the window into a passage, and from thence, finding all the doors locked, into an upper open loft. At this moment the funeral was passing through the village, which had been all freshly strewed with leaves. Nanny saw her mistress plainly close below her, more plainly, more entirely, than any one in the procession underneath; she appeared to be lifted above the earth, borne as it were on clouds or waves, and the girl fancied she was making signs to her; her senses swam, she tottered, swayed herself for a moment on the edge, and fell to the ground. The crowd fell asunder on all sides with a cry of horror. In the tumult and confusion, the bearers were obliged to set down the coffin; the girl lay close by it: it seemed as if every limb was broken. They lifted her up, and by accident or providentially she was allowed to lean over the body; she appeared, indeed, to be endeavouring with what remained to her of life to reach her beloved mistress. Scarcely, however, had the loosely hanging limbs touched Ottilie's robe, and the powerless finger rested on the folded hands, than the girl started up, and first raising her arms and eyes towards heaven, flung herself down upon her knees before the coffin, and gazed with passionate devotion at her mistress.

At last she sprang, as if inspired, from off the ground, and cried with a voice of ecstasy: " Yes, she has forgiven me; what no man, what I myself could never have forgiven. God forgives me through her look, her motion, her lips. Now she is lying again so still and quiet, but you saw how she raised herself up, and unfolded her hands and blessed me, and how kindly she looked at me. You all heard, you can witness that she said to me: ' You are forgiven.' I am not a murderess any more. She has forgiven me. God has forgiven me, and no one may now say anything more against me.' "

The people stood crowding around her. They were amazed; they listened and looked this way and that, and no one knew what should next be done. " Bear her on to her rest," said the girl. " She has done her part; she has suffered, and cannot now remain any more among us." The bier moved on, Nanny now following it; and thus they reached the church and the chapel.

So now stood the coffin of Ottilie, with the child's coffin at her head, and her box at her feet, inclosed in a resting-place of massive oak. A woman had been provided to watch the body for the first part of the time, as it lay there so beautifully beneath its glass covering. But Nanny would not permit this duty to be taken from herself. She would remain alone without a companion, and attend to the lamp which was now kindled for the first time; and she begged to be allowed to do it with so much eagerness and perseverance, that they let her have her way, to prevent any greater evil that might ensue.

But she did not long remain alone. As night was falling, and the hanging lamp began to exercise its full right and shed abroad a larger lustre, the door opened and the Architect entered the chapel. The chastely ornamented walls in the mild light looked more strange, more awful, more antique, than he was prepared to see them. Nanny was sitting on one side of the coffin. She recognized him immediately; but she pointed in silence to the pale form of her mistress. And there stood he on the other side, in the vigour of youth and of grace, with his arms drooping, and his hands clasped piteously together, motionless, with head and eye inclined over the inanimate body.

Once already he had stood thus before in the Belisarius; he had now involuntarily fallen into the same attitude. And this time how naturally! Here, too, was something of inestimable worth thrown down from its high estate. *There* were courage, prudence, power, rank, and wealth in one single man, lost irrevocably; *there* were qualities which, in decisive moments, had been of indispensable service to the nation and the prince; but which, when the moment was passed, were no more valued, but flung aside and neglected, and cared for no longer. And *here* were many other silent virtues, which had been summoned but a little time before by nature out of the depths of her treasures, and now swept rapidly away again by her careless hand—rare, sweet, lovely virtues, whose peaceful workings the thirsty world had welcomed, while it had them, with gladness and joy; and now was sorrowing for them in unavailing desire.

Both the youth and the girl were silent for a long time. But when she saw the tears streaming fast down his cheeks, and he appeared to be sinking under the burden of his sorrow, she spoke to him with so much truthfulness and power, with such kindness and such confidence, that, astonished at the flow of her words, he was able to recover himself, and he saw his beautiful friend floating before him in the new life of a higher world. His tears ceased flowing; his sorrow grew lighter: on his knees he took leave of Ottilie, and with a warm pressure of the hand of Nanny, he rode away from the spot into the night without having seen a single other person.

The surgeon had, without the girl being aware of it, remained all night in the church; and when he went in the morning to see her, he found her cheerful and tranquil. He was prepared for wild aberrations. He thought that she would be sure to speak to him of conversations which she had held in the night with Ottilie, and of other such apparitions. But she was natural, quiet, and perfectly self-possessed. She remembered accurately what had happened in her previous life; she could describe the circumstances of it with the greatest exactness, and never in anything which she said stepped out of the course of what was real and natural, except in her account of what had passed with the body, which she delighted to repeat again and again, how Ottilie had raised herself up, had blessed her, had forgiven her, and thereby set her at rest for ever.

Ottilie remained so long in her beautiful state, which more resembled sleep than death, that a number of persons were attracted there to look at her. The neighbours and the villagers wished to see her again, and every one desired to hear Nanny's incredible story from her own mouth. Many laughed at it, most doubted, and some few were found who were able to believe.

Difficulties, for which no real satisfaction is attainable, compel us to faith. Before the eyes of all the world, Nanny's limbs had been broken, and by touching the sacred body she had been restored to strength again. Why should not others find similar good fortune? Delicate mothers first privately brought their children who were suffering from obstinate disorders, and they believed that they could trace an immediate improvement. The confidence of the people increased, and at last there was no one so old or so weak as not to have come to seek fresh life and health and strength at this place, The concourse became so great, that they were obliged, except at the hours of divine service, to keep the church and chapel closed.

Edward did not venture to look at her again; he lived on mechanically; he seemed to have no tears left, and to be incapable of any further suffering; his power of taking interest in what was going on diminished every day; his appetite gradually failed. The only refreshment which did him any good was what he drank out of the glass, which to him, indeed, had been but an untrue prophet. He continued to gaze at the intertwining initials, and the earnest cheerfulness of his expression seemed to signify that he still hoped to be united with her at last. And as every little circumstance combines to favour the fortunate, and every accident contributes to elate him; so do the most trifling occurrences love to unite to crush and overwhelm the unhappy. One day as Edward raised the beloved glass to his lips, he put it down and thrust it from him with a shudder. It was the same and not the same. He missed a little private mark upon it. The valet was questioned, and had to confess that the real glass had not long since been broken, and that one like it belonging to the same set had been substituted in its place.

Edward could not be angry. His destiny had spoken out with sufficient clearness in the fact, and how should he be affected by the shadow? and yet it touched him deeply. He seemed now to dislike drinking, and thenceforward purposely to abstain from food and from speaking.

But from time to time a sort of restlessness came over him; he would desire to eat and drink something, and would begin again to speak. "Ah!" he said, one day to the Major, who now seldom left his side, "how unhappy I am that all my efforts are but imitations ever, and false and fruitless. What was blessedness to her, is pain to me; and yet for the sake of this blessedness I am forced to take this pain upon myself. I must go after her; follow her by the same road. But my nature and my promise hold me back. It is a terrible difficulty, indeed, to imitate the inimitable. I feel clearly, my dear friend, that genius is required for everything; for martyrdom as well as the rest."

What shall we say of the endeavours which in this hopeless condition were made for him? his wife, his friends, his physician, incessantly laboured to do something for him. But it was all in vain : at last they found him dead. Mittler was the first to make the melancholy discovery; he called the physician, and examined closely, with his usual presence of mind, the circumstances under which he had been found. Charlotte rushed in to them ; she was afraid that he had committed suicide, and accused herself and accused others of unpardonable carelessness. But the physician on natural, and Mittler on moral grounds, were soon able to satisfy her of the contrary. It was quite clear that Edward's end had taken him by surprise. In a quiet moment he had taken out of his pocket-book and out of a casket everything which remained to him as memorials of Ottilie, and had spread them out before him ; a lock of hair; flowers which had been gathered in some happy hour, and every letter which she had written to him from the first, which his wife had ominously happened to give him. It was impossible that he would intentionally have exposed these to the danger of being seen, by the first person who might happen to discover him.

But so lay the heart, which but a short time before had been so swift and eager, at rest now, where it could never be disturbed ; and falling asleep, as he did, with his thoughts on one so saintly, he might well be called blessed. Charlotte gave him his place at Ottilie's side, and arranged that thenceforth no other person should be placed with them in the same vault.

In order to secure this, she made it a condition under which she settled considerable sums of money on the church and the school.

So lie the lovers, sleeping side by side. Peace hovers above their resting-place. Fair angel faces gaze down upon them from the vaulted ceiling, and what a happy moment that will be when one day they wake again together !

THE SORROWS OF YOUNG WERTHER.

———◆———

I HAVE carefully collected whatever I have been able to learn of the story of poor Werther, and here present it to you, knowing that you will thank me for it. To his spirit and character you cannot refuse your admiration and love; to his fate you will not deny your tears.

And thou, good soul, who sufferest the same distress as he once endured, draw comfort from his sorrows; and let this little book be thy friend, if from fortune or thine own fault thou canst find no dearer companion.

———

BOOK I.

May 4th.

How happy am I to be away! My dear friend, what a thing is the heart of man! To leave you, from whom I have been inseparable, whom I love so dearly, and yet to feel happy! I know you will forgive me. Have not other attachments been specially appointed by fate to torment a head like mine? Poor Leonora! and yet I was not to blame. Was it my fault that whilst the peculiar charms of her sister afforded me an agreeable entertainment, a passion for me was engendered in her feeble heart? And yet am I wholly blameless? Did I not encourage her emotions? Did I not feel charmed at those truly genuine expressions of nature, which, though but little mirthful in reality, so often amused us? Did I not——, but oh, what is man, that he dares so to accuse himself? My dear friend, I promise you I will improve; I will no longer, as has ever been my habit, continue to ruminate on every pretty vexation which fortune may dispense; I will enjoy the present, and the past shall be for me the past. You are doubtless right, my best of friends, there would be far less suffering amongst mankind, if men —and God knows why they are so fashioned—did not employ their imaginations so assiduously in recalling the memory of past sorrow, instead of bearing their present lot with equanimity.

Be kind enough to inform my mother that I shall attend to her business to the best of my ability, and shall give her the earliest information about it. I have seen my aunt, and find her very far from the disagreeable person our friends allege her to be. She is a lively, cheerful woman, with the best of hearts. I explained to her my mother's wrongs with regard to that part of her portion which has been withheld from her. She told me the motives and reasons of her own con-duct, and the terms upon which she is willing to give up the whole, and do more than we have asked. In short, I cannot write further upon this subject at present, only assure my mother that all will go on well. And I have again observed, my dear friend, in this trifling affair, that misunderstandings and neglect occasion more mischief in the world than even malice and wickedness. At all events, the two latter are of less frequent occurrence.

In other respects, I am very happy here. Solitude in this terrestrial paradise is a genial balsam to my mind, and the young spring cheers with its bounteous promises my often-times misgiving heart. Every tree, every bush, is full of flowers, and one might wish himself transformed into a but-terfly, to float about in this ocean of perfume and find his whole existence therein.

The town itself is disagreeable, but then, all around, you find an inexpressible beauty of nature. This induced the late Count M—— to lay out a garden on one of the sloping hills which here intersect each other with the most charming variety, and form the most lovely valleys. The garden is simple, and it is easy to perceive, even upon your first en-trance, that the plan was not designed by a scientific gar-dener, but by a sensitive heart, who wished here to study its own enjoyment. Many a tear have I already shed to the memory of its departed master, in a summer-house, now reduced to ruins, which was his favourite resort, and is now mine. I shall soon be master of the place. The gardener has become attached to me within the last few days, and he will be no loser thereby.

May 10*th.*

A wonderful serenity has taken possession of my entire soul, like these sweet mornings of Spring which I enjoy with my whole heart. I am alone, and feel the charm of existence in this spot, which was created for the bliss of souls like mine. I am so happy, my dear friend, so absorbed in the exquisite sense of mere tranquil existence, that I neglect my talents. I should be incapable of drawing a single stroke at the present moment, and yet I feel that I never was a greater artist than now. When the lovely valley teems with vapour around me, and the meridian sun strikes the upper surface of the impenetrable foliage of my trees, and but a few stray gleams steal into the inner sanctuary, than I throw myself down in the tall grass by the trickling stream, and as I lie close to the earth, a thousand unknown plants discover themselves to me. When I hear the buzz of the little world among the stalks, and grow familiar with the countless indescribable forms of the insects and flies, then I feel the presence of the Almighty, who formed us in His own image, and the breath of that universal love which bears and sustains us, as it floats round us in an eternity of bliss; and then, my friend, when darkness overspreads my eyes, and heaven and earth seem to dwell in my soul, and absorb its power, like the idea of a beloved mistress, then I often long and think: O! that you could describe these conceptions, that you could impress upon paper all that lives so full and warm within you, that it might be the mirror of your soul, as your soul is the mirror of the infinite God! O, my friend—but it is too much for my strength—I sink under the weight of the grandeur of these visions.

May 12*th.*

I know not whether some deceiving spirits haunt this spot, or whether it be the warm celestial fancy in my own heart,

which makes everything around me seem like Paradise.   In
front of the house is a fountain—a fountain to which I am
bound by a charm like Melusina and her sisters.   Descending
a gentle slope, you come to an arch, where, some twenty
steps lower down, water of the clearest crystal gushes from the
marble rock.   The narrow wall which incloses it above, the
tall trees which encircle the spot, and the coolness of the
place itself,—everything imparts a pleasant but sublime impression.   Not a day passes that I do not spend an hour
there.   The young maidens come from the town to fetch
water,—innocent and necessary employment, and formerly
the occupation of the daughters of kings.   As I take my
rest there, the idea of the old patriarchal life is awakened
around me.   I see them, our old ancestors, how they formed
their friendships and contracted alliances at the fountain-side,
and I feel how fountains and streams were guarded by
beneficent spirits.   He who is a stranger to these sensations
has never really enjoyed cool repose at the side of a fountain
after the fatigue of a weary summer day.

May 25th.

You ask if you shall send me books.   My dear friend, I
beseech you, for the love of God, relieve me from such a yoke.
I need no more to be guided, agitated, heated.   My heart
ferments sufficiently of itself.   I want strains to lull me, and
I find them to perfection in my Homer.   Often do I strive
to allay the burning fever of my blood, and you have never
witnessed anything so unsteady, so uncertain, as my heart.
But need I confess this to you, my dear friend, who have so
often endured the anguish of witnessing my sudden tran-
sitions from sorrow to immoderate joy, and from sweet
melancholy to violent passions?   I treat my poor heart like a
sick child, and gratify its every fancy.   Do not mention this
again; there are people who would censure me for it.

May 13th.

The common people of the place know me already, and
love me, particularly the children.   At first when I associated
with them, and inquired in a friendly tone about their various
trifles, some fancied that I wished to ridicule them, and turned

from me in exceeding ill-humour. I did not allow that circumstance to grieve me; I only felt most keenly what I have often before observed. Persons of some pretension to rank keep themselves coldly aloof from the common people, as though they feared to lose their importance by the contact, whilst wanton idlers and poor pretenders to understanding affect to descend to their level only to make the poor people feel their impertinence more keenly.

I know very well that we are not and cannot be all equal; but in my opinion he who avoids the common people in order to command their respect, is as culpable as a coward who hides himself from his enemy because he fears defeat.

The other day I went to the fountain, and found a young servant-girl, who had set her pitcher on the lowest step, and looked round to see if one of her companions was approaching to place it on her head. I ran down and looked at her. "Shall I help you, pretty lass?" said I. She blushed deeply. "O, sir!" she exclaimed. "No ceremony!" I replied. She placed herself properly, and I helped her. She thanked me, and went up the steps.

May 17th.

I have made all sorts of acquaintance, but as yet have found no society. I know not what attraction I possess for the people, so many of them like me, and attach themselves to me, and then I feel sorry when our road together only goes a short distance. If you inquire what the people are like here, I must answer, "The same as everywhere!" The human race is but a monotonous affair. Most of them labour the greater part of their time for mere subsistence, and the small portion of freedom which remains unemployed so troubles them that they use every exertion to get rid of it. O, the destiny of man!

But they are a right good sort of people! If I occasionally forget myself, and take part in the innocent pleasures which are not yet forbidden to the peasantry, and enjoy myself, for instance, with genuine freedom and sincerity, round a well-covered table, or arrange an excursion or dance opportunely, and so forth, all this produces a good effect upon my disposition; only I must forget that so many other qualities lie dormant within me, which moulder uselessly, and which I am obliged to keep carefully concealed. Ah! this thought affects my spirits fearfully. And yet to be misunderstood is the fate of us all.

Alas, that the friend of my youth is gone! Alas, that I ever knew her! I might say to myself, "You are a dreamer to seek what is not to be found here below." But she has been mine. I have possessed that heart, that noble soul, in whose presence I seemed to be more than I really was, because I was all that I could be. Good Heaven! did a single power of my soul remain then unexercised? In her presence could I not display the entire of that mysterious feeling with which my heart embraces nature? Was not our intercourse a perpetual web of the finest emotions, of the keenest wit, whose varieties, even in their very eccentricity, bore the stamp of genius? Alas! the few years by which she was my senior, brought her to the grave before me. Never can I forget her strong sense or her heavenly patience.

A few days ago I met a certain young V——, a frank open fellow, with a most happy expression of face. He has just left the University. He does not fancy himself overwise, but believes he knows more than other people. He has worked hard, as I can perceive from many circumstances, and, in short, possesses a large stock of information. When he heard that I drew a good deal, and could read Greek, (two wonderful things for this part of the country,) he came to see me, and displayed his whole store of learning, from Batteaux to Wood, from De Piles to Winkelmann: he assured me had read through the first part of Sultzer's theory, and also possessed a manuscript of Heyne, on the study of the antique. I allowed it all to pass.

I have become acquainted also with a very worthy person, the district judge, a frank and open-hearted man. I am told it is a most delightful thing to see him in the midst of his children, of whom he has nine. His eldest daughter is much spoken of. He has invited me to go and see him, and I intend to do so the first opportunity. He lives at one of the royal hunting-lodges, an hour and a half's walk from hence, which he obtained leave to inhabit after the loss of his wife, as his residence in town and at the court was so painful to him.

A few other originals, of a questionable sort, have come in my way, who are in all respects undesirable, and most intolerable in their demonstrations of friendship. Good bye. This letter will please you: it is quite a history.

May 22nd.

That the life of man is but a dream is the opinion of many, and this feeling pursues me everywhere. When I consider the narrow limits within which our active and enquiring faculties are confined,—when I see how all our energies are wasted in providing for mere necessities, which again have no further end than to prolong a wretched existence,—and then that all our satisfaction upon certain subjects of investigation ends in nothing better than a passive resignation, whilst we amuse ourselves with painting our prison-walls with bright figures and brilliant landscapes,—when I consider all this, Wilhelm, I am silent. I examine my own being, and find there a world, but a world rather of imagination and dim desires, than of distinctness and living power. Then everything swims before my senses; I smile and dream my way back into existence.

All learned professors and doctors are agreed, that children do not comprehend the cause of their desires; but that grown people should wander about this earth like children, without knowing whence they come or whither they go, influenced as little by fixed motives, but guided like them by biscuits, sugar-plums, and chastisements,—this is what nobody is willing to acknowledge, and yet I think it can be made palpable.

I know what you will say in reply, and I am ready to admit, that the happiest are those who, like children, amuse themselves with their playthings, dress and undress their dolls, and attentively watch the cupboard where mamma has locked her sweet things, and when at last they get a delicious morsel, eat it greedily and cry for more. These are certainly happy beings; but others also are objects of envy, who dignify their paltry employments, and sometimes even their passions, with pompous titles, representing them to mankind as achievements of a superior order, accomplished for their welfare and glory. But the man who humbly acknowledges the vanity of all this, who observes with what pleasure the thriving citizen converts his little garden into a paradise, and how patiently even the poor man pursues his weary way under his burden, and how all wish equally to behold the light of the sun a little longer;—yes, such a man is at peace, and creates his own world within himself; and he is also happy, because he is a man. And then, however limited his sphere, he still preserves in his bosom the sweet feeling of liberty, and knows that when he will he can burst his prison.

May 26th.

You know of old my ways of finding amusement; how I select a little cottage in some sequestered spot, and there put up with every inconvenience. I have just discovered such a spot here, which possesses peculiar charms for me.

About a league from the town is a place called Walheim.* It is delightfully situated on the side of a hill, and by proceeding along one of the footpaths which lead out of the village, you can have a view of the whole valley. A good old woman lives there, who keeps a small inn. She sells wine, beer, and coffee, and is cheerful and pleasant notwithstanding her age. The chief charm of this spot consists in two linden-trees, which spread their enormous branches over the little green before the church, which is entirely surrounded by peasants' cottages, with their barns and homesteads. I have seldom seen a place so retired and peaceable, and I often have my table and chair brought out from the little inn, and there I drink my coffee and read my Homer. Accident brought me to the spot one fine afternoon, and I found it perfectly deserted. Everybody was in the fields, except a little boy about four years old, who was sitting on the ground and held between his knees a child about six months old; he pressed it to his bosom with both arms, which thus formed a sort of arm-chair, and notwithstanding the liveliness which sparkled in its black eyes, it remained perfectly still. The sight charmed me. I sat down upon a plough opposite, and sketched with great delight this little picture of brotherly tenderness. I added the neighbouring hedge, the barn-door, and some broken cart-wheels, just as they happened to lie;

---

* The reader need not take the trouble to look for the place thus designated. We have found it necessary to change the names as they stood in the original.

and I found in about an hour that I had made a very correct and interesting drawing, without putting in the slightest thing of my own. This confirmed me in my resolution of adhering for the future entirely to nature. She alone is inexhaustible, and capable of forming the greatest masters. Much may be alleged in favour of rules, as much may be likewise advanced in favour of the laws of society; an artist formed upon them will never produce anything absolutely bad or disgusting, as a man who observes the laws and obeys decorum, can never be an absolutely intolerable neighbour, nor a decided villain; but yet say what you will of rules, they destroy the genuine feeling of nature as well as its true expression. Do not tell me " that this is too hard, that they only restrain and prune superfluous branches, &c." My good friend, I will illustrate this by an analogy. These things resemble love. A warm-hearted youth becomes strongly attached to a maiden, he spends every hour of the day in her company, wears out his health, and lavishes his fortune, to afford continual proof that he is wholly devoted to her. Then comes a man of the world, a man of place and respectability, and addresses him thus :—" My good young friend, love is natural, but you must love within bounds. Divide your time, devote a portion to business, and give the hours of recreation to your mistress. Calculate your fortune, and out of the superfluity you may make her a present, only not too often, on her birthday and such occasions." Pursuing this advice, he may become a useful member of society, and I should advise some prince to give him an appointment; but his love is annihilated, and if he be an artist, his genius is fled. Oh, my friends, why is it that the torrent of genius so seldom bursts forth, so seldom rolls in full flowing stream, overwhelming your wondering soul? Because, on either side of this stream, cold and respectable persons have taken up their abodes, and forsooth their summer-houses and tulip-beds would suffer from the torrent, wherefore they dig trenches and raise embankments betimes, in order to avert the impending danger.

May 27th.

I find I have fallen into raptures, declamation, and similes, and have forgotten in consequence to tell you what became of the children. Absorbed in my artistic contemplations, which I briefly described in my letter of yesterday, I continued sitting on the plough for two hours. Towards evening, a young woman, with a basket on her arm, came running towards the children, who had not moved all that time. She exclaimed, from a distance, "You are a good boy, Philip." She saluted me; I returned it, rose and approached her. I inquired if she was the mother of those pretty children? "Yes," she said; and, giving the eldest a piece of bread, she took the little one in her arms, and kissed it with a mother's tenderness. "I left my child with Philip to take care of," she said, "whilst I went into the town with my eldest boy to buy some white bread, some sugar, and an earthen pot." I saw the various articles in the basket, from which the cover had fallen. "I shall make some broth to-night for my little Hans (which was the name of the youngest); that wild fellow, the big one, broke the pot for me yesterday, whilst he was scrambling with Philip for what remained of the contents." I inquired for the eldest, and she had scarcely time to tell me that he was driving a couple of geese home from the meadow, when he ran up, and handed Philip an ozier-twig. I talked a little longer with the woman, and found that she was the daughter of the schoolmaster, and that her husband was gone on a journey into Switzerland for some money a relation had left him. "They wanted to cheat him," she said, "and would not answer his letters, so he is gone there himself; I hope he has met with no accident, as I have heard nothing of him since his departure." I left the woman with regret, giving each of the children a kreutzer, with an additional one for the youngest, to buy some white bread for his broth when she went to town next, and so we parted.

I assure you, my dear friend, when my thoughts are all in tumult, the sight of such a creature as this tranquillizes my disturbed mind. She moves in a happy thoughtlessness within the confined circle of her existence; she supplies her wants from day to day; and when she sees the leaves fall, they raise no other idea in her mind than that winter is approaching.

Since that time I have gone out there frequently. The children have become quite familiar with me; and each get a lump of sugar when I drink my coffee, and they share my milk and bread and butter in the evening. They always receive their kreutzer on Sundays, for when I do not go there after evening service, the good woman has orders to give it to them.

They are quite at home with me, tell me everything, and I am particularly amused with observing their tempers, and the simplicity of their behaviour, when some of the other village children are assembled with them.

It has given me a deal of trouble to satisfy the anxiety of the mother, lest (as she says) " they should inconvenience the gentleman."

May 30*th.*

What I have lately said of painting is equally true with respect to poetry. It is only necessary for us to know what is really excellent, and venture to give it expression, and that is saying much in few words. To-day I have had a scene, which if literally related, would make the most beautiful idyl in the world. But why should I talk of poetry, and scenes, and idyls? Can we never take pleasure in nature, without requiring the assistance of art?

If you expect anything grand or magnificent from this introduction, you will be sadly mistaken. It relates merely to a peasant-lad who has excited in me the warmest interest. As usual, I shall tell my story badly; and you, as usual, will think me extravagant. It is Walheim once more—always Walheim—which produces these wonders.

A party had assembled outside the house under the linden-trees, to drink coffee. The company did not exactly please me, and under one pretext or another, I lingered behind.

A peasant came from an adjoining house, and set to work arranging some part of the same plough which I had lately sketched. His appearance pleased me, and I spoke to him; inquired about his circumstances, made his acquaintance, and, as is usual with me amongst persons of that class, was soon admitted into his confidence. He said he was servant to a young widow, with whom he was in high favour. He spoke so much of his mistress, and praised her so extravagantly, that I could soon see he was desperately in love with

8

her. "She is no longer young," he said; "and she was treated so badly by her former husband, that she does not mean to marry again." From his account, it was plain she possessed incomparable charms for him, and that he wished ardently she would select him to extinguish the recollection of her first husband's ill-conduct. But I should repeat his own words, to describe the depth of the poor fellow's attachment, truth, and devotion. It would, in fact, require the gifts of a great poet to convey the expression of his features, the harmony of his voice, and the heavenly fire of his eye. No words can pourtray the tenderness of his every movement, and of every feature: no effort of mine could do justice to the scene. His alarm lest I should misconceive his relation towards his mistress, or question the propriety of her conduct, particularly touched me. The charming manner with which he described her form and her person, which, without possessing the graces of youth, won and attached him to her, are inexpressible, and must be left to the imagination. I have never in my life witnessed, or fancied, or conceived the possibility of such intense devotion, such ardent affections united with so much purity. Do not blame me if I say, that the recollection of this innocence and truth is deeply impressed upon my very soul; that this picture of fidelity and tenderness haunts me incessantly, and that my own heart, enkindled by the flame, glows and burns within me.

I mean now to try and see her as soon as I can, or, perhaps, on second thoughts, I had better not. It is better I should behold her through the eyes of her lover. To my sight, perhaps, she would not appear as she now stands before me; and why should I destroy so sweet a picture?

June 16th.

"Why do I not write to you?" You pretend to penetration, and ask such a question. You should have guessed that I was well, but that—in a word, I have made an acquaintance who has won my heart; I have found—I know not what.

To give you a regular account of the manner in which I have become acquainted with the most amiable of women, would be a difficult task.   I am a happy and contented mortal, but a poor historian.

An angel! Nonsense! Everybody so describes his mistress: and yet I find it impossible to tell you how perfect she is, or why she is so perfect; enough to say she has captivated all my senses.

So much simplicity, with so much understanding—so mild, and yet so resolute—a mind so placid, and a life so active.

But this is all mere common-place abstract ideas, which express no single character or feature.   Some other time—but no, not some other time, but now, this very instant, will I tell you all about it.   Now or never.   Well, between ourselves, since I commenced my letter, I have been on the point three times of throwing down my pen, ordering my horse, and riding out.   And yet I vowed this morning that I would not ride to-day, and I run every moment to the window to see how high the sun is.

    ✤   *   *   *   *

I could not restrain myself—go to her I must.   I have just returned, Wilhelm, and whilst I am taking supper I will write to you.   What a delight it was for my soul to see her in the midst of her dear, beautiful children—eight brothers and sisters!

But if I proceed thus, you will be no wiser at the end of my letter than you were at the beginning.   Attend then, and I will compel myself to give you the details.

I mentioned to you the other day that I had become acquainted with S——, the district judge, and that he had invited me to go and visit him in his retirement, or rather in his little kingdom.   But I neglected going, and perhaps should never have gone if chance had not discovered to me the treasure which lay concealed in that retired spot.   Some of our young people had proposed giving a ball in the country, at which I consented to be present.   I offered my hand for the evening to a pretty and agreeable, but rather common-place sort of girl, from the immediate neighbourhood; and it was agreed that I should engage a carriage, and call upon Charlotte, with my partner and her aunt, to convey them to the ball.   My companion informed me, as we drove along through the park to the hunting-lodge, that I should make the acquaintance of a very charming young lady.   "Take

s 2

care," added the aunt, "that you do not lose your heart."
" Why ?" said I. " Because she is already engaged to a
very worthy man," she replied, "who is gone to settle his
affairs upon the death of his father, and will succeed to a very
considerable inheritance." This information possessed no
interest for me. When we arrived at the gate, the sun was
setting behind the tops of the mountains. The atmosphere
was heavy, and the ladies expressed their fears of an approaching storm, as masses of low black clouds were gathering
in the horizon. I relieved their anxieties by pretending to
be weather-wise, although I myself had some apprehensions
lest our pleasure should be interrupted.

I alighted, and a maid came to the door and begged us
to wait a moment for her mistress. I walked across the
court to a well-built house, and ascending the flight of steps
in front, opened the door, and saw before me the most
charming spectacle I had ever witnessed. Six children, from
eleven to two years old, were running about the hall, and surrounding a lady of middle height, with a lovely figure, dressed
in a robe of simple white, trimmed with pink ribands. She
held a brown loaf in her hand, and was cutting slices for the
little ones all round in proportion to their age and appetite.
She performed her task in a graceful and affectionate manner,
each claimant awaiting his turn with outstretched hands, and
boisterously shouting his thanks. Some of them ran away at
once to enjoy their evening meal, whilst others of a gentler
disposition retired to the courtyard to see the stranger, and
survey the carriage which was to carry away their Charlotte.
" Pray forgive me for giving you the trouble to come for me,
and for keeping the ladies waiting, but dressing and the arranging some household duties before I leave had made me
forget my children's supper, and they do not like to take it
from any one but me." I uttered some unmeaning compliment,
but my whole soul was absorbed by her air, her voice, her
manner, and I had scarcely recovered myself when she ran
into her room to fetch her gloves and fan. The young ones
threw inquiring glances at me from a distance, whilst I approached the youngest, a most delicious little creature. He
drew back, and Charlotte entering at the very moment, said,
" Louis, shake hands with your cousin." The little fellow
obeyed willingly, and I could not resist giving him a hearty

kiss. "Cousin," said I, to Charlotte, as I handed her down; "do you think I deserve the happiness of being related to you?" She replied, with an arch smile, "Oh, I have such a number of cousins, that I should be sorry if you were the most undeserving of them." In taking leave, she desired her next sister, Sophy, a girl about eleven years old, to take great care of the children, and to say good-bye to papa for her when he came home from his ride. She desired the little ones to obey their sister Sophy, as they would herself, upon which some promised that they would, but a little fair-haired girl, about six years old, looked discontented, and said, ''But Sophy is not you, Charlotte, and we like you best." The two eldest boys had clambered up the carriage, and at my request she permitted them to accompany us a little way through the forest, upon their promising to sit very still and hold fast.

We were hardly seated, and the ladies had scarcely exchanged compliments, making the usual remarks upon each each other's dress, and upon the company they expected to meet, when Charlotte stopped the carriage, and made her brothers get down. They insisted upon kissing her hands once more, which the eldest did with all the tenderness of a youth of fifteen, but the other in a lighter and more careless manner. She desired them again to give her love to the children, and we drove off.

The aunt inquired of Charlotte whether she had finished the book she had last sent her. "No," said Charlotte, "I did not like it; you can have it again; and the one before was not much better." I was surprised, upon asking the title, to hear that it was*———. I found penetration and character in everything she said; every expression seemed to brighten her features with new charms—with new rays of genius—which unfolded by degrees, as she felt herself understood.

"When I was younger," she observed, "I loved nothing so much as romances. Nothing could equal my delight when, on some holiday, I could settle down quietly in a corner, and enter with my whole heart and soul into the joys or sorrows of some fictitious Leonora. I do not deny that they even possess some charms for me yet. But I read so seldom, that

* We feel obliged to suppress the passage in the letter, to prevent any one from feeling aggrieved; although no author need pay much attention to the opinion of a mere girl, or that of an unsteady young man.

I prefer books suited exactly to my taste. And I like those authors best whose scenes describe my own situation in life, and the friends who are about me, whose stories touch me with interest, from resembling my own homely existence, which, without being absolutely Paradise, is on the whole a source of indescribable happiness."

I endeavoured to conceal the emotion which these words occasioned, but it did not last long, for when she had expressed her opinion truly and beautifully of the Vicar of Wakefield, and of other works, whose names I omit,* I could no longer contain myself, but gave utterance to all my own thoughts on the subject; and it was not until Charlotte had addressed herself to the two other ladies, that I remembered their presence, and observed them sitting mute with astonishment. The aunt looked at me several times with an air of raillery, which, however, I did not at all mind.

We talked of the pleasures of dancing. " If it is a fault to love it," said Charlotte, " I confess myself extremely guilty, as no amusement is more agreeable to me. If any thing disturbs me, I go to the piano, play an air to which I have danced, and all goes right again directly."

You who know me can fancy how steadfastly I gazed upon her rich dark eyes during these remarks; how my very soul gloated over her warm lips, and fresh glowing cheeks; how I became lost in the delightful meaning of her words, to such a degree, that I scarcely heard the actual expressions. In fine, I alighted from the carriage like a person in a dream, and was so lost to the dim world around me, that I scarcely heard the music which resounded from the illuminated saloon.

The two Messrs. Andran and a certain N. N.,—(I cannot trouble myself with the names)—who were the Aunt's and Charlotte's partners, received us at the carriage door, and took possession of their ladies, whilst I followed with mine.

We commenced with a minuet. I led out one lady after another, and precisely those who were the most disagreeable could not bring themselves to leave off. Charlotte and her partner began an English country dance, and you must imagine

---

* Though the names are omitted, yet the authors mentioned deserve Charlotte's approbation, and will feel it in their hearts when they read this passage. It concerns no other person.

my delight when it came to their turn to dance the figure
with us.   You should see Charlotte dance.   She dances with
her whole heart and soul; her figure is all harmony, elegance,
and grace, as if she were conscious of nothing else, and had
no other thought or feeling, and doubtless for the moment
every other sensation is extinct.

She was engaged for the second country dance, but she
promised me the third, and she assured me, with the most
agreeable freedom, that she was very fond of waltzing.   " It
is the custom here," she said, " for the previous partners to
waltz together; but my partner is an indifferent waltzer, and
will feel delighted if I save him the trouble.   Your partner
is not allowed to waltz, and indeed is equally incapable ; but
I observed during the country dance that you waltz well, so
if you will waltz with me, I beg you to propose it to my
partner, and I will propose it to yours."   We agreed, and it
was arranged that our partners should mutually entertain
each other.

We set off, and at first delighted ourselves with the usual
graceful motions of the arms.   With what grace, with what
ease she moved.   When the waltz commenced, and the
dancers whirled round each other in the giddy maze, there
was a little confusion arising from the incapacity of some.
But we judiciously remained still, allowing the others to
weary themselves, and when the awkward dancers had withdrawn, we joined in and kept it up famously together with
one other couple, Andran and his partner.   Never did I dance
more lightly.   I felt myself more than mortal, holding this
loveliest of creatures in my arms, flying with her as rapidly
as the wind, till I lost sight of every other object; and, oh !
Wilhelm, I vowed at that moment, that a maiden whom I
loved, or for whom I felt the slightest attachment, never,
never should waltz with another than with me, if I went to
perdition for it—you will understand this.

We took a few turns in the room to recover our breath.
Charlotte sat down and felt refreshed by partaking of some
oranges, which I had privately brought with me, and were
difficult to procure ; but every slice which she kindly offered
to her neighbours was a dagger to my heart.

We were the second couple in the third country dance.
As we were going down (and Heaven knows with what

ectasy I gazed upon her arms and her eyes, which beamed
with the sweetest feeling of pure and genuine enjoyment), we
passed a lady whom I had noticed for her charming expression of countenance, although she was no longer young.   She
looked at Charlotte with a smile; then holding up her finger
in a threatening attitude, repeated twice in a very significant.
tone of voice the name of "Albert."

"Who is Albert," said I to Charlotte, "if it is not impertinent to ask?"   She was about to answer, when we were
obliged to separate, by a figure in the dance, and as we crossed
over again in front of each other, I perceived she looked a
little pensive.   "Why need I conceal it from you," she said,
as she gave me her hand for the promenade, "Albert is a
worthy man, to whom I am engaged."   Now there was
nothing new to me in this (for the girls had told me of it on
the way), but it was so far new that I had not thought of it in
connection with her, whom in so short a time I had learned
to prize so highly.   Enough, I became confused, got out in
the figure, and occasioned general confusion, so that it required all Charlotte's presence of mind to set me right, by
pulling and pushing me into my proper place.

The dance was not yet finished when the lightning, which
had for some time been seen in the horizon, and which I had
asserted to proceed entirely from heat, grew more violent,
and the thunder was heard above the music.   When any
distress or terror surprises us in the midst of our amusements, it naturally makes a deeper impression than at other
times, either because the contrast makes us more keenly susceptible, or rather perhaps because our senses are then more
open to impressions, and the shock is consequently stronger.
To this cause I must ascribe the fright and shrieks of the
ladies.   One sagaciously sat down in a corner with her back
to the window, and held her fingers to her ears; a second
knelt down before her, and hid her face in her lap; a third
threw herself between them and embraced her sister with a
thousand tears; some insisted upon going home, others, unconscious of their actions, wanted sufficient presence of mind
to repress the impertinence of their young partners, who
sought to direct to themselves those sighs which the lips of
our agitated beauties intended for Heaven.   Some of the gentlemen had gone down stairs to smoke a quiet cigar, and the

rest of the company gladly embraced a happy suggestion of the hostess to retire into another room, which was provided with shutters and curtains. We had hardly got there when Charlotte placed the chairs in a circle, and when the company had sat down in compliance with her request, she forthwith proposed a round game.

I observed some of the company prepare their mouths and draw themselves up at the prospect of some agreeable forfeit. "Let us play at counting," said Charlotte. "Observe now, I go round the circle from right to left, and each person is to count, one after the other, the number that comes to him, and must count fast; whoever stops or mistakes is to have a box on the ear, and so on, till we have counted a thousand." It was delightful to see the fun. She went round the circle with upraised arm. "One," said the first; "two," the second; "three," the third, and so on, till Charlotte went faster and faster. One made a mistake, instantly a box on the ear; and amid the laughter that ensued came another box, and so on, faster and faster. I myself came in for two. I fancied they were harder than the rest, and felt quite delighted. A general laughter and confusion put an end to the play long before we had reached a thousand. The party broke up into little separate knots, the storm had ceased, and I followed Charlotte into the saloon. On the way she said: "The game banished their fears of the storm." I could make no reply. "I myself," she continued, "was as much frightened as any of them; but by affecting courage, to keep up the spirits of the others, I forgot my apprehensions." We went to the window. It still thundered at a distance; a soft rain was pouring down over the country, and filled the air around us with delicious odours. Charlotte leaned forward upon her arm; her eyes wandered over the scene; she raised them to Heaven, and then turned them upon me; they were moistened with tears; she placed her hand upon mine, and said: "Klopstock!" at once I remembered the magnificent ode which was in her thoughts; I felt oppressed with the weight of my sensations, and sank under them. It was more than I could bear. I bent over her hand and kissed it in a stream of delicious tears. As I raised myself, I looked steadfastly in her face. Divine Klopstock! why didst thou not see thy apotheosis in those eyes? And thy name, so often profaned, why should I ever desire to hear it again repeated?

June 19th.

I no longer remember where I broke off with my narrative; I only know it was two in the morning when I went to bed, and if you had been with me that I might have talked instead of writing to you, in all probability I should have kept you up till daylight.

I believe I have not related what happened on our way home from the ball, and I have not time to tell you now. It was a most magnificent sunrise; the whole country was refreshed, and the rain fell drop by drop from the trees in the forest. Our companions were asleep. Charlotte asked me if I did not wish to sleep too, and desired I would not make any ceremony on her account. Looking steadfastly at her I answered, "As long as those eyes continue open, there is no fear of mine." We both continued awake till we reached her door. The maid opened it softly, and assured her, in answer to her inquiries, that her father and the children were well, and still asleep. I left her, asking permission to visit her in the course of the day. She consented, and I went; and since that time, sun, moon, and stars may pursue their course; I know not whether it is day or night; the whole world is nothing to me.

June 21st.

My days are as happy as those reserved by God for his elect, and whatever be my fate hereafter, I can never say that I have not tasted joy,—the purest joy of life. You know Walheim. I am now completely settled there. In that spot I am only half a league from Charlotte, and there I enjoy myself, and taste all the pleasure which can fall to the lot of man.

Little did I imagine when I selected Walheim for my pedestrian excursions, that all heaven lay so near it. How often in my wanderings from the hill-side or from the meadows across the river, have I beheld this hunting-lodge, which now contains within it all the joy of my heart!

I have often, my dear Wilhelm, reflected on the eagerness

men feel to wander and make new discoveries, and upon that secret impulse which afterwards inclines them to return back to their narrow circle, to conform to the laws of custom, and to embarrass themselves no longer with what passes around them.

It is so strange how, when I came here first and gazed upon that lovely valley from the hill-side, I felt charmed with the entire scene around me.   The little wood opposite,—how delightful to sit under its shade!   How fine the view from that point of rock!   Then that delightful chain of hills and the exquisite valleys at their feet!   Could I but wander and lose myself amongst them!   I went and returned without finding what I wished.   Distance, my friend, is like futurity. A dim vastness is spread before our souls ; the perceptions of our mind are as obscure as those of our vision, and we desire earnestly to surrender up our whole being, that it may be filled with the complete and perfect bliss of one glorious emotion.   But, alas ! when we have attained our object, when the distant *there* becomes the present *here*, all is changed again ; we are as poor and circumscribed as ever, and our souls still languish for unattainable happiness.

So the restless traveller pants for his native soil, and finds in his own cottage, in the arms of his wife, in the affections of his children, and in the labour necessary for their support, that happiness which he had sought in vain through the wide world.

When I go out at sunrise in the morning to Walheim, and with my own hands gather the peas in the garden, which are to serve for my dinner, when I sit down to shell them and read my Homer during the intervals, and then selecting a saucepan from the kitchen, fetch my own butter, put my mess on the fire, cover it up, and sit down to stir it as occasion requires, I figure to myself the illustrious suitors of Penelope, killing, dressing, and preparing their own oxen and swine. Nothing fills me with a more pure and genuine sense of happiness than those traits of patriarchal life which, thank Heaven! I can imitate without affectation.   Happy is it, indeed, for me that my heart is capable of feeling the same simple and innocent pleasure as the peasant, whose table is covered with food of his own rearing, and who not only enjoys his meal, but remembers with delight the happy days and sunny mornings when he planted it, the soft evenings when he watered it, and the pleasure he experienced in watching its daily growth.

June 29th.

The day before yesterday, the physician came from the town to pay a visit to the Judge. He found me on the floor playing with Charlotte's children. Some of them were scrambling over me, and others romped with me, and as I caught and tickled them they made a great noise. The Doctor is a formal sort of personage; he adjusts the plaits of his ruffles, and continually settles his frill whilst he speaks with you, and he thought my conduct beneath the dignity of a sensible man. I could perceive this by his countenance. But I did not suffer myself to be disturbed. I allowed him to continue his wise conversation whilst I rebuilt the children's card-houses for them as fast as they threw them down. He went about the town, afterwards, complaining that the Judge's children were spoiled enough before, but that now Werther was completely ruining them.

Nothing on this earth, my dear Wilhelm, affects my heart so much as children. When I consider them, when I mark in the little creatures the seeds of all those virtues and qualities which they will one day find so indispensable; when I behold in the obstinate all the future firmness and constancy of a noble character; in the capricious, that levity and gaiety of temper which will carry them lightly over the dangers and troubles of life, their whole nature simple and unpolluted; then I call to mind the golden words of the Great Teacher of mankind, "If you become not like one of these!" And now, my friend, these children, who are our equals, whom we ought to consider as our models, we treat them as subjects. They are allowed no will of their own! And have we then none ourselves? Whence comes our exclusive right? Is it because we are older and more experienced? Great God! from the height of thy heaven, thou beholdest great children and little children, and no others; and thy Son has long since declared which afford Thee greatest pleasure. But they believe in Him, and hear Him not,—that too is an old story; and they train their children after their own image, &c.

Adieu, Wilhelm, I will not further bewilder myself with this subject.

July 1st.

The consolation which Charlotte can bring to an invalid, I experience from my own heart, which suffers more from her absence, than many a poor creature who lingers on a bed of sickness. She is gone to spend a few days in the town, with a very worthy woman, who is given over by the physicians, and wishes to have Charlotte near her in her last moments. I accompanied her last week on a visit to the vicar of S——, a small village in the mountains, about a league from hence. We arrived about four o'clock; Charlotte had taken her little sister with her. When we entered the vicarage court, we found the good old man sitting upon a bench before the door, under the shade of two large walnut-trees. At the sight of Charlotte he seemed to gain new life, rose up, forgot his stick, and ventured to walk towards her. She ran to him, and made him sit down again; then placing herself by his side, she gave him a number of messages from her father, and then caught up his youngest child, a dirty, ugly little thing, the joy of his old age, and kissed it. I wish you could have witnessed her attention to this old man,—how she raised her voice on account of his deafness,—how she told him of healthy young people, who had been carried off when it was least expected; praised the virtues of Carlsbad, and commended his determination to spend the ensuing summer there; and assured him that he looked better and stronger than he did when she saw him last. I, in the mean time, paid attention to his good lady. The old man seemed quite in spirits; and, as I could not help admiring the beauty of the walnut-trees which formed such an agreeable shade over our heads, he began, though with some little difficulty, to tell us their history. "As to the oldest," said he, "we do not know who planted it,—some say one clergyman, and some another; but the younger one, there behind us, is exactly the age of my wife, fifty years old next October; her father planted it in the morning, and in the evening she came into the world. My wife's father was my predecessor here, and I cannot tell you how fond he was of that tree, and it is fully as dear to me. Under the shade of that very tree, upon a log of wood, my wife was seated knitting, when I, a poor student, came into this court for the first time, just seven-and-twenty years ago." Charlotte inquired for his daughter. He said she was gone with Herr Schmidt to the meadows, and was with the haymakers. The old man then resumed his story, and told us how his predecessor had taken a fancy to him, as had his daughter likewise; and how he had become first his curate, and subsequently his successor. He had scarcely finished his story, when his daughter returned through the garden, accompanied by the above-mentioned Herr Schmidt. She welcomed Charlotte affectionately, and I confess I was much taken with her appearance. She was a lively-looking, good humoured brunette, quite competent to amuse one for a short time in the country. Her lover (for such Herr Schmidt evidently appeared to be) was a polite, reserved personage, and would not join our conversation, notwithstanding all Charlotte's endeavours to draw him out. I was much annoyed at observing, by his countenance, that his silence did not arise from want of talent, but from caprice and ill-humour. This subsequently became very evident, when we set out to take a walk, and Frederica joining Charlotte, with whom I was talking, the worthy gentleman's face, which was naturally rather sombre, became so dark and angry, that Charlotte was obliged to touch my arm, and remind me that I was talking too much to Frederica. Nothing distresses me more than to see men torment each other; particularly when in the flower of their age, in the very season of pleasure, they waste their few short days of sunshine in quarrels and disputes, and only perceive their error when it is too late to repair it. This thought dwelt upon my mind; and in the evening, when we returned to the vicar's, and were sitting round the table, with our bread and milk, the conversation turned on the joys and sorrows of the world, I could not resist the temptation to inveigh bitterly against ill-humour. "We are apt," said I, "to complain, but with very little cause, that our happy days are few, and our evil days many. If our hearts were always disposed to receive the benefits which Heaven sends us, we should acquire

strength to support evil when it comes." "But," observed
the vicar's wife, "we cannot always command our tempers,
so much depends upon the constitution: when the body
suffers, the mind is ill at ease." "I acknowledge that," I
continued; "but we must consider such a disposition in the
light of a disease, and inquire whether there is no remedy
for it." "I should be glad to hear one," said Charlotte;
"at least I think very much depends upon ourselves: I know
it is so with me. When anything annoys me, and disturbs
my temper, I hasten into the garden, hum a couple of
country dances, and it is all right with me directly." "That
is what I meant," I replied; "ill-humour resembles indolence; it is natural to us: but if once we have courage to
exert ourselves, we find our work run fresh from our hands,
and we experience in the activity from which we shrank a
real enjoyment." Frederica listened very attentively, and
the young man objected, that we were not masters of ourselves, and still less so of our feelings. "The question is
about a disagreeable feeling," I added, "from which every
one would willingly escape, but none know their own power
without trial. Invalids are glad to consult physicians, and
submit to the most scrupulous regimen, the most nauseous
medicines, to recover their health." I observed that the
good old man inclined his head, and exerted himself to hear
our discourse; so I raised my voice, and addressed myself
directly to him. "We preach against a great many crimes,"
I observed, "but I never remember a sermon delivered
against ill-humour." "That may do very well for your
town clergymen," said he; "country people are never ill-
humoured; though, indeed, it might be useful, occasionally,
to my wife, for instance, and the Judge." We all laughed,
as did he likewise very cordially, till he fell into a fit of
coughing, which interrupted our conversation for a time.
Herr Schmidt resumed the subject. "You call ill-humour a
crime," he remarked, "but I think you use too strong a
term." "Not at all," I replied, "if that deserves the name,
which is so pernicious to ourselves and our neighbours. Is it
not enough that we want the power to make one another
happy,—must we deprive each other of the pleasure which
we can all make for ourselves? Show me the man who has
the courage to hide his ill-humour, who bears the whole

burden himself, without disturbing the peace of those around him. No; ill-humour arises from an inward consciousness of our own want of merit,—from a discontent, which ever accompanies that envy which foolish vanity engenders. We see people happy, whom we have not made so, and cannot endure the sight." Charlotte looked at me with a smile; she observed the emotion with which I spoke; and a tear in the eyes of Frederica stimulated me to proceed. "Woe unto those," I said, "who use their power over a human heart, to destroy the simple pleasures it would naturally enjoy! All the favours, all the attentions in the world cannot compensate for the loss of that happiness which a cruel tyranny has destroyed." My heart was full as I spoke. A recollection of many things which had happened pressed upon my mind, and filled my eyes with tears. "We should daily repeat to ourselves," I exclaimed, "that we should not interfere with our friends, unless to leave them in possession of their own joys, and increase their happiness by sharing it with them. But when their souls are tormented by a violent passion, or their hearts rent with grief, is it in your power to afford them the slightest consolation?

And when the last fatal malady seizes the being whose untimely grave you have prepared, when languid and exhausted she lies before you, her dim eyes raised to heaven, and the damp of death upon her pallid brow, then you stand at her bed-side like a condemned criminal, with the bitter feeling that your whole fortune could not save her; and the agonizing thought wrings you, that all your efforts are powerless to impart even a moment's strength to the departing soul, or quicken her with a transitory consolation."

At these words the remembrance of a similar scene at which I had been once present, fell with full force upon my heart. I buried my face in my handkerchief and hastened from the room, and was only recalled to my recollection by Charlotte's voice, who reminded me that it was time to return home. With what tenderness she chid me on the way, for the too eager interest I took in everything! She declared it would do me injury, and that I ought to spare myself.—Yes, my angel! I will do so for your sake.

July 6th.

She is still with her dying friend, and is still the same bright, beautiful creature, whose presence softens pain and sheds happiness around whichever way she turns.   She went out yesterday with her little sisters; I knew it, and went to meet them, and we walked together.   In about an hour and a half we returned to the town.   We stopped at the spring I am so fond of, and which is now a thousand times dearer to me than ever.   Charlotte seated herself upon the low wall, and we gathered about her.   I looked around and recalled the time when my heart was unoccupied and free.—" Dear fountain !" I said, " since that time, I have no more come to enjoy cool repose by thy fresh stream; I have passed thee with careless steps, and scarcely bestowed a glance upon thee."   I looked down and observed Charlotte's little sister, Jane, coming up the steps with a glass of water.   I turned towards Charlotte, and I felt her influence over me.   Jane at the moment approached with the glass.   Her sister, Marianne, wished to take it from her.   " No !" cried the child, with the sweetest expression of face, " Charlotte must drink first."

The affection and simplicity with which this was uttered so charmed me, that I sought to express my feelings by catching up the child and kissing her heartily.   She was frightened and began to cry.—" You should not do that," said Charlotte: I felt perplexed.—" Come, Jane," she continued, taking her hand and leading her down the steps again, " it is no matter; wash yourself quickly in the fresh water."   I stood and watched them, and when I saw the little dear rubbing her cheeks with her wet hands, in full belief that all the impurities contracted from my ugly beard would be washed off by the miraculous water, and how, though Charlotte said it would do, she continued still to wash with all her might, as though she thought too much were better than too little, I assure you, Wilhelm, I never attended a baptism with greater reverence; and when Charlotte came up from the well, I could have prostrated myself as before the prophet of an eastern nation.

In the evening I could not resist telling the story to a person, who I thought possessed some natural feeling, because he was a man of understanding.   But what a mistake

T

I made! He maintained it was very wrong of Charlotte,— that we should not deceive children,—that such things occasioned countless mistakes and superstitions, from which we were bound to protect the young. It occurred to me then, that this very man had been baptized only a week before, so I said nothing further, but maintained the justice of my own convictions. We should deal with children as God deals with us, —we are happiest under the influence of innocent delusions.

July 8th.

What a child is man! that he should be so solicitous about a look! What a child is man! We had been to Walheim: the ladies went in a carriage, but during our walk I thought I saw in Charlotte's dark eyes—I am a fool—but forgive me! you should see them—those eyes ;—however, to be brief, (for my own eyes are weighed down with sleep,) you must know, when the ladies stepped into their carriage again, young W. Seldstadt, Andran, and I were standing about the door. They are a merry set of fellows, and they were all laughing and joking together. I watched Charlotte's eyes ; they wandered from one to the other, but they did not light on me,—on me, who stood there motionless, and who saw nothing but her! My heart bade her a thousand times adieu, but she noticed me not. The carriage drove off, and my eyes filled with tears. I looked after her ; suddenly I saw Charlotte's bonnet leaning out of the window, and she turned to look back,—was it at me? My dear friend, I know not, and in this uncertainty I find consolation. Perhaps she turned to look at me. Perhaps! Good night,— what a child I am!

July 10th,

You should see how foolish I look in company when her name is mentioned, particularly when I am asked plainly how I like her? How I like her!—I detest the phrase. What sort of creature must he be who merely liked Charlotte, whose whole heart and senses were not entirely absorbed by her. Like her! Some one asked me lately how I liked Ossian.

July 11*th.*

Madame M. is very ill. I pray for her recovery, because Charlotte shares my sufferings. I see her occasionally at my friend's house, and to-day she has told me the strangest circumstance. Old M. is a covetous, miserly fellow, who has long worried and annoyed the poor lady sadly; but she has borne her afflictions patiently. A few days ago, when the physician informed us that her recovery was hopeless, she sent for her husband, (Charlotte was present,) and addressed him thus: " I have something to confess, which, after my decease, may occasion trouble and confusion. I have hitherto conducted your household as frugally and economically as possible, but you must pardon me for having defrauded you for thirty years. At the commencement of our married life, you allowed a small sum for the wants of the kitchen, and the other household expenses. When our establishment increased and our property grew larger, I could not persuade you to increase the weekly allowance in proportion; in short you know that when our wants were greatest, you required me to supply everything with seven florins a week. I took the money from you without an observation, but made up the weekly deficiency from the money-chest, as nobody would suspect your wife of robbing the household bank. But I have wasted nothing, and should have been content to meet my eternal Judge without this confession, if she, upon whom the management of your establishment will devolve after my decease, would be free from embarrassment upon your insisting that the allowance made to me, your former wife, was sufficient."

I talked with Charlotte of the inconceivable manner in which men allow themselves to be blinded; how any one could avoid suspecting some deception, when seven florins only were allowed to defray expenses twice as great. But I have myself known people who believed, without any visible astonishment, that their house possessed the prophet's never-failing cruise of oil.

July 13*th.*

No, I am not deceived. In her dark eyes I read a genuine interest in me and in my fortunes. Yes, I feel it, and I may

T 2

believe my own heart which tells me—dare I say it?—dare I pronounce the divine words?—that she loves me!

That she loves me! How the idea exalts me in my own eyes! and as you can understand my feelings, I may say to you, how I honour myself since she loves me!

Is this presumption, or is it a consciousness of the truth? I do not know a man able to supplant me in the heart of Charlotte; and yet when she speaks of her betrothed with so much warmth and affection, I feel like the soldier who has been stripped of his honours and titles, and deprived of his sword.

July 16*th.*

How my heart beats when by accident I touch her finger, or my feet meet hers under the table! I draw back as if from a furnace, but a secret force impels me forward again, and my senses become disordered. Her innocent, unconscious heart never knows what agony these little familiarities inflict upon me! Sometimes when we are talking she lays her hand upon mine, and in the eagerness of conversation comes closer to me, and her balmy breath reaches my lips,—when I feel as if lightning had struck me, and that I could sink into the earth. And yet, Wilhelm! with all this heavenly confidence,—if I know myself and should ever dare—you understand me——No, no, my heart is not so corrupt,—it is weak, weak enough—but is not that a degree of corruption?

She is to me a sacred being. All passion is still in her presence; I cannot express my sensations when I am near her. I feel as if my soul beat in every nerve of my body. There is a melody which she plays on the piano with angelic skill,—so simple is it and yet so spiritual! It is her favourite air; and when she plays the first note, all pain, care, and sorrow disappear from me in a moment.

I believe every word that is said of the magic of ancient music. How her simple song enchants me! Sometimes, when I am ready to commit suicide, she sings that air, and instantly the gloom and madness which hung over me are dispersed, and I breathe freely again.

July 18*th.*

Wilhelm! what is the world to our hearts without love? What is a magic lantern without light? You have but to kindle the flame within, and the brightest figures shine on the white wall; and if love only show us fleeting shadows, we are yet happy when, like mere children, we behold them, and are transported with the splendid phantoms. I have not been able to see Charlotte to-day. I was prevented by company from which I could not disengage myself. What was to be done? I sent my servant to her house, that I might, at least, see somebody to-day who had been near her. Oh! the impatience with which I waited for his return—the joy with which I welcomed him! I should certainly have caught him in my arms and kissed him, if I had not been ashamed.

It is said that the Bonona stone, when placed in the sun, attracts the rays, and for a time appears luminous in the dark. So was it with me and this servant. The idea that Charlotte's eyes had dwelt on his countenance, his cheek, his very apparel, endeared them all inestimably to me, so that at the moment I would not have parted from him for a thousand crowns. His presence made me so happy! Beware of laughing at me, Wilhelm. Can that be a delusion which makes us happy?

July 19*th.*

" I shall see her to-day!" I exclaim with delight, when I rise in the morning, and look out with gladness of heart at the bright, beautiful sun.—" I shall see her to day!" and then I have no further wish to form; all—all is included in that one thought.

July 20*th.*

I cannot assent to your proposal that I should accompany the Ambassador to———. I do not love subordination, and we all know that he is a rough, disagreeable person to be connected with. You say my mother wishes me to be employed. I could not help laughing at that. Am I not sufficiently employed? And is it not in reality the same, whether I shell peas or count lentils? The world runs on from one folly to another, and the man who, solely from regard to the opinion of others, and without any wish or necessity of his own, toils after gold, honour, or any other phantom, is no better than a fool.

You insist so much on my not neglecting my drawing, that it would be as well for me to say nothing as to confess how little I have lately done.

I never felt happier; I never understood nature better, even down to the veriest stem, or smallest blade of grass; and yet I am unable to express myself; my powers of execution are so weak, everything seems to swim and float before me, so that I cannot make a clear, bold outline; but I fancy I should succeed better if I had some clay or wax to model. I shall try, if this state of mind continues much longer, and will take to modelling, if I only knead dough.

I have commenced Charlotte's portrait three times, and have as often disgraced myself. This is the more annoying, as I was formerly very happy in taking likenesses. I have since sketched her profile, and must content myself with that.

Yes, dear Charlotte! I will order and arrange everything. Only give me more commissions,—the more the better. One thing, however, I must request. Use no more writing-sand with the dear notes you send me. To-day I raised your letter hastily to my lips, and it set my teeth on edge.

I have often determined not to see her so frequently. But who could keep such a resolution? Every day I am exposed to the temptation, and promise, faithfully, that to-morrow I will really stay away; but, when to-morrow comes, I find some irresistible reason for seeing her; and, before I can account for it, I am with her again. Either she has said on the previous evening, " You will be sure to call to-morrow!" —and who could stay away then?—or she gives me some commission, and I find it essential to take her the answer in person; or the day is fine and I walk to Walheim, and when I am there it is only half a league further to her. I am within the charmed atmosphere, and soon find myself at her side. My grandmother used to tell us a story of a mountain of load-stone. When any vessels came near it, they were deprived instantly of their ironwork, the nails flew to the mountain, and the unhappy crew perished amongst the disjointed planks.

July 30*th.*

Albert is arrived and I must take my departure. Were he the best and noblest of men and I in every respect his inferior, I could not endure to see him in possession of such a perfect being. Possession!—enough, Wilhelm; her betrothed is here! A fine, worthy fellow, whom one cannot help liking. Fortunately I was not present at their meeting. It would have broken my heart! And he is so considerate.; he has not given Charlotte one kiss in my presence. Heaven reward him for it! I must love him for the respect with which he treats her. He shows a regard for me, but for this I suspect I am more indebted to Charlotte than to his own fancy for me. Women have a delicate tact in such matters; and it should be so. They cannot always succeed in keeping two rivals on terms with each other; but when they do, they are the only gainers.

I cannot help esteeming Albert. The coolness of his temper contrasts strongly with the impetuosity of mine, which I cannot conceal. He has a great deal of feeling, and is fully sensible of the treasure he possesses in Charlotte. He is free from ill-humour, which you know is the fault I detest most.

He regards me as a man of sense, and my attachment to Charlotte, and the interest I take in all that concerns her, augment his triumph and his love. I shall not inquire whether he may not at times teaze her with some little jealousies, as I know that were I in his place, I should not be entirely free from such sensations.

But be that as it may, my pleasure with Charlotte is over. Call it folly, or infatuation, what signifies a name? The thing speaks for itself. Before Albert came, I knew all that I know now. I knew I could make no pretensions to her, nor did I offer any; that is, as far as it was possible in the presence of so much loveliness, not to pant for its enjoyment. And now, behold me, like a silly fellow, staring with astonishment when another comes in and deprives me of my love.

I bite my lips and feel infinite scorn for those who tell me to be resigned, because there is no help for it. Let me escape from the yoke of such silly subterfuges! I ramble through the woods, and when I return to Charlotte, and find Albert sitting by her side in the summer-house in the garden, I am unable to bear it; behave like a fool; and commit a thousand extravagancies. "For Heaven's sake," said Charlotte to-day, "let us have no more scenes like those of last night. You terrify me when you are so violent." Between ourselves, I am always away now when he visits her, and I feel delighted when I find her alone.

August 8th.

Believe me, dear Wilhelm, I did not allude to you when I spoke so severely of those who advise resignation to inevitable fate. I did not think it possible for you to indulge such a sentiment. But in fact you are right. I only suggest one objection. In this world one is seldom reduced to make a selection between two alternatives. There are as many varieties of conduct and opinion as there are turns of feature between an aquiline nose and a flat one.

You will, therefore, permit me to concede your entire argument, and yet contrive means to escape your dilemma.

Your position is this : " Either you have hopes of obtaining Charlotte, or you have none. Well, in the first case, pursue your course, and press on to the fulfilment of your wishes. In the second, be a man, and shake off a miserable passion, which will enervate and destroy you." My dear friend, this is well and easily said.

But would you require a wretched being, whose life is slowly wasting under a lingering disease, to despatch himself at once by the stroke of a dagger? Does not the very disorder which consumes his strength, deprive him of the courage to effect his deliverance?

You may answer me, if you please, with a similar analogy. " Who would not prefer the amputation of an arm to the perilling of life by doubt and procrastination?" But I know not if I am right, and let us leave these comparisons.

Enough!—There are moments, Wilhelm, when I could rise up and shake it all off, and when, if I only knew where to go, I could fly from this place.

———

The same evening.

My diary, which I have for some time neglected, came before me to-day, and I am amazed to see how deliberately I have entangled myself step by step. To have seen my position so clearly, and yet to have acted so like a child! Even still I behold the result plainly, and yet have no thought of acting with greater prudence.

———

August 10th.

If I were not a fool, I could spend the happiest and most delightful life here. So many agreeable circumstances, and of a kind to ensure a worthy man's happiness, are seldom united. Alas! I feel it too sensibly—the heart alone makes our happiness. To be admitted into this most charming family, to be loved by the father as a son, by the children as a father, and by Charlotte!—then the noble Albert, who never disturbs my happiness by any appearance of ill-humour, receiving me with the heartiest affection, and loving me next to Charlotte, better than all the world! Wilhelm, you would be delighted to hear us in our rambles and conversations about Charlotte; nothing in the world can be more absurd than our connection, and yet the thought of it often moves me to tears.

He tells me sometimes of her excellent mother—how upon her death-bed she had committed her house and children to Charlotte, and had given Charlotte herself in charge to him—how since that time a new spirit had taken possession of her—how in care and anxiety for their welfare she became a real mother to them—how every moment of her time was devoted to some labour of love in their behalf—and yet her mirth and cheerfulness had never forsaken her. I walk by his side, pluck flowers by the way, arrange them carefully into a nosegay, then fling them into the first stream I pass, and watch them as they float gently away. I forget whether I told you that Albert is to remain here. He has received a government appointment, with a very good salary, and I understand he is in high favour at court. I have met few persons so punctual and methodical in business.

August 12*th.*

Certainly Albert is the best fellow in the world. I had a strange scene with him yesterday. I went to take leave of him, for I took it into my head to spend a few days in these mountains, from whence I now write to you. As I was walking up and down his room, my eye fell upon his pistols. "Lend me those pistols," said I, "for my journey." "By all means," he replied, "if you will take the trouble to load them, for they only hang there for form." I took down one of them, and he continued: "Ever since I was near suffering for my extreme caution, I have had nothing to do with such things." I was curious to hear the story. "I was staying," said he, "some three months ago, at a friend's house in the country. I had a brace of pistols with me unloaded, and I slept without any anxiety. One rainy afternoon I was sitting by myself, doing nothing, when it occurred to me—I do not not know how—that the house might be attacked—that we might require the pistols—that we might—in short, you know how we go on fancying, when we have nothing better to do. I gave the pistols to the servant to clean and load. He was playing with the maid, and trying to frighten her, when the pistol went off—God knows how!—the ramrod was in the barrel, and it went straight through her right hand, and shattered the thumb. I had to endure all the lamentation and the surgeon's bill to pay; so since that time I have kept all my weapons unloaded. But, my dear friend, what is the use of prudence? We can never be on our guard against all possible dangers. However,"—now you must know I can tolerate all men till they come to "however," for it is self-evident that every universal rule must have its exceptions. But he is so exceedingly accurate, that if he only fancies he has said a word too precipitate, or too general, or only half true, he never ceases to qualify, to modify, and extenuate, till at last he appears to have said nothing at all. Upon this occasion Albert was deeply immersed in his subject; I ceased to hear him, and became lost in reverie. With a sudden motion I pointed the mouth of the pistol to my forehead, over the right eye.

"What do you mean?" cried Albert, turning back the pistol.
"It is not loaded," said I. "And even if not," he answered
with impatience, "what can you mean? I cannot comprehend
how a man can be so mad as to shoot himself, and the bare
idea of it shocks me."

"But why should any one," said I, "in speaking of an
action, venture to pronounce it mad, or wise, or good, or
bad? What is the meaning of all this? Have you carefully
studied the secret motives of our actions? Do you understand—can you explain the causes which occasion them, and
make them inevitable? If you can, you will be less hasty
with your decision."

"But you will allow," said Albert, "that some actions are
criminal, let them spring from whatever motives they may."
I granted it, and shrugged my shoulders.

"But still, my good friend," I continued, "there are some
exceptions here too. Theft is a crime, but the man who
commits it from extreme poverty, with no design but to save
his family from perishing, is he an object of pity or of
punishment? Who shall throw the first stone at a husband,
who, in the heat of just resentment, sacrifices his faithless
wife and her perfidious seducer? or at the young maiden,
who in her weak hour of rapture, forgets herself in the
impetuous joys of love? Even our laws, cold and cruel as
they are, relent in such cases, and withhold their punishment."

"That is quite another thing," said Albert; "because a
man under the influence of violent passion, loses all power of
reflection, and is regarded as intoxicated or insane."

"O! you people of sound understandings," I replied,
smiling, "are ever ready to exclaim, 'Extravagance and
madness, and intoxication!' You moral men are so calm
and so subdued! You abhor the drunken man, and detest
the extravagant; you pass by like the Levite, and thank
God, like the Pharisee, that you are not like one of them. I
have been more than once intoxicated, my passions have
always bordered on extravagance; I am not ashamed to confess it, for I have learnt, by my own experience, that all
extraordinary men, who have accomplished great and astonishing actions, have ever been decried by the world as
drunken or insane. And in private life, too, is it not in-

tolerable that no one can undertake the execution of a noble or generous deed, without giving rise to the exclamation that the doer is intoxicated or mad? Shame upon you, ye sages!"

"This is another of your extravagant humours," said Albert; "you always exaggerate a case, and in this matter your are undoubtedly wrong, for we were speaking of suicide, which you compare with great actions, when it is impossible to regard it as anything but a weakness. It is much easier to die than to bear a life of misery with fortitude."

I was on the point of breaking off the conversation, for nothing puts me so completely out of patience as the utterance of a wretched common-place, when I am talking from my inmost heart. However, I composed myself, for I had often heard the same observation with sufficient vexation, and I answered him, therefore, with a little warmth: "You call this a weakness—beware of being led astray by appearances. When a nation which has long groaned under the intolerable yoke of a tyrant, rises at last and throws off its chains,—do you call that weakness? The man, who to rescue his house from the flames, finds his physical strength redoubled, so that he lifts burdens with ease, which in the absence of excitement he could scarcely move; he who under the rage of an insult attacks and puts to flight half a score of his enemies—are such persons to be called weak? My good friend, if resistance be strength, how can the highest degree of resistance be a weakness?"

Albert looked steadfastly at me, and said, "Pray forgive me, but I do not see that the examples you have adduced bear any relation to the question." "Very likely," I answered, "for I have often been told that my style of illustration borders a little on the absurd. But let us see if we cannot place the matter in another point of view, by inquiring what can be a man's state of mind, who resolves to free himself from the burden of life,—a burden often so pleasant to bear,—for we cannot otherwise reason fairly upon the subject."

"Human nature," I continued, "has its limits. It is able to endure a certain degree of joy, sorrow, and pain, but becomes annihilated as soon as this measure is exceeded. The question, therefore, is, not whether a man is strong or weak, but whether he is able to endure the measure of his sufferings? The suffering may be moral or physical; and in my opinion it is just as absurd to call a man a coward who destroys himself as to call a man a coward who dies of a malignant fever."

"Paradox, all paradox!" exclaimed Albert. "Not so paradoxical as you imagine," I replied. "You allow that we designate a disease as mortal, when nature is so severely attacked, and her strength so far exhausted, that she cannot possibly recover her former condition, under any change that may take place.

"Now, my good friend, apply this to the mind; observe a man in his natural isolated condition, consider how ideas work, and how impressions fasten upon him, till at length a violent passion seizes him, destroying all his powers of calm reflection, and provoking his utter ruin.

"It is in vain that a man of sound mind and cool temper understands the condition of such a wretched being, in vain he counsels him! He can no more communicate his own wisdom to him than a healthy man can instil his strength into the invalid, by whose bed-side he is seated."

Albert thought this too general. I reminded him of a girl who had drowned herself a short time previously, and I related her history.

She was a good creature, who had grown up in the narrow sphere of household industry and weekly-appointed labour; one who knew no pleasure beyond indulging in a walk on Sundays, arrayed in her best attire, accompanied by her friends, or perhaps joining in the dance now and then at some festival, and chatting away her spare hours with a neighbour, discussing the scandal or the quarrels of the village—trifles sufficient to occupy her heart. At length the warmth of her nature is influenced by certain new and unknown wishes. Inflamed by the flatteries of men, her former pleasures become by degrees insipid, till at length she meets with a youth to whom she is attracted by an indescribable feeling: upon him she now rests all her hopes; she forgets the world around her; she sees, hears, desires nothing but him, and him only. He alone occupies all her thoughts. Uncorrupted by the idle indulgence of an enervating vanity, her affection moving steadily towards its object, she hopes to become his, and to realise in an everlasting union with him, all that happiness which she sought, all that bliss for which she longed. His repeated promises confirm her hopes; embraces and endearments, which increase the ardour of her desires, overmaster her soul. She floats in a dim delusive anticipation of her happiness, and her feelings become excited to their utmost tension. She stretches out her arms finally to embrace the object of all her wishes——— and her lover forsakes her. Stunned and bewildered, she stands upon a precipice. All is darkness around her. No prospect, no hope, no consolation—forsaken by him in whom her existence was centred! She sees nothing of the wide world before her, thinks nothing of the many individuals who might supply the void in her heart; she feels herself deserted, forsaken by the world; and blinded and impelled by the agony which wrings her soul, she plunges into the deep, to end her sufferings in the broad embrace of death. See here, Albert, the history of thousands, and tell me, is not this a case of physical infirmity? Nature has no way to escape from the labyrinth, her powers are exhausted, she can contend no longer, and the poor soul must die.

Shame upon him who can look on calmly and exclaim, "The foolish girl! she should have waited; she should have allowed time to wear off the impression; her despair would have been softened, and she would have found another lover to comfort her." One might as well say, "The fool, to die of a fever!—why did he not wait till his strength was restored, till his blood became calm?—all would then have gone well, and he would have been alive now."

Albert, who could not see the justice of the comparison, offered some further objections, and amongst others, urged that I had taken the case of a mere ignorant girl. But how any man of sense, of more enlarged views and experience, could be excused, he was unable to comprehend. "My friend," I exclaimed, "man is but man, and whatever be the extent of his reasoning powers, they are of little avail when passion rages within, and he feels himself confined by the narrow limits of nature. It were better, then——But we will talk of this some other time," I said, and caught up my hat. Alas! my heart was full; and we parted without conviction on either side. How rarely in this world do men understand each other!

August 15*th*.

There can be no doubt that in this world nothing is so indispensable as love. I observe that Charlotte could not lose me without a pang, and the very children have but one wish; that is, that I should visit them again to-morrow. I went this afternoon to tune Charlotte's piano. But I could not do it, for the little ones insisted on my telling them a story; and Charlotte herself urged me to satisfy them. I waited upon them at tea, and they are now as fully contented with me as with Charlotte, and I told them my very best tale of the princess who was waited upon by dwarfs. I improve myself by this exercise, and am quite surprised at the impression my stories create. If I sometimes invent an incident which I forget upon the next narration, they remind me directly that the story was different before; so that I now endeavour to relate with exactness the same anecdote in the same monotonous tone, which never changes. I find by this how much an author injures his works by altering them, even though they be improved in a poetical point of view. The first impression is readily received. We are so constituted, that we believe the most incredible things, and once they are engraved upon the memory, woe to him who would endeavour to efface them.

August 18*th*.

Must it ever be thus—that the source of our happiness must also be the fountain of our misery? The full and ardent sentiment which animated my heart with the love of nature, overwhelming me with a torrent of delight, and which brought all paradise before me, has now become an insupportable torment—a demon which perpetually pursues and harrasses me. When in bye-gone days I gazed from these rocks upon yonder mountains across the river, and upon the green flowery valley before me, and saw all nature budding and bursting around—the hills clothed from foot to peak with tall, thick forest trees—the valleys in all their varied windings, shaded with the loveliest woods, and the soft river gliding along amongst the lisping reeds, mirroring the beautiful clouds which the soft evening breeze wafted across the sky,—when I heard the groves about me melodious with the music of birds, and saw the million swarms of insects dancing in the last golden beams of the sun, whose setting rays awoke the humming bettles from their grassy beds, whilst the subdued tumult around directed my attention to the ground, and I there observed the arid rock compelled to yield nutriment to the dry moss, whilst the heath flourished upon the barren sands below me,—all this displayed to me the inner warmth which animates all nature, and filled and glowed within my heart.   I felt myself exalted by this overflowing fullness to the perception of the Godhead, and the glorious forms of an infinite universe became visible to my soul! Stupendous mountains encompassed me, abysses yawned at my feet, and cataracts fell headlong down before me; impetuous rivers rolled through the plain, and rocks and mountains resounded from afar.   In the depths of the earth I saw innumerable powers in motion, and multiplying to infinity, whilst upon its surface, and beneath the heavens, there teemed ten thousand varieties of living creatures.   Everything around is alive with an infinite number of forms, while mankind fly for security to their petty houses, from the shelter of which they rule in their imaginations over the wide-extended universe.   Poor fool! in whose petty estimation all things are little.   From the inaccessible mountains, across the desert which no mortal foot has trod, far as the confines of the unknown ocean, breathes the spirit of the eternal Creator, and every atom to which he has given existence finds favour in his sight.   Ah, how often at that time has the flight of a bird, soaring above my head, inspired me with the desire of being transported to the shores of the immeasurable waters, there to quaff the pleasures of life from the foaming goblet of the Infinite; and, to partake, if but for a moment, even with the confined powers of my soul, the beatitude of that Creator, who accomplishes all things in himself, and through himself.

My dear friend, the bare recollection of those hours still consoles me.   Even this effort to recal those ineffable sensations, and give them utterance, exalts my soul above itself, and makes me doubly feel the intensity of my present anguish.

It is as if a curtain had been drawn from before my eyes; and, instead of prospects of eternal life, the abyss of an ever open grave yawned before me. Can we say of anything that it exists when all passes away—when time, with the speed of a storm, carries all things onward—and our transitory existence, hurried along by the torrent, is either swallowed up by the waves or dashed against the rocks. There is not a moment but preys upon you, and upon all around you—not a moment in which you do not yourself become a destroyer. The most innocent walk deprives of life thousands of poor insects; one step destroys the fabric of the industrious ant, and converts a little world into chaos. No; it is not the great and rare calamities of the world, the floods which sweep away whole villages, the earthquakes which swallow up our towns, that affect me. My heart is wasted by the thought of that destructive power which lies concealed in every part of universal nature. Nature has formed nothing that does not consume itself, and every object near it; so that, surrounded by earth and air, and all the active powers, I wander on my way with aching heart, and the universe is to me a fearful monster, for ever devouring its own offspring.

August 21*st*.

In vain do I stretch out my arms towards her when I awaken in the morning from my weary slumbers. In vain do I seek for her at night in my bed, when some innocent dream has happily deceived me, and placed her near me in the fields, when I have seized her hand and covered it with countless kisses. And when I feel for her in the half confusion of sleep, with the happy sense that she is near me, tears flow from my oppressed heart, and bereft of all comfort, I weep over my future woes.

August 22*nd*.

What a misfortune, Wilhelm! My active spirits have degenerated into contented indolence. I cannot be idle, and yet I am unable to set to work. I cannot think: I have no longer any feeling for the beauties of nature, and books are distasteful to me. Once we give ourselves up, we are

U

totally lost.   Many a time and oft I wish I were a common labourer; that, awakening in the morning, I might have but one prospect, one pursuit, one hope, for the day which has dawned.   I often envy Albert when I see him buried in a heap of papers and parchments, and I fancy I should be happy were I in his place.   Often impressed with this feeling, I have been on the point of writing to you and to the minister, for the appointment at the embassy, which you think I might obtain. I believe I might procure it.   The minister has long shown a regard for me, and has frequently urged me to seek employment.   It is the business of an hour only.   Now and then the fable of the horse recurs to me.   Weary of liberty, he suffered himself to be saddled and bridled, and was ridden to death for his pains.   I know not what to determine upon.   For is not this anxiety for change the consequence of that restless spirit which would pursue me equally in every situation of life?

August 28th.

If my ills would admit of any cure, they would certainly be cured here.   This is my birthday, and early in the morning I received a packet from Albert.   Upon opening it, I found one of the pink ribands which Charlotte wore in her dress the first time I saw her, and which I had several times asked her to give me.   With it were two volumes in duodecimo of Wetstein's Homer, a book I had often wished for, to save me the inconvenience of carrying the large Ernestine edition with me upon my walks.   You see how they anticipate my wishes, how well they understand all those little attentions of friendship, so superior to the costly presents of the great, which are humiliating.   I kissed the riband a thousand times, and in every breath inhaled the remembrance of those happy and irrevocable days, which filled me with the keenest joy. Such, Wilhelm, is our fate.   I do not murmur at it: the flowers of life are but visionary!   How many pass away, and leave no trace behind—how few yield any fruit—and the fruit itself, how rarely does it ripen!   And yet there are flowers enough!—and, is it not strange, my friend, that we should suffer the little that does really ripen, to rot, decay, and perish unenjoyed?   Farewell!   It is a glorious summer.   I often climb into the trees in Charlotte's orchard and shake down the pears that hang on the highest branches. She stands below, and catches them as they fall.

August 30th.

Unhappy being that I am! Why do I thus deceive myself? What is to come of all this wild, aimless, endless passion? I cannot pray except to her. My imagination sees nothing but her, all surrounding objects are of no account, except as they relate to her. In this dreamy state I enjoy many happy hours, till at length I feel compelled to tear myself away from her. Ah! Wilhelm, to what does not my heart often compel me! When I have spent several hours in her company, till I feel completely absorbed by her figure, her grace, the divine expression of her thoughts, my mind becomes gradually excited to the highest excess, my sight grows dim, my hearing confused, my breathing oppressed as if by the hand of a murderer, and my beating heart seeks to obtain relief for my aching senses. I am sometimes unconscious whether I really exist. If in such moments I find no sympathy, and Charlotte does not allow me to enjoy the melancholy consolation of bathing her hand with my tears, I feel compelled to tear myself from her, when I either wander through the country, climb some precipitous cliff, or force a path through the trackless thicket, where I am lacerated and torn by thorns and briars, and thence I find relief. Sometimes I lie stretched on the ground, overcome with fatigue and dying with thirst; sometimes late in the night, when the moon shines above me, I recline against an aged tree, in some sequestered forest, to rest my weary limbs; when, exhausted and worn, I sleep till break of day. O Wilhelm! the hermit's cell, his sackcloth, and girdle of thorns would be luxury and indulgence compared with what I suffer. Adieu! I see no end to this wretchedness except the grave.

September 3rd.

I must away. Thank you, Wilhelm, for determining my wavering purpose. For a whole fortnight I have thought of leaving her. I must away. She is returned to town, and is at the house of a friend. And then, Albert——yes, I must go.

————

Oh, what a night, Wilhelm! I can henceforth bear anything. I shall never see her again. Oh, why cannot I fall on your neck, and with floods of tears and raptures, give utterance to all the passions which distract my heart! Here I sit gasping for breath, and struggling to compose myself. I wait for day, and at sunrise the horses are to be at the door.

And she is sleeping calmly, little suspecting that she has seen me for the last time. I am free. I have had the courage, in an interview of two hours' duration, not to betray my intention. And oh! Wilhelm, what a conversation it was!

Albert had promised to come to Charlotte in the garden, immediately after supper. I was upon the terrace under the tall chestnut-trees, and watched the setting sun,—I saw him sink for the last time beneath this delightful valley and silent stream. I had often visited the same spot with Charlotte, and witnessed that glorious sight, and now—I was walking up and down the very avenue which was so dear to me. A secret sympathy had frequently drawn me thither, before I knew Charlotte, and we were delighted when, in our early acquaintance, we discovered that we each loved the same spot, which is indeed as romantic as any that ever captivated the fancy of an artist.

From beneath the chestnut-trees there is an extensive view. But I remember that I have mentioned all this in a former letter, and have described the tall mass of beech-trees at the end, and how the avenue grows darker and darker as it winds its way among them, till it ends in a gloomy recess which has all the charm of a mysterious solitude. I still remember the strange feeling of melancholy which came over me, the first time I entered that dark retreat, at bright midday. I felt some secret foreboding that it would, one day, be to me the scene of some happiness or misery.

I had spent half an hour struggling between the contending thoughts of going and returning, when I heard them coming up the terrace. I ran to meet them; I trembled as I took her hand and kissed it. As we reached the top of the terrace, the moon rose from behind the wooded hill. We conversed on many subjects, and without perceiving it, we approached the gloomy recess. Charlotte entered and sat down. Albert seated himself beside her; I did the same, but my agitation did not suffer me to remain long seated. I got up and stood before her, then walked backwards and forwards, and sat down again. I was restless and miserable. Charlotte drew our attention to the beautiful effect of the moonlight, which threw a silver hue over the terrace, in front of us beyond the beech-trees. It was a glorious sight, and was rendered more striking by the darkness which surrounded the spot where we were. We remained for some time silent, when Charlotte observed: " Whenever I walk by moonlight, it brings to my remembrance all my beloved and departed friends, and I am filled with thoughts of death and futurity. We shall live again, Werther!" she continued, with a firm but feeling voice; " but shall we know one another again— what do you think, what do you say?"

" Charlotte!" I said, as I took her hand in mine, and my eyes filled with tears, "we shall see each other again—here and hereafter we shall meet again." I could say no more. Why, Wilhelm, should she put this question to me, just at the moment when the fear of our cruel separation filled my heart?

" And oh! do those departed ones know how we are employed here, do they know when we are well and happy, do they know when we recal their memories with the fondest love? In the silent hour of evening the shade of my mother hovers round me; when seated in the midst of my children, I see them assembled near me as they used to assemble near her! and then I raise my anxious eyes to heaven, and wish she could look down upon us and witness how I fulfil the promise I made to her in her last moments, to be a mother to her children. With what emotion do I then exclaim, ' Pardon, dearest of mothers, pardon me, if I do not adequately supply your place. Alas! I do my utmost; they are clothed and fed, and still better, they are loved and educated. Could you but see, sweet saint! the peace and harmony that dwells amongst us, you would glorify God with the warmest feelings of gratitude, to whom, in your last hour, you addressed such fervent prayers for our happiness.' " Thus did she express herself, but O! Wilhelm, who can do justice to her language, how can cold and passionless words convey the heavenly expressions of the spirit? Albert interrupted her gently. " This affects you too deeply, my dear Charlotte: I know your soul dwells on such recollections with intense delight, but I implore"——"O, Albert," she continued, " I am sure you do not forget the evenings when we three used to sit at the little round table, when papa was absent, and the little ones had retired. You often had a good book with you, but seldom read it; the conversation of that noble being was preferable to everything—that beautiful, bright, gentle, and yet ever-toiling woman. God alone knows how I have supplicated with tears on my nightly couch that I might be like her."

I threw myself at her feet, and seizing it, bedewed it with a thousand tears. " Charlotte!" I exclaimed, " God's blessing and your mother's spirit are upon you." "O! that you had known her," she said, with a warm pressure of the hand; " she was worthy of being known to you." I thought I should have fainted; never had I received praise so flattering. She continued: "and yet she was doomed to die in the flower of her youth, when her youngest child was scarcely six months old. Her illness was but short, but she was calm and resigned—and it was only for her children, especially the youngest, that she felt unhappy. When her end drew nigh, she bade me bring them to her. I obeyed, the younger ones knew nothing of their approaching loss, while the elder ones were quite overcome with grief. They stood around the bed, and she raised her feeble hands to heaven, and prayed over them, then kissing them in turn, she dismissed them, and said to me, " Be you a mother to them." I gave her my hand. " You are promising much, my child," she said, " a mother's fondness, and a mother's care! I have often witnessed, by your tears of gratitude, that you know what is a mother's tenderness; show it to your brothers and sisters, and be dutiful and faithful to your father as a wife: you will be his comfort." She inquired for him. He had retired to conceal his intolerable anguish—he was heartbroken.

" Albert! you were in the room. She heard some one

moving, she inquired who it was, and desired you to approach. She surveyed us both with a look of composure and satisfaction expressive of her conviction that we should be happy—happy with one another." Albert fell upon her neck, and kissed her, and exclaimed, "We are so, and we shall be so." Even the composure of Albert was moved, and I was excited beyond expression.

"And such a being," she continued, "was to leave us, Werther! Great God, must we thus part with everything we hold dear in this world? Nobody felt this more acutely than the children; they cried and lamented for a long time afterwards, complaining that black men had carried away their dear mamma."

Charlotte stood up. It aroused me, but I continued sitting, and held her hand. "Let us go," she said; "it grows late." She attempted to withdraw her hand; I held it still. "We shall see each other again," I exclaimed, "we shall recognise each other under every possible change. I am going," I continued, "going willingly, but should I say for ever, perhaps I may not keep my word, Adieu, Charlotte! adieu, Albert; we shall meet again." "Yes, to-morrow, I think," she answered, with a smile. To-morrow! how I felt the word! Ah! she little thought, when she drew her hand away from mine. They walked down the avenue. I stood gazing after them in the moonlight. I threw myself upon the ground, and wept; I then sprang up, and ran out upon the terrace, and saw, under the shade of the linden-trees, her white dress disappearing near the garden gate. I stretched out my arms, and she vanished.

BOOK II.

October 20th

WE arrived here yesterday. The ambassador is indisposed, and will not go out for some days. If he were less peevish and morose, all would be well. I see but too plainly that heaven has destined me to severe trials; but, courage! a light heart may bear anything. A light heart! I smile to find such a word proceeding from my pen. A little more lightheartedness would render me the happiest being under the sun. But must I despair of my talents and faculties, whilst others of far inferior abilities parade before me with the utmost self-satisfaction? Gracious Providence! to whom I owe all my powers, why didst thou not withhold some of those blessings I possess, and substitute in their place a feeling of self-confidence and contentment?

But patience! all will yet be well; for I assure you, my dear friend, you were right; since I have been obliged to associate continually with other people, and observe what they do, and how they employ themselves, I have become far better satisfied with myself. For we are so constituted by nature, that we are ever prone to compare ourselves with others, and our happiness or misery depends very much on the objects and persons around us. On this account, nothing is more dangerous than solitude; there our imagination, always disposed to rise, taking a new flight on the wings of fancy, pictures to us a chain of beings, of whom we seem the most inferior. All things appear greater than they really are, and all seem superior to us. This operation of the mind is quite natural; we so continually feel our own imperfections, and fancy we perceive in others the qualities we do not possess, attributing to them also all that we enjoy ourselves, that by this process we form the idea of a perfect, happy man—a man, however, who only exists in our own imagination.

But when, in spite of weakness and disappointments, we set to work in earnest, and persevere steadily, we often find that, though obliged continually to tack, we make more way than others who have the assistance of wind and tide; and, in truth, there can be no greater satisfaction than to keep pace with others, or outstrip them in the race.

November 26th.

I begin to find my situation here more tolerable. I find a great advantage in being much occupied, and the number of persons I meet, and their different pursuits, create a varied entertainment for me. I have formed the acquaintance of the Count C——, and I esteem him more and more every day. He is a man of strong understanding and great discernment; but though he sees further than other people, he is not on that account cold in his manner, but is capable of inspiring and returning the warmest affection. He appeared interested in me, on one occasion, when I had to transact some business with him. He perceived, at the first word, that we understood each other, and that he could converse with me in a different tone from what he used with others. I cannot sufficiently esteem his frank and open kindness to me. It is the greatest and most genuine of pleasures to observe a great mind in sympathy with our own.

December 24th.

As I anticipated, the ambassador occasions me infinite annoyance. He is the most punctilious blockhead under heaven. He does everything step by step, with the trifling minuteness of an old woman, and he is a man whom it is impossible to please, because he is never pleased with himself. I like to do business regularly and cheerfully, and when it is finished, to leave it. But he constantly returns my papers to me, saying, "They will do," but recommending me to look over them again, as "one may always improve, by using a better word, or a more appropriate particle." I then lose all patience, and wish myself at the devil. Not a conjunction, not an adverb must be omitted; he has a deadly antipathy to all those transpositions of which I am so fond, and if the music of our periods is not tuned to the established official key, he cannot comprehend our meaning. It is deplorable to be connected with such a fellow.

My acquaintance with the Count C—— is the only compensation for such an evil. He told me frankly, the other day, that he was much displeased with the difficulties and delays of the ambassador; that people like him are obstacles both to themselves and to others; but," added he, "one must submit, like a traveller who has to ascend a mountain; if the mountain was not there, the road would be both shorter and pleasanter, but there it is, and he must get over it."

The old man perceives the Count's partiality for me; this annoys him, and he seizes every opportunity to depreciate the Count in my hearing. I naturally defend him, and that only renders matters worse. Yesterday he made a blow at me, in allusion to him. "The Count," he said, " is a man of the world, and a good man of business; his style is good, and he writes with facility; but like other geniuses, he has no solid learning." He looked at me with an expression that seemed to ask if I felt the blow? But it did not produce the desired effect: I despise a man who can think and act in such a manner. However, I made a stand, and answered, with no little warmth. The Count, I said, was a man entitled to respect alike for his character and his acquirements. I had never met a person whose mind was stored with more useful and extensive knowledge—who had, in fact, mastered such an infinite variety of subjects, and who yet retained all his activity for the details of ordinary business. This was altogether beyond his comprehension, and I took my leave, lest my anger should be too highly excited by some new absurdity on his part.

And you are to blame for all this, you who persuaded me to bend my neck to this yoke, by preaching a life of activity to me. If the man who plants vegetables, and carries his corn to town on market days, is not more usefully employed than I am, then let me work ten years longer at the galleys to which I am now chained.

Oh! the brilliant wretchedness, the weariness that one is doomed to witness among the silly people whom we meet in society here! The ambition of rank; how they watch, how they toil to gain precedence. What poor and contemptible passions are displayed in their utter nakedness! We have a woman here, for example, who never ceases to entertain the company with accounts of her family and her estates. Any stranger would consider her a silly being, whose head was turned by her pretensions to rank and property; but she is in reality even more ridiculous—the daughter of a mere magistrate's clerk from this neighbourhood. I cannot understand how human beings can so debase themselves.

Every day I observe more and more the folly of judging of others by ourselves; and I have so much trouble with myself, and my own heart is in such constant agitation, that I am well content to let others pursue their own course, if they only allow me the same privilege.

What provokes me most, is the unhappy extent to which distinctions of rank are carried. I know perfectly well how necessary are inequalities of condition, and I am sensible of the advantages I myself derive therefrom—but I would not have these institutions prove a barrier to the small chance of happiness which I may enjoy on this earth.

I have lately become acquainted with a Miss B——, a very agreeable girl, who has retained her natural manners in the midst of artificial life. Our first conversation pleased us both equally, and at taking leave, I requested permission to visit her. She consented in so obliging a manner, that I waited with impatience for the arrival of the happy moment. She is not a native of this place, but resides here with her aunt. The countenance of the old lady is not prepossessing. I paid her much attention, addressing the greater part of my conversation to her, and in less than half an hour I discovered what her niece subsequently acknowledged to me, that her aged aunt, having but a small fortune, and a still smaller share of understanding, enjoys no satisfaction, except in the pedigree of her ancestors, no protection save in her noble birth, and no enjoyment, but in looking from her castle over the heads of the humble citizens. She was, no doubt, handsome in her youth, and in her early years probably trifled away her time in rendering many a poor youth the sport of her caprice; in her riper years she has submitted to the yoke of a veteran officer, who, in return for her person and her small independence, has spent with her what we may designate her age of brass. He is dead, and she is now a widow and deserted. She spends her iron age alone, and would not be approached, except for the loveliness of her niece.

January 8th, 1772.

What beings are men, whose whole thoughts are occupied with form and ceremony, who for years together devote their mental and physical exertions to the task of advancing themselves but one step, and endeavouring to occupy a higher place at the table. Not that such persons would otherwise want employment; on the contrary, they give themselves much trouble by neglecting important business for such petty trifles. Last week a question of precedence arose, at a sledging party, and all our amusement was spoilt.

The silly creatures cannot see that it is not place which

constitutes real greatness, since the man who occupies the first place but seldom plays the principal part. How many kings are governed by their ministers—how many ministers by their secretaries? Who, in such cases, is really the chief? He, as it seems to me, who can see through the others, and possesses strength or skill enough to make their power or passions subservient to the execution of his own designs.

January 20th.

I must write to you from this place, my dear Charlotte, from a small room in a country inn, where I have taken shelter from a severe storm. During my whole residence in that wretched place D ——, where I lived amongst strangers, —strangers, indeed, to this heart—I never at any time felt the smallest inclination to correspond with you; but in this cottage, in this retirement, in this solitude, with the snow and hail beating against my lattice-pane, you are my first thought. The instant I entered, your figure rose up before me, and the remembrance! O my Charlotte, the sacred, tender remembrance! Gracious Heaven! restore to me the happy moment of our first acquaintance.

Could you but see me, my dear Charlotte, in the whirl of dissipation; how my senses are dried up, but my heart is at no time full. I enjoy no single moment of happiness; all is vain—nothing touches me. I stand, as it were, before the raree-show, I see the little puppets move, and I ask whether it is not an optical illusion. I am amused with these puppets, or rather, I am myself one of them, but when I sometimes grasp my neighbour's hand, I feel that it is not natural, and I withdraw mine with a shudder. In the evening I say I will enjoy the next morning's sunrise, and yet I remain in bed; in the day I promise to ramble by moonlight, and I, nevertheless, remain at home. I know not why I rise, nor why I go to sleep.

The leaven which animated my existence is gone, the charm which cheered me in the gloom of night, and aroused me from my morning slumbers, is for ever fled.

I have found but one being here to interest me, a Miss B——. She resembles you, my dear Charlotte, if any one can possibly resemble you. "Ah!" you will say, " he has learnt to pay fine compliments." And this is partly true. I have been very agreeable lately, as it was not in my power to be otherwise. I have, moreover, a deal of wit, and the ladies say that no one understands flattery better—or falsehoods, you will add, since the one accomplishment invariably accompanies the other. But I must tell you of Miss B. She has abundance of soul, which flashes from her deep blue eyes. Her rank is a torment to her, and satisfies no one desire of her heart. She would gladly retire from this whirl of fashion, and we often picture to ourselves a life of undisturbed happiness in distant scenes of rural retirement; and then we speak of you, my dear Charlotte, for she knows you, and renders homage to your merits, but her homage is not exacted, but voluntary—she loves you, and delights to hear you made the subject of conversation.

Oh, that I were sitting at your feet in your favourite little room, with the dear children playing around us. If they became troublesome to you, I would tell them some appalling goblin story, and they would crowd round me with silent attention. The sun is setting in glory; his last rays are shining on the snow, which covers the face of the country; the storm is over, and I must return to my dungeon. Adieu! —Is Albert with you, and what is he to you? God forgive the question.

February 8th.

For a week past we have had the most wretched weather, but this to me is a blessing, for during my residence here, not a single fine day has beamed from the heavens, but has been lost to me by the intrusion of somebody. During the severity of rain, sleet, frost, and storm, I congratulate myself that it cannot be worse in doors than abroad, nor worse abroad than it is within doors, and so I become reconciled. When the sun rises bright in the morning, and promises a glorious day, I never omit to exclaim, " There now, they have another blessing from Heaven, which they will be sure to destroy; they spoil everything—health, fame, happiness, amusement—and they do this generally through folly, ignorance, or imbecility, and always, according to their own account, with the best intentions. I could often beseech them, on my bended knees, to be less resolved upon their own destruction.

———

I fear that my ambassador and I shall not continue much longer together. He is really growing past endurance. He transacts his business in so ridiculous a manner, that I am often compelled to contradict him, and do things my own way, and then, of course, he thinks them very ill done. He complained of me lately on this account at Court, and the Minister gave me a reprimand,—a gentle one it is true, but still a reprimand. In consequence of this, I was about to tender my resignation, when I received a letter, to which I submitted with great respect, on account of the high, noble, and generous spirit which dictated it. He endeavoured to soothe my excessive sensibility, paid a tribute to my extreme ideas of duty, of good example, and of perseverance in business, as the fruit of my youthful ardour,—an impulse which he did not seek to destroy but only to moderate, that it might have proper play and be productive of good. So now I am at rest for another week, and no longer at variance with myself. Content and peace of mind are valuable things. I could wish, my dear friend, that these precious jewels were less transitory.

———

God bless you, my dear friends, and may He grant you that happiness which He denies to me!

I than you, Albert, for having deceived me. I waited for the news that your wedding-day was fixed, and I intended on that day, with solemnity, to take down Charlotte's profile from the wall, and to bury it with some other papers I possess. You are now united, and her picture still remains here. Well, let it remain! Why should it not? I know that I am still one of your society, that I still occupy a place uninjured in Charlotte's heart, that I hold the second place therein, and I intend to keep it. O! I should become mad if she could forget.—Albert! that thought is hell. Farewell, Albert—farewell, angel of Heaven—farewell, Charlotte!

———

March 15th.

I have just had a sad adventure, which will drive me from hence. I lose all patience!—Death!—It is not to be remedied, and you are alone to blame, who urged and impelled me to fill a post for which I was by no means suited. I have now reason to be satisfied, and so have you! But that you may not again attribute this fatality to my impetuous temper, I send you, my dear sir, a plain and simple narration of the affair, as a mere chronicle of facts would describe it.

The Count of O—— likes me, and distinguishes me: it is well known, and I have mentioned this to you a hundred times. Yesterday I dined with him; it is the day on which the nobility are accustomed to assemble at his house in the evening. I never once thought of the assembly, nor that we subalterns did not belong to such society. Well! I dined with the Count, and after dinner we adjourned to the large hall; we walked up and down together, and I conversed with him and with Colonel B. who joined us, and in this manner the hour for the assembly approached. God knows I was thinking of nothing, when who should enter but the honourable Lady S., accompanied by her noble husband and their silly, scheming daughter, with her small waist and flat neck—and with disdainful looks and a haughty air, they passed me by. As I heartily detest the whole race, I determined upon going away, and only waited till the Count had disengaged himself from their impertinent prattle to take leave, when the agreeable Miss B. came in. As I never meet her without experiencing a heartfelt pleasure, I stayed and talked to her, leaning over the back of her chair, and did not perceive till after some time that she seemed a little confused, and ceased to answer me with her usual ease of manner. I was struck with it. "Heavens!" I said to myself, "can she too be like the rest?" I felt annoyed, and was about to withdraw; but I remained, notwithstanding, forming excuses for her conduct, fancying she did not mean it, and still hoping to receive some friendly recognition. The rest of the company now arrived. There was the Baron F—— in an entire suit that dated from the coronation of Francis I., the Chancellor N—— with his deaf wife, the shabbily dressed I——, whose old-fashioned coat bore evidence of modern

repairs—this crowned the whole. I conversed with some of
my acquaintance, but they answered me laconically. I was
engaged in observing Miss B——, and did not notice that
the women were whispering at the end of the room, that the
murmur extended by degrees to the men, that Madame S——
addressed the Count with much warmth, (this was all related
to me subsequently by Miss B.,) till at length the Count
came up to me and took me to the window.—"You know our
ridiculous customs," he said; "I perceive the company is rather
displeased at your being here; I would not on any account"
——"I beg your excellency's pardon," I exclaimed; "I
ought to have thought of this before, but I know you will forgive this little inattention. I was going," I added, "some
time ago, but my evil genius detained me," and I smiled and
bowed to take my leave. He shook me by the hand in a manner
which expressed everything. I hastened at once from the illustrious assembly, sprang into a carriage and drove to M——. I
contemplated the setting sun from the top of the hill, and read
that beautiful passage in Homer, where Ulysses is entertained
by the hospitable herdsmen. This was indeed delightful.

I returned home to supper in the evening. But few persons were assembled in the room; they had turned up a
corner of the table-cloth, and were playing at dice. The
good-natured A—— came in; he laid down his hat when he
saw me, approached me and said, in a low tone,—"You
have met with a disagreeable adventure." "I!" I exclaimed.
"The Count obliged you to withdraw from the assembly!"
"Deuce take the assembly," said I, "I was very glad to be
gone." "I am delighted," he added, "that you take it so
lightly; I am only sorry that it is already so much spoken
of." The circumstance then began to pain me. I fancied
that every one who sat down, and even looked at me, was
thinking of this incident, and my heart became embittered.

And now I could plunge a dagger into my bosom, when
I hear myself everywhere pitied, and observe the triumph
of my enemies, who say that this is always the case with
vain persons, whose heads are turned with conceit, who affect
to despise forms and such petty, idle nonsense.

Say what you will of fortitude, but show me the man who
can patiently endure the laughter of fools, when they have
obtained an advantage over him. 'Tis only when their non-

sense is without foundation that one can suffer it without complaint.

———

March 16*th*.

Everything conspires against me. I met Miss B—— walking to-day. I could not help joining her; and when we were at a little distance from her companions, I expressed my sense of her altered manner towards me. "O Werther!" she said, in a tone of emotion, you who know my heart, how could you so ill interpret my distress? What did I not suffer for you from the moment you entered the room! I foresaw it all—a hundred times was I on the point of mentioning it to you. I knew that the S——s and T——s, with their husbands, would quit the room rather than remain in your company; I knew that the Count would not break with them: and now so much is said about it." "How!" I exclaimed, and endeavoured to conceal my emotion, for all that Adelin had mentioned to me yesterday recurred to me painfully at that moment. "Oh, how much it has already cost me!" said this amiable girl, while her eyes filled with tears. I could scarcely contain myself, and was ready to throw myself at her feet. "Explain yourself!" I cried. Tears flowed down her cheeks. I became quite frantic. She wiped them away, without attempting to conceal them. "You know my aunt," she continued—"she was present, and in what light does she consider the affair! Last night and this morning, Werther, I was compelled to listen to a lecture upon my acquaintance with you. I have been obliged to hear you condemned and depreciated, and I could not—I dared not—say much in your defence."

Every word she uttered was a dagger to my heart. She did not feel what a mercy it would have been to conceal everything from me. She told me, in addition, all the impertinence that would be further circulated, and how the malicious would triumph; how they would rejoice over the punishment of my pride, over my humiliation for that want of esteem for others with which I had often been reproached. To hear all this, Wilhelm, uttered by her in a voice of the most sincere sympathy, awakened all my passions, and I am still in a state of extreme excitement. I wish I could find a man to jeer me about this event. I would sacrifice him to my

x

resentment : the sight of his blood might possibly be a relief to my fury. A hundred times have I seized a dagger to give ease to this oppressed heart. Naturalists tell of a noble race of horses that instinctively open a vein with their teeth, when heated and exhausted by a long course, in order to breathe more freely. I am often tempted to open a vein to procure for myself everlasting liberty.

March 24*th.*

I have tendered my resignation to the Court. I hope it will be accepted, and you will forgive me for not having previously consulted you. It is necessary I should leave this place. I know all you will urge to induce me to stay, and therefore———. I beg you will soften this news to my mother. I am unable to do anything for myself; how, then, should I be competent to assist others? It will afflict her that I should have interrupted that career which would have made me first a privy councillor, and then minister, and that I should look behind me in place of advancing. Argue as you will, combine all the reasons which should have induced me to remain—I am going ; that is sufficient. But that you may not be ignorant of my destination, I may mention that the Prince of——— is here. He is much pleased with my company ; and having heard of my intention to resign, he has invited me to his country house to pass the spring months with him. I shall be left completely my own master ; and as we agree on all subjects but one, I shall try my fortune, and accompany him.

April 19*th.*

Thanks for both your letters. I delayed my reply, and withheld this letter, till I should obtain an answer from the Court. I feared my mother might apply to the minister to defeat my purpose. But my request is granted—my resignation is accepted. I shall not recount with what reluctance it was accorded, nor relate what the minister has written ; you would only renew your lamentations. The Crown Prince has sent me a present of five-and-twenty ducats ; and indeed such goodness has affected me to tears. For this reason I shall not require from my mother the money for which I lately applied.

May 5th.

I leave this place to-morrow; and as my native place is only six miles from the high road, I intend to visit it once more, and recall the happy dreams of my childhood. I shall enter at the same gate through which I came with my mother, when, after my father's death, she left that delightful retreat to immure herself in your melancholy town. Adieu, my dear friend; you shall hear of my future career.

May 9th.

I have paid my visit to my native place with all the devotion of a pilgrim, and have experienced many unexpected emotions. Near the great elm-tree, which is a quarter of a league from the village, I got out of the carriage, and sent it on before, that alone, and on foot, I might enjoy vividly and heartily all the pleasure of my recollections. I stood there under that same elm which was formerly the term and object of my walks. How things have since changed! Then, in happy ignorance, I sighed for a world I did not know, where I hoped to find every pleasure and enjoyment which my heart could desire; and now, on my return from that wide world, O my friend, how many disappointed hopes and unsuccessful plans have I brought back!

I contemplated the mountains which lay stretched out before me, and I thought how often they had been the object of my dearest desires. Here used I to sit for hours together with my eyes bent upon them, ardently longing to wander in the shade of those woods—to lose myself in those valleys, which form so delightful an object in the distance! With what reluctance did I leave this charming spot when my hour of recreation was over, and my leave of absence expired! I drew near to the village—all the well-known old summer-houses and gardens were recognised again; I disliked the new ones, and all other alterations which had taken place. I entered the village, and all my former feelings returned. I cannot, my dear friend, enter into details, charming as were my sensations: they would be dull in the narration. I had

x 2

intended to lodge in the market-place, near our old house. As soon as I entered, I perceived that the school-room, where our childhood had been taught by that good old woman, was converted into a shop. I called to mind the sorrow, the heaviness, the tears and oppression of heart which I experienced in that confinement. Every step produced some particular impression. A pilgrim in the Holy Land does not meet so many spots pregnant with tender recollections, and his soul is hardly moved with greater devotion. One incident will serve for illustration. I followed the course of a stream to a farm, formerly a delightful walk of mine, and I paused at the spot where as boys we used to amuse ourselves with making ducks and drakes upon the water. I recollected so well how I used formerly to watch the course of that same stream, following it with enquiring eagerness, forming romantic ideas of the countries it was to pass through; but my imagination was soon exhausted, while the water continued flowing farther and farther on, till my fancy became bewildered by the contemplation of an invisible distance. Exactly such, my dear friend, so happy and so confined, were the thoughts of our good ancestors. Their feelings and their poetry were fresh as childhood. And when Ulysses talks of the immeasurable sea and of the boundless earth, his epithets are true, natural, deeply felt, and mysterious. Of what importance is it that I have learnt with every schoolboy that the world is round? Man needs but little earth for enjoyment, and still less for his final repose.

I am at present with the Prince at his hunting-lodge. He is a man with whom one can live happily. He is honest and unaffected. There are, however, some strange characters about him, whom I cannot at all understand. They do not seem vicious, and yet they do not carry the appearance of thoroughly honest men. Sometimes I am disposed to believe them honest, and yet I cannot persuade myself to confide in them. It grieves me to hear the Prince occasionally talk of things which he has only read or heard of, and always with the same view in which they have been represented by others.

He values my understanding and talents more highly than he does my heart, and I am alone proud of the latter. It is the sole source of everything, of our strength, of our happiness, and our misery. All the knowledge I possess, every one else can acquire, but my heart is exclusively my own.

May 25th.

I have had a plan in my head, of which I did not intend to speak to you until it was accomplished; now that it has failed I may as well mention it. I wished to enter the army, and had long been desirous of taking the step. This, indeed, was the chief reason for my coming here with the Prince, as he is a General in the ———— service. I communicated my design to him during one of our walks together. He disapproved of it, and it would have been actual madness not to have listened to his reasons.

June 11th.

Say what you will, I can remain here no longer. Why should I remain? I am weary of it. The Prince is as gracious to me as any one could be, and yet I am not at my ease. There is, indeed, nothing in common between us. He is a man of understanding, but quite of the ordinary kind. His conversation affords me no more amusement than I should derive from the perusal of a well-written book. I shall remain here a week longer, and then start again on my travels. My drawings are the best things I have done since I came here. The Prince has a taste for the arts, and would improve if his mind were not fettered by cold rules and mere technical ideas. I often lose patience when, with a glowing imagination I am giving expression to art and nature, he interferes with learned suggestions, and uses at random the technical phraseology of artists.

July 16th.

Once more I am a wanderer, a pilgrim, through the world But what else are you?

July 18th.

Whither am I going? I will tell you in confidence. I am obliged to continue a fortnight longer here, and then I think it would be better for me to visit the mines in ————. But

I am only deluding myself thus.   The fact is, I wish to be
near Charlotte again,—that is all.   I smile at the suggestions
of my heart, and obey its dictates.

July 29th.

No! no! it is yet well—all is well!   I, her husband!
——O God! who gave me being, if thou hadst destined this
happiness for me, my whole life would have been one continual thanksgiving!   But I will not murmur——forgive
these tears; forgive these fruitless wishes.   She—my wife!
Oh, the very thought of folding that dearest of Heaven's
creatures in my arms!——Dear Wilhelm! my whole frame
feels convulsed when I see Albert put his arms round her
slender waist.

And shall I avow it?   Why should I not, Wilhelm?   She
would have been happier with me than with him!   Albert is
not the man to satisfy the wishes of such a heart.   He wants
a certain sensibility; he wants——in short, their hearts do
not beat in unison!   How often, my dear friend, in reading
a passage from some interesting book, when my heart and
Charlotte's seemed to meet, and in a hundred other instances,
when our sentiments were unfolded by the story of some
fictitious character, have I felt that we were made for each
other!   But, dear Wilhelm! he loves her with his whole
soul, and what does not such a love deserve?

I have been interrupted by an insufferable visit.   I have
dried my tears and composed my thoughts.   Adieu, my best
friend!

August 4th.

I am not alone unfortunate!   All men are disappointed in
their hopes and deceived in their expectations.   I have paid
a visit to my good old woman under the lime-trees.   The
eldest boy ran out to meet me; his exclamation of joy
brought out his mother, but she had a very melancholy look.
Her first word was, "Alas! dear sir, my little John is dead."
He was the youngest of her children.   I was silent.   "And
my husband has returned from Switzerland without any
money, and if some kind people had not assisted him, he must
have begged his way home.   He was taken ill with fever on

his journey." I could answer nothing, but made the little one a present. She invited me to take some fruit; I complied, and left the place with a sorrowful heart.

August 21st.

My sensations are constantly changing. Sometimes a happy prospect opens before me; but, alas! it is only for a moment, and then when I am lost in reverie, I cannot help saying to myself, " If Albert were to die ?—Yes, she would become—and I should be——," and so I pursue a chimera, till it leads me to the edge of a precipice at which I shudder.

When I pass through the same gate and walk along the same road which first conducted me to Charlotte, my heart sinks within me at the change that has since taken place. All, all, is altered! No sentiment, no pulsation of my heart is the same. My sensations are such as would occur to some departed Prince whose spirit should return to visit the superb palace which he had built in happy times, adorned with costly magnificence, and left to a beloved son, but whose glory he should find departed and its halls deserted and in ruins.

September 3rd.

I sometimes cannot understand how she can love another, how she dares love another, when I love nothing in this world so completely, so devotedly, as her, when I know only her, and have no other possession than her in the world.

September 4th.

It is even so! As nature puts on her autumn tints, it becomes autumn with me and around me. My leaves are sere and yellow, and the neighbouring trees are divested of their foliage. Do you remember my writing to you about a peasant boy, shortly after my arrival here? I have just made inquiries about him in Walheim. They say he has been dismissed from his service, and is now avoided by every one. I met him yesterday on the road, going to a neighbouring village. I spoke to him, and he told me his story. It interested me exceedingly, as you will easily understand when I

repeat it to you. But why should I trouble you? Why
should I not reserve all my sorrow for myself? Why should
I continue to give you occasion to pity and blame me? But
no matter; this also is part of my destiny.

At first the peasant lad answered my inquiries with a
sort of subdued melancholy, which seemed to me the mark
of a timid disposition; but as we grew to understand each
other, he spoke with less reserve, and openly confessed his
faults and lamented his misfortune. I wish, my dear friend,
I could give proper expression to his language. He told me
with a sort of pleasurable recollection, that after my departure his passion for his mistress increased daily, until at last
he neither knew what he did nor what he said, nor what was
to become of him. He could neither eat, nor drink, nor
sleep; he felt a sense of suffocation; he disobeyed all orders,
and forgot all commands involuntarily; he seemed as if
pursued by an evil spirit; till one day, knowing that his
mistress had gone to an upper chamber, he followed her, or
rather felt attracted after her. As she proved deaf to his
entreaties, he had recourse to violence. He knows not what
happened, but he called God to witness that his intentions to
her were honourable, and that he desired nothing more sincerely than that they should marry and pass their lives together. When he had come to this point, he began to hesitate,
as if there was something which he had not courage to utter,
till at length he acknowledged with some confusion certain
little confidences which she had encouraged and freedoms
which she had allowed. He broke off two or three times in
his narration, and assured me most earnestly that he had no
wish to make her bad, as he termed it, for he loved her still
as sincerely as ever; that the tale had never before escaped
his lips, and was only now told, to convince me that he was
not utterly lost and abandoned. And here, my dear friend,
I must commence the old song, which you know I utter
eternally. If I could only represent the man as he stood
and stands now before me,—could I only give his true
expressions, you would feel compelled to sympathise in his
fate. But enough; you, who know my misfortune and my
disposition, can easily comprehend the attraction which draws
me towards every unfortunate being, but particularly towards him whose story I have recounted.

Upon perusing this letter a second time, I find I have omitted the conclusion of my tale, but it is easily supplied. She became reserved towards him, at the instigation of her brother, who had long hated him, and desired his expulsion from the house, fearing that his sister's second marriage might deprive his children of the handsome fortune which they expected from her, as she is childless. He was dis-missed at length, and the whole affair occasioned so much scandal, that the mistress dared not take him back, even if she had wished it. She has since hired another servant, with whom, they say, the brother is equally displeased, and whom she is likely to marry; but my informant assures me that he himself is determined not to survive such a catastrophe.

This story is neither exaggerated nor embellished; indeed, I have weakened and impaired it in the narration, by the necessity of using the more refined expressions of society.

This love, then, this constancy, this passion is no poetical fiction. It is actual, and dwells in its greatest purity amongst that class of mankind whom we term rude, uneducated. We are the educated, not the perverted! But read this story with attention, I implore you. I am tranquil to-day, for I have been employed upon this narration; you see by my writing that I am not so agitated as usual. Read and re-read this tale, Wilhelm! it is the history of your friend. My fortune has been and will be similar; and I am neither half so brave nor half so determined as the poor wretch with whom I hesitate to compare myself.

September 5th.

Charlotte had written a letter to her husband in the country, where he was detained by business. It commenced "My dearest love, return as soon as possible; I await you with a thousand raptures." A friend, who arrived, brought word that, for certain reasons, he could not return imme-diately. Charlotte's letter was not forwarded, and the same evening it fell into my hands. I read it and smiled. She asked the reason. "What a heavenly treasure is imagina-tion!" I exclaimed; "I fancied for a moment that this was written to me !" She paused and seemed displeased. I was silent.

———

It cost me much to part with the blue coat which I wore the first time I danced with Charlotte. But I could not possibly wear it any longer. But I have ordered a new one, precisely similar, even to the collar and sleeves, as well as a new waistcoat and pantaloons.

But it does not produce the same effect upon me. I know not how it is; but I hope in time I shall like it better.

———

She has been absent for some days. She went to meet Albert. To-day I visited her; she rose to receive me, and I kissed her hand most tenderly.

A canary at the moment flew from a mirror and settled upon her shoulder. "Here is a new friend," she observed, while she made him perch upon her hand; "he is a present for the children. What a dear he is! Look at him! When I feed him, he flutters with his wings, and pecks so nicely. He kisses me, too—only look!"

She held the bird to her mouth, and he pressed her sweet lips with so much fervour, that he seemed to feel the excess of bliss which he enjoyed.

"He shall kiss you, too," she added, and then she held the bird towards me. His little beak moved from her mouth to mine, and the delightful sensation seemed like the forerunner of the sweetest bliss.

"A kiss," I observed, "does not seem to satisfy him; he wishes for food, and seems disappointed by these unsatisfactory endearments."

"But he eats out of my mouth," she continued, and extended her lips to him containing seed, and she smiled with all the charm of a being who has allowed an innocent participation of her love.

I turned my head away. She should not act thus. She ought not to excite my imagination with such displays of heavenly innocence and happiness, nor awaken my heart from its slumbers, in which it dreams of the worthlessness of life! And why not? Because she knows how much I love her.

———

September 15th.

It makes me wretched, Wilhelm, to think that there should be men incapable of appreciating the few things which possess a real value in life. You remember the walnut-trees at S————, under which I used to sit with Charlotte during my visits to the worthy old Vicar. Those glorious trees, the very sight of which has so often filled my heart with joy, how they adorned and refreshed the parsonage yard, with their wide extended branches! and how pleasing was our remembrance of the good old pastor, by whose hands they were planted so many years ago! The schoolmaster has frequently mentioned his name. He had it from his grandfather. He must have been a most excellent man, and under the shade of those old trees his memory was ever venerated by me. The schoolmaster informed us yesterday, with tears in his eyes, that those trees had been felled. Yes, cut to the ground! I could, in my wrath, have slain the monster who struck the first stroke. And I must endure this!—I who, if I had had two such trees in my own court, and one had died from old age, should have wept with real affliction. But there is some comfort left—such a thing is sentiment—the whole village murmurs at the misfortune, and I hope the Vicar's wife will soon find, by the cessation of the villagers' presents, what a wound she has inflicted upon the feelings of the neighbourhood. It was she who did it,—the wife of the present incumbent (our good old man is dead)—a tall, sickly creature, who is so far right to disregard the world, as the world totally disregards her. The silly being affects to be learned, pretends to examine the canonical books, lends her aid towards the new-fashioned reformation of Christendom, moral and critical, and shrugs up her shoulders at the mention of Lavater's enthusiasm. Her health is destroyed, which prevents her from having any enjoyment here below. Such a creature alone could have cut down my walnut-trees! I can never pardon it. Hear her reasons. The falling leaves made the court wet and dirty, the branches obstructed the light, boys threw stones at the nuts when they were ripe, and the noise affected her nerves and disturbed

her profound meditations, when she was weighing the difficulties of Kennicot, Semler, and Michaelis. Finding that all
the parish, particularly the old people, were displeased, I
asked "why they allowed it?" "Ah, sir!" they replied,
"when the steward orders, what can we poor peasants do?"
But one thing has happened well. The steward and the
Vicar (who for once thought to reap some advantage from the
caprices of his wife) intended to divide the trees between
them. The revenue-office being informed of it, revived an
old claim to the ground where the trees had stood, and sold
them to the best bidder. There they still lie on the ground.
If I were the sovereign, I should know how to deal with
them all—Vicar, steward, and revenue-office. Sovereign did
I say? I should in that case care little about the trees that
grew in the country.

October 10*th.*

Only to gaze upon her dark eyes is to me a source of happiness! And what grieves me is, that Albert does not seem
so happy as he—hoped to be—as I should have been,—if
——I am no friend to these pauses, but here I cannot
express myself otherwise; and probably I am explicit
enough.

October 12*th.*

Ossian has superseded Homer in my heart. To what a
world does the illustrious bard carry me! To wander over
pathless wilds, surrounded by impetuous whirlwinds, where,
by the feeble light of the moon, we see the spirits of our
ancestors; to hear from the mountain-tops, mid the roar of
torrents, their plaintive sounds issuing from deep caverns,
and the sorrowful lamentations of a maiden who sighs and
expires on the mossy tomb of the warrior by whom she was
adored. I meet this bard with silver hair; he wanders in
the valley, he seeks the footsteps of his fathers, and, alas!
he finds only their tombs. Then contemplating the pale
moon, as she sinks beneath the waves of the rolling sea, the
memory of bygone days strikes the mind of the hero,—
days, when approaching danger invigorated the brave, and
the moon shone upon his bark laden with spoils, and returning in triumph. When I read in his countenance deep

sorrow, when I see his dying glory sink, exhausted, into the grave, as he inhales new and heart-thrilling delight from his approaching union with his beloved, and he casts a look on the cold earth and the tall grass which is so soon to cover him, and then exclaims, " The traveller will come,—he will come who has seen my beauty, and he will ask, where is the bard,—where is the illustrious son of Fingal? He will walk over my tomb, and will seek me in vain!" Then, O my friend, I could instantly, like a true and noble knight, draw my sword, and deliver my prince from the long and painful languor of a living death, and dismiss my own soul to follow the demigod whom my hand had set free.

October 19*th.*

Alas! the void—the fearful void, which I feel in my bosom! Sometimes I think, if I could only once—but once, press her to my heart, this dreadful void would be filled.

October 26*th.*

Yes, I feel certain, Wilhelm, and every day I become more certain, that the existence of any being whatever is of very little consequence. A friend of Charlotte's called to see her just now; I withdrew into a neighbouring apartment, and took up a book; but finding I could not read, I sat down to write. I heard their conversation; they spoke upon ordinary topics, and retailed the news of the town. One was going to be married, another was ill, very ill—she had a dry cough; her face was growing thinner daily, and she had occasional fits. " N —— is very unwell, too," said Charlotte. "His limbs begin to swell already," answered the other, and my lively imagination carried me at once to the beds of the infirm. There I see them struggling against death, with all the agonies of pain and horror; and these women, Wilhelm, talk of all this with as much indifference as one would mention the death of a stranger. And when I look around the apartment where I now am,—when I see Charlotte's apparel lying before me, and Albert's writings, and all those articles of furniture which are so familiar to me, even to the very inkstand which I am using,—when I think what I am to this family—everything. My friends esteem me; I often contribute to their happiness, and my heart seems as if it could not beat without them; and yet—if I were to die, if I were to be summoned from the midst of this circle, would they feel,—or how long would they feel, the void which my loss would make in their existence? How long! Yes, such is the frailty of man, that even there, where he has the greatest consciousness of his own being, where he makes the strongest and most forcible impression, even in the memory, in the heart of his beloved, there also he must perish—vanish—and that quickly.

October 27th.

I could tear open my bosom with vexation to think how little we are capable of influencing the feelings of each other. No one can communicate to me those sensations of love, joy, rapture, and delight which I do notnaturally possess; and though my heart may glow with the most lively affection, I cannot make the happiness of one in whom the same warmth is not inherent.

October 27th. Evening.

I possess so much, but my love for her absorbs it all. I possess so much, but without her I have nothing.

October 30th.

One hundred times have I been on the point of embracing her. Heavens! what a torment it is to see so much loveliness passing and repassing before us, and yet not dare to touch it! And to touch is the most natural of human insticts. Do not children touch everything they see? And I!

November 3rd.

Witness Heaven how often I lie down in my bed, with a wish, and even a hope, that I may never awaken again! and in the morning, when I open my eyes, I behold the sun once more, and am wretched. If I were whimsical, I might blame the weather, or an acquaintance, or some personal disappointment, for my discontented mind, and then this insupportable load of trouble would not rest entirely upon myself. But, alas! I feel it too sadly. I am alone the cause of my own woe,—am I not? Truly, my own bosom contains the source of all my sorrow, as it previously contained the source of all my pleasure. Am I not the same being who once enjoyed an excess of happiness—who, at every step, saw Paradise open before him, and whose heart was ever expanded towards the whole world? And this heart is now dead; no sentiment can revive it: my eyes are dry, and my senses, no more refreshed by the influence of soft tears, wither and consume my brain. I suffer much, for I have lost the only charm of life; that active sacred power which created worlds around me,—it is no more. When I look from my window at the distant hills, and behold the morning sun breaking through the mists, and illuminating the country around, which is still wrapt in silence, whilst the soft stream winds gently through the willows which have shed their leaves; when glorious Nature displays all her beauties before me, and her wondrous prospects are ineffectual to extract one tear of joy from my withered heart; I feel that in such a moment I stand like a reprobate before Heaven, hardened, insensible, and unmoved. Oftentimes do I then bend my knee to the earth, and implore God for the blessing of tears, as the desponding labourer, in some scorching climate, prays for the dews of heaven to moisten his parched corn.

But I feel that God does not grant sunshine or rain to our importunate entreaties. And O those bygone days, whose memory now torments me, why were they so fortunate? Because I then waited with patience for the blessings of the Eternal, and received his gifts with the grateful feelings of a thankful heart.

November 8th.

Charlotte has reproved me for my excesses with so much tenderness and goodness. I have lately drunk more wine than usual. "Don't do it!" she said; "think of Charlotte!" "Think of you!" I answered; "can such advice be necessary—do I not ever think of you? And yet mine are not thoughts; you live within my soul. This very morning I was sitting in the spot where, a few days ago, you descended from the carriage, and ———." She immediately changed the subject, to prevent me from pursuing it further. My dear friend, my energies are all prostrated; she can do with me what she pleases.

November 15th.

I thank you, Wilhelm, for your cordial sympathy, for your excellent advice, and I implore you to be quiet. Leave me to my sufferings. In spite of my wretchedness, I have still strength enough for endurance. I revere religion,—you know I do. I feel that it can impart strength to the feeble, and comfort to the afflicted; but does it affect all men equally? Consider this vast universe; you will see thousands for whom it has never existed, thousands for whom it will never exist, whether it be preached to them or not; and must it then necessarily exist for me? Does not the Son of God himself say, that they are his whom the Father has given to him? Have I been given to him? What if the Father will retain me for himself, as my heart sometimes suggests? I pray you do not misinterpret this. Do not extract derision from my harmless words. I pour out my whole soul before you. Silence were otherwise preferable to me: but I need not shrink from a subject of which few know more than I do myself. What is the destiny of man, but to fill up the measure of his sufferings, and to drink his allotted cup of bitterness? And if that same cup proved bitter to the God of Heaven, under a human form, why should I affect a foolish pride and call it sweet? Why should I be ashamed of shrinking at that fearful moment, when my whole being will tremble between existence and annihilation; when a remembrance of the past, like a flash of lightning, will illuminate the dark gulph of futurity, when everything shall dissolve around me, and the whole world vanish away? Is not this the voice of a creature oppressed beyond all resource, self-deficient, about to plunge into inevitable destruction, and groaning deeply at its inadequate strength— "My God! my God! why hast thou forsaken me?" And should I feel ashamed to utter the same expression? Should I not shudder at a prospect which had its fears, even for him who spread out the heavens like a garment?

November 21st.

She does not feel, she does not know, that she is preparing a poison which will destroy us both; and I drink deeply of the draught which is to prove my destruction. What mean those looks of kindness with which she often—often—no, not often, but sometimes regards me,—that complacency with which she hears the involuntary sentiments which frequently escape me, and the tender pity for my sufferings which appears in her countenance?

Yesterday, when I took leave, she seized me by the hand and said, "Adieu, dear Werther!" Dear Werther!—It was the first time she ever called me dear; the sound sunk deep into my heart. I have repeated it a hundred times, and yesterday night, on going to bed, and talking to myself of various things, I suddenly said, "Good night, dear Werther!" I recollected myself and laughed.

November 22nd.

I cannot pray for strength to renounce her, for she seems to belong to me. I cannot pray that she may be given to me, for she is the property of another. In this way I affect mirth over my troubles, and if I had time, I could compose a whole litany of antitheses.

November 24th.

She is sensible of my sufferings. This morning her look pierced my very soul. I found her alone, and she was silent; she steadfastly surveyed me. I no longer saw in her face the charms of beauty or the fire of genius—these had disappeared. But I was affected by an expression much more touching—a look of the deepest sympathy and of the softest pity. Why was I afraid to throw myself at her feet? Why did I not dare to take her in my arms, and answer her by a thousand kisses? She had recourse to her piano for relief, and in a low and sweet voice accompanied the music with delicious sounds. Her lips never appeared so lovely; they seemed but just to open that they might imbibe the sweet tones which issued from the instrument, and return the heavenly vibration from her lovely mouth. Oh! who can express my sensations? I was quite overcome, and bending

Y

down, pronounced this vow: "Beautiful lips, which the angels guard, never will I seek to profane your purity with a kiss." And yet my friend, O, I wish——but my heart is darkened by doubt and indecision——could I but taste felicity and then die to expiate the sin. What sin?

November 26th.

Oftentimes I say to myself, "Thou alone art wretched; all other mortals are happy—none are distressed like thee! Then I read a passage in an ancient poet, and I seem to understand my own heart. I have so much to endure! Have men before me ever been so wretched?

November 30th.

I shall never be myself again! Wherever I go, some fatality occurs to distract me. Even to day—alas, for our destiny! alas, for human nature!

About dinner-time I went to walk by the river side, for I had no appetite. Everything around seemed gloomy; a cold and damp easterly wind blew from the mountains, and black heavy clouds spread over the plain. I observed a man at a distance in a tattered coat; he was wandering among the rocks, and seemed to be looking for plants. When I approached, he turned round at the noise, and I saw that he had an interesting countenance, in which a settled melancholy, strongly marked by benevolence, formed the principal feature. His long black hair was divided, and flowed over his shoulders. As his garb betokened a person of the lower order, I thought he would not take it ill if I inquired about his business, and I therefore asked what he was seeking for. He replied, with a deep sigh, that he was looking for flowers and could find none. "But it is not the season," I observed, with a smile. "Oh, there are so many flowers," he answered, as he came nearer to me. "In my garden, there are roses and honeysuckles of two sorts: one sort was given to me by my father; they grow as plentifully as weeds; I have been looking for them these two days and cannot find them. There are flowers above there, yellow, blue, and red, and that centaury has a very pretty blossom; but I can find none of them." I observed his peculiarity, and therefore asked him, with an air of indifference, what he intended to do with his flowers. A strange smile overspread his countenance. Holding his finger to his mouth, he expressed a hope that I would not betray him, and he then informed me that he had promised to gather a nosegay for his mistress. "That is right," said I. "O," he replied, "she possesses many other things as well; she is very rich." "And yet," I continued, "she likes your nosegays." "O, she has jewels and crowns!" he exclaimed. I asked who she was. "If the States-General would but pay me," he added, "I should be quite another man. Alas! there was a time when I was so happy, but that is past, and I am now——." He raised his swimming eyes to Heaven. "And you were happy once?" I observed. "Ah, would I were so still!" was his reply. "I was then as gay and contented as a man can be." An old woman, who was coming towards us, now called out, "Henry, Henry! where are you? We have been looking for you everywhere: come to dinner." "Is he your son?" I inquired, as I went towards her. "Yes," she said, "he is my poor, unfortunate son. The Lord has sent me a heavy affliction." I asked whether he had been long in this state. She answered, "He has been as calm as he is at present for about six months. I thank Heaven that he is so far recovered; he was for one whole year quite raving, and chained down in a madhouse. Now he injures no one, but talks of nothing else than kings and queens. He used to be a very good, quiet youth, and helped to maintain me; he wrote a very fine hand; but all at once he became melancholy, was seized with a violent fever, grew distracted, and is now as you see. If I were only to tell you, sir ——" I interrupted her by asking what period it was in which he boasted of having been so happy. "Poor boy!" she exclaimed, with a smile of compassion, "he means the time when he was completely deranged—a time he never ceases to regret—when he was in the madhouse, and unconscious of everything." I was thunderstruck: I placed a piece of money in her hand, and hastened away.

"You were happy!" I exclaimed, as I returned quickly to the town—"as gay and contented as a man can be!" God of Heaven! and is this the destiny of man? Is he only happy before he has acquired his reason, or after he has lost it! Unfortunate being! and yet I envy your fate—I

delusion to which you are a victim.   You go forth with joy
to gather flowers for your princess—in winter—and grieve
when you can find none, and cannot understand why they do
not grow.   But I wander forth without joy, without hope,
without design, and I return as I came.   You fancy what a
man you would be if the States-General paid you.   Happy
mortal, who can ascribe your wretchedness to an earthly
cause !   You do not know, you do not feel, that in your own
distracted heart, and disordered brain, dwells the source of
that unhappiness, which all the potentates on earth cannot
relieve.

Let that man die unconsoled who can deride the invalid
for undertaking a journey to distant healthful springs, where
he often finds only a heavier disease and a more painful death,
or who can exult over the despairing mind of a sinner, who
to obtain peace of conscience and an alleviation of misery,
makes a pilgrimage to the Holy Sepulchre !   Each laborious
step which galls his wounded feet in rough and untrodden
paths pours a drop of balm into his troubled soul, and the
journey of many a weary day brings a nightly relief to his
anguished heart.   Will you dare call this enthusiasm, ye
crowd of pompous declaimers ?   Enthusiasm ! O God ! thou
seest my tears.   Thou hast allotted us our portion of misery ;
must we also have brethren to persecute us, to deprive us of
our consolation, of our trust in thee, and in thy love and
mercy.   For our trust in the virtue of the healing root, or in
the strength of the vine, what is it else than a belief in thee,
from whom all that surrounds us derives its healing and restoring powers.   Father, whom I know not—who wert once
wont to fill my soul, but who now hidest thy face from me—
call me back to thee ; be silent no longer ; thy silence shall
not delay a soul which thirsts after thee.   What man, what
father, could be angry with a son for returning to him suddenly, for falling on his neck, and exclaiming, " I am here
again, my father ! forgive me if I have anticipated my journey, and returned before the appointed time !   The world is
everywhere the same—a scene of labour and of pain, of pleasure and reward ; but what does it all avail ?   I am happy
only where thou art ; and in thy presence am I content to
suffer or enjoy.   And wouldst thou, heavenly Father, banish
such a child from thy presence ?

December 1st.

Wilhelm, the man about whom I wrote to you—that man so enviable in his misfortunes—was secretary to Charlotte's father, and an unhappy passion for her which he cherished, concealed, and at length discovered, caused him to be dismissed from his situation. This made him mad. Think, whilst you peruse this plain narration, what an impression the circumstance has made upon me. But it was related to me by Albert, with as much calmness, as you will probably peruse it.

December 4th.

I implore your attention. It is all over with me. I can support this state no longer! To-day I was sitting by Charlotte. She was playing upon her piano a succession of delightful melodies, with such intense expression! Her little sister was dressing her doll upon my lap. The tears came into my eyes. I leaned down, and looked intently at her wedding ring—my tears fell—immediately she began to play that favourite, that divine air, which has so often enchanted me. I felt comfort from a recollection of the past, of those bygone days when that air was familiar to me, and then I recalled all the sorrows and the disappointments which I had since endured. I paced with hasty strides through the room; my heart became convulsed with painful emotions. At length I went up to her, and with eagerness exclaimed, "For Heaven's sake, play that air no longer." She stopped, and looked steadfastly at me. She then said, with a smile, which sunk deep into my heart, "Werther, you are ill; your dearest food is distasteful to you. But go, I entreat you, and endeavour to compose yourself." I tore myself away. God, thou seest my torments, and wilt end them!

December 6th.

How her image haunts me! Waking or asleep, she fills my entire soul! Soon as I close my eyes—here—in my brain, where all the nerves of vision are concentrated, her dark eyes are imprinted. Here—I do not know how to describe it—but if I shut my eyes, hers are immediately before me; dark as an abyss, they open upon me, and absorb my senses.

And what is man—that boasted demigod? Do not his powers fail when he most requires their use? And whether he soar in joy or sink in sorrow, is not his career in both inevitably arrested? and whilst he fondly dreams that he is grasping at infinity, does he not feel compelled to return to a consciousness of his cold, monotonous existence?

THE EDITOR TO THE READER.

It is a matter of extreme regret that we want original evidence of the last remarkable days of our friend, and we are, therefore, obliged to interrupt the progress of his correspondence, and to supply the deficiency by a connected narration.

I have felt it my duty to collect accurate information from the mouths of persons well acquainted with his history. The story is simple; and all the accounts agree, except in some unimportant particulars. It is true that, with respect to the characters of the persons spoken of, opinions and judgments vary.

We have only then to relate conscienciously the facts which our diligent labour has enabled us to collect, to give the letters of the deceased, and to pay particular attention to the slightest fragment from his pen, more especially as it is so difficult to discover the real and correct motives of men who are not of the common order.

. Sorrow and discontent had taken deep root in Werther's soul, and gradually imparted their character to his whole being. The harmony of his mind became completely disturbed; a perpetual excitement and mental irritation, which weakened his natural powers, produced the saddest effects upon him, and rendered him at length the victim of an exhaustion against which he struggled, with still more painful efforts than he had displayed, even in contending with his other misfortunes. His mental anxiety weakened his various good qualities, and he was soon converted into a gloomy companion—always unhappy and unjust in his ideas, the more wretched he became. This was at least the opinion of Albert's friends. They assert, moreover, that the character of Albert himself had undergone no change in the mean time; he was still the same being whom Werther had loved, honoured, and respected from the commencement. His love for Charlotte was unbounded; he was proud of her, and desired that she should be recognised by every one as the noblest of created beings. Was he, however, to blame for wishing to avert from her every appearance of suspicion, or for his unwillingness to share his rich prize with another, even for a moment, and in the most innocent manner? It is asserted that Albert frequently retired from his wife's apartment during Werther's visits; but this did not arise from hatred or aversion to his friend, but only from a feeling that his presence was oppressive to Werther.

Charlotte's father, who was confined to the house by indisposition, was accustomed to send his carriage for her, that she might take excursions in the neighbourhood. One day the weather had been unusually severe, and the whole country was covered with snow.

Werther went for Charlotte the following morning, in order that, if Albert were absent, he might conduct her home.

The beautiful weather produced but little impression upon his troubled spirit. A heavy weight lay upon his soul, deep melancholy had taken possession of him, and his mind knew no change save from one painful thought to another.

As he now never enjoyed internal peace, the condition of his fellow-creatures was to him a perpetual source of trouble and distress. He believed he had interrupted the happiness of Albert and his wife, and whilst he censured himself strongly for this, he began to entertain a secret dislike to Albert.

His thoughts were directed occasionally to this point. "Yes," he would repeat to himself, with ill-concealed dissatisfaction—" yes, this is, after all the extent of that confiding, dear, tender, and sympathetic love, that calm and eternal fidelity! What do I behold but satiety and indifference? Does not every frivolous engagement attract him, more than his charming and lovely wife? Does he know how to prize his happiness? Can he value her as she deserves? He possesses her, it is true—I know that, as I know much more—and I have become accustomed to the thought, that he will drive me mad, or, perhaps, murder me. Is his friendship towards me unimpaired? Does he not view my attachment

to Charlotte as an infringement upon his rights, and consider
my attention to her as a silent rebuke to himself? I know,
and indeed feel, that he dislikes me—that he wishes for my
absence—that my presence is hateful to him."

He often paused on his way to visit Charlotte, stood
doubtingly still, and seemed desirous of returning, but he
nevertheless proceeded; and, engaged in such thoughts and
soliloquies as we have described, he finally reached the
hunting-lodge with a sort of involuntary consent.

Upon one occasion he entered the house, and inquiring for
Charlotte, he observed that the inmates were in unusual
confusion. The eldest boy informed him that a dreadful
misfortune had occurred at Walheim—that a peasant had
been murdered! But this made little impression upon him.
Entering the apartment, he found Charlotte engaged reasoning with her father, who, in spite of his infirmity, insisted on
going to the scene of the crime, in order to instinute an
inquiry. The criminal was unknown,—the victim had been
found dead at his own door, that morning. Suspicions were
excited; the murdered man had been in the service of a
widow, and the person who had previously filled the situation
had been dismissed from her employment.

As soon as Werther heard this, he exclaimed with great
excitement, " Is it possible! I must go to the spot—I cannot delay a moment!" He hastened to Walheim; every
incident returned vividly to his remembrance—and he entertained not the slightest doubt that that man was the murderer
to whom he had so often spoken, and for whom he entertained
so much regard. His way took him past the well-known
lime-trees, to the house where the body had been carried,
and his feelings were greatly excited at the sight of the fondly
recollected spot. That threshhold where the neighbours'
children had so often played together, was stained with blood;
love and attachment, the noblest feelings of human nature,
had been converted into violence and murder. The huge
trees around were bare and leafless; the beautiful hedgerows
which surrounded the old churchyard-wall were withered,
and the grave-stones, half covered with snow, were visible
through the openings.

As he approached the little inn, near to which the whole
village was assembled, there suddenly arose a wild cry.

A troop of armed peasants was seen approaching, and a general shout arose that the criminal had been apprehended. Werther looked, and was not long in doubt. The prisoner was no other than the servant, who had been formerly so attached to the widow, and whom he had met prowling about, with that suppressed anger and ill-concealed despair which we have before described.

"What have you done, unfortunate man?" inquired Werther, as he advanced towards the prisoner. The latter turned his eyes upon him in silence, and then replied with perfect composure, "No one will now marry her, and she will marry no one." The prisoner was secured in the inn, and Werther left the place.

The mind of Werther was fearfully excited by this shocking occurrence. He ceased, however, to be oppressed by his usual feeling of melancholy, moroseness, and indifference to everything that passed around him. He entertained a strong degree of pity for the prisoner, and was seized with an indescribable anxiety to save him from his impending fate. He considered him so unfortunate, he deemed his crime so excusable, and thought his own condition so nearly similar, that he felt convinced he could make every one else view the matter in the light in which he saw it himself. He now became anxious to undertake his defence, and commenced composing an eloquent speech for the occasion, and on his way to the hunting-lodge, he could not refrain from speaking aloud the statement which he resolved to make to the Judge.

Upon his arrival, he found Albert had been before him, and he was a little perplexed by this meeting; but he soon recovered himself, and expressed his opinion with much warmth to the Judge. The latter shook his head doubtingly; and although Werther urged his case with the utmost zeal, feeling, and determination in defence of his client, yet, as we may easily suppose, the Judge was not much influenced by his appeal. On the contrary, he interrupted him in his address, reasoned with him seriously, and even administered a rebuke to him for becoming the advocate of a murderer: He demonstrated that, according to this precedent, every law might be violated, and the public security utterly destroyed. He added, moreover, that in such a case he could himself do nothing, without incurring the greatest responsibility; that everything must follow in the usual course, and pursue the ordinary channel.

Werther, however, did not abandon his enterprise, and even besought the Judge to connive at the flight of the prisoner. But this proposal was peremptorily rejected. Albert, who had taken some part in the discussion, coincided in opinion with the Judge. At this Werther became enraged, and took his leave in great anger, after the Judge had more than once assured him that the prisoner could not be saved!

The excess of his grief at this assurance may be inferred from a note we have found amongst his papers, and which was doubtless written upon this very occasion.

"Unhappy being! you cannot be saved! I see clearly that we cannot be saved!"

Werther was highly incensed at the observations which Albert had made to the Judge in this matter of the prisoner. He thought he could detect therein a little bitterness towards himself personally; and although, upon reflection, it could not escape his sound judgment that their view of the matter was correct, he felt the greatest possible reluctance to make such an admission.

A memorandum of Werther's upon this point, expressive of his general feelings towards Albert, has been found amongst his papers.

"What is the use of my continually repeating that he is a good and estimable man? He is an inward torment to me—and I am incapable of being just towards him."

One fine evening in winter, when the weather seemed inclined to thaw, Charlotte and Albert were returning home together. The former looked from time to time about her, as if she missed Werther's company. Albert began to speak of him, and censured him for his prejudices. He alluded to his unfortunate attachment, and wished it were possible to discontinue his acquaintance. "I desire it on our own account," he added, " and I request you will compel him to alter his deportment towards you, and to visit you less frequently. The world is censorious, and I know that here and there we are spoken of." Charlotte made no reply, and Albert seemed to feel her silence. At least, from that time, he never again spoke of Werther, and when she introduced the subject, he allowed the conversation to die away, or else he directed the discourse into another channel.

The vain attempt which Werther had made to save the unhappy murderer was the last feeble glimmering of a flame about to be extinguished. He sank almost immediately afterwards into a state of gloom and inactivity, until he was at length brought to perfect distraction by learning that he was to be summoned as a witness against the prisoner, who asserted his complete innocence.

His mind now became oppressed by the recollection of every misfortune of his past life. The mortification he had suffered at the Ambassador's, and his subsequent troubles, were revived in his memory. He became utterly inactive. Destitute of energy, he was cut off from every pursuit and occupation which compose the business of common life, and he became a victim to his own susceptibility, and to his restless passion for the most amiable and beloved of women, whose peace he destroyed. In this unvarying monotony of existence his days were consumed, and his powers became exhausted without aim or design, until they brought him to a sorrowful end.

A few letters which he left behind, and which we here subjoin, afford the best-proofs of his anxiety of mind and of the depth of his passion, as well as of his doubts and struggles and of his weariness of life.

December 12*th.*

Dear Wilhelm! I am reduced to the condition of those unfortunate wretches who believe they are pursued by an evil spirit. Sometimes I am oppressed—not by apprehension or fear—but by an inexpressible internal sensation, which weighs upon my heart and impedes my breath! Then I wander forth at night, even in this tempestuous season, and feel pleasure in surveying the dreadful scenes around me.

Yesterday evening I went forth.   A rapid thaw had suddenly set in; I had been informed that the river had risen, that the brooks had all overflowed their banks, and that the whole vale of Walheim was under water!   Upon the stroke of twelve I hastened forth.   I beheld a fearful sight.   The foaming torrents rolled from the mountains in the moonlight. —fields and meadows, trees and hedges, were confounded together, and the entire valley was converted into a deep lake, which was agitated by the roaring wind!   And when the moon shone forth and tinged the black clouds with silver, and the impetuous torrent at my feet foamed and resounded with awful and grand impetuosity, I was overcome by a mingled sensation of apprehension and delight.   With extended arms I looked down into the yawning abyss and cried "Plunge!"   For a moment my senses forsook me, in the intense delight of ending my sorrows and my sufferings by a plunge into that gulph!   And then I felt as if I were rooted to the earth, and incapable of seeking an end to my woes! But my hour is not yet come; I feel it is not.   O Wilhelm, how willingly could I abandon my existence to ride the whirlwind or to embrace the torrent! and then might not rapture perchance be the portion of this liberated soul?

I turned my sorrowful eyes towards a favourite spot, where I was accustomed to sit with Charlotte beneath a willow, after a fatiguing walk.   Alas! it was covered with water, and with difficulty I found even the meadow.   And the fields around the hunting-lodge, thought I!—has our dear bower been destroyed by this unpitying storm?   And a beam of past happiness streamed upon me, as the mind of a captive is illumined by dreams of flocks and herds and bygone joys of home!   But I am free from blame.   I have courage to die!   Perhaps I have——but I still sit here, like a wretched pauper who collects faggots and begs her bread from door to door, that she may prolong for a few days a miserable existence, which she is willing to resign.

December 15th.
What is the matter with me, dear Wilhelm?   I am afraid of myself!   Is not my love for her of the purest, most holy, and most brotherly nature?   Has my soul ever been sullied

by a single sensual desire—but I will make no protestations. And now, ye nightly visions, how truly have those mortals understood you, who ascribe your various contradictory effects to some invincible power! This night—I tremble at the avowal—I held her in my arms, locked in a close embrace; I pressed her to my bosom, and covered with countless kisses, those dear lips, which murmured in reply soft protestations of love. My sight became confused by the delicious intoxication of her eyes. Heavens! is it sinful to revel again in such happiness, to recall once more those rapturous moments with intense delight? Charlotte! Charlotte! I am lost! My senses are bewildered, my recollection is confused, mine eyes are bathed in tears—I am ill, and yet I am well—I wish for nothing—I have no desires—it were better I were gone!

Under the circumstances narrated above, a determination to quit this world had now taken fixed possession of Werther's soul. Since Charlotte's return, this thought had been the final object of all his hopes and wishes; but he had resolved that such a step should not be taken with precipitation, but with calmness and tranquillity, and with the most perfect deliberation.

His doubts and internal struggles may be understood from the following fragment, which was found without any date, amongst his papers, and appears to have formed the beginning of a letter to Wilhelm.

" Her presence, her fate, her sympathy for me, have power still to extract tears from my withered brain.

" One lifts up the curtain, and passes to the other side,— that is all! And why all these doubts and delays? Because we know not what is behind—because there is no returning— and because our mind infers that all is darkness and confusion, where we have nothing but uncertainty."

His appearance at length became quite altered by the effect of his melancholy thoughts, and his resolution was now finally and irrevocably taken, of which the following ambiguous letter, which he addressed to his friend, may appear to afford some proof.

December 20*th.*

I am grateful to your love, Wilhelm, for having repeated your advice so seasonably. Yes, you are right; it is undoubtedly better that I should depart! But I do not entirely approve your scheme of returning at once to your neighbourhood; at least, I should like to make a little excursion on the way, particularly as we may now expect a continued frost, and consequently good roads. I am much pleased with your intention of coming to fetch me, only delay your journey for a fortnight, and wait for another letter from me. One should gather nothing before it is ripe, and a fortnight sooner or later makes a great difference. Entreat my mother to pray for her son, and tell her I beg her pardon for all the unhappiness I have occasioned her. It has ever been my fate to give pain to those whose happiness I should have promoted. Adieu, my dearest friend! May every blessing of Heaven attend you! Farewell.

We find it difficult to express the emotions with which Charlotte's soul was agitated during the whole of this time, whether in relation to her husband or to her unfortunate friend, although we are enabled, by our knowledge of her character, to understand their nature.

It is certain that she had formed a determination, by every means in her power, to keep Werther at a distance; and if she hesitated in her decision, it was from a sincere feeling of friendly pity, knowing how much it would cost him—indeed, that he would find it almost impossible to comply with her wishes. But various causes now urged her to be firm. Her husband preserved a strict silence about the whole matter, and she never made it a subject of conversation, feeling bound to prove to him by her conduct that her sentiments agreed with his.

The same day, which was the Sunday before Christmas, after Werther had written the last-mentioned letter to his friend, he came in the evening to Charlotte's house, and found her alone. She was busy preparing some little gifts for her brothers and sisters, which were to be distributed to them on Christmas Day. He began talking of the delight of the children, and of that age when the sudden appearance of the Christmas-tree, decorated with fruit and sweetmeats, and lighted up with wax candles, causes such transports of joy. "You shall have a gift, too, if you behave well," said Charlotte, hiding her embarrassment under a' sweet smile. "And what do you call behaving well? What should I do —what can I do; my dear Charlotte," said he. ": Thursday night," she answered, "is Christmas Eve; the children are all to be here, and my father, too: there is a present for each;—do you come likewise, but do not come before that time." Werther started. "I desire you will not—it must be so," she continued. "I ask it of you as a favour—for my own peace and tranquillity. We cannot go on in this manner any longer." He turned away his face, walked hastily up and down the room, muttering indistinctly, "We cannot go on in this manner any longer!" Charlotte, seeing the violent agitation into which these words had thrown him, endeavoured to divert his thoughts by different questions, but in vain. "No, Charlotte!" he exclaimed: "I will never see you any more." "And why so?" she answered; "we may —we must see each other again, only let it be with more discretion. O, why were you born with that excessive, that ungovernable passion for everything that is dear to you?" Then, taking his hand, she said, "I entreat of you to be more calm; your talents, your understanding, your genius, will furnish you with a thousand resources. Be a man, and conquer an unhappy attachment towards a creature who can do nothing but pity you." He bit his lips, and looked at her with a gloomy countenance. She continued to hold his hand. "Grant me but a moment's patience, Werther," she said; "do you not see that you are deceiving yourself,—that you are seeking your own destruction? Why must you love me—me only, who belong to another? I fear, I much fear, that it is only the impossibility of possessing me which makes your desire for me so strong." He drew back his hand, whilst he surveyed her with a wild and angry look. "'Tis well," he exclaimed, "'tis very well; did not Albert furnish you with this reflection?—it is profound, a very profound remark." "A reflection that any one might easily make," she answered; "and is there not a woman in the whole world, who is at liberty, and has the power to make you happy? Conquer yourself; look for such a being, and believe me when I say that you will certainly find her. I have long felt for you, and for us all; you have confined yourself too long within the limits of too narrow a circle. Conquer yourself; make an effort, a short journey will be of service to you. Seek and find an object worthy of your love; then return hither, and let us enjoy together all the happiness of the most perfect friendship."

"This speech," replied Werther, with a cold smile—"this speech should be printed, for the benefit of all teachers. My dear Charlotte, allow me but a short time longer, and all will be well." "But, however, Werther," she added, "do not come again before Christmas." He was about to make some answer, when Albert came in. They saluted each other coldly, and with mutual embarrassment paced up and down the room. Werther made some common remarks; Albert did the same; and their conversation soon dropped. Albert asked his wife about some household matters, and finding that his commissions were not executed, he used some expressions which, to Werther's ear, savoured of extreme harshness. He wished to go, but had not power to move; and in this situation he remained till eight o'clock, his uneasiness and discontent continually increasing. At length the cloth was laid for supper, and he took up his hat and stick. Albert invited him to remain, but Werther, fancying that he was merely paying a formal compliment, thanked him coldly, and left the house.

Werther returned home, took the candle from his servant, and retired to his room alone. He talked for some time with great earnestness to himself, wept aloud, walked in a state of great excitement through his chamber, till at length, without undressing, he threw himself on the bed, where he was found by his servant at eleven o'clock, when the latter ventured to enter the room and take off his boots. Werther did not prevent him, but forbade him to come in the morning till he should ring.

On Monday morning, the 21st of December, he wrote the following letter to Charlotte, which was found, sealed, on his bureau after his death, and was given to her. I shall insert it in fragments, as it appears, from several circumstances, to have been written in that manner.

"It is all over, Charlotte, I am resolved to die! I make this declaration deliberately and coolly, without any romantic passion, on this morning of the day when I am to see you for the last time. At the moment you read these lines, O best of women! the cold grave will hold the inanimate remains of that restless and unhappy being who, in the last moments of his existence, knew no pleasure so great as that of conversing with you. I have passed a dreadful night, or rather let me say, a propitious one, for it has given me resolution—it has fixed my purpose. I am resolved to die. When I tore myself from you yesterday, my senses were in tumult and disorder; my heart was oppressed, hope and pleasure had fled from me for ever, and a petrifying cold had seized my wretched being. I could scarcely reach my room. I threw myself on my knees, and Heaven, for the last time, granted me the consolation of shedding tears. A thousand ideas, a thousand schemes arose within my soul; till at length one last, fixed, final thought took possession of my heart. It was to die. I lay down to rest, and in the morning—in the quiet hour of awakening, the same determination was upon me. To die! It is not despair—it is conviction that I have filled up the measure of my sufferings—that I have reached my appointed term, and that I must sacrifice myself for thee. Yes, Charlotte, why should I not avow it? One of us three must die—it shall be Werther. O beloved Charlotte! this heart, excited by rage and fury, has often conceived the horrid idea of murdering your husband—you—myself. The lot at length is cast! And in the bright, quiet evenings of summer, when you sometimes wander towards the mountains, let your thoughts then turn to me; recollect how often you have watched me coming to meet you from the valley—then bend your eyes upon the churchyard, which contains my grave, and by the light of the setting sun, mark how the evening breeze waves the tall grass which grows above my tomb. I was calm when I began this letter, but the recollection of these scenes makes me weep like a child."

About ten in the morning, Werther called his servant, and whilst he was dressing, told him that in a few days he intended to set out upon a journey, and bade him therefore lay his

z

clothes in order, and prepare them for packing up, call in all his accounts, fetch home the books he had lent, and give two months' pay to the poor dependents who were accustomed to receive from him a weekly allowance.

He breakfasted in his room, and then mounted his horse, and went to visit the steward, who however was not at home. He walked pensively in the garden, and seemed anxious to renew all the ideas that were most painful to him.

The children did not suffer him to remain long alone. They followed him, skipping and dancing before him, and told him that after to-morrow—and to-morrow—and one day more, they were to receive their Christmas gift from Charlotte; and they then recounted the all wonders of which they had formed ideas in their little imaginations. "To-morrow—and to-morrow," said he—"and one day more!"—and he kissed them tenderly. He was going—but the younger boy stopped him, to whisper something in his ear. He told him that his elder brothers had written splendid New-Year's wishes—so large!—one for papa, and another for Albert and Charlotte, and one for Werther, and they were to be presented early in the morning on New-Year's Day. This quite overcame him; he made each of the children a present, mounted his horse, left his compliments for papa and mamma, and, with tears in his eyes, rode away from the place.

He returned home about five o'clock, ordered his servant to keep up his fire, desired him to pack his books and linen at the bottom of the trunk, and to place his coats at the top. He then appears to have made the following addition to his letter to Charlotte.

———

"You do not expect me. You think I will obey you, and not visit you again till Christmas Eve. O Charlotte, to-day or never! On Christmas Eve you will hold this paper in your hand; you will tremble, and moisten it with your tears. I will—I must! Oh, how happy I feel to be determined!"

In the meantime Charlotte was in a pitiable state of mind. After her last conversation with Werther, she found how painful it would be to herself to decline his visits, and knew how severely he would suffer from their separation.

She had mentioned casually, in conversation with Albert,

that Werther would not return before Christmas Eve; and soon afterwards, Albert rode over to a person in the neighbourhood, with whom he had some business to transact, which would detain him from home all night.

Charlotte was sitting alone. None of her family were near, and she abandoned herself to the reflections which silently took possession of her mind. She was eternally united to a husband whose love and fidelity she had proved, to whom she was heartily devoted, and who seemed to be a special gift from Heaven to insure her happiness. On the other hand, Werther had become dear to her; from the very first hour of their acquaintance, there was a cordial unanimity of sentiment between them, and their long association and repeated interviews had made an indelible impression upon her heart. She had been accustomed to communicate to him every thought and feeling which interested her, and his absence threatened to open a void in her existence which it might be impossible to fill. How heartily she wished that she might convert him into a brother—that she could induce him to marry one of her own friends—or that she could re-establish his intimacy with Albert.

She passed all her intimate friends in review before her mind, but found something objectionable in each, and could decide upon none to whom she would consent to give him.

Amid all these considerations she felt deeply but indistinctly that her own real but unexpressed wish was to retain him for herself; and her pure and amiable heart felt from this thought a sense of oppression which seemed to forbid a prospect of happiness. She was wretched—a dark cloud obscured her mental vision.

It was now half-past six o'clock, and she heard Werther's step upon the stairs; she immediately recognised his voice, inquiring if she was at home. Her heart beat audibly—we could almost say for the first time—at his arrival. It was too late to deny herself, and, as he entered, she exclaimed, with a sort of ill-concealed confusion, " You have not kept your word." " I did not promise anything," he answered. " But you should have complied at least for my sake," she continued. " I implore it of you, for both our sakes."

She scarcely knew what she said or what she did, and sent for some one of her female friends, that she might

not be left alone with Werther.   He placed some books down,
which he had brought with him, then made inquiries about
some others, until she began to hope that her friends might
shortly arrive, entertaining at the same time a desire that
they might remain away.

At one moment she felt anxious that the servant should
remain in the adjoining room, then she wished differently.
Werther meanwhile walked impatiently backwards and for-
wards.   She went to the piano, and determined not to retire.
She then collected her thoughts and sat down quietly at
Werther's side, who had taken his usual place upon the sofa.

"Have you brought nothing to read?" she inquired.   He
had nothing.   "There in my drawer," she continued; "you
will find your own translation of some of the songs of Ossian.   I
have not yet read them, as I have still hoped to hear you recite
them; but for some time past I have not been able to accomplish
such a wish."   He smiled, and went to fetch the manuscript,
and with a shudder he took it up.   He sat down, and with
eyes swimming in tears, he began to read.

"Star of descending night! fair is thy light in the west!
thou liftest thy unshorn head from thy cloud; thy steps are
stately on thy hill.   What dost thou behold in the plain?
The stormy winds are laid.   The murmur of the torrent comes
from afar.   Roaring waves climb the distant rock.   The flies
of evening are on their feeble wings; the hum of their
course is on the field.   What dost thou behold, fair light?
But thou dost smile and depart.   The waves come with joy
around thee: they bathe thy lovely hair.   Farewell, thou
silent beam!   Let the light of Ossian's soul arise.

"And it does arise in its strength.   I behold my departing
friends.   Their gathering is on Lora, as in the days of other
years.   Fingal comes like a watery column of mist: his
heroes are around: and see the bards of song, grey-haired
Uullin! stately Rhyno! Alpin with the tuneful voice! the
soft complaint of Minona!   How are ye changed, my friends,
since the days of Selma's feast! when we contended like gales
of spring as they fly along the hill, and bend by turns the
feebly-whistling grass.

"Minona came forth in her beauty with downcast look
and tearful eye.   Her hair flew slowly on the blast that
rushed unfrequent from the hill.   The souls of the heroes

were sad when she raised the tuneful voice. Oft had she seen the grave of Salgar, the dark dwelling of white-bosomed Colma. Colma left alone on the hill with all her voice of song! Salgar promised to come: but the night descended around. Hear the voice of Colma, when she sat alone on the hill!

"*Colma*. It is night; I am alone, forlorn on the hill of storms. The wind is heard on the mountain. The torrent pours down from the rock. No hut receives me from the rain: forlorn on the hill of winds!

"Rise moon! from behind thy clouds. Stars of the night, arise! Lead me, some light, to the place where my love rests from the chase alone! His bow near him unstrung, his dogs panting around him! But here I must sit alone by the rock of the mossy stream. The stream and the wind roar aloud. I hear not the voice of my love! Why delays my Salgar; why the chief of the hill his promise? Here is the rock and here the tree! here is the roaring stream! Thou didst promise with night to be here. Ah! whither is my Salgar gone? With thee I would fly from my father, with thee from my brother of pride. Our race have long been foes: we are not foes, O Salgar!

"Cease a little while, O wind! stream, be thou silent awhile! let my voice be heard around! let my wanderer hear me! Salgar! it is Colma who calls. Here is the tree and the rock. Salgar, my love, I am here! Why delayest thou thy coming? Lo! the calm moon comes forth. The flood is bright in the vale. The rocks are grey on the steep. I see him not on the brow. His dogs come not before him with tidings of his near approach. Here I must sit alone!

"Who lie on the beach beside me? Are they my love and my brother? Speak to me, O my friends. To Colma they give no reply. Speak to me: I am alone! My soul is tormented with fears. Ah, they are dead! Their swords are red from the fight. O my brother! my brother! why hast thou slain my Salgar? Why, O Salgar! hast thou slain my brother? Dear were ye both to me! what shall I say in your praise? Thou wert fair on the hill. Among thousands he was terrible in fight! Speak to me! hear my voice! hear me, sons of my love! They are silent! silent for ever! Cold, cold, are their breasts of clay   Oh, from the rock on the hill, from the top of the windy steep, speak, ye ghosts of the dead! Speak, I will not be afraid! Whither are ye gone to rest? In what cave of the hill shall I find the departed? No feeble voice is on the gale: no answer half drowned in the storm!

"I sit in my grief: I wait for morning in my tears! Rear the tomb, ye friends of the dead. Close it not till Colma come. My life flies away like a dream. Why should I stay behind? Here shall I rest with my friend, by the streams of the sounding rock. When night comes on the hill—when the loud winds arise, my ghost shall stand in the blast, and mourn the death of friends. The hunter shall hear from his booth; he shall hear, but love my voice! For sweet shall my voice be for my friends: pleasant were her friends to Colma.

"Such was thy song, Minona, softly-blushing daughter of Torman. Our tears descended for Colma, and our souls were sad! Ullin came with his harp; he gave the song of Alpin. The voice of Alpin was pleasant, the soul of Rhyno was a beam of fire! But they had rested in the narrow house; their voice had ceased in Salma! Ullin had returned one day from the chase before the heroes fell. He heard their strife on the hill: their song was soft, but sad! They mourned the fall of Morar, first of mortal men! His soul was like the soul of Fingal: his sword like the sword of Oscar. But he fell, and his father mourned: his sister's eyes were full of tears. Minona's eyes were full of tears, the sister of car-borne Morar. She retired from the song of Ullin, like the moon in the west, when she foresees the shower and hides her fair head in a cloud. I touched the harp with Ullin: the song of mourning rose!

"*Rhyno*. The winds and the rain are past, calm is the noon of day. The clouds are divided in heaven. Over the green hills flies the inconstant sun. Red through the stony vale comes down the stream of the hill. Sweet are thy murmurs, O stream! but more sweet is the voice I hear. It is the voice of Alpin, the son of song, mourning for the dead! Bent is his head of age: red his tearful eye. Alpin, thou son of song, why alone on the silent hill? why complainest thou, as a blast in the wood—as a wave on the lonely shore?

"*Alpin*. My tears, O Rhyno! are for the dead—my voice for those that have passed away. Tall thou art on the hill;

fair among the sons of the vale. But thou shalt fall like
Morar: the mourner shall sit on thy tomb. The hills shall
know thee no more: thy bow shall lie in thy hall unstrung!

"Thou wert swift, O Morar! as a roe on the desert: terrible
as a meteor of fire. Thy wrath was as the storm. Thy
sword in battle as lightning in the field. Thy voice was a
stream after rain, like thunder on distant hills. Many fell
by thy arm: they were consumed in the flames of thy wrath.
But when thou didst return from war, how peaceful was thy
brow. Thy face was like the sun after rain: like the moon
in the silence of night: calm as the breast of the lake when
the loud wind is laid.

"Narrow is thy dwelling now! dark the place of thine
abode! With three steps I compass thy grave, O thou who
wast so great before! Four stones, with their heads of moss,
are the only memorial of thee. A tree with scarce a leaf,
long grass which whistles in the wind, mark, to the hunter's
eye, the grave of the mighty Morar. Morar! thou art low
indeed. Thou hast no mother to mourn thee, no maid with
her tears of love. Dead is she that brought thee forth.
Fallen is the daughter of Morglan.

"Who on his staff is this? Who is this whose head is
white with age, whose eyes are red with tears, who quakes at
every step? It is thy father, O Morar! the father of no son
but thee. He heard of thy fame in war, he heard of foes
dispersed. He heard of Morar's renown, why did he not
hear of his wound? Weep, thou father of Morar! Weep,
but thy son heareth thee not. Deep is the sleep of the dead,
—low their pillow of dust. No more shall he hear thy voice
—no more awake at thy call. When shall it be morn in the
grave, to bid the slumberer awake? Farewell, thou bravest
of men! thou conqueror in the field! but the field shall see
thee no more, nor the dark wood be lightened with the splendour of thy steel. Thou hast left no son. The song shall
preserve thy name. Future times shall hear of thee—they
shall hear of the fallen Morar!

"The grief of all arose, but most the bursting sigh of
Armin. He remembers the death of his son, who fell in the
days of his youth. Carmor was near the hero, the chief of
the echoing Galmol. Why bursts the sigh of Armin? he
said. Is there a cause to mourn? The song comes with its

music to melt and please the soul. It is like soft mist that, rising from a lake, pours on the silent vale; the green flowers are filled with dew, but the sun returns in his strength, and the mist is gone. Why art thou sad, O Armin, chief of sea-surrounded Gorma?

"Sad I am! nor small is my cause of woe! Carmor, thou hast lost no son; thou hast lost no daughter of beauty. Colgar the valiant lives, and Annira, fairest maid. The boughs of thy house ascend, O Connar! but Armin is the last of his race. Dark is thy bed, O Daura! deep thy sleep in the tomb! When shalt thou wake with thy songs?—with all thy voice of music?

"Arise, winds of Autumn, arise: blow along the heath. Streams of the mountains, roar; roar, tempests in the groves of my oaks! Walk through broken clouds, O Moon! show thy pale face at intervals; bring to my mind the night, when all my children fell, when Arindal the mighty fell—when Daura the lovely failed. Daura, my daughter, thou wert fair, fair as the moon on Fura, white as the driven snow, sweet as the breathing gale. Arindal, thy bow was strong, thy spear was swift in the field, thy look was like mist on the wave, thy shield a red cloud in a storm! Armar, renowned in war, came and sought Daura's love. He was not long refused; fair was the hope of their friends.

"Erath, son of Odgal, repined: his brother had been slain by Armar. He came disguised like a son of the Sea: fair was his cliff on the wave, white his locks of age, calm his serious brow. Fairest of women, he said, lovely daughter of Armin! a rock not distant in the sea bears a tree on its side: red shines the fruit afar. There Armar waits for Daura. I come to carry his love! she went—she called on Armar. Nought answered, but the son of the rock. Armar, my love, my love! why tormentest thou me with fear? Hear, son of Amar, hear! it is Daura who calleth thee. Erath, the traitor, fled laughing to the land. She lifted up her voice—she called for her brother and her father. Arindal! Armin! none to relieve you, Daura.

"Her voice came over the sea. Arindal, my son, descended from the hill, rough in the spoils of the chase. His arrows rattled by his side; his bow was in his hand, five dark-grey dogs attended his steps. He saw fierce Erath on the shore;

he seized and bound him to an oak. Thick wind the thongs of the hide around his limbs; he loads the wind with his groans. Arindal ascends the deep in his boat to bring Daura to land. Armar came in his wrath, and let fly the grey-feathered shaft. It sung, it sunk in thy heart, O Arindal, my son! for Erath the traitor thou diest. The oar is stopped at once: he panted on the rock, and expired. What is thy grief, O Daura, when round thy feet is poured thy brother's blood. The boat is broken in twain. Armar plunges into the sea to rescue his Daura, or die. Sudden a blast from the hill came over the waves; he sank, and he rose no more.

"Alone, on the sea-beat rock, my daughter was heard to complain; frequent and loud were her cries. What could her father do? All night I stood on the shore: I saw her by the faint beam of the moon. All night I heard her cries. Loud was the wind; the rain beat hard on the hill. Before morning appeared, her voice was weak; it died away like the evening breeze among the grass of the rocks. Spent with grief, she expired, and left thee, Armin, alone. Gone is my strength in war, fallen my pride among women. When the storms aloft arise, when the north lifts the wave on high, I sit by the sounding shore, and look on the fatal rock.

"Often by the sitting moon I see the ghosts of my children; half viewless they walk in mournful conference together."

A torrent of tears which streamed from Charlotte's eyes, and gave relief to her bursting heart, stopped Werther's recitation. He threw down the book, seized her hand, and wept bitterly. Charlotte leaned upon her hand, and buried her face in her handkerchief; the agitation of both was excessive. They felt that their own fate was pictured in the misfortunes of Ossian's heroes—they felt this together, and their tears redoubled. Werther supported his forehead on Charlotte's arm; she trembled, she wished to be gone, but sorrow and sympathy lay like a leaden weight upon her soul. She recovered herself shortly, and begged Werther, with broken sobs, to leave her—implored him with the utmost earnestness to comply with her request. He trembled; his heart was ready to burst: then taking up the book again, he recommenced reading, in a voice broken by sobs.

"Why dost thou waken me, O spring? Thy voice woos

me, exclaiming, I refresh thee with heavenly dews; but
the time of my decay is approaching, the storm is nigh
that shall wither my leaves. To-morrow the traveller
shall come,—he shall come, who beheld me in beauty; his eye
shall seek me in the field around, but he shall not find me."

The whole force of these words fell upon the unfortunate
Werther. Full of despair he threw himself at Charlotte's
feet, seized her hands, and pressed them to his eyes and to
his forehead. An apprehension of his fatal project now
struck her for the first time. Her senses were bewildered;
she held his hands, pressed them to her bosom; and leaning towards him, with emotions of the tenderest pity, her
warm cheek touched his. They lost sight of everything.
The world disappeared from their eyes. He clasped her in
his arms, strained her to his bosom, and covered her trembling
lips with passionate kisses. "Werther! she cried with a
faint voice, turning herself away—"Werther!" and with a
feeble hand she pushed him from her. At length, with the
firm voice of virtue, she exclaimed, "Werther!" He resisted
not, but tearing himself from her arms, fell on his knees
before her. Charlotte rose and with disordered grief, in
mingled tones of love and resentment, she exclaimed, "It is
the last time, Werther!—you shall never see me more!"
then casting one last tender look upon her unfortunate lover,
she rushed into the adjoining room, and locked the door.
Werther held out his arms, but did not dare to detain her.
He continued on the ground, with his head resting on the sofa
for half an hour, till he heard a noise which brought him to
his senses. The servant entered. He then walked up and
down the room, and when he was again left alone, he went
to Charlotte's door, and in a low voice said, "Charlotte,
Charlotte! but one word more—one last adieu!" She returned no answer. He stopped, and listened, and entreated—
but all was silent. At length he tore himself from the place,
crying, "Adieu, Charlotte! adieu, for ever!"

Werther ran to the gate of the town. The guards, who
knew him, let him pass in silence. The night was dark
and stormy—it rained and snowed. He reached his own
door about eleven. His servant perceived, as he entered the
house, that he was without a hat, but did not venture to say
anything; and as he undressed his master, he found that his

clothes were wet. His hat was found afterwards upon the point of a rock which overhangs the valley; and it is inconceivable how he could have climbed to the summit on such a dark, tempestuous night without losing his life.

He retired to bed, and slept to a late hour. The next morning his servant, upon being called to bring his coffee, found him writing. He was adding what we here annex to Charlotte's letter.

"For the last, last time, I open these eyes. Alas! they will behold the sun no more. It is covered by a thick, impenetrable cloud. Yes, Nature! put on mourning; your child, your friend, your lover, draws near his end! This thought, Charlotte! is without parallel, and yet it seems like a mysterious dream, when I repeat—this is my last day! The last! Charlotte, no word can adequately express this thought! The last!——To-day I stand erect, in all my strength—to-morrow, cold and stark, I shall lie extended upon the ground. To die! What is death? We do but dream in our discourse upon it. I have seen many human beings die, but so straitened is our feeble nature, we have no clear conception of the beginning or the end of our existence. At this moment I am my own—or rather I am thine—thine—my adored!—and the next, we are parted—severed—perhaps for ever! No, Charlotte, no—how can I—how can you be annihilated? We exist. What is annihilation? A mere word, an unmeaning sound, that fixes no impression on the mind. Dead, Charlotte! laid in the cold earth, in the dark and narrow grave!—I had a friend once, who was everything to me in early youth—she died. I followed her hearse, I stood by her grave when the coffin was lowered—and when I heard the creaking of the cords as they were loosened and drawn up—when the first shovelful of earth was thrown in, and the coffin returned a hollow sound, which grew fainter and fainter till all was completely covered over, I threw myself on the ground—my heart was smitten, grieved, shattered, rent—but I neither knew what had happened, nor what was to happen to me. Death!—the grave!—I understand not the words.—Forgive, O forgive me! Yesterday—ah! that day should have been the last of my life. Thou angel!—for the first—first time in my existence, I felt rapture glow within my inmost soul. She loves, she loves me! Still burns upon my lips the sacred fire they received from thine. **New torrents** of delight overwhelm my soul. Forgive me, O forgive!

"I knew that I was dear to you; I saw it in your first entrancing look, knew it by the first pressure of your hand; but when I was absent from you, when I saw Albert at your side, my doubts and fears returned.

"Do you remember the flowers you sent me, when at that crowded assembly you could neither speak nor extend your hand to me. Half the night I was on my knees before those flowers, and I regarded them as the pledges of your love; but those impressions grew fainter, and were at length effaced.

"Everything passes away, but a whole eternity could not extinguish the living flame which was yesterday kindled by your lips, and which now burns within me. She loves me! these arms have encircled her waist; these lips have trembled upon hers. She is mine! Yes, Charlotte, you are mine for ever!

"And what do they mean by saying Albert is your husband? He may be so for this world; and in this world it is a sin to love you—to wish to tear you from his embrace. Yes, it is a crime, and I suffer the punishment—but I have enjoyed the full delight of my sin. I have inhaled a balm that has revived my soul. From this hour you are mine; yes, Charlotte, you are mine! I go before you. I go to my Father, and to your Father. I will pour out my sorrows before Him, and He will give me comfort till you arrive. Then will I fly to meet you. I will claim you, and remain in your eternal embrace, in the presence of the Almighty.

"I do not dream; I do not rave. Drawing nearer to the grave, my perceptions become clearer. We shall exist; we shall see each other again; we shall behold your mother; I shall behold her, and expose to her my inmost heart. Your mother—your image!"

About eleven o'clock, Werther asked his servant if Albert had returned. He answered, "Yes;" for he had seen him pass on horseback; upon which Werther sent him the following note, unsealed.

"Be so good as to lend me your pistols for a journey. Adieu."

Charlotte had slept little during the past night. All her

apprehensions were realised in a way that she could neither foresee nor avoid. Her blood boiled in her veins, and a thousand painful sensations rent her pure heart. Was it the ardour of Werther's passionate embraces that she felt within her bosom? Was it anger at his daring? Was it the sad comparison of her present condition with former days of innocence, tranquillity, and self-confidence? How could she approach her husband, and confess a scene which she had no reason to conceal, and which she yet felt nevertheless unwilling to avow? They had preserved so long a silence towards each other—and should she be the first to break it by so unexpected a discovery? She feared that the mere statement of Werther's visit would trouble him, and his distress would be heightened by her perfect candour. She wished that he could see her in her true light, and judge her without prejudice,—but was she anxious that he should read her inmost soul? On the other hand, could she deceive a being, to whom all her thoughts had ever been exposed as clearly as crystal, and from whom no sentiment had ever been concealed? These reflections made her anxious and thoughtful. Her mind still dwelt on Werther, who was now lost to her, but whom she could not bring herself to resign, and for whom she knew nothing was left but despair, if she should be lost to him for ever.

A recollection of that mysterious estrangement which had lately subsisted between herself and Albert, and which she could never thoroughly understand, was now beyond measure painful to her. Even the prudent and the good have, before now, hesitated to explain their mutual differences, and have dwelt in silence upon their imaginary grievances, until circumstances have become so entangled, that in that critical juncture, when a calm explanation would have saved all parties, an understanding was impossible. And thus if domestic confidence had been earlier established between them, if love and kind forbearance had mutually animated and expanded their hearts, it might not, perhaps, even yet have been too late to save our friend.

But we must not forget one remarkable circumstance. We may observe from the character of Werther's correspondence, that he had never affected to conceal his anxious desire to quit this world. He had often discussed the subject with

Albert, and between the latter and Charlotte it had not un-
frequently formed a topic of conversation. Albert was so
opposed to the very idea of such an action, that, with a degree
of irritation unusual in him, he had more than once given
Werther to understand that he doubted the seriousness of
his threats, and not only turned them into ridicule, but caused
Charlotte to share his feelings of incredulity. Her heart was
thus tranquillized when she felt disposed to view the melancholy subject in a serious point of view, though she never
communicated to her husband the apprehensions she sometimes experienced.

Albert, upon his return home, was received by Charlotte
with ill-concealed embarrassment. He was himself out of
humour, his business was unfinished, and he had just discovered that the neighbouring official, with whom he had to
deal, was an obstinate and narrow-minded personage. Many
things had occurred to irritate him.

He inquired whether anything had happened during his
absence, and Charlotte hastily answered, that Werther had
been there on the evening previously. He then inquired for
his letters, and received for answer, that several packages had
been left in his study. He thereupon retired, and Charlotte
remained alone.

The presence of the being whom she loved and honoured,
produced a new impression upon her heart. The recollection
of his generosity, his kindness, and his affection, had calmed
her agitation; a secret impulse prompted her to follow him;
she took her work and went to his study, as was often her
custom. He was busily employed in opening and reading
his letters. It seemed as if the contents of some were disagreeable. She asked some questions; he gave short answers,
and sat down to write.

Several hours passed over in this manner, and Charlotte's
feelings became more and more melancholy. She felt the
extreme difficulty of explaining to her husband, under any
circumstances, the weight that lay upon her heart, and her
depression became every moment greater, in proportion as
she endeavoured to hide her grief and to conceal her tears.

The arrival of Werther's servant occasioned her the greatest
embarrassment. He gave Albert a note, which the latter
coldly handed to his wife, saying, at the same time, " Give

him the pistols. I wish him a pleasant journey," he added,
turning to the servant. These words fell upon Charlotte like
a thunderstroke; she rose from her seat, half fainting, and
unconscious of what she did. She walked mechanically towards
the wall, with a trembling hand took down the pistols, slowly
wiped off the dust from them, and would have delayed longer,
had not Albert hastened her movements by an impatient look.
She then delivered the fatal weapons to the servant, without
being able to utter a word. As soon as he had departed, she
folded up her work, and retired at once to her room, her heart
overcome with the most fearful forebodings. She anticipated
some dreadful calamity. She was at one moment on the
point of going to her husband, throwing herself at his feet, and
acquainting him with all that had happened on the previous
evening—that she might acknowledge her fault, and explain
her apprehensions; then she saw that such a step would be
useless, as she would certainly be unable to induce Albert to
visit Werther. Dinner was served, and a kind friend, whom
she had persuaded to remain, assisted to sustain the conversation, which was carried on by a sort of compulsion, till
the events of the morning were forgotten.

When the servant brought the pistols to Werther, the
latter received them with transports of delight, upon hearing
that Charlotte had given them to him with her own hand.
He ate some bread, drank some wine, sent his servant to
dinner, and then sat down to write as follows:—

"They have been in your hands—you wiped the dust from
them. I kiss them a thousand times—you have touched
them. Yes, Heaven favours my design—and you, Charlotte,
provide me with the fatal instruments. It was my desire to
receive my death from your hands, and my wish is gratified.
I have made inquiries of my servant. You trembled when
you gave him the pistols, but you bade me no adieu. Wretched,
wretched that I am—not one farewell! How could you shut
your heart against me in that hour which makes you mine
for ever? O Charlotte, ages cannot efface the impression—I
feel you cannot hate the man who so passionately loves you!"

After dinner he called his servant, desired him to finish the
packing up, destroyed many papers, and then went out to

pay some trifling debts. He soon returned home, then went out again notwithstanding the rain, walked for some time in the Count's garden, and afterwards proceeded farther into the country. Towards evening he came back once more, and resumed his writing.

"Wilhelm, I have for the last time beheld the mountains, the forests, and the sky. Farewell! And you, my dearest mother, forgive me! Console her, Wilhelm. God bless you! I have settled all my affairs! Farewell! We shall meet again, and be happier than ever."

"I have requited you, badly, Albert; but you will forgive me. I have disturbed the peace of your home. I have sowed distrust between you. Farewell! I will end all this wretchedness. And, oh, that my death may render you happy! Albert, Albert! make that angel happy, and the blessing of Heaven be upon you!"

He spent the rest of the evening in arranging his papers; he tore and burned a great many; others he sealed up, and directed to Wilhelm. They contained some detached thoughts and maxims, some of which I have perused. At ten o'clock he ordered his fire to be made up and a bottle of wine to be brought to him. He then dismissed his servant, whose room, as well as the apartments of the rest of the family, was situated in another part of the house. The servant lay down without undressing, that he might be the sooner ready for his journey in the morning, his master having informed him that the post horses would be at the door before six o'clock.

"Past eleven o'clock! All is silent around me, and my soul is calm. I thank thee, O God, that thou bestowest strength and courage upon me in these last moments. I approach the window, my dearest of friends, and through the clouds, which are at this moment driven rapidly along by the impetuous winds, I behold the stars which illumine the eternal heavens! No, you will not fall, celestial bodies! the hand of the Almighty supports both you and me! I have looked for the last time upon the constellation of the Greater Bear; it is my favourite star; for when I bade you farewell at night, Charlotte, and turned my steps from your door, it always shone upon me. With what rapture have I at times beheld it! How often have I implored it with uplifted hands to witness my felicity? and even still—But what object is there, Charlotte, which fails to summon up your image before me? Do you not surround me on all sides? and have I not, like a child, treasured up every trifle which you have consecrated by your touch?

" Your profile, which was so dear to me, I return to you, and I pray you to preserve it. Thousands of kisses have I imprinted upon it, and a thousand times has it gladdened my heart on departing from, and returning to my home.

" I have implored your father to protect my remains. At the corner of the churchyard, looking towards the fields, there are two lime-trees—there I wish to lie. Your father can, and doubtless will, do thus much for his friend. Implore it of him. But perhaps pious Christians will not choose that their bodies should be buried near the corpse of a poor unhappy wretch like me. Then let me laid in some remote valley, or near the highway, where the priest and Levite may bless themselves as they pass by my tomb, whilst the Samaritan will shed a tear for my fate.

" See, Charlotte, I do not shudder to take the cold and fatal cup, from which I shall drink the draught of death. Your hand presents it to me, and I do not tremble. All, all is now concluded; the wishes and the hopes of my existence are fulfilled. With cold, unflinching hand I knock at the brazen portals of Death.

" Oh, that I had enjoyed the bliss of dying for you! how gladly would I have sacrificed myself for you, Charlotte! And could I but restore peace and joy to your bosom, with what resolution, with what joy would I not meet my fate! But it is the lot of only a chosen few to shed their blood for their friends, and by their death to augment, a thousand times, the happiness of those by whom they are beloved.

" I wish, Charlotte, to be buried in the dress I wear at present; it has been rendered sacred by your touch. I have begged this favour of your father. My spirit soars above my sepulchre. I do not wish my pockets to be searched. The knot of pink ribbon which you wore on your bosom the first time I saw you, surrounded by the children!—O kiss them a thousand times for me, and tell them the fate of their unhappy friend. I think I see them playing around me. The dear children! How warmly have I been attached to you, Charlotte! Since the first hour I saw you, how impossible have I found it to leave you. This ribbon must be buried with me; it was a present from you on my birthday. How confused it all appears! Little did I then think that I should journey this road. But, peace! I pray you, peace!

"They are loaded—the clock strikes twelve. I say amen. Charlotte, Charlotte! farewell, farewell!"

A neighbour saw the flash, and heard the report of the pistol, but as everything remained quiet, he thought no more of it.

In the morning, at six o'clock, the servant went into Werther's room with a candle. He found his master stretched upon the floor, weltering in his blood, and the pistols at his side. He called, he took him in his arms, but received no answer. Life was not yet quite extinct. The servant ran for a surgeon, and then went to fetch Albert. Charlotte heard the ringing of the bell; a cold shudder seized her. She wakened her husband, and they both rose. The servant, bathed in tears, faltered forth the dreadful news. Charlotte fell senseless at Albert's feet.

When the surgeon came to the unfortunate Werther, he was still lying on the floor, and his pulse beat, but his limbs were cold. The bullet, entering the forehead, over the right eye, had penetrated the skull. A vein was opened in his right arm; the blood came, and he still continued to breathe.

From the blood which flowed from the chair, it could be inferred that he had committed the rash act sitting at his bureau, and that he afterwards fell upon the floor. He was found, lying on his back, near the window. He was in full-dress costume.

The house, the neighbourhood, and the whole town, was immediately in commotion. Albert arrived. They had laid Werther on the bed; his head was bound up, and the paleness of death was upon his face. His limbs were motionless; but he still breathed, at one time strongly, then weaker—his death was momently expected.

He had drunk only one glass of the wine. 'Emilia Galotti' lay open upon his bureau.

I shall say nothing of Albert's distress, or of Charlotte's grief.

The old steward hastened to the house immediately upon hearing the news; he embraced his dying friend amid a flood of tears. His eldest boys soon followed him on foot. In speechless sorrow they threw themselves on their knees by the bedside, and kissed his hands and face. The eldest, who was his favourite, hung over him till he expired, and even then he was removed by force. At twelve o'clock Werther breathed his last. The presence of the steward, and the precautions had adopted, prevented a disturbance; and that night, at the hour of eleven, he caused the body to be interred in the place which Werther had selected for himself.

The steward and his sons followed the corpse to the grave. Albert was unable to accompany them. Charlotte's life was despaired of. The body was carried by labourers. No priest attended.

THE RECREATIONS OF
THE GERMAN EMIGRANTS.

At that unhappy period, so fruitful in disasters to Germany, to Europe, and indeed to the whole world, when the French army overran the Continent, a family of distinction was compelled to forsake their property on the first invasion, and to fly beyond the Rhine. They sought to escape those calamities to which persons of noble birth were inevitably exposed, in whom it was considered criminal to be descended from an honourable line of ancestors, and to inherit those privileges and possessions which the virtues or the valour of their forefathers had bequeathed to them.

The Baroness of C——, a widow lady, of middle age, distinguished for every domestic virtue which could promote the comfort or independence of her family, evinced, upon the occasion of this unforeseen calamity, the most noble spirit of activity and resolute determination. Brought up amid a wide circle of acquaintance, and already experienced, to some extent, in the reverses of life, she was considered perfect in her private and domestic character; and she was remarkable for the real delight which she ever felt in the active employment of her faculties. Indeed, the great purpose of her life seemed to consist in rendering services to others, and it is easy to suppose that her numerous friends never failed to provide her with employment. She was summoned, at the time we speak of, to take the lead of a little band of emigrants. Even for this duty she was prepared; and the same solicitous though cheerful temper, which had invariably distinguished her at home, did not forsake her in this hour of general terror and distress. But cheerfulness was not an entire stranger to our band of fugitives; many an unexpected incident and strange event afforded occasion for the indulgence of mirth and laughter, of which their easily-excited minds readily took advantage. The very flight itself was a circumstance well calculated to call out the peculiar character of each individual in a remarkable manner. The mind of one, for instance, was distracted by vain fear and terror ; another fell a prey to idle apprehensions ; and the extravagances and deficiencies, the weakness, irresolution, or impetuosity which was on all sides displayed, produced so many instances of vexation and bad temper, that the real trouble of the whole party afforded more mirth than an actual tour of pleasure could possibly have occasioned.

As we may sometimes preserve our composure even during the performance of a farce, without smiling at the most positive drolleries, though we find it impossible to restrain our laughter when anything absurd occurs in the representation of a tragedy, so in this real world, the generality of accidents of a serious nature are accompanied by circumstances either ridiculous at the moment, or infallibly productive of subsequent mirth.

We must observe that the Baroness's eldest daughter, Louisa, a cheerful, lively, and, in her hour of prosperity, an imperious young lady, had to endure an unusual degree of suffering. She is said to have been quite overwhelmed with terror at the first alarm, and in her distraction and absence of mind, to have packed together the most useless things with the greatest seriousness, and actually to have made an offer of marriage to one of the old servants of the establishment.

She defended herself for this step with much obstinacy, and would not allow her intended to be made a subject of ridicule. In her opinion she suffered enough from her daily fear of the allied army, and from the apprehension that her wished-for marriage might be delayed, or even frustrated by a general engagement.

Her elder brother, Frederick, who was a youth of decisive character, executed his mother's orders with precision and exactitude, accompanied the procession on horseback, and discharged, at times, the various duties of courier, conductor, and guide. The tutor of the Baroness's younger son, who was a well-educated young man, accompanied her in her carriage ; whilst uncle Charles, and an elderly clergyman, who had long been an indispensable friend of the family, followed in another vehicle, which was also occupied by two female relations, one young, the other somewhat advanced in years.

The servants followed, in an open carriage, and the procession was closed by a heavily packed waggon, which occasionally loitered behind.

The whole party, as it is easy to suppose, had abandoned their dwellings with great reluctance, but uncle Charles had forsaken his residence on this side of the Rhine even more unwillingly than the others; not that he had left his mistress behind, as one might, perhaps, have conjectured from his youth, his figure, and the warmth of his nature : he had rather been seduced by the brilliant phantom, which, under the denomination of freedom, had secured so many adherents, first in secret, then in public, and which, notwithstanding that she was a harsh mistress to some, was all the more devotedly honoured by the others.

Just as lovers are generally blinded by their passion, did it happen in the case of uncle Charles. They pant for the possession of a single happiness, and fancy that for this they can endure the privation of every other blessing. Position, fortune, and all advantages, vanish into nothing, compared with the one benefit which is to supply their place. Parents, relatives, and friends are now looked upon as strangers. One desire fills and absorbs their whole being, to which everything else is to give way.

Uncle Charles abandoned himself to the intensity of his passion, and did not conceal it in his conversation. He thought he might express his conviction the more freely, because he was of noble birth, and although the second son, yet the presumptive heir to a noble fortune. Even this fortune, which was to be his future inheritance, was at present in the enemy's hands, by whom it had been shamefully wasted. But in spite of all this, Charles could not hate a nation which promised such advantages to the world at large, and whose principles he approved, according to his own admission, and the evidence of some of his associates. He constantly disturbed the peace of the little community (seldom as they enjoyed such a blessing), by an indiscriminate praise of everything, good or bad, which happened amongst the French, and by his noisy delight at their success. By this means he irritated his companions, 'who felt their own grievances doubly aggravated by the malicious triumphs of their friend and relation.

Frederick had been already engaged in frequent disputes with him, and latterly they had ceased to hold communication with each other. But the Baroness, by her prudent management, had secured his moderation, at least for a time. Louisa gave him the greatest trouble, for she often used the most unfair methods to cast a slur upon his character and judgment. The tutor silently pronounced him right—the clergyman silently pronounced him wrong; and the female attendants, who were charmed with his figure and his liberality, heard him with delight, because, whilst they listened to his lectures, they could honourably fix upon him those loving eyes, which, until that time, had ever been modestly bent upon the ground.

Their daily necessities, the obstacles of the journey, and their disagreeable quarters, generally led the whole company to a consideration of their immediate interests; and the great number of French and German fugitives whom they constantly met, and whose conduct and fortunes were various, often made them consider how much occasion existed at such times for the practice of every virtue, but particularly of liberality and forbearance.

The Baroness, upon one occasion, observed aloud, that nothing could show more clearly the deficiencies of men in these virtues, than the opportunity afforded for their exercise, by occasions of general confusion and distress. Our whole constitution, she maintained, resembled a ship chartered in a season of tempest, to convey a countless crowd of men, old and young, healthy and infirm, across a stormy sea; but only in the hour of shipwreck could the capabilities of the crew be displayed, an emergency when even the good swimmer often perished.

Fugitives, for the most part, carry their faults and ridiculous peculiarities along with them, and we wonder at this circumstance. But as the English traveller never leaves his tea-kettle behind in any quarter of the globe, so are the generality of mankind invariably accompanied by their stock of proud pretensions, vanity, intolerance, impatience, obstinacy, prejudices, and envy. Thus, the thoughtless enjoyed this flight as they would have enjoyed a party of pleasure, and the discontented required, even now in their moments of abject poverty, that their every want should be supplied.

How rare is the display of that pure virtue, which incites us to live and to sacrifice ourselves for others.

In the mean time, whilst numerous acquaintances were formed, which gave occasion to reflections of this nature, the season of winter was brought to a close. Fortune once more smiled on the German arms, the French were again driven across the Rhine, Frankfort was relieved, and Mainz was invested.

Trusting to the further advance of our victorious troops, and anxious to take possession of a part of their recovered property, the family we speak of set out for an estate which lay in one of the most beautiful parts of the country, on the right bank of the Rhine. We can ill describe the rapture with which they once more beheld the silver stream flowing beneath their windows, the joy with which they took possession of every part of their house, and hailed the sight of their well-known furniture, their old family pictures, and of every trifle which they had long given up as totally lost ; and they indulged the fondest anticipations of finding everything flourishing as heretofore on their side of the Rhine.

The arrival of the Baroness was scarcely announced in the village, when all her former acquaintances, friends, and dependants hastened to welcome her, to recount the various vicissitudes of the last few months, and in more than one instance, to implore her advice and assistance.

In the midst of these interviews, she was most agreeably surprised by a visit from the Privy Councillor S. and his family, a man who from his earliest youth had followed business as a pursuit of pleasure, and who had both merited and acquired the confidence of his Sovereign. His principles were firm, and he indulged his own peculiar notions upon many subjects. He was precise both in his conversation and conduct, and required others to be the same. A dignified deportment was, in his opinion, the highest virtue a man could possess.

His Sovereign, his country, and himself, had suffered much from the irruption of the French. He had experienced the despotic character of that nation, which was perpetually boasting of justice, and had felt the tyranny of men who always had the cry of freedom on their lips. He had observed, however, the general consistency of character which prevailed, and had marked how many persons witnessed with feelings of angry disappointment, the substitution of mere words for practice, and of empty appearance for reality. The consequences to be expected from an unfortunate campaign did not escape his acute penetration, any more than the results of the general maxims and opinions we have quoted; though it must be admitted, his views upon all subjects were neither cheerful nor dispassionate.

His wife, who had been an early friend of the Baroness, after the experience of so much adversity, found a perfect paradise in the arms of her former companion. They had grown up together, had been educated together, and had always shared each other's confidence. The early inclinations of their youth, their more important matrimonial interests, their joys and cares and domestic anxieties, had always been communicated, either personally or by correspondence, as they had for years maintained an uninterrupted intimacy with each other; but this was at length broken by the general troubles of the eventful times. Their present intercourse was, for this reason, the more affectionate, and their interviews the more frequent; and the Baroness observed with pleasure, that the intimacy of Louisa with the daughters of her friend was daily increasing.

Unfortunately, however, the complete enjoyment of the delightful neighbourhood around was often disturbed by the roar of cannon which was heard in the distance, sometimes loudly and sometimes indistinctly, according to the point of the wind. Moreover, it was impossible to avoid conversations upon political subjects, which were introduced by the perpetual rumours of the day, and which generally disturbed the temporary tranquillity of society, as the various ideas and opinions of all parties were usually propounded without reserve.

And as intemperate men seldom refrain from wine or injurious food on account of their experience of the evil consequences which such enjoyments occasion, so, in this instance, the several members of the society we speak of, in place of imposing restraint upon their conversation, abandoned themselves to the irresistible impulse of vexing each other, and thus eventually opened a channel of most disagreeable reflections.

We can readily suppose that the Privy Councillor adopted the opinions of those who advocated the old *régime*, and that Charles took the opposite side, in expectation that the approaching changes would heal and reanimate the old shattered constitution of the country.

The conversation was carried on at first with some degree of moderation, particularly as the Baroness sought, by her well-timed and graceful interruptions, to maintain the balance equal between both parties ; but when the important crisis of the conversation arrived, and the investment of Mainz was about to change to an actual siege, and the fears of all increased for that beautiful city and its abandoned inhabitants, both sides asserted their opinions with unrestrained violence.

The members of the clubs who had remained in the town were particularly discussed, and each expressed his hope of their liberation or punishment, according as he approved or condemned their conduct.

Amongst the latter class was the Privy Councillor, whose observations were especially displeasing to Charles, as he assailed the sound judgment of those people, and charged them with a thorough ignorance of the world and of themselves.

" What blind dolts they must be," he exclaimed, one afternoon when the discussion became warm, " to think that a great nation, employed in an effort to suppress its own internal commotions, and which in sober moments has no other object than its own prosperity, can look down upon them with any sort of sympathy. Used as temporary tools, they will be thrown away at last or utterly neglected. How grossly they err in thinking that they will ever be admitted into the ranks of the French nation.

" Nothing is more ridiculous to the strong and powerful, than to see weakness and inefficiency setting up its pretensions to equality, wrapped in the obscurity of its own fancies and in the ignorance of itself, its powers and its qualities. And can you suppose that the great nation, with that good fortune with which it has been hitherto favoured, will be less haughty and overbearing than any other royal conqueror ?

" Many a person who now struts about in his municipal robes and gaudy attire, will heartily curse the masquerade when, after having assisted to oppress his own countrymen, by a new and disadvantageous change of things, he finds himself at last, in his new character, despised by those in whom he wholly confided. Indeed, it is my firm opinion, that upon the surrender of the town, which must soon take place, those people will be abandoned or given up to us. I hope they will then receive their reward in that punishment they so richly deserve, according to my opinion, which is as unprejudiced as possible."

"Unprejudiced!" exclaimed Charles with vehemence; "I beg I may never hear that word again. How can we so unequivocally condemn these men? Have they not actually devoted their whole lives to the old pursuit of serving the more favoured classes of mankind? Have they not occupied the few habitable rooms of the old mansion, and toiled diligently therein; or rather have they not felt the inconvenience of the deserted part of your State Palace, by the obligation of living there in a state of misery and oppression? Uncorrupted by frivolous pursuits, they do not consider their own occupation to be alone noble,—but in silence they deplore the prejudice, the irregularity, the indolence and ignorance upon which your statesmen build their foolish claims to reverence, and in silence they pray for a more equal division of labour and enjoyment. And who can deny that their ranks contain at least some such men of intelligence and virtue, who, if they cannot now realize universal good, can fortunately aid in modifying evil and in preparing for a happy future? and if there be such noble beings amongst them, should we not deplore the approach of that evil hour, which must destroy, perhaps for ever, their fondest anticipations?"

The Privy Councillor, upon this, sneered with some degree of bitterness at certain youths who were in the habit of idealizing upon practical subjects, whilst Charles was equally severe upon men whose thoughts were merely formed upon antiquated precedents, and who never adopted any but compulsory reforms.

By reciprocal contradictions of this nature, the dispute became gradually more violent, and every topic was introduced which has for so many years tended to dismember society. In vain did the Baroness endeavour to establish a truce, if not to make peace between the contending parties;

and the wife of the Privy Councillor, who from her estimable qualities had acquired some influence over Charles's
disposition, interposed also to no effect, more particularly
as her husband continued to launch his poisoned shafts
against youth and inexperience, and enlarged upon the especial
aptitude of children to play with fire, a dangerous element
which they were wholly unable to control.

Charles, forgetting prudence in his anger, now declared
openly that he wished every success to the French arms, and
called upon all his countrymen to aid in putting an end to their
general slavery, expressing his conviction that their so-called
enemies would protect every noble German who should join
them, would regard them and treat them as their own countrymen, and crown them with honours, fortune, and rewards,
in place of sacrificing or leaving them in misery.

But the Councillor maintained it was ridiculous to suppose
that the French would bestow a thought upon them, whether
they capitulated or not; that they would probably fall into
the hands of the allies, by whom he hoped they would all be
hanged.

Charles was provoked by this speech, and expressed his
wish that the guillotine might find a rich harvest in Germany,
and that no guilty head might escape. He added some
cutting observations which were aimed at the Councillor personally, and were in every sense offensive.

"I shall take leave of a society," interrupted the latter,
"in which everything is now slighted which once seemed
worthy of respect. I lament that I should be for the second
time expelled, and now by a fellow-countryman; but I am
well aware that less pity may be expected from this new foe
than from the French themselves; and I find here a confirma-
tion of the old proverb, that it is better to fall into the hands
of the Turks than of renegades."

So saying, he rose and left the apartment. He was
followed by his wife, and a general silence ensued. The
Baroness expressed her displeasure in a few words of strong
import. Charles walked up and down the room. The
Councillor's wife returned in tears, and stated that her husband had given directions for leaving, and had actually
ordered the carriage. The Baroness went to pacify him,
whilst the young ladies wept and kissed each other, dis-

tressed beyond measure that they were compelled so suddenly and so unexpectedly to separate. The Baroness returned without succeeding in her wishes. Gradually all those troubles approached which it is ever the lot of strangers to encounter. The sad moments of separation and departure were bitter beyond expression. Hope vanished with the appearance of the post-horses, and the general sorrow was redoubled.

The carriage drove off. The Baroness followed it with her eyes full of tears. She left the window and sat down to her embroidery frame. The silence, and even despair, was universal. Charles showed his sorrow by sitting in a corner and intently turning over the leaves of a book, directing at intervals a melancholy look towards his aunt. At length he rose and took his hat, as if about to depart, but turned round on reaching the door, and approaching his aunt, he exclaimed with a countenance truly noble : " I have offended you, my dear aunt, I have distressed you ; but pardon my thoughtlessness, I acknowledge my fault, and am deeply sensible of its sad consequences."

" I forgive you," replied the Baroness ; " I entertain no ill-feeling towards you—you are a good and noble being, but you can never repair the injury you have done. Your error has deprived me of a friend to whom, after a long separation, I had been restored by the accident of our joint misfortunes, and in whose society I have forgotten much of the misery which has pursued and threatens us. She herself, driven from her home under most painful circumstances, and long a fugitive, after a short repose in the society of old and beloved friends, in this delightful spot and comfortable dwelling, is again compelled to wander forth; and we lose the company of her husband, who, in spite of some peculiarities, is a man of noble integrity, possessing an inexhaustible knowledge of society and of the world, of facts and experiences which he is ever ready to communicate with the most cheerful and delightful willingness. Of all these enjoyments we have been deprived by your fault, and how can you restore what we have lost ?"

Charles.—Spare me, my dear Aunt. I feel deeply the weight of my fault ; cease to explain to me its evident consequences.

Baroness.—Rather contemplate them as closely as possible.

Talk not of sparing you; only inquire how your mind may be corrected. It is not the first time you have erred, nor will it be the last. Ye inexplicable men! cannot a common suffering, which brings you together under one roof, and confines you in one narrow dwelling, induce you to practice forbearance towards each other? Do you need any additional calamities than those which are perpetually bursting upon you? Consider your condition, and act sensibly and justly towards those who, in truth, would deprive you of nothing. Restrain your tempers from working and fermenting blindly, like some storm or other natural phenomenon which disturbs the world.

Charles made no reply. The tutor advanced from the window, where he had been standing, towards the Baroness, and said his pupil would improve; that this event would act as a warning, that he should test his progress daily, that he would remember the distress the Baroness had endured, and would afford convincing evidence of the self-restraint he could practice.

Baroness.—How easily men deceive themselves, especially in this particular. Authority is so delightful a word, and it sounds so noble to promise to control ourselves. Men speak of it with pleasure, and would persuade us that they can seriously practice the virtue. I wish I had ever known a man capable of subduing himself in the smallest particular. In indifferent matters they affect resolution, as if the loss occasioned actual suffering; whilst their real desires are considered as supremely essential, unavoidable, and indispensable. I have never known a man capable of enduring the smallest privation.

Tutor.—You are seldom unjust, and I have never seen you so overpowered by anger and disappointment as at present.

Baroness.—Well, I need not be ashamed of my anger. When I think of my friend, who is now pursuing her journey in discomfort, weeping, probably, at the recollection of our inhospitality, my heart burns with indignation.

Tutor.—In your greatest trouble, I have never seen you so agitated and exasperated as now.

Baroness.—A small evil, which follows closely upon a greater, can fill the cup; though, in truth, it is no small evil to lose a friend.

Tutor.—Be comforted, and rely upon our improvement, and that we will do all in our power to content you.

Baroness.—No; I shall rely upon none of you. But, for the future, I will demand obedience from all. I will command in my own house.

" Command, certainly," exclaimed Charles, " and you shall not have to complain of our disobedience."

" My severity will scarcely be very harsh," rejoined the Baroness with a smile, as she recovered herself; " I am not fond of commanding. particularly democrats; but I will give you some advice, and make one request."

Tutor.—Both shall be strictly observed.

Baroness.—It would be ridiculous, if I thought to impair the interest which you all take in the great events of the world, of which we ourselves are indeed the victims. I cannot change the opinions which exist and are established in the mind of each of you, according to his peculiar disposition; and it would be no less harsh than foolish, to require you to suppress them. But I can demand this at least from the circle in which I live, that those of similar sentiments shall associate peaceably together, and converse in harmony. In your private apartments, during your walks, and wherever else you meet, you may communicate together at will, support your respective opinions, and enjoy the gratification of an ardent conviction. But my dear friends, let us not forget how much we were accustomed to sacrifice of our own individual opinions, for the sake of general harmony, long before these new topics became the fashion; and as long as the world lasts, we must all, for the general benefit, practice some outward self-control. It is not, therefore, for the sake of virtue, but in the name of common politeness, that I implore you now to concede to me a favour, which I think I may safely say you have always allowed to the veriest stranger.

It seems to me strange (continued the Baroness), that we should have so far forgotten ourselves. What has become of our politeness? It used to be the custom in society to avoid topics disagreeable to others. Protestants, in the company of Catholics, never asserted that church ceremonies were ridiculous; and the most bigotted Catholic never maintained before a Protestant, that the old religion afforded the only chance of salvation. In the presence of a mother who had lost her son, no one displayed the deep delight he took in his children, and an inappropriate word occasioned general embarrassment. It seemed the duty of each to repair the accidental evil; but now the very reverse of all this seems to be the rule. We appear to seek the opportunity of introducing subjects calculated to give pain. Oh! my dear friends, let us try and restore the old system. We have much to endure already; and who knows how soon the column of smoke by day, or the pillar of flame by night, may announce the destruction of our dwellings, and of our most valued possessions. Let us, at least, forbear to announce this intelligence with triumph; let us cease, by our own bitter observations, to impress our souls with calamities, which it is painful enough to endure in silence.

When your father died, was it your habit to renew my grief upon every opportunity, by a reference to the sad subject? Did you not rather avoid all improper allusion to his memory, and seek by your love, your silent sympathy, and your incessant attentions, to soften my sorrow, and relieve my pain? Should we not now practice the same kind forbearance, which often brings more consolation than the offices of active friendship, more particularly at this time, when ours is not the grief of an individual in the midst of a happy multitude, where sorrow disappears amid the general content, but the grief of thousands, where but few indeed are capable of experiencing an accidental or artificial consolation.

Charles.—My dear aunt, you have sufficiently humiliated us: may we take your hand in token of reconciliation?

Baroness.—Here it is, on condition that you will obey its guidance. We proclaim a general amnesty, which we cannot conclude with sufficient speed.

The young ladies, who had all been dissolved in tears since the event we have related, now made their appearance, but could not be persuaded to be reconciled to Charles.

"You are welcome, children," said the Baroness, addressing them. "We have just had a serious conversation, which I trust will establish peace and harmony amongst us; perhaps it was never more important that we should be friends, and enjoy even one brief portion of the day. Let us make this resolution, to banish from our conversation all reference to the mere

2 B

events of the time. How long have we been deprived of all instruction and entertaining intercourse! How long it seems, dear Charles, since you have amused us with accounts of distant lands, with whose productions, inhabitants, manners, and customs, you are so well acquainted. And you (continued the Baroness, addressing the tutor), you have not lately instructed us in history, ancient or modern, in the comparison of centuries, or of remarkable men. And you, young ladies! where are the pretty poems which you used to bring forth from their hiding-places for the delight of your friends? what has become of all your free philosophic observations? Have you no more ambition to surprise us with some wonderful mineral specimen, some unknown plant, or remarkable insect, brought home from your walks, and affording occasion for pleasing speculations on the mysterious connection of all the productions of Nature? Let us restore all those charming amusements, by an agreement, a resolution, a rule, to be useful, instructive, and, above all things, companionable towards each other; for all these advantages we can enjoy even in the most extreme adversity. Your promise, children."

They promised eagerly. "And now, I dismiss you," added the Baroness; "the evening is fine, amuse yourselves as you please, and at supper-time let us enjoy a friendly communion together, after so long an interruption."

The company separated. Louisa alone remained with her mother. She could not so easily forget the misfortune of losing her companion, and she allowed Charles, whom she had invited to accompany her upon a walk, to set out alone. For some time the Baroness and her daughter remained together, when the clergyman entered, after a long absence, entirely ignorant of what had, in the meantime, happened. Laying by his hat and stick, he took a seat, and was about to narrate something, when Louisa, pretending to continue a conversation with her mother, interrupted his intention with the following observations :—

"Some of our company will, I think, find the arrangement we have come to rather disagreeable. When we lived in the country, it is true, we were sometimes at a loss for conversation, for it did not happen so often, as in town, that a girl could be slandered, or a young man traduced; but still we had an alternative in describing the follies of two great nations, in finding the Germans as absurd as the French, and in representing first one, and then the other, as Jacobins and Radicals. But if these topics are forbidden, some of our society will be rendered stupid."

"Is your observation directed to me, young lady?" asked the old clergyman with a smile. "You know how ready I am to be sacrificed for the benefit of the company. For though upon all occasions you do credit to your instructors, and every one finds your society both amiable and delightful, yet there is a certain little malicious spirit within you, which, notwithstanding all your efforts, you cannot entirely subdue, which prompts you to take your revenge at my expense. Tell me, gracious lady," he continued, turning towards the Baroness, "what has occurred during my absence, and what topics have been forbidden to our society?"

The Baroness informed him of all that had taken place. He listened attentively, and then observed that "this regulation would probably enable many persons to entertain the company better than others."

"We shall be able to endure it," said Louisa.

"Such an arrangement," he added, "will not be grievous to those who have been accustomed to rely upon their own resources; on the contrary, they will find it pleasant, since they can amuse the company with pursuits which they have followed in private. And do not be offended, young lady, if I attribute to society the very existence of all newsmongers, spies, and slanderers. For my part I never see persons so lively and so animated either at a learned meeting or at a public lecture convened for general instruction, as in a society where some piece of scandal is introduced which reflects on the character of a neighbour. Ask yourself or ask others, what invests a piece of news with its greatest charm? Not its importance, nor its influence, but its mere novelty. Nothing old is cared for; novelty by itself excites our surprise, awakens the imagination, gently agitates the feelings, and requires no exertion of the reasoning powers. Every man can take the most lively interest in a piece of news with the least trouble to himself; indeed since a succession of new events carries us rapidly from one circumstance to another, nothing is more welcome to the generality of mankind than this inducement to constant dissipation, and this opportunity of venting their spleen and malice in an agreeable and varied manner."

"Well!" exclaimed Louisa, "you shew some skill at explanation; just now you censured individuals, at present you condemn mankind in general."

"I do not require," he answered, "that you should render me justice; but this I must say, we who depend upon society must act according to its rules, and it would be safer to provoke its resentment than its ennui, by requiring it to think or reflect. We must avoid everything that would tend to this result, and pursue by ourselves in private whatever would prove unpalateable to the public."

"By yourselves in private," said Louisa, "many a bottle of wine will, I suppose, be drunk, and many a nap taken in the daytime."

"I have never," continued the old clergyman, "set much value upon my own actions, for I know how little I have done for others; but, however, I am in possession of something which may, perhaps, afford agreeable relaxation to this society, circumstanced as it is at present."

"To what do you allude?" inquired the Baroness.

"Rely upon it," interrupted Louisa, "he has made some marvellous collection of scandals."

"You are mistaken," replied the clergyman.

"We shall see," answered Louisa.

"Suffer him to continue, my dear," said the Baroness, "and do not accustom yourself to act in a hard and unfriendly manner towards others even in jest, as they may take it ill. We have no need to increase our evil habits by practising them for entertainment. Tell me, my dear friend, of what does your collection consist? Will it conduce to our amusement? Have you been long employed about it? Why have you never mentioned it before?"

"I will give you an account of the whole matter," rejoined the old clergyman. "I have lived long in the world, and have paid much attention to public occurrences. I have neither talent nor inclination for chronicling great actions, and worldly affairs in general are troublesome to me; but amongst the many private histories, true and false, which sometimes happen in public, or are related in private, there are some which possess a greater attraction than the charm of mere novelty, some which are calculated to improve us by their moral application, some which display at a glance the secret springs of human nature, and others again whose very absurdities are amusing. Amongst the multitude of occurrences which attract our attention and our malice in ordinary life, and which are as common as the individuals to whom they relate, I have noted down a few on account of their peculiar character, because they engaged and excited my attention and feelings, and the very recollection of them has never failed to produce a momentary sensation of pure and tranquil pleasure."

" I am curious to hear," said the Baroness, " the nature of your anecdotes, and to learn their peculiar character."

" You may easily suppose," replied the clergyman, " that they are not about disputes or family matters. Such things have little interest except for those who are engaged in them."

Louisa.—And what are yours about?

Clergyman.—Why, for the most part, they treat of those emotions by which friends become attached or disunited, happy or miserable, and by which they are more frequently entangled than improved.

Louisa.—Indeed! I suppose you will produce a collection of merry adventures for our instruction and improvement. Excuse me for making this observation, dear mamma; it seems so evident, and it is, of course, allowable to speak the truth.

Clergyman.—I suspect that you will not find anything in the whole collection which may be styled merry.

Louisa.—And what would you consider of that description?

Clergyman.—Scandalous dialogues or situations are my abhorrence. I object equally that common adventures, which are unworthy of engaging our attention, should be told with exaggerated importance; they excite our expectations unduly, in place of giving real pleasure to the mind. They make a mystery of that which should be wholly unveiled, or from which we should altogether turn our eyes.

Louisa.—I do not understand you. You will, however, relate your stories with some degree of elegance. I hope our ears will not be offended by any coarse adventures. You must consider us in the light of a ladies' seminary, and look for our thanks as your recompense.

Clergyman.—Nothing of the sort. But in truth, you will hear nothing new, particularly as I have, for some time back, observed that you never miss the perusal of certain criticisms in some of the learned reviews.

Louisa.—You are really too bad.

Clergyman.—You are engaged to be married, and I therefore pardon you. But I am obliged to show that I also possess arrows which I know how to use. .

Baroness.—I see your object plainly, but you must let her see it likewise.

Clergyman.—Then I must repeat what I said at the beginning of this conversation. But it seems you had not the politeness to pay attention.

Louisa.—What is the use of attention, or of much argument? Look at the matter in any light, they will be scandalous stories, in some shape or other, and nothing else.

Clergyman.—Must I repeat, young lady, that a well-regulated mind only perceives scandal, when it reads of wickedness, arrogance, a desire to injure, and an unwillingness to oblige; and from such spectacles he should avert his eyes. He finds pleasure in the narration of trifling faults and failings, and contemplates with satisfaction those points of the story where good men contend with themselves, with their desires and their intentions, where silly and conceited mortals are rebuked, corrected, or deceived, and where hopes, wishes, and designs are disturbed, interrupted, and frustrated, or unexpectedly fulfilled, accomplished, and confirmed. But on those scenes where accident combines with human weakness and inefficiency, he dwells with the greatest delight, and none of the heroes whose history he authenticates, has either blame to apprehend, or praise to expect from him.

Baroness.—Your introduction excites our wish to hear a specimen. We have spent the greater part of our lifetime in one circle, and have never experienced anything worthy to find a place in such a collection.

Clergyman.—Much undoubtedly depends upon the observer, and upon the peculiar view he takes of occurrences.

But, however, I will not deny that I have made large extracts from old books and traditions. Perhaps you will have no objection to see some of your old friends with new faces. And this gives me a privilege of which I must not be deprived ——that none of my tales shall be doubted.

Louisa.——But we are not to be prevented from recognising our friends and acquaintances, or, if we please, from expounding the enigma.

Clergyman.——Certainly not. But you will allow me, under such circumstances, to produce an old folio, to prove that the identical occurrence happened, and was made matter of record, some centuries ago. And I must be permitted to smile, when some narration is pronounced to be an old fable, though it may have taken place amongst ourselves, without our being able to recognise the characters.

Louisa.——We shall never begin. Had we not better declare a truce for this evening, and do you commence a story at once, by way of specimen?

Clergyman.——Permit me, in this instance, to be guilty of disobedience. The entertainment is intended for the whole assembled company. We must not deprive them of it, and I must premise beforehand, that whatever I have to say, possesses no value in itself. But when my audience, after some serious occupation, wishes for a brief repose, and already sated with good things, desires the addition of a light dessert, then I shall be ready, and only hope that what I shall provide may not prove unpalatable.

Baroness.——In that case, we had better postpone the amusement till to-morrow.

Louisa.——I am beyond measure curious to know what it will be.

Clergyman.——You must not be so, young lady; for high expectations are seldom satisfied.

That same evening, after dinner, the Baroness retired early to her apartment, whilst the rest of the company remained together, and discussed the many reports which were current, and the various incidents which had happened. As is generally the case in such circumstances, few of them knew what to doubt, or what to believe.

The old Clergyman had his remedy for such an emergency. " I propose," said he, " as the most convenient plan, that we all believe implicitly whatever we find pleasant, and that we reject, without ceremony, whatever we find unpleasant, and that we allow everything to be true which can prove itself."

It was then remarked by some one, that men generally acted in this way; and after some desultory conversation, they commented upon that strange propensity of our nature to believe in the marvellous. They talked of romances and visions; and when the old Clergyman had promised at a future time to relate some interesting anecdotes upon these subjects, Louisa exclaimed, "It will be extremely good of you, and you will merit our gratitude, by telling us a story of that description now, for we are all in the proper humour for it; we shall pay attention and be thankful. Without needing further entreaties, the old Clergyman commenced at once, as follows :—

During my residence in Naples, an event happened which attracted universal attention, and with regard to which public opinion varied exceedingly. Some persons maintained that the circumstance had actually occurred; whilst others asserted, that though true in general, it was founded upon a gross deceit. The latter class of persons were at further variance amongst themselves,—they could not agree who was the deceiver. Others held it to be far from clear that spiritual natures were incapable of influencing the elements and human bodies, and maintained that we were not justified in pronouncing every marvellous occurrence to be a fraud or a delusion. But now to the facts themselves.

At the time I speak of, a singer named Antonelli was the favourite of the Neapolitan public. In the bloom of youth, beauty, and talents, she was deficient in none of those enchantments by which women can allure and captivate, and render a certain class of their favourites happy. She was not insensible to the charms of love and flattery, but naturally temperate and sensible, she knew how to enjoy the delights of both, without losing that self-respect which was so essential to her happiness. The young, the distinguished, and the rich, flocked to her in crowds, but she admitted few to her friendship; and if she pursued her own inclination in the choice of her admirers, she evinced, upon all occasions, so firm and resolute a character, that she attached every person to her. I had an opportunity of observing her upon one occasion, in consequence of my close intimacy with one of her especial favourites.

Some years had elapsed; her friends were numerous, and amongst the number were many foolish, simple, and fickle personages. It was her opinion, that a lover who, in a certain sense, is everything to woman, generally proves deficient in those very emergencies when she most needs his assistance; as, for example, in the difficulties of life, in domestic necessities, and upon the occurrence of sudden disasters. In such times, she maintained, that his own self-love often proved absolutely prejudicial to his mistress, and his advice became positively dangerous.

Her former attachments were insufficient to satisfy her soul The void required to be filled. She wished for a friend, and scarcely had she felt this want, than she found a youth amongst those who sought her favours, upon whom she bestowed her confidence, of which in every respect he seemed worthy.

He was a native of Genoa, who had taken up his residence in Naples, to transact the mercantile business of a firm to which he belonged. His natural talents had been improved by a most excellent education. His knowledge was extensive, his mind and body were sound and active, and his general conduct might serve as a model, and in his attention to others he ever seemed forgetful of himself. He was imbued with the commercial spirit for which his native town was distinguished. All his speculations were upon a large scale. His condition, however, was none of the happiest. The firm had entered into some unfortunate transactions, and became entangled in ruinous law-suits. Time only increased the difficulties, and the anxiety which he endured gave him an air of melancholy, which was not unbecoming, and made Antonelli still more desirous of his acquaintance, from the idea that he stood in need of a friend.

Until now he had only seen Antonelli in public, but at his first request, she granted him the entrée to her house, even inviting him to visit her, a favour which he did not fail to accept.

She lost no time in communicating to him her confidence and her wishes. He was no less surprised than delighted at her proposals. She implored him earnestly to be her friend, but to make no pretensions to the privileges of a lover. She

made him acquainted with some embarrassments in which
she had become involved, and his great experience enabled
him to offer advice and assistance for her speedy release.
In return for this confidence, he unfolded to her his own
situation, and whilst she endeavoured to cheer and console him, many new plans occurred to him, which he had not
thought of before, and she thus appeared to be his adviser,
and a reciprocal friendship, founded on the highest regard
and respect, was established between them.

Unfortunately we do not always consider the practicability
of the obligations we incur. He had promised to be her
friend, and to make no pretensions to the privileges of a
lover. But he could not deny that her visitors, in that character, were not only unwelcome to, but were detested by
him; and he felt it extremely painful when she thought
to amuse him with the description of their various characters.

It soon happened, fortunately, or perhaps unfortunately,
that her heart was again free. This was a source of extreme
delight to our young friend, who lost no time in entreating
that the vacant place might be allotted to him. With some
reluctance she listened to his proposals. " I fear," she said,
"that in making this concession, I shall lose my friend." Her
anticipation was correct, for scarcely had he for a short time
filled this double character, than he found her temper change.
As her friend he had been content with her respect—
as a lover he demanded her affection, and as an intelligent and
accomplished man, he sought for constant entertainment.
But this was more than Antonelli expected. She was unwilling to make an entire sacrifice of herself, and had no wish to
surrender her absolute liberty to any one. She soon adopted
ingenious expedients for curtailing the length of his visits,
for avoiding his presence, and for making him sensible that
she would not consent to forego her independence for any
consideration.

This discovery was to him a source of the greatest misery,
and unfortunately the calamity did not come alone. His
domestic affairs became more and more involved, and he
found reason for reproaching himself with having always considered his income as inexhaustible, and with having neglected
his business in order to engage in foreign travel, and to make

a greater figure in the world than he was entitled to do, either from the advantages of his birth or income. The law-suits from which he expected so much, were tardy and expensive. They took him frequently to Palermo, and upon the occasion of his last journey thither, Antonelli adopted means to change the nature of her establishment, for the purpose of becoming gradually disengaged from him. On his return, he found her in another residence, at some distance from his; and he saw that the Marquis of S., who at that time exercised great influence in the world of fashion, had unreserved admission to her house. He was greatly affected by this discovery. which brought on a serious illness. Upon hearing this sad intelligence, Antonelli hastened to him, attended him, and as she was fully aware that his purse was but scantily supplied, she left a large sum of money, which supplied his necessities for a considerable time.

In consequence of his efforts to restrain her freedom, he had fallen considerably in her estimation. As her attachment diminished, her suspicions increased, and she at length began to think that a person who had managed his own affairs so badly, was not entitled to a high character for good sense. But he was unaware of the great change which had taken place in her feelings towards him; and he attributed her anxiety for his recovery, and the constancy of her attentions which induced her to spend whole days at his bedside, rather to her love for him than to compassion for his sufferings; and he hoped upon his recovery, to find himself once more reinstated in her favour.

But he was grievously mistaken. With his restoration to health and strength, all semblance of affection disappeared, and he now seemed as odious in her eyes as he had formerly proved agreeable. In addition to this, his temper had unconsciously become soured and unbearable. He attributed to others all the blame of his own misfortunes, and justified himself fully from their evil consequences. He considered himself an injured and persecuted invalid, and looked for a complete recompense for all his troubles, in the devoted affection of his mistress.

With these exalted expectations he visited Antonelli immediately upon his recovery. He would be satisfied with nothing short of her entire affection, the dismissal of all her

·other friends and acquaintance, her complete retirement from
the stage, and the devotion of herself to him alone. She demonstrated the impossibility of complying with these requests,
at first in a playful, and afterwards in a more serious tone.
At length she communicated to him the sad intelligence that
their connection must end.   He left her and never returned.

He lived for several years afterwards in a retired manner, in
the house of a pious old lady, who had a small independence.
At this period he gained his first law-suit, and soon afterwards he was successful in another; but this change of
fortune came too late, his health was undermined, and the
joy of his existence had vanished.   A slight accident brought
on a relapse, and the physician announced to him his approaching death.   He heard his fate without a murmur,
and merely expressed a wish to see his beautiful friend once
more.   He sent his servant to her—the same messenger who,
in happier days, had been the bearer of many a delightful
answer to him.   He entreated an interview; she refused.
He sent a second time, and implored her to consent ; she was
still inexorable.   At length, at midnight, he sent a third
time. She was embarrassed, and communicated her situation
to me, as I had been invited, along with the Marquis and
some other friends, to spend the evening at her house.   I
advised her, indeed begged her, to show some last attentions
to her friend.   She appeared undecided at first, but after a
short reflection, she made up her mind, and dismissed the
servant with a refusal.   He did not return.

After supper we were all engaged in social conversation,
and general animation and hilarity reigned around. Suddenly,
a little after midnight, a piercing shriek of bitter, painful lamentation was heard. We rose from the table, looked at each
other, and wondered what this strange event could possibly
mean.   The sound seemed to come from the middle of the
room in which we were assembled, and to re-echo again from
the wall.   The Marquis rushed to the window, whilst we
endeavoured to support Antonelli, who had fainted.   By degrees she came to herself.   She had scarcely opened her eyes
than the jealous and passionate Marquis loaded her with the
bitterest reproaches.   " If you choose to have these mysterious understandings with your friends," said he, " at least
let them be of a less fearful nature."   She replied, with her

wonted presence of mind, "that as she had always enjoyed the right of seeing her friends whenever she pleased, she would scarcely select such appalling sounds as they had just heard, to indicate approaching happiness.

And in truth the cry had something in it unspeakably appalling. The long-continued scream of anguish dwelt upon our ears, and made our very limbs tremble. Antonelli was pale, motionless, and in a continual faint. We sat with her for half the night; but we heard nothing further. On the following night, the same company, who had met together not quite so cheerful as usual, though with a reasonable supply of courage, about the same hour of midnight, heard the same identical loud and appalling shriek.

We had, in the meantime, wearied our imaginations in framing conjectures as to the cause of the cry, and thinking from whence it could proceed. But why should I weary you? Whenever Antonelli supped at home, at the self-same hour the same shriek was heard, sometimes louder, and sometimes fainter. It was spoken of all over Naples. The mystery excited universal attention. The police were called out. Spies were placed in every direction, to detect the cause of the mystery. To persons in the street, the shriek appeared to come from the open air, whilst in the house it seemed to proceed from the very room in which Antonelli was sitting. When she supped abroad nothing whatsoever occurred; but as often as she supped at home, the horrid shriek was invariably heard.

But her absence from home did not upon all occasions protect her from this fearful visitation. Her many personal recommendations secured her a welcome reception in the most distinguished families. A pleasant companion, she was everywhere well received, and it had lately become her custom, in order to escape the fearful visitation we have described, to spend her evenings from home.

One evening a gentleman of great respectability, from his age and position, accompanied her to her house in his carriage. When in the act of taking leave of him at the door, a loud shriek was heard, which seemed to come from between them; and the gentlemen, who, like many others, had often heard of this mysterious occurrence, was lifted into his carriage more like a corpse than a living person.

Upon another occasion, a young singer, to whom she was partial, drove through the town with her at evening, to visit a friend. He likewise had frequently heard of the wonderful phenomenon we have related, and, with the spirits of a light-hearted youth, had expressed his doubts of its reality. They spoke of the circumstance. " I wish extremely," said he, " that I could hear the voice of your invisible companion; call him, perhaps he will come; we are two, and need not fear him." From thoughtlessness, or indifference to danger, I know not which, she called the spirit, and instantly the piercing shriek issued, as it were, from the middle of the carriage: three times it was heard, and then died away gradually. Arrived at the house of their friend, both parties were found insensible in the carriage; with difficulty they recovered their senses sufficiently to relate what had happened.

It was some time before Antonelli completely recovered. Her health became impaired by the constantly recurring fright she sustained; but when, at length, her fearful visitor appeared to intend that she should enjoy some repose, she began to hope for a complete cessation from this annoyance; but this expectation was premature.

At the end of the Carnival, accompanied by a young female acquaintance and a servant, she set out upon an excursion of pleasure. It was her intention to visit a friend in the country. Night came on before she reached her destination: an accident occurred to the carriage, and she was necessitated to take refuge in a small country inn, and to put up with the indifferent accommodation it afforded.

Her companion had already gone to bed, and the servant, having arranged the night-light, was about to retire, when her mistress observed jestingly—" I think we are at the end of the world, it is a dreadful night, should he only find us out ?" That very instant the shriek was heard more piercing and louder than ever. Her companion was terrified beyond expression, sprang from her bed, rushed down stairs, and alarmed the whole house. No one that night closed an eye. It was, however, the last time the shriek was heard. But the unwelcome visitor soon found another more frightful mode of indicating his presence.

He was quiet for a short time, when one evening, at the accustomed hour, as Antonelli sat with her companions at table, a shot from a gun, or from a heavily loaded pistol, was fired in at the window. Every one heard the report, every one saw the flash, but upon the closest inspection the window was found not to have sustained the slightest injury. But the circumstance seemed to every one of the most alarming importance, and all thought that an attempt had been made upon Antonelli's life. The police were called, and the neighbouring house was searched ; but as nothing suspicious was found, guards were placed in it, next day, from top to bottom. Her own dwelling was carefully examined, and spies were even dispersed about the streets.

But all this precaution was useless. For three months in succession, at the very same hour, the shot was fired through the same window; without the slightest injury to the glass ; and what was especially remarkable, this always took place exactly one hour before midnight, although in Naples time is counted after the Italian fashion, and the term midnight is never used.

But custom at length reconciled all parties to this occurrence, as it had done to the previous one, and the ghost began to lose credit by reason of his very harmless tricks. The shot ceased to alarm the company, or even to interrupt their conversation.

One evening, at the end of a very sultry day, Antonelli opened the window, without thinking of the hour, and went out with the Marquis upon the balcony. They had scarcely been in the air a couple of minutes when the shot exploded between them, and drove them back into the house, where for some time they lay apparently lifeless on the floor. When they recovered, each felt the pain of a violent blow upon the cheek, one on the right side, the other on the left ; but as no further injury was apparent, the singularity of the circumstance merely occasioned a few jocular observations.

From this time the shot was not repeated in the house, and Antonelli thought she was at last completely delivered from her invisible tormentor ; when one evening, upon making a little excursion with a friend, she was terrified beyond measure by a most unexpected incident. Her way lay through the Chiaja, where her Genoese friend had formerly lived. It was bright moonlight. A lady who sat near her asked, " Is not that the house in which Signor —— died ?"

" As well as I can recollect, it is one of those two," answered
Antonelli;—the words were scarcely uttered when the shot
was fired from one of the two houses alluded to, and it penetrated the carriage. The driver thought he was wounded,
and drove forward with all possible speed. Arrived at their
destination, the two ladies were lifted lifeless from the carriage.

But this was the last alarm of that kind. The unseen foe
now changed his plan, and one evening, shortly afterwards, a
loud clapping of hands was heard before the window. As a
popular singer and favourite actress, she was more familiar
with sounds of this description. They did not inspire terror,
and might have proceeded, perhaps, from one of her numerous admirers. She paid no attention to them. Her friends,
however, were more watchful, and distributed their guards as
before. They continued to hear the noise, but saw nobody,
and began to indulge a hope that the unaccountable mystery
would soon completely end.

After a short time it became changed in character, and
assumed the form of agreeable sounds. They were not
strictly speaking melodious, but were, however, of a soft
and pleasing character. To an accurate observer they
seemed to proceed from the corner of the street, to float about
in the empty space before Antonelli's window, and there to
die away in the most soft and delightful manner. It seemed
as if some heavenly spirit wished, by means of a sweet prelude, to draw attention to a lovely melody which he designed
to play. But these sounds also ceased at length, and were
heard no more after the wonder had lasted for about a year
and a half.

The Clergyman here paused for a few moments in his narrative, and the entire company began to express their opinions,
and their doubts about the truth of the tale.

The narrator answered that the story ought to be true, if it
was intended to be interesting, as a manufactured tale could
possess but little merit. Some one here observed that he
thought it singular no one had inquired about Antonelli's
deceased friend, or the circumstances of his death, as perhaps
some light might by this means have been thrown upon the
whole affair.

" But this was done," replied the Clergyman ; " I was myself
curious enough, immediately after the first mysterious occur-

rence, to go to the house under the pretext of visiting the lady who had attended him in his last moments with a mother's care. This lady informed me that the deceased was passionately attached to Antonelli, that during the last hours of his existence he had spoken of nothing but her; that at one time he addressed her as an adorable angel, and at another as little better than a demon.

When his sickness became desperate, his whole thoughts were fixed on seeing her once more before his death, perhaps in the hope of obtaining from her an expression of affection, of pity, of attachment, or of love. Her unwillingness to see him afflicted him exceedingly, and her last decisive refusal hastened his decease. In despair he cried out, "No! it shall not avail her. She avoids me, but after my death, she shall have no rest from me." In a paroxysm of this kind he expired, and only too late do we learn, that the dead can keep their word on the other side of the grave.

The company began once more to express their opinions about the story. At length Fritz observed: "I have a suspicion, but I shall not tell it till I have thought over all the circumstances again, and put my combinations to the proof."

Being somewhat strongly pressed, he endeavoured to avoid giving an answer, by requesting that he might be allowed to relate an anecdote, which, though it might not equal the preceding one in interest, was of the same character, inasmuch as it could not be explained with any certainty.

"A gallant nobleman," he commenced, "who inhabited an ancient castle, and was father of a large family, had taken into his protection an orphan girl, who, when she attained the age of fourteen years, was employed in attending the mistress of the house, in duties immediately about her person. She gave complete satisfaction, and her whole ambition seemed to consist in a wish to evince her gratitude to her benefactor, by attention and fidelity. She possessed various charms both of mind and person, and was not without suitors for her hand. But none of these proposals seemed likely to conduce to her happiness, and the girl herself did not evince the least inclination to change her condition.

"On a sudden it happened that as she went through the house, intent upon her various duties, she heard sounds of knocking, which came from about her and beneath her. At

2 c

first this seemed accidental, but as the knocking never ceased, and beat almost in unison with her footsteps, she became alarmed, and scarcely left the room of her mistress, where alone she found she could enjoy security.

"These sounds were heard by every one who accompanied her, or who stood near her. At first the subject was treated as a jest, but at length it was regarded in a more serious light. The master of the house, who was of a cheerful disposition, now took the matter in hand. The knocking was never heard when the maiden remained motionless, and when she walked, was perceived not so evidently when she put her foot to the ground, as when she raised it to advance another step. But the sounds were often irregular, and they were observed to be more than usually loud when the maiden went transversely across a certain large apartment in the castle.

"The old nobleman, one day having workmen in the house, caused the flooring to be suddenly raised behind the maiden, when the knocking sounds were at the loudest. Nothing, however, was found but a couple of rats, who, disturbed by the search, gave occasion to a chase, and to considerable uproar in the house.

"Provoked by this circumstance and by the disappointment, the nobleman determined upon adopting strong measures. He took down his large whip from the wall, and swore that he would flog the maiden to death if he heard the knocking any more. From this time forth she could go through the house without the slightest molestation, and the knocking was never heard again."

"Whereby," observed Louisa, sagaciously, "we may conclude that the young maiden was her own ghost, and practised this joke, and played the fool with the family, to indulge some whim of her own."

"Not at all," answered Fritz; "for those who ascribed the mysterious occurrence to a ghost, believed that the maiden's guardian angel wished her to leave the house, but was anxious also to protect her from injury. Others took another view, and maintained that one of the girl's lovers had the cleverness to occasion these sounds, in order to drive her out of the house into his arms. But be this as it may, the poor child became quite ill in consequence, and was reduced to a melancholy spectre, though she had formerly been the most cheerful and lively and merry person in the whole establishment. But such a change in personal appearance can be explained in more ways than one."

" It is a pity," observed Fritz, " that these occurrences are not always more particularly examined, and that in judging of events which so much interest us, we are obliged to hesitate between different appearances, because the circumstances under which they happen have not been all observed."

" True," replied the old Clergyman, " but it is so extremely difficult to make this examination at the very moment when anything of the kind happens, and to take every precaution that nothing shall escape, in which deceit or fraud may be concealed. Can we, for example, detect a conjuror so easily, though we are perfectly conscious that he is deluding us ?"

He had scarcely finished this observation, than a loud report was suddenly heard in one corner of the apartment. Every one leaped up, whilst Charles said, jokingly, " Surely the noise does not proceed from some dying lover."

He would willingly have recalled the expression, for Louisa became suddenly pale, and stammered forth that she felt apprehension about the safety of her intended.

Fritz, to divert her attention, took up the light, and went towards a reading-desk, which stood in a corner of the apartment. The semicircular top was split through—this, then, was the cause of the report which they had heard ; but it immediately occurred to them, that the reading-desk was of the best workmanship, and had occupied the very same spot for years, and they were all, therefore, astonished that it should be so suddenly split asunder. It had even been praised more than once, as a very model piece of furniture ; and how, therefore, could this accident have occurred, without even the slightest change having taken place in the temperature ?

" Quick !" said Charles, " let us settle this point at once, by examining the barometer." The quicksilver maintained the same point it had held for some days. And even the thermometer had not fallen more than could be reconciled with the difference of the temperature between day and night. " It is a pity that we have not a hygrometer at hand," he exclaimed, " the very instrument that would have been most serviceable.

" It seems," said the old Clergyman, "that the most valuable instrument always fails when we are engaged in supernatural inquiries." They were interrupted in their reflections by the entry of a servant, who announced that a great fire was visible in the heavens, though no one could say whether it was raging in the town, or in the neighbourhood.

The circumstances we have just related made the whole party more susceptible of terror, and they were therefore much agitated by the news. Fritz hastened up to the belvidere of the house, where a map of the adjacent country was suspended, by means of which he was enabled, even at night, to point out with tolerable accuracy, the various positions of the surrounding places. The rest of the party remained together, not without some sensations of fear and anxiety.

Fritz announced, upon his return, that he had no good news to tell. "The fire does not seem to be in the town, but upon the property of our aunt. I am well acquainted," said he, " with the locality, and believe I am not mistaken." Each one lamented the destruction of the fine building, and calculated the loss. " A strange thought has just occurred to me," said Fritz, " which may quiet our minds as to the mystery of the reading-desk. Consider how long it is since we heard the report." They counted the minutes, and thought it had occurred about half-past twelve. " Now you will probably laugh," continued Fritz, " when I tell you my conjecture. You know that our mother, a good many years ago, made our aunt a present of a reading-desk, in every respect similar to this one. They were both finished with the greatest care, by the same workman, at the same time, and cut out of one piece of wood. Both have lasted well until now; and I will lay a wager, that at this very instant, the second reading-desk is actually burning at the house of my aunt, and its twin-brother here is afflicted at the disaster. To-morrow I will set out and investigate this singular fact, as thoroughly as I am able."

Whether Frederick really entertained the above opinion, or whether his wish to tranquillize his sister suggested the idea, we are unable to decide; they, however, seized the opportunity to speak of many undeniable sympathies, and ended by discovering that a sympathy actually existed between pieces of timber formed from one tree, and pronounced it probable that the same sympathy subsisted between pieces of work completed by the same hand. They agreed that these things resembled natural phenomena, fully as much as other things which were often adduced, and which, although quite evident, are incapable of explanation. "And in my opinion," added Charles, "every phenomenon, as well as every fact, is peculiarly interesting for its own sake. Whoever explains it, or connects it with other circumstances, only makes a jest of it, or deludes us: this is done, for example, by the natural philosopher and the historian. But an unconnected fact or event is interesting, not because it is explicable or probable, but because it is true. When at midnight the flames consumed your aunt's reading-desk, the extraordinary splitting of ours, at the very same time, was a palpable fact, however explicable or connected with other things it may be."

Though night was by this time far advanced, none of the company felt any inclination to retire; and Charles, in his turn, asked permission to tell a story, which, though equally interesting, might seem perhaps more natural and explicable than the previous ones. "Marshal Bassompierre," he said, "relates it in his Memoirs, and I may be permitted to tell it in his name.

"I had remarked for five or six months, that whenever I crossed the little bridge (for at that time the Pont Neuf had not been built), a very handsome shopkeeper, over the door of whose establishment was painted the sign of "The Two Angels," always saluted me with a low and respectful bow, and followed me with her eyes as far as she could see me. This conduct on her part surprised me extremely, but I always directed my looks to her, and saluted her in return. I rode on one occasion from Fontainbleau to Paris, and when I had arrived at the little bridge, she appeared at the door of her shop, and said, 'Your servant, sir!' I returned the salute, and as I looked back from time to time, I observed that she was as usual leaning forward, to keep me in view as long as possible.

" My servant was following with a postilion, as I wished to send some letters back to some ladies in Fontainbleau the same day. I ordered the servant to alight, to go to the pretty shopkeeper, and to tell her from me, that I had noticed her wish to speak to me, and that if she desired my acquaintance, I would visit her whenever she wished. She answered that I could have sent her no more delightful news, that she would meet me whenever I should appoint, on condition that she might be allowed to pass a night under the same roof with me. I accepted the proposal, and asked the servant to find a place where I might appoint an assignation. He said he would lead me to a friend's house, but advised me, as fever was then very prevalent, to provide myself with my own house-linen. When evening came, I went to the appointed house, where I found a very beautiful young woman awaiting my arrival. She was attired in a charming head-dress, and wore the finest linens. Her tiny feet were adorned with slippers, worked in gold and silk, and her person was covered with a loose mantle of the softest satin texture. Suffice it to say, that I never saw a more charming person. In the morning I asked when I could see her again, as it was then Thursday night, and it was not my intention to leave the town before the following Sunday.

" She replied, that she was more anxious for a fresh appointment than I could possibly be ; but that it would be impracticable, unless I could postpone my departure, as I could only see her on Sunday night. To this I made some difficulty, which caused her to complain that I was tired of her, and therefore wished to set out on Sunday ; ' but,' she added, ' you will soon think of me again, and will be glad to forfeit a day, to pass a night with me.'

" I was easily persuaded. I promised to stay during Sunday, and to meet her in the evening, at the same place. She answered me as follows : ' I am quite aware, that on your account, I have allowed myself to meet you under circumstances calculated to ruin my character ; but I have done this in obedience to an irresistible desire to enjoy your society. But so great an indiscretion cannot be repeated. I shall excite the jealousy of my husband, though one might risk even that for the satisfaction of an irresistible passion. For your sake I have come to this house, which has been honoured by your presence. But if you desire to see me again, you must meet me at the residence of my Aunt.'

" She described the house with great particularity, and then added, 'I shall expect you at ten o'clock. From that time till midnight the door shall be open. You will find a small entrance, through which you must advance, as my Aunt's door is at the farther end. You will then see a flight of stairs opposite to you. They lead to the first floor, and there I shall be expecting you with open arms.'

" I made all my arrangements. I sent away my things, dismissed my servants, and waited impatiently the arrival of Sunday night, when I was to see my charming companion once more. At ten o'clock I was at the appointed place. I found the door which she had described, close shut, and observed lights in the house, which seemed every now and then to blaze up into a flame. I knocked impatiently in order to announce my arrival, and I was immediately saluted by the hoarse voice of a man inquiring what I wanted? I retired disappointed, and paced restlessly up and down the street. At length I returned to the house, and found the door then wide open. I hurried through the passage and ascended the stairs. Judge of my astonishment at finding the room occupied by two men, who were employed in burning a mattress and some bed-clothes, while I saw before me two naked corpses stretched upon the floor. I hastened away instantly, and in rushing down stairs, knocked against two men carrying a coffin, who asked me angrily what I wanted. I drew my sword to protect myself, and finally reached my home in a state of the greatest excitement. I swallowed half a dozen glasses of wine, as a preservative against the fever, and on the following day continued my journey.

" All the inquiries I afterwards instituted to discover who this woman was, were in vain. I even visited the shop where the 'Two Angels' were painted, but the new-comers could not inform who their predecessors had been. The chief character in this adventure was doubtless a person from the lower orders, but I can assure you, that but for the disagreeable finale, it would have proved one of the most delightful incidents that has ever happened to me, and that I never think of my charming heroine without feelings of the warmest affection."

Charles observed, upon the conclusion of the anecdote, that the mystery which enveloped the story was not easily explained. The woman might either have died of the fever, or have kept away from the house on account of the infection.

"But if she was alive," answered Charles, "she would have met her lover in the street, as no fear could, under the circumstances, have kept her from him. I fear," he added, "that her corpse was stretched on the floor."

"Oh! no more of this," said Louisa: "this story is too frightful. What a night we shall pass, if we retire with our imaginations full of these pictures!"

"I recollect an anecdote," interrupted Charles, "of rather a more cheerful description, which the same Bassompierre relates of some of his ancestors.

"A very beautiful woman, who loved one of her relations passionately, visited him every Monday at his country house, where they spent much time together, his wife believing in the meanwhile that her husband was engaged on a hunting-party. Two years uninterruptedly had passed in this way, when the wife's suspicions being roused, she stole one morning to the country house, and found her husband asleep with his companion. Being unwilling or afraid to disturb them, she untied her veil, threw it over the feet of the sleeping couple, and retired. When the lady awoke and observed the veil, she uttered a piercing cry, and with loud lamentations complained that she would now never be able to see her lover again. She then took leave of him, having first given him three presents, a small fruit-basket, a ring, and a goblet, being a present for each of his three daughters, and desired him to take great care of them. They were accepted with thanks, and the children of these three daughters believe that they are indebted to their respective gifts for whatever good fortune has attended them."

"This somewhat resembles the story of the beautiful Melusina, and such like fairy tales," observed Louisa.

"But there is just such a tradition in our family," said Frederick, "and we have possession of a similar talisman."

"What do you mean?" asked Charles.

"That is a secret," replied the former. "It can be told to no one but the eldest son, and that during the lifetime of his father, and he is then to hold the charm."

" Are you the present possessor ?" inquired Louisa.

" I have told too much already," answered Frederick, as he lighted his candle, previous to retiring.

———

The family had assembled to breakfast according to their usual custom, and the Baroness afterwards took her seat at her embroidery-frame. After a short silence, the Clergyman observed, with a slight smile, " It is seldom indeed that singers, poets, or story-tellers, who enter into an agreement to amuse a company, do it at the right time; they often require pressing, when they should begin voluntarily; whilst, on the other hand, they are frequently eager and urgent to commence at a time when the entertainment could be dispensed with. I hope, however, to prove an exception to this custom, and I shall be glad to know whether it will prove agreeable to you that I should relate a story."

" Particularly so," answered the Baroness, " and I feel sure that I express the general opinion. But if it is your intention to relate an anecdote as a specimen, I will tell you for what sort of story I have no inclination."

" I take no pleasure in stories which, like the Arabian Nights, connect one tale with another, and so confound the interest of both, where the narrator finds himself compelled to excite our attention by interruptions, and instead of satisfying us by detailing a course of consecutive adventures, seeks to attract us by rare and often unworthy artifices. I cannot but censure the attempt to convert stories which should possess the unity of a poem, into unmeaning puzzles, which only have the effect of destroying our taste. I leave you to choose your own subjects, but I hope you will pay a little attention to the style, since it must be remembered that we are members of good society. Commence with some narrative in which but few persons are concerned or few events described, in which the plot is good and natural, though possessing as much action and contrivance as is necessary, which shall not prove dull, nor be confined to one spot, but in which, however, the action shall not progress too rapidly. Let your characters be pleasing, and if not perfect, at least good,— not extravagant, but interesting and amiable. Let your story be amusing in the narration, in order that when concluded, we may remember it with pleasure."

"If I were not well acquainted with you, gracious lady," said the Clergyman, "I should be of opinion that it was your wish, by thus explaining how much you require of me, to bring my wares into disrepute, before I have exposed them for sale. I see how difficult it will be to reach your standard of excellence. Even now," he continued, after a short pause, "you compel me to postpone the tale which I had intended to relate, till another time, and I fear I shall commit a mistake in extemporizing an anecdote for which I have always felt a great partiality :—

In a sea-coast town in Italy, once lived a merchant, who from his youth had been distinguished for activity and industry. He was, in addition, a first-rate sailor, and had amassed considerable wealth by trading to Alexandria, where he was accustomed to purchase or exchange merchandize, which he afterwards either brought home or forwarded to the northern parts of Europe. His fortune increased from year to year. Business was his greatest pleasure, and he found no time for the indulgence of extravagant dissipation.

His life was employed in active pursuits of this nature till he was fifty years old, and he had been, during all this time, a total stanger to those social pleasures with which luxurious citizens are accustomed to diversify their lives. Even the charms of the fair sex had never excited his attention, notwithstanding the attractions of his countrywomen. His knowledge of them was confined to their love for ornaments and jewellery, a taste of which he never failed to take proper advantage.

He was surprised, therefore, at the change which took place in his disposition, when, after a long voyage, his richly laden ship entered the port of his native town, upon the occurrence of a great festival, in which the children of the place took a prominent part. The youths and maidens had attended the church in their gayest attire, and had joined in the sacred processions. They afterwards mingled through the town in separate companies, or dispersed through the country in search of amusements, or they assembled in the large square, engaging in various active pursuits, and exhibiting feats of skill and dexterity, for which small prizes were bestowed.

The merchant became delighted with all he saw. But after he had for some time observed the happiness of the children, and the delight of their parents, and witnessed so many persons in the full enjoyment of present bliss, and the indulgence of the fondest hopes, he could not help reflecting upon the wretchedness of his own condition. The thought of his own solitary home began for the first time to be distressing to him, and he thus gave vent to his melancholy thoughts.

" Unhappy being that I am! Why are my eyes opened so late? Why, in my old age, do I first become acquainted with those blessings which can alone ensure the happiness of mankind? What toil have I endured! What labours have I borne! And what have they done for me? 'Tis true, my cellars are filled with merchandize, my chests with valuable metals, and my caskets with jewellery and precious stones; but these treasures can neither console nor satisfy my heart. The more I have, the more I want,—one coin requires another, and one diamond wishes for its fellow. I am not the master of my riches. They command me in imperious tone. ' Go and get more,' they exclaim. Gold delights in gold, and jewels in their fellows. They have ruled me all my life; and now I find, too late, that they possess no real value. Now when age approaches, I begin for the first time to reflect, and to complain, that I enjoy none of the treasures which I possess, and that no one will enjoy them after me. Have I ever used them to adorn the person of a beloved wife?—to provide a marriage-portion for a daughter? Have I ever, by their means, enabled a son to win and to dower the maiden of his heart? Never! None of these treasures have ever enriched me or mine; and what I have collected with so much toil, some stranger, after my death, will thoughtlessly dissipate.

" Oh! with what different feelings will those happy parents whom I see around me, assemble their children this evening, praise their address, and encourage them to virtue! What joy have I beheld beaming from their eyes, and what hopes from the happiness of their beloved offspring! And must I ever be a stranger to hope? Am I grown grey? Is it not enough to see my error, before the final evening of my days arrives? No, in my ripe years, it is not foolish to dream of love. I will enrich a fair maiden with my wealth, and make her happy. And should my house ever become blest with children, those late fruits will render me happy, instead of proving a plague and a torment, as they often do, to those who too early receive such gifts from Heaven."

Thus communing with himself, he silently formed his determination. He then called two of his intimate companions, and opened his mind to them. They were ever ready to aid him in all emergencies, and were not wanting upon the present occasion. They hastened, therefore, into the town, to make inquiries after the fairest and most beautiful maidens; for they knew their master was a man, who, whatever goods he might wish to acquire, would never be satisfied with any but the best. He was himself active, went about, inquired, saw, and listened, and soon found what he sought, in the person of a young maiden about sixteen years of age, accomplished and well-educated. Her person and disposition pleased him, and gave him every hope of happiness. In fact, at this time no maiden in the whole town was more admired for her beauty.

After a short delay, during which the most perfect independence of his intended bride, not only during his own life, but after his decease, was secured, the nuptial ceremony was performed with great pomp and triumph, and from that day, the merchant felt himself, for the first time in his life, in actual possession and enjoyment of his riches. His rarest and most costly silks were devoted to the adornment of his bride, and his diamonds gleamed more brilliantly upon the neck and amid the tresses of his love, than they had ever shone in his caskets; and his rings acquired an inexpressible value from the beauty of the hand by which they were adorned. And thus he felt that he was not only as wealthy, but even wealthier than before; and all he possessed acquired a new value from being shared with her whom he loved. The happy couple spent a year together in the most perfect contentment, and he seemed to experience a real joy in having exchanged his active and wandering course of life for the calm content of domestic bliss. But he could not so easily divest himself of his nature; and he found that a habit acquired in early youth, though it may for a time be interrupted, can never be completely laid aside.

After some time the sight of some of his old companions, when they had safely brought their ships into harbour, after a long and perilous voyage, excited anew his old inclinations, and he began now, even in the company of his bride, to experience sensations of restlessness and discontent. These feelings increased daily, and were gradually converted into so intense a longing for his old course of life, that at last he became positively miserable, and a serious illness was the result.

" What will now become of me ?" he asked himself. " I learn too late, the folly, in old age, of entering upon a new system of life. How can we separate ourselves from our thoughts and our habits ? What have I done ? Once I possessed the perfect freedom which a bird enjoys in open air, and now I am imprisoned in a dwelling with all my wealth and jewels, and my beauteous wife. I thought thus to win contentment, and enjoy my riches ; but I feel that I lose everything so long as I cannot increase my stores. Unjustly are men considered fools who add to their wealth by ceaseless activity,— for activity itself is happiness, and riches themselves are valueless in comparison with the delight of the toil by which they are acquired. I am wretched from idleness, sick from inactivity, and if I do not determine upon some other course, I may soon bid farewell to life.

" I know, however, how much I risk in separating from a young and lovely wife. I know how unjust it is to win the affections of a charming maiden, and, after a brief possession, to abandon her to the wearisome society of her own desires and emotions. I know, even now, how many vain and frivolous youths display their conceited persons before my windows. I know that in church, and in the public promenades, they seek to attract the notice, and engage the attention, of my wife. What may not take place, then, if I absent myself? Can I hope for the intervention of some miracle to save her from her almost inevitable fate ? It were vain to expect that at her age, and with her warm affections, she can withstand the seductions of love. If I depart, I know that upon my return I shall have lost the attachment of my wife, and that she will have forfeited her fidelity, and tarnished the honour of my house."

Such reflections as these, and the doubts to which he became a prey, embittered his condition tenfold. His wife, no less than his relations and friends, sympathized deeply with him, without being able to comprehend the cause of his illness. At length he sought relief from his own thoughts, and thus communed with himself:—"Fool! to trouble yourself so much about the protection of a wife, whom, if your illness continues, you must leave behind you for the enjoyment of another. Is it not better to preserve your life, even though in the effort you risk the loss of the greatest treasure which a woman can possess. How many find their very presence ineffectual to preserve this treasure, and patiently endure a privation which they cannot prevent! Why cannot you summon up courage to be independent of so precarious a blessing, since upon this resolution your very existence depends?"

He felt invigorated by these thoughts, and forthwith summoned together his former crew. He instructed them without delay to charter a vessel, to load it, and to hold themselves ready to set sail with the first favourable wind. He then unburthened himself in the following terms to his wife:—

"Be not astonished at any commotion you may shortly observe in our house, but conclude from thence that I am making preparations for a journey. Be not overcome with grief when I inform you that I am once more bent upon a sea voyage. My love is still unchanged towards you, and so it will doubtless remain during my life. I am sensible of the bliss I have enjoyed in your society, and should feel it still more powerfully, but for the silent censures of idleness and inactivity with which my conscience reproves me. My old disposition returns, and my former habits are still alive. Let me once more visit the markets of Alexandria, to which I shall repair with the greater joy, because I can there procure for you the richest merchandize and most valuable treasures. I leave you in possession of all my fortune and of all my goods; make use of them without restraint, and enjoy yourself in the company of your relatives and friends. The period of our separation will roll swiftly by, and we shall see each other once more with inexpressible delight."

Dissolved in tears, his loving wife assured him, with the most tender endearments, that during his absence she should never be able to enjoy one happy moment; and entreated him, since she wished neither to control nor to detain him, that she might, at least, share his affectionate thoughts during the sad time of their separation.

He then gave some general directions on business and household matters, and added, after a short pause: " I have something to say, which lies like a burden upon my heart, and you must permit me to utter it; I only implore you earnestly not to misinterpret my meaning, but in my anxiety for you to discern my love."

" I can guess your thoughts," interrupted his wife; " you are suspicious of me, I know; and after the fashion of men, you always rail against the universal weakness of our sex. I am, it is true, young and of a cheerful disposition, and you fear that, in your absence, I shall be found inconstant and unfaithful. I do not find fault with your suspicions: it is the habit of your sex; but if I know my own heart, I may assure you that I am not so susceptible of impressions as to be induced, lightly, to stray from the paths of love and duty, through which I have hitherto journeyed. Fear not; you shall find your wife as true and faithful on your return, as you have ever found her hitherto, when you have come to her arms at evening after a short absence."

" I believe the truth of the sentiments you utter," added the husband, "and I beseech you to be constant to them. But let us conceive the possibility of the worst. Why should we shrink from it? You know yourself how the beauty of your person attracts the admiration of all our young fellow-citizens. During my absence, they will be more attentive to you than ever. They will redouble their efforts to attract and to please you. The image of your husband will not prove as effective as his presence, in banishing them from my doors and from your heart. I know you are a noble being; but the blandishments of love are powerful, and oftentimes overcome the firmest resolutions. Interrupt me not. Your very thoughts of me during my absence may inflame your passions. I may, for some time, continue to be the object of your dearest wishes; but who can foretell what opportunities may occur, and allow a stranger to enjoy those privileges which were destined for me. Be not impatient, I beseech you, but hear me out.

"Should that time arrive, the possibility of which you deny, and which I am by no means anxious to hasten, in which you feel that you need society, and can no longer defer the requirements of love, then make me one promise. Permit no thoughtless youth to supplant me, whatever may be the attractions of his person, for such lovers are more dangerous to the honour than to the virtue of a woman. Incited rather by vanity than by love, they seek the general favours of the sex, and are ever ready to transfer their transitory affections. If you wish for the society of a friend, look out for one who is worthy of the name, whose modesty and discretion understands the art of exalting the joys of love by the virtue of secrecy."

His beautiful wife could suppress her agony no longer, and the tears which she had till now restrained, flowed in copious torrents from her eyes. "Whatever may be your opinion of me," she cried, after a passionate embrace, "nothing can be at this hour farther from my thoughts than the crime which you seem to consider as inevitable. If such an idea shall ever suggest itself to my imagination, may the earth in that instant open and swallow me up, and all hope of that joy for ever vanish, which promises a blessed immortality! Banish this mistrust from your bosom, and let me enjoy the full and delightful hope of seeing you again return to these arms."

Leaving no effort untried to comfort and console his wife, he set sail the next day. His voyage was prosperous, and he soon arrived in Alexandria.

In the meantime our heroine lived in the tranquil enjoyment of a large fortune, in possession of every luxury, though, with the exception of her relatives and immediate friends, no person was admitted to her society. The business of her absent husband was discharged by trustworthy servants, and she inhabited a large mansion, in whose splendid salons she was able to enjoy the daily pleasure of recalling the remembrance of his love.

But notwithstanding her quiet and retired mode of life, the young gallants of the town did not long remain inactive. They frequented the street, passed incessantly before her windows, and in the evening sought by means of music and serenades to attract her attention. The pretty prisoner at first found these attentions troublesome and annoying, but gradually she became reconciled to the vexation, and when the long evenings arrived, she began to consider the serenades in the light of an agreeable entertainment, and could scarcely suppress an occasional sigh, which, strictly speaking, belonged to her absent husband.

But her unknown admirers, in place of gradually wearying in their attentions, as she had once expected, became more assiduous in their devotion to her. She began, at last, to recognize the oft-repeated instruments and voices, to grow familiar with the melodies, and to feel an anxiety to know the names of her most constant serenaders. She might innocently indulge so harmless a curiosity. She now peeped occasionally through her curtains and half-closed shutters, to notice the pedestrians, and to observe more particularly the youths whose eyes were constantly directed towards her windows. They were invariably handsome, and fashionably dressed; but their manner and whole deportment were unmistakably marked by frivolity and vanity. They sought rather to make themselves remarkable by directing their attention to the house of so beautiful a woman, than to display towards her a feeling of peculiar respect.

"Really," the lady would sometimes say to herself in a tone of raillery, "really my husband showed a deal of penetration. The condition under which he allowed me to enjoy the privilege of a lover, excludes all those who care in the least for me, or to whom I am likely to take a fancy. He seems to have well understood that prudence, modesty, and silence are qualities which belong to demure old age, when men can value the understanding, but are incapable of awakening the fancy, or exciting the desires. I am pretty sure, at least, that amongst the youths who lay perpetual siege to my mansion, there is not one entitled to my confidence; and those who might lay some claim to that virtue, fall lamentably short in other attractions."

Supported by these reflections, she allowed herself to take more and more pleasure daily in the music and in the attentions of her young admirers; till, at length, unperceived by herself, a restless desire gradually sprung up in her bosom, with which she was too late compelled to struggle. Solitude and idleness, combined with comfort and luxury, gave birth

2 D

to an unruly passion, long before the thoughtless victim had
any suspicion of her danger.

Amongst the numerous endowments of her husband, she
now saw ample reason to admire his profound knowledge of
the world and of mankind, and his thorough acquaintance
with woman's heart.   She now perceived the possibility of
that occurrence which she had formerly so strenuously
denied, and acknowledged his wisdom in preaching the
necessity of prudence and caution.   But what could these
virtues avail, where pitiless chance seemed to be in con-
spiracy with her own unaccountable passions?   How could
she select one from a crowd of strangers, and was she permitted, in case of disappointment, to make a second choice?

Innumerable thoughts of this nature increased the perplexity of our solitary heroine.   In vain she sought for
recreation, and tried to forget herself.   Her mind was perpetually excited by agreeable objects, and her imagination thus
became impressed with the most delightful pictures of fancied
happiness.

In this state of mind, she was informed one day by a relation, amongst other pieces of news, that a young lawyer who
had just finished his studies at Bologna, had lately arrived in
his native town.   His talents were the topic of general
admiration and encomium.   His universal knowledge was
accompanied by a modesty and reserve very uncommon in
youth, and his personal attractions were of a high order.   In
his office of Procurator he had already won, not only the
confidence of the public, but the respect of the judges.   He
had daily business to transact at the court-house, so great was
the increase of his professional practice.

Our heroine could not hear the talents of this youth so
generally extolled, without feeling a wish to become acquainted
with him, accompanied by a secret hope that he might prove
a person upon whom, in conformity with the permission of
her husband, she might bestow her heart.   She soon learnt
that he passed her dwelling daily, on his way to the court
house, and she carefully watched for the hour when the
lawyers were accustomed to assemble for the discharge of
business.   With beating heart she at length observed him
pass, and if his handsome figure and youthful attractions, on
the one hand, excited her admiration, his apparent reserve

and modesty, on the other, gave her much reason for doubt and anxiety. For several days she watched him silently, till at length, she was no longer able to resist her desire to gain his attention. She dressed herself with care, went out upon the balcony, and marked his approach with feelings of suspense. But she grew troubled and, indeed, felt ashamed when she saw him pass, in contemplative mood, with thoughtful steps and downcast eyes pursuing his quiet way, without deigning to bestow the slightest notice upon her. Vainly did she endeavour thus to win his attention for several successive days. In the same undeviating course he continued to pass by, without raising his eyes or looking to the right or to the left. But the more she observed him, the more did he appear to be the very person she desired. Her wish to know him now grew stronger and, at length, became irresistible. How! she thought within herself—when my noble, sensible husband actually foresaw the extremity to which his absence would reduce me, when his keen perception knew that I could not live without a friend,—must I droop and pine away at the very time when fortune provides me with one whom not only my own heart, but even the choice of my husband would approve, in whose society I may enjoy the delights of love in inviolable secrecy? Fool should I be, to miss such an opportunity, fool, to resist the powerful impulses of love.

With such reflections did she endeavour to decide upon some fixed course, and she did not long remain a prey to uncertainty. It happened with her, as it usually does with every one who is conquered by a passion, that she looked without apprehension upon all such trifling objections as shame, fear, timidity, and duty, and came at length to the bold resolution of sending her servant maid to the young lawyer at any risk, and inviting him to visit her.

She found him in the company of several friends, and delivered her message punctually in the terms in which she had been instructed. The Procurator was not at all surprised at the invitation. He had known the merchant previously, was aware of his absence at present, and presumed that the lady required the aid of his professional services about some important matter of business. He promised the servant, therefore, that he would wait upon her mistress without delay.

The latter heard with unspeakable joy, that she would soon
be allowed an opportunity of seeing and speaking to her
beloved. She prepared carefully for his reception, and had
her saloons arranged with the utmost elegance. Orange-leaves
and flowers were strewn around in profusion, and the most
costly furniture was displayed for the occasion. And thus
the brief intervening time hastened by, which would otherwise have been unbearable.

Who can describe the emotion with which she witnessed
his arrival, or her agitation upon inviting him to take a
seat at her side? She hesitated how to address him now
that he had arrived, and found a difficulty in remembering
what she had to say. He sat still and silent. At length,
she took courage and addressed him, not without some visible
perplexity.

" I understand, Sir, that you are but lately returned to
your native city, and I learn that you are universally admired
as a talented and incomparable man. I am ready to bestow
my utmost confidence upon you, in a matter of extraordinary
importance, but which, upon reflection, would seem adapted
rather for the ear of the Confessor than that of the Lawyer.
I have been for some years married to a husband who is both
rich and honourable, and who, as long as we have lived
together, has never failed to tenderly love me, and of whom
I should not have a single word of complaint to utter, if an
irresistible desire for travelling and for trade had not torn
him, for some time, from my arms.

" As a sensible and just man, he no doubt felt conscious of
the injury which his absence must necessarily inflict upon me.
He knew that a young wife must be preserved in a different
manner from jewellery and pearls. He knew that she resembled a garden, full of the choicest fruits, which would
be lost not only to him, but to every one else, if the door
were kept locked for years. For this reason, he addressed
me in serious but friendly tones before his departure, and
assured me, that he knew I should not be able to live without
the society of a friend, and therefore not only permitted, but
made me promise, that I would, in a free and unrestrained
manner, follow the inclination which I should soon find
springing up within my heart."

. She paused for a moment,—but an eloquent look, which

the young Lawyer directed towards her, encouraged her to proceed.

" One only condition was imposed upon me by my indulgent husband. He recommended me to use the most extreme caution, and impressed upon me strongly the necessity of choosing a steady, prudent, silent, and confidential friend. But, you will excuse my continuing—excuse the embarrassment with which I must confess how I have been attracted by your numerous accomplishments, and conceive, if possible, from the confidence I have reposed in you, the nature of my hopes and wishes."

The worthy young Lawyer was silent for a short time, and then replied, in a thoughtful tone. " I am deeply indebted for the high mark of confidence with which you both honour and delight me. I wish to convince you that I am not unworthy of your favour. But let me first answer you in a professional capacity, and I must confess my admiration for your husband, who so clearly saw the nature of the injustice he committed against you ; for there can be no doubt of this —that a husband who leaves his young wife, in order to visit distant countries, must be viewed in the light of a man who relinquishes a valuable treasure, to which, by his own conduct, he abandons all manner of claim. And as the first finder may then lawfully take possession—so I hold it to be natural and just, that a young woman, under the circumstances you describe, should bestow her affections and herself, without scruple, upon any friend who may prove worthy of her confidence.

" But particularly when the husband, as in this case, conscious of the injustice he himself commits, expressly allows his forsaken wife a privilege, of which he could not deprive her, it must be clear that he can suffer no wrong from an action to which he has given his own consent.

" Wherefore if you," continued the young lawyer, with a different look and the most express emphasis, and the most affectionate pressure of the hand, " if you select me for your servant, you enrich me with a happiness, of which, till now‘ I could have formed no conception. And be assured," he added, while at the same time he warmly kissed her hand, " that you could not have found a more true, loving, prudent, and devoted servant."

This declaration tranquillized the agitated feelings of our tender heroine. She at once expressed her love without reserve. She pressed his hand, drew him nearer to her, and reclined her head upon his shoulder. They had remained but a short time in this position, when he sought to disengage himself gently, and not without emotion expressed himself thus :—" Did ever happy mortal find himself in such embarrassment? I am compelled to leave you, and to do violence to myself in the very moment when I might surrender myself to the most divine enchantment. I cannot now partake the bliss which is prepared for me,' and I earnestly pray that a temporary postponement may not altogether frustrate my fondest hopes.

She inquired hastily the cause of this strange speech :

" When I was in Bologna," he replied, " and had just completed my studies, preparing to enter upon the practice of my profession, I was seized with a dangerous illness, from which it appeared, that even if I should escape with my life, my bodily and mental faculties must sustain irreparable injury. Reduced to despair, and tortured by the pangs of disease, I made a solemn vow to the Virgin, that should I recover, I would persist for one whole year in practising the strictest fast and abstinence from enjoyment of every description. For ten months I have already adhered to my vow, and considering the wonderful favour I have enjoyed, the time has not passed wearily, and I have not found it difficult to abstain from many accustomed pleasures. But the two months which still remain, will now seem an eternity, since, till their expiration, I am forbidden to partake a happiness whose delights are inconceivable. And though you may think the time long, do not, I beseech you, withdraw the favour which you have so bountifully bestowed upon me."

Not much consoled by this announcement, she felt a little more encouraged when her friend added, after a few minutes' reflection, " I scarcely dare to make a proposal, and suggest a plan, which may, perhaps, release me a little earlier from my vow. If I could only find some one as firm and resolute as myself in keeping a promise, and who would divide with me the time that still remains, I should then be the sooner free, and nothing could impede our enjoyment. Are you willing, my sweet friend, to assist in hastening our happiness by removing one-half of the obstacle which opposes us? I can only share my vow with one upon whom I can depend with full confidence. And it is severe,—nothing but bread and water twice a-day, and at night a few hours' repose on a hard bed, and notwithstanding my incessant professional occupation, I must devote many hours to prayer. If I am obliged to attend a party, I am not thereby released from my duty, and I must avoid the enjoyment of every dainty. If you can resolve to pass one month in the observance of these rules, you will find yourself the sooner in possession of your friend's society, which you will relish the more from the consciousness of having deserved it by your praiseworthy resolution."

The beautiful lady was not insensible of the difficulty she had to encounter; but, the very presence of her beloved so increased her attachment, that no trial appeared to her too difficult which should ensure the possession of so valuable a prize. She assured him, therefore, in the most affectionate manner, of her readiness to share the responsibility of his vow, and addressed him thus: "My sweet friend! the miracle through which you have recovered your health, is to me an event of so much value and importance, that it is not only my duty, but my joy, to partake the vow by which you are still bound. I am delighted to offer so strong a proof of my sincerity. I will imitate your example in the strictest manner, and, until you discharge me from my obligation, no consideration shall induce me to stray from my path of duty."

The young lawyer once more repeated the conditions under which he was willing to transfer to her the obligation of one half of his vow, and then took his leave, with the assurance that he would soon visit her again, to inquire after her constancy and resolution. And she was then obliged to witness his departure, without receiving so much as one kiss or pressure of the hand, and scarcely with a look of ordinary recognition. She found some degree of happy relief in the strange employment which the performance of her new duties imposed upon her, for she had much to do in the preparation for her unaccustomed course of life. In the first place, all her beautiful exotics and flowers were removed, which had been procured to grace the reception of her beloved. Then a hard mattress was substituted for her downy bed, to which she retired at evening, after having scarcely satisfied her hunger with a frugal meal of bread and water. The following morning found her busily employed in plain work, and in making wearing apparel for a certain number of poor inmates of the town hospital. During this new occupation, she entertained her fancy by dwelling upon the image of her dear friend, and indulging the hope of future happiness ; and these thoughts reconciled her to the greatest privations, and to the humblest fare.

At the end of the first week, the roses began to fade from her beautiful cheeks, her person to fall away, and her strength to become weak and languid ; but a visit from her friend imparted new animation and fortitude. He encouraged her to persist in her resolution, by the example of his own perseverance, and by shewing her the approaching certainty of uninterrupted happiness. His visit was brief, but he promised to return again speedily.

With cheerful resignation, she continued her new and strict course of life, but her strength soon declined so much that the most severe illness could scarcely have reduced her to such extreme weakness. Her friend, whose visit was repeated at the end of the week, sympathized with her condition, but comforted her by an assurance that one half the period of her trial was already over. But the severe fasting, continual praying, and incessant work, became every day more unbearable, and her excessive abstemiousness threatened to ruin the health of one who had ever been accustomed to a life of the greatest luxury. At length she found a difficulty in walking, and she was compelled, notwithstanding the sultriness of the season, to wrap herself up in the warmest clothing, to preserve even an ordinary degree of heat, till finally she was obliged to take to her bed.

Reduced to this extremity, it would be difficult to describe the course of her reflections, as she thought over the whole of this extraordinary occurrence, and it is impossible to imagine her distress when ten tedious days wearily passed without the appearance of the friend, for whose sake she had consented to make this unheard-of sacrifice. But those hours of trouble sufficed to recal her to reason, and she formed her resolution. Her friend visited her after the lapse of some few days more, and seating himself at her bed-side, upon the very sofa which he had occupied when she made her first declaration of love to him, he encouraged and implored her in the most tender and affectionate tones, to persist for a short time longer; but she interrupted him with a sweet smile, and assured him that she needed no persuasion to continue, for a few days, the performance of a vow which she knew full well had been appointed for her advantage. "I am, as yet, too feeble," she said, "to express my thanks to you as I could wish. You have saved me from myself. You have restored me to myself, and I confess, that from this moment I am indebted to you for my existence. My husband was, indeed, gifted with prudence and good sense, and well knew the nature of woman's heart! And he was, moreover, just enough not to condemn a passion which he saw might spring up within my bosom, through his own fault, and he was generous enough to make allowance for the weakness of my nature! But you, Sir, are truly virtuous and good. You have taught me that we possess within us an antidote equivalent to the force of our passions; that we are capable of renouncing luxuries to which we have been accustomed, and of suppressing our strongest inclinations. You have taught me this lesson by means of hope, and of delusion. Neither are any longer necessary; you have made me acquainted with the existence of that ever-living conscience, which, in peaceful silence, dwells within our souls, and never ceases with gentle admonitions to remind us of its presence, till its sway becomes irresistibly acknowledged. And now farewell. May your influence over others be as effective as it has been over me. Do not confine your labours to the task of unravelling legal perplexities, but show mankind, by your own gentle guidance and example, that within every bosom the germ of hidden virtue lies concealed. Esteem and fame will be your reward, and, far better than any statesman or hero, you will earn the glorious title of father of your country."

"We must all extol the character of your young lawyer," said the Baroness, at the conclusion of the Clergyman's tale; "polished, wise, interesting, and instructive, I wish every preceptor were like him, who undertakes to restrain or recal youth from the path of error. I think such a tale is peculiarly entitled to be styled a moral anecdote. Relate some more of the same nature, and your audience will have ample reason to be thankful."

Clergyman.—I am delighted that my tale has earned your approbation, but I am sorry you wish to hear more of such moral anecdotes; for, to say the truth, this is the first and last of the kind.

Louisa.—It certainly does not do you much credit, to say that your best collection only furnishes a single specimen.

Clergyman.—You have not understood me. It is not the only moral tale I can relate, but they all bear so close a resemblance, that each would seem only to repeat the original.

Louisa.—Really, you should give up your paradoxical style, which so much obscures your conversation, and express yourself more clearly.

Clergyman.—With pleasure, then. No anecdote deserves to be called moral, which does not prove that man possesses within himself that power to subdue his inclinations, which may be called out by the persuasion of another. My story teaches this doctrine, and no moral tale can teach otherwise.

Louisa.—Then, in order to act morally, I must act contrary to my inclinations?

Clergyman.—Undoubtedly.

Louisa.—Even when they are good?

Clergyman.—No inclinations are abstractedly good—but only so, as far as they effect good.

Louisa.—Suppose I have an inclination for benevolence?

Clergyman.—Then you should subdue your inclination for benevolence, if you find that your domestic happiness suffer from its exercise.

Louisa.—Suppose I felt an irresistible impulse to gratitude?

Clergyman.—It is wisely ordained that gratitude can never be an impulse. But if it were, it would be better to prove ungrateful, than to commit a crime to oblige your benefactor.

Louisa.—Then there may be a thousand moral stories?

Clergyman.—Yes, in your sense. But none of them would read a lesson different from the one our lawyer taught, and in this sense there can be but one story of the kind: you are right, however, if you mean that the incidents can be various.

Louisa.—If you had expressed your meaning more precisely at first, we had not disagreed.

Clergyman.—And we should have had no conversation. Errors and misunderstandings are the springs of action, of life, and of amusement.

Louisa.—I cannot agree with you. Suppose a brave man saves another at the risk of his own life, is that not a moral action?

Clergyman.—Not according to my mode of thinking. But suppose a cowardly man were to overcome his fears and do the same, that would be a moral action.

Baroness.—I wish, my dear friend, you would give us some examples, and convince Louisa of the truth of your theory. Certainly, a mind disposed to good must delight us, when we become acquainted with it. Nothing in the world can be more pleasing than a mind under the guidance of reason and conscience. If you know a tale upon such a subject, we should like to hear it. I am fond of stories which illustrate a doctrine. They give a better explanation of one's meaning, than dry words can possibly do.

Clergyman.—I certainly can relate some anecdotes of that kind; for I have paid some attention to those qualities of the human mind.

Louisa.—I would just make one observation. I must confess I do not like stories which oblige us to travel, in imagination, to foreign lands. Why must every adventure take place in Italy, in Sicily, or in the East? Are Naples, Palermo, and Smyrna, the only places where any thing interesting can happen? One may transpose the scene of our fairy tales to Ormus and Samarcand for the purpose of perplexing the imagination; but if you would instruct the understanding or the heart, do it by means of domestic stories,—family portraits—in which we shall recognize our own likeness, and our hearts will more readily sympathize with sorrow.

Clergyman.—You shall be gratified. But there is something peculiar, too, about family stories. They bear a strong resemblance to each other, and besides, we daily see every incident and situation of which they are capable, fully worked out upon the stage. However, I am willing to make the attempt, and shall relate a story, with some of the incidents of which you are already familiar; and it will only prove interesting so far as it is an exact representation of the picture in your own minds.

We may often observe in families, that the children inherit not only the personal appearance, but even the mental qualities of their parents, and it sometimes happens that one child combines the dispositions of both father and mother in a peculiar and remarkable manner.

A youth, whom I may name Ferdinand, was a strong instance of this fact. In his appearance he resembled both parents, and one could distinguish in his mind the separate disposition of each. He possessed the gay, thoughtless manner of his father, in his strong inclination to enjoy the present moment, and, in most cases, to prefer himself to others; but he also inherited the tranquil and reflective mind of his mother, no less than her love for honesty and justice, and a willingness, like her, perpetually to sacrifice himself for the advantage of others. To explain his contradictory conduct upon many occasions, his companions were often reduced to the necessity of believing that he had two souls. I must pass by many adventures which happened in his youth, and shall content myself with relating one anecdote, which not only explains his character fully, but forms a remarkable epoch in his life.

His youth was passed in every species of enjoyment. His parents were affluent, and brought up their children extravagantly. If the father indulged in unreasonable expenditure, either in company, at the gaming-table, or in other dissipations, it was the habit of the mother to restrain her own, and the household expenses, so as to supply the deficiency, though she never allowed an appearance of want to be observed. Her husband was fortunate in his business; he was successful in several hazardous speculations which he had undertaken, and, as he was fond of society, he had the happiness to form many pleasant and advantageous connections.

The children of a family usually copy those members of the household who seem to live most happily, and enjoy themselves. They see in the example of a father who follows such a course, a model worthy of imitation, and, as they are seldom slow in obeying their inclinations, their wishes and desires often increase very much in disproportion to their means of enjoyment. Obstacles to their gratification soon arise; each new addition to the family forms a new claim upon the capabilities of the parents, who frequently surrender their own pleasures for the sake of their children, and, by common consent, a more simple and less expensive mode of living is adopted.

Ferdinand grew up with a consciousness of the disagreeable truth, that he was often deprived of many luxuries which his more fortunate companions enjoyed. It distressed him to appear inferior to any of them in the richness of his apparel, or the liberality of his expenditure. He wished to resemble his father, whose example was daily before him, and who appeared to him a two-fold model, first, as a parent, in whose favour a son is usually prejudiced; and secondly, as a man, who led a pleasant and luxurious life, and was, therefore, apparently loved and esteemed by a numerous acquaintance. It is easy to suppose that all this occasioned great vexation to his mother; but in this way Ferdinand grew up, with his wants daily increasing, until at length, when he had attained his eighteenth year, his requirements and his wishes were sadly out of proportion to his condition.

He had hitherto avoided contracting debts, a vice for which his mother had impressed him with the greatest abhorrence, and, in order to win his confidence, she had, in numerous instances, exerted herself to gratify his desires and relieve him from occasional embarrassments. But it happened, unfortunately, that she was now compelled to practise the most rigid economy in her household expenditure, and this at a time when his wants, from many causes, had increased. He had commenced to enter more generally into society, sought to win the affections of a very attractive girl, and to rival, and even surpass his companions in the elegance of his attire. His mother, being unable any longer to satisfy his demands, appealed to his duty and filial affection to induce him to restrain his expenses. He admitted the justice of her expostulations, but being unable to follow her advice, was soon reduced to a state of the greatest mental embarrassment.

Without forfeiting the object of his dearest wishes, he found it impossible to change his mode of life. From earliest youth he had been addicted to his present pursuits, and he could alter no iota of his habits or practices without running the risk of losing an old friend, a desirable companion, or what was worse, abandoning the society of his dearest love.

His attachment became stronger, as the love which was bestowed upon him, not only flattered his vanity, but complimented his understanding.

It was something to be preferred before a host of suitors, by a handsome and agreeable girl, who was acknowledged to be the richest heiress in the city. He boasted of the preference with which he was regarded, and she also seemed proud of the delightful bondage in which she was held. It now became indispensable that he should be in constant attendance upon her, that he should devote his time and money to her service, and that he should afford perpetual proofs of the value he set upon her affection. All these inevitable results of his attachment occasioned Ferdinand to indulge in more expense than he would otherwise have incurred. His lady love (who was named Ottilia) had been entrusted to the care of an aunt by her parents, and no exertions had been spared to introduce her to society under the most favourable circumstances. Ferdinand exhausted every resource to furnish her with the enjoyments of society, into all of which she entered with the greatest delight, and of which she herself proved one of the greatest attractions.

No situation could possibly be more wretched, than that to which Ferdinand was now reduced. His mother, whom he sincerely loved and respected, had pointed out to him the necessity of embarking in very different duties from those which he had hitherto practised; she could no longer assist him in a pecuniary way. He felt a horror at the debts which were daily becoming more burdensome to him; and he saw before him the difficult task of reconciling his impoverished condition with his anxiety to appear rich and to practise generosity. No mind could be a prey to greater unhappiness.

His mind was now forcibly impressed with thoughts which had formerly only indistinctly suggested themselves to his imagination. Certain unpleasant reflections became to him the source of great unhappiness. He had once looked upon his father as a model, he now began to regard him as a rival. What the son wished to enjoy, the parent actually possessed, and the latter felt none of the anxieties or grievances wherewith the former was tortured. Ferdinand, however, was in full possession of every comfort of life, but he envied his father the luxuries which he enjoyed, and with which he thought his parent might very well dispense. But the latter was of a different opinion. He was one of those beings whose desires are wholly insatiable, and who, for their own gratification, subject their family and dependents to the greatest privations. His son received from him a certain pecuniary allowance, but a regular account of his expenditure was strictly exacted.

The eye of the envious is sharpened by restrictions; and dependants are never more censorious than when the commands of superiors are at variance with their practice. Thus Ferdinand came strictly to watch the conduct of his father, particularly upon points which concerned his expenditure. He listened attentively when it was rumoured that his parent had lost heavily at the gambling-table and expressed great dissatisfaction at any unwonted extravagance which he might indulge. " Is it not astonishing?" he would say to himself, "that whilst parents revel in every luxury that can spring from the possession of a property which they accidentally enjoy, they can debar their children of those reasonable pleasures which their season of youth most urgently requires! And by what right do they act thus? How have they acquired this privilege? Does it not arise from mere chance, and can that be a right which is the result of accident? If my grandfather were still alive, who loved me as his own son, I should be better provided for. He would not see me in want of common necessaries, those things I mean which we have had from our birth. He would no more let me want, than he would approve the extravagance of my parent. Had he lived longer, had he known how worthy his grandchild would prove to inherit a fortune, he would have provided in his will for my earlier independence. I have heard that his death was unexpected, that he had intended to make a will, and I am probably indebted to mere chance for the postponement of a fortune, which, if my father continue his present course, will, probably, be lost to me for ever."

With such discontented thoughts did Ferdinand often perplex himself in those hours of solitude and unhappiness, in which he was prevented, by the want of money, from joining his companions upon some agreeable party of pleasure. Then it was that he discussed those dangerous questions of right and property, and considered how far individuals are bound by laws to which they have given no consent, or whether they may lawfully burst through the restraints of society. But all these were mere pecuniary sophistries, for every article of value which he formerly possessed had gradually disappeared, and his daily wants had now far outgrown his allowance.

He soon became silent and reserved, and at such times, even his respect for his mother disappeared, as she could afford him no assistance, and he began to entertain a hatred for his father, who, according to his sentiments, was perpetually in his way.

Just at this period he made a discovery, which increased his discontent. He learnt that his father was not only an irregular, but an improvident manager of his household. He observed that his parent often took money hastily from his desk, without entering it in his account-book, and that he was afterwards perplexed with private calculations, and annoyed at his inability to balance his accounts. More than once did Ferdinand make this remark, and his father's carelessness was the more galling to him, as it often occurred at times when he himself was suffering severely from the want of money.

Whilst he was in this state of mind, an unlucky accident happened, which afforded an opportunity for the commission of a crime, to which he had long felt himself impelled by a secret and ungovernable impulse.

His father had desired him to examine and arrange a collection of old letters. One Sunday, when he was alone, he set to work in a room which contained his father's writing desk, and in which his money was usually kept. The box of letters was heavy, and in the act of lifting it from the ground, he pushed unintentionally against the desk, when the latter suddenly flew open. The rolls of money lay temptingly displayed before him. Without allowing time for a moment's reflection, he took a roll of gold from that part of the desk where he thought his father kept a supply of money for his own occasional wants. He shut the desk again, and repeated the experiment of opening it. He once more succeeded, and saw that he could now command the treasure as completely as if he had possessed the key.

He soon plunged once more into all those dissipations which he had lately been obliged to renounce. He became more constant than ever in his attentions to Ottilia, and more passionate in the pursuit of pleasure. His former graceful animation was even converted into a species of excitement, which, though it was far from unbecoming, was deficient in that kind attention to others which is so agreeable.

Opportunity is to passion what a spark is to gunpowder, and those desires which we gratify contrary to the dictates of conscience always rule with the most ungovernable power. Ferdinand's own convictions loudly condemned his conduct, but he endeavoured to justify himself by specious arguments, and though his manner became in appearance more free and unrestrained than before, he was in reality a captive to the influence of his evil inclinations.

Just at this time the wearing of extravagant trifles came into fashion. Ottilia was fond of personal ornaments, and Ferdinand endeavoured to discover a mode of gratifying her taste without apprising her where her supply of presents came from. Her suspicions fell upon an old uncle, and Ferdinand's gratification was indescribable at observing the satisfaction of his mistress and the course of her mistaken suspicions. But unfortunately for his peace of mind, he was now obliged to have frequent recourse to his father's desk, in order to gratify Ottilia's fancy and his own inclinations, and he pursued this course now the more boldly, as he had lately observed that his father grew more and more careless about entering in his account-book the sums which he himself required.

The time now arrived for Ottilia's return to her parents. The young couple were overpowered with grief at the prospect of their separation, and one circumstance added to their sorrow. Ottilia had accidentally learnt that the presents we have spoken of had come from Ferdinand; she questioned

2 E

him upon the subject, and he confessed the truth with feelings of evident sorrow. She insisted upon returning them, and this request occasioned him the bitterest anguish. He declared his determination not to live without her, prayed that she would preserve her attachment to him, and implored that she would not refuse her hand as soon as he should have provided an establishment. She loved him, was moved at his entreaties, promised what he wished, and sealed her vow with the warmest embraces and a thousand passionate kisses.

After her departure, Ferdinand was reduced to sad solitude. The company in which he had found delight pleased him no more, as she was absent. From the mere force of habit he mingled with his former associates, and had recourse to his father's desk to supply those expenses which in reality he felt but slight inclination to indulge. He was now frequently alone, and his natural good disposition began to obtain the mastery over him. In moments of calm reflection he felt astonished how he could have listened to that deceitful sophistry about justice and right, and his claim to the goods of others, and he wondered at his approval of those evil arguments by which he had been led to justify his dishonest conduct. But in the meantime, before these correct ideas of truth and uprightness produced a practical effect upon his conduct, he yielded more than once to the temptation of supplying his wants, in extreme cases, from his father's treasury. This plan, however, was now adopted with more reluctance, and he seemed to be under the irresistible impulse of an evil spirit.

At length he took courage and formed the resolution of rendering a repetition of the practice impossible, by informing his father of the facility with which his desk could be opened. He took his measures cautiously, and once, in the presence of his father, he carried the box of letters we have mentioned into the room, pretended to stumble accidentally against the desk, and astonished his father by causing it to spring open. They examined the lock without delay, and found that it had become almost useless from age. It was at once repaired, and Ferdinand soon enjoyed a return of his peace of mind, when he saw his father's rolls of money once more in safe custody.

But he was not content with this. He formed the resolution of restoring the money which he had abstracted. He commenced the most economical course of life for this purpose, with a view of saving from his allowance all that could be possibly spared from the merest necessities. It is true that this was but little, but it appeared large as it was the commencement of a system of restitution, and there will always be a wonderful difference between the last guinea borrowed and the first guinea saved. He had pursued this upright course for but a short time, when his father determined to settle him in business. His intention was to form a connection with a manufactory at some distance from his residence. The design was to establish a company in a part of the country where labour and provisions were cheap, to appoint an agent, and extend the business as widely as possible by means of money and credit. It was determined that Ferdinand should inquire into the practicability of the scheme, and forward a circumstantial report of his proceedings. His father furnished him with money for his journey, but placed a moderate limit upon his expenditure. The supply was, however, sufficient for his wants, and Ferdinand had no reason to complain of a deficiency.

Ferdinand used the utmost economy upon his journey, and found upon the closest calculation that he could live upon one-third of his allowance, by practising strict restraint. He was now anxious to find means of gradually saving a certain sum, and it soon presented itself; for opportunity comes indifferently to the good and to the bad, and favours all parties alike. In the neighbourhood which he designed to visit, he found every article of life cheaper than he had expected. No new habits of expense had as yet been introduced. A moderate capital alone had been invested in business, and the manufacturers were satisfied with small profits. Ferdinand soon saw that with a large capital, and the advantages of a new system, by purchasing the raw material by wholesale, and erecting machinery under the guidance of experienced workmen, large and solid advantages might be secured.

The prospect of a life of activity gave him the greatest delight. The image of his beloved Ottilia was ever before him, and the charming and picturesque character of the country made him wish anxiously that his father might be induced to establish him in this spot, commit the conduct of the new manufactory to him, and thus afford him the means of attaining independence. His attention to business was secured by the demands of his own personal interests. He now found an opportunity, for the first time in his life, for the exercise of his understanding and judgment, and for exerting his other mental powers. Not only the beautiful neighbourhood, but his business and occupation, were full of attractions for him, they acted as balm and cordial to his wounded heart, whenever he recalled the painful remembrance of his father's house, in which, influenced by a species of insanity, he had acted in a manner which now seemed to him in the highest degree criminal.

His constant companion was a friend of his family, a person of strong mind, but delicate health, who had first conceived the project of founding this establishment. He instructed Ferdinand in all his own views and projects, and seemed to take great pleasure in the thorough harmony of mind which existed between them. This latter personage led a simple and retired life, partly from choice, and partly because his health required it. He had no family of his own. His household establishment was conducted by a niece, who, he intended, should inherit his fortune, and it was his wish to see her united to a person of active and enterprising disposition, who, by means of capital and persevering industry, might carry on the business which his infirm health and want of means disqualified him from conducting. His first interview with Ferdinand suggested that he had found the man he wanted, and he was the more strongly confirmed in this opinion, upon observing his fondness for business, and his attachment to the place. His niece became aware of his intentions, and seemed to approve of them. She was a young and interesting girl, of sweet and engaging disposition. Her care of her uncle's establishment had imparted to her mind the valuable qualities of activity and decision, whilst her attention to his health had softened down these traits by a proper union of gentleness and affection. It would have been difficult to find a person better calculated to make a lover happy.

But Ferdinand's mind was engrossed with the thoughts of Ottilia's love; he saw no attractions in the charms of this country beauty, or at least, his admiration was circumscribed by the wish that if ever Ottilia settled down as his wife in this part of the country, she might have the assistance of such a person as assistant and housekeeper. But he was free and unrestrained in his intercourse with the young lady, he valued her more as he came to know her better, and his conduct became more respectful and attentive, and both she and her uncle soon put their own interpretations upon his behaviour.

Ferdinand had in the meantime made all the requisite inquiries about his father's business. The uncle's suggestions had enabled him to form certain projects which, with his usual thoughtlessness, he made the subject of conversation. He had more than once uttered certain gallant speeches to the niece, until her uncle and herself fancied that he actually indulged intentions which gave them both unfeigned satisfaction. To Ferdinand's great joy, he had learned that he could not only derive great advantage from his father's plan, but that another favourable project would enable him to make restitution of the money he had abstracted, and the recollection of which pressed like a heavy burden upon his conscience. He communicated his intentions to his friend, who tendered not only his cordial congratulations, but every possible assistance to carry out his views. He even proposed to furnish his young friend with the necessary merchandize upon credit, a part of which offer was thankfully accepted, some portion of the goods being paid for with money Ferdinand had saved from his travelling expenses, and a short period of credit being taken for the remainder.

It would be difficult to describe the joy with which Ferdinand prepared for his return home. There can be no greater delight than is experienced by a man who, by his own unaided resources, frees himself from the consequences of error. Heaven looks down with satisfaction upon such a spectacle, and we cannot deny the force of the seeming paradox, which assures us that there is more joy before God over one returning sinner, than over ninety-nine just.

But, unfortunately, neither the good resolutions nor the repentance and improvement of Ferdinand could remove the evil consequences of his crime, which were destined once more to disturb and agitate his mind with the most painful reflections. The storm had gathered during his absence, and it was destined to burst over his head upon his return home.

We have already had reason to observe, that Ferdinand's father was most irregular in his habits; but his business was under the superintendence of a clever manager. He had not himself missed the money which had been abstracted by his son, with the exception of one roll of foreign money, which he had won from a stranger at play. This he had missed, and the circumstance seemed to him unaccountable. He was afterwards somewhat surprised to perceive that several rolls of ducats could not be found, money which he had some time before lent to a friend, but which he knew had been repaid. He was aware of the previous insecurity of his desk, and felt convinced, therefore, that he had been robbed. This feeling rendered him extremely unhappy. His suspicions fell upon every one. In anger and exasperation, he related the circumstance to his wife. The entire household was thereupon strictly examined, and neither servants nor children were allowed to escape. The good wife exerted herself to tranquillize her husband; she represented the discredit which a mere report of this circumstance would bring upon the family; that no one would sympathize in their misfortune, further than to humiliate them with their compassion; that neither he nor she could expect to escape the tongue of scandal; that strange observations would be made, if the thief should remain undiscovered; and she suggested, that perhaps if they continued silent, they might recover their lost money without reducing the wretched criminal to a state of misery for life. In this manner she prevailed upon her husband to remain quiet, and to investigate the affair in silence.

But the discovery was unfortunately soon made. Ottilia's aunt had of course been informed of the engagement of the young couple. She had heard of the presents which her niece had received. The attachment was not approved by her, and she had only maintained silence in consequence of her niece's absence. She would have consented to her marriage with Ferdinand, but she did not like uncertainty on such a subject; and as she knew that he was shortly to return, and her niece was expected daily, she determined to inform the parents of the state of things, to inquire their opinion, to ask whether Ferdinand was to have a settlement, and if they would consent to the marriage.

The mother was not a little astonished at this information, and she was shocked at hearing of the presents which Ferdinand had made to Ottilia. But she concealed her surprise, and requesting the aunt to allow her some time to confer with her husband upon the matter, she expressed her own concurrence in the intended marriage, and her expectation that her son would be advantageously provided for.

The aunt took her leave, but Ferdinand's mother did not deem it advisable to communicate the circumstance to her husband. She now had to undertake the sad duty of discovering whether Ferdinand had purchased Ottilia's presents with the stolen money. She went straight to the shopkeeper who dealt in such goods, made some general inquiries, and said at last, "that he ought not to overcharge her, particularly as her son, who had bought some similar articles, had procured them from him at a more reasonable charge." This the tradesman denied, producing the account, and further observing that he had even added something for the exchange, as Ferdinand had paid for the goods partly in foreign money. He specified the exact nature of the coin, and to her inexpressible grief, it was the very same which had been stolen from her husband. She left the shop with sorrowful heart. Ferdinand's crime was but too evident. The sum which her husband had lost was large, and she saw in all its force the extent of the crime and its evil results. But she had prudence enough to conceal her discovery. She waited for the return of her son, with feelings of mingled fear and anxiety. She wished for an explanation, and yet dreaded the consequences of a farther inquiry.

At length he arrived in the highest spirits. He expected the greatest praise from the manner in which he transacted his business, and was the bearer of a sum of money sufficient to make compensation for what he had criminally abstracted. His father heard his statement with pleasure, but did not manifest so much delight as the son expected. His late losses had irritated his temper, and he was the more distressed from having some large payments to make at the moment. Ferdinand felt hurt at his father's depression of mind,

and his own peace was further disturbed by the sight of
everything around him; the very room in which he was, the
furniture, and the sight of the fatal desk, those silent witnesses of his crime, spoke loudly to his guilty conscience.
His satisfaction was at an end. He shrunk within himself
and felt like a culprit.

After a few days' delay he was about to distract his attention from these thoughts by examining the merchandize which
he had ordered, when his mother finding him alone, addressed
him upon the subject, in a tone of affectionate earnestness,
which did not allow the smallest opportunity for prevarica-
tion. He was overcome with grief. He threw himself at
her feet, imploring her forgiveness, acknowledging his crime,
and protesting that nothing but his affection for Ottilia had
misled him; he assured her, in conclusion, that it was the
only offence of the kind of which he had ever been guilty.
He related the circumstances of his bitter repentance, of his
having acquainted his father with the insecurity of his desk,
and finally informed her how, by personal privations and a
fortunate speculation, he was in a condition to make restitution.

His mother heard him calmly, but insisted on knowing
how he had disposed of so much money, as the presents
would account but for a small part of the sum abstracted.
She produced to his dismay an account of what his father
had missed, but he denied having taken even so much silver;
the missing gold he solemnly protested he had never touched.
His mother became exasperated at this denial. She rebuked
him for his attempt to deceive her, and that at a moment
when he laid claim to the virtue of repentance, asserting that
if he could be guilty in one respect, she must doubt his innocence in another. She suggested that he might perhaps have
accomplices amongst his dissipated companions; that perhaps
the business he had carried on was transacted with the stolen
money, and that probably he would have confessed nothing,
if his crime had not been accidentally discovered. She
threatened him with the anger of his father, with judicial
punishment, with her highest displeasure, but nothing affected
him more than his learning that his projected marriage with
Ottilia had been already spoken of. She left him in the
most wretched condition. His real crime had been discovered, and he was suspected of even greater guilt. How

could he ever persuade his parents that he had not stolen the gold? He dreaded the public exposure which was likely to result from his father's irritable temper, and he now had time to compare his present wretched condition with the happiness which he might have attained. All his prospects of an active life and of a marriage with Ottilia were at an end. He saw his utter wretchedness, abandoned, a fugitive in foreign lands, exposed to every species of misfortune.

But these reflections were not the worst evil he had to encounter, though they bewildered his mind, wounded his pride, and crushed his affections. His most severe pangs arose from the thought, that his honest resolution, his noble intention to repair the past, was suspected, repudiated, and denied. And even if these thoughts gave birth to a feeling resembling despair, he could not deny that he had deserved his fate, and to this conviction must be added his knowledge of the fatal truth, that one crime is sufficient to destroy the character for ever. Such meditations as these, and the apprehension that his firmest resolutions of amendment might be looked upon as insincere, made life itself a burden.

In this moment of abandonment he appealed to Heaven for assistance. He sank upon his knees, and moistening the ground with his tears of contrition, implored help from his Divine Maker. His prayer was worthy of being heard. Man, throwing off his load of crimes, has a claim upon Heaven. He who has exhausted every effort of his own, may, as a last resource, appeal to God. He was for some time engaged in earnest prayer, when the door opened and some one entered his apartment. It was his mother, who approached him with a cheerful look, saw his agitation, and addressed him with consoling words. "How happy I am," she said, "to find that I may credit your assertions, and regard your sorrow as sincere. The missing sum of gold has been found ; your father, when he received it from his friend, handed it to his secretary, who forgot the circumstance, amid the numerous transactions of the day. And with respect to the silver, you are also right, as the amount taken is less than I had supposed. Unable to conceal my joy, I promised your father to replace the missing sum, if he would consent to forbear making any further inquiry into the matter."

Ferdinand's joy was indescribable. He completed at once

his business arrangements, gave his mother the promised money, and in addition replaced the amount which his father had lost through his own irregularity. He became gradually more cheerful and happy, but the whole circumstance produced a serious impression upon his mind. He became convinced that every man has power to accomplish good, and that our Divine Maker will infallibly extend to him His assistance in the hour of trial—a truth which he himself had learned from late experience. He now unfolded to his father his plan of establishing himself in the neighbourhood from which he had lately returned. He fully explained the nature of the intended business. His father consented to his proposals, and his mother at a proper time related to her husband the attachment of Ferdinand to Ottilia. He was delighted at the prospect of having so charming a daughter-in-law, and felt additional pleasure at the idea of being able to establish his son without the necessity of incurring much expense.

"This story pleases me," said Louisa, when the old Clergyman had finished his narration, "and though the incidents are taken from low life, yet the tone is sufficiently elevated to prove agreeable. And it seems to me, that if we examine ourselves, or observe others, we shall find that men are seldom influenced by their own reflections either to pursue or to abandon a certain course, but are generally impelled by extraneous circumstances."

"I wish for my part," said Charles, "that we were not obliged to deny ourselves anything, and that we had no knowledge of those blessings which we are not allowed to possess. But unfortunately we walk in an orchard, where though all the trees are loaded with fruit, we are compelled to leave them untouched, to satisfy ourselves with the enjoyment of the shade, and forego the greatest indulgence."

"Now," continued Louisa to the Clergyman, "let us hear the end of the story."

Clergyman.—It is finished.

Louisa.—The dénouement may be finished, but we should like to hear the very end.

Clergyman.—Your distinction is just, and since you seem interested in the fate of my friend, I will tell you briefly what happened to him.

Relieved from the oppressive weight of so dreadful a crime, and enjoying some degree of satisfaction at his own conduct, his thoughts were now directed to his future happiness, and he expected with anxiety the return of Ottilia, that he might explain his position and perform his promise to her. She came, accompanied by her parents. He hastened to meet her, and found her more beautiful than ever. He waited with impatience for an opportunity of speaking to her alone, and of unfolding all his future projects. The moment arrived, and with a heart full of tenderness and love, he spoke of his hopes, of his expectations of happiness, and of his wish to share it with her. But what was his surprise and astonishment to find that she heard his announcement with indifference and even with contempt, and that she indulged in disagreeable jokes about the hermitage prepared for their reception, and the interest they would excite by enacting the characters of shepherd and shepherdess in a pastoral abode.

Her conduct occasioned bitter reflections. He was hurt and grieved at her indifference. She had been unjust to him, and he now began to observe faults in her conduct, which had previously escaped his attention. In addition, it required no very keen perception to remark that a cousin, who had accompanied her, had made an impression upon her and won a large portion of her affections.

But Ferdinand soon perceived the necessity of struggling with this new source of sorrow, and as victory had attended his exertions in one instance, he hoped to be successful upon a second occasion. He saw Ottilia frequently and determined to observe her closely. His conduct towards her was attentive and affectionate, and her deportment was of a similar nature, but her attractions had become diminished for him ; he soon found that her professions were not cordial or sincere, and that she could be affectionate and cold, attractive and repulsive, charming and disagreeable, according to the mere whim of the moment. He gradually became indifferent to her, and he resolved at length to break the last link of their connection.

But this was more difficult than he had anticipated. He found her one day alone, and took courage to remind her of her engagement to him, and of those happy moments in which, under the influence of the most delightful feelings, they had discoursed with joyful anticipations of their future happiness. She was in a tender mood, and he began to hope that he might perhaps have been deceived in the estimate he had lately formed of her. He thereupon began to describe his worldly prospects and the probable success of his intended establishment. She expressed her satisfaction, accompanied, however, with regret that their union must on this account be postponed still longer. She gave him to understand that she had not the least wish to leave the pleasures of a city life, but expressed her hopes that he might be able, after some years' active industry in the country, to return home and become a citizen of consequence. She gave him, moreover, to understand that she expected he would play a more respectable and honest part in life than his father.

Ferdinand saw plainly that he could expect no happiness from such a connection, and yet he felt the difficulty of wholly disengaging himself. In this state of mind he would probably have parted from her in uncertainty about the future, had he not been finally influenced by the conduct of Ottilia's cousin, towards whom he thought she displayed too much tenderness. Ferdinand, thereupon, wrote a letter assuring her that it was still in her power to make him happy, but that it could not be advisable to encourage indefinite hopes, or to enter into engagements for an uncertain future.

He trusted that this letter would produce a favourable answer; but he received a reply which his heart deplored, but his judgment approved. She released him from his promise, without rejecting his love, and adverted to her own feelings in the same ambiguous manner. She was still bound by the sense of her letter, but free by its literal meaning. But why should I delay communicating the inevitable result? Ferdinand hastened back to the peaceful abode he had left, and formed his determination at once. He became attentive and diligent in business, and was encouraged in this course by the affections of the kind being, of whom we have already spoken, and the exertions of her uncle to employ every means in his power to render them happy. I knew him afterwards, when he was surrounded by a numerous and prosperous family. He related his own story to me himself;

and as it often happens with individuals whose early life has been marked by some uncommon accident, his own adventures had become so indelibly impressed upon his mind, that they exerted a deep influence on his conduct. Even as a man and as a father, he constantly denied himself the enjoyment of many gratifications, in order not to forget the practice of self-restraint ; and the whole course of his children's education was founded upon this principle, that they must accustom themselves to a frequent denial of their most ardent inclinations.

I once had an opportunity of witnessing an instance of the system he adopted. One of his children was about to eat something at table, of which he was particularly fond. His father forbade it, apparently without reason. To my astonishment, the child obeyed with the utmost cheerfulness, and dinner proceeded as if nothing had occurred. And in this manner, even the eldest members of the family often allowed a tempting dish of fruit or some other dainty to pass them untasted. But, notwithstanding this, a general freedom reigned in his house, and there was at times a sufficient display both of good and bad conduct. But Ferdinand was for the most part indifferent to what occurred, and allowed an almost unrestrained licence. At times, however, when a certain week came about, orders were given for precise punctuality, the clocks were regulated to the second, every member of the family received his orders for the day, business and pleasure had their turn, and no one dared to be a single second in arrear. I could detain you for hours in describing his conversation and remarks on this extraordinary system of education. He was accustomed to jest with me upon my vows as a catholic priest, and maintained that every man should make a vow to practise self-restraint, as well as to require obedience from others ; but he observed that the exercise of these vows, in place of being perpetually demanded, was only suitable for certain occasions.

The Baroness observed, that she thought Ferdinand was perfectly right, and she compared the authority of a parent to the executive power in a kingdom, where, if the influence of the latter is weak, the legislative authority can be of little avail.

Louisa, at this moment, rushed hastily to the window,

having heard Ferdinand ride past. She ran to meet him, and accompanied him into the salon. He seemed cheerful, notwithstanding he had just come from a scene of trouble and distress. In place of entering into a detailed description of the fire which had seized the house of his aunt, he assured the company that he had established beyond doubt the fact that the desk there had been burnt at the very same time when theirs had been split asunder in so strange a manner.

He stated, that when the fire approached the room where the desk was, one of the servants saved a clock which stood upon it; that in carrying it out, some accident had happened to the works, and it had stopped at the hour of half-past eleven, and thus the coincidence of time was placed beyond all question. The Baroness smiled, and the Tutor observed, that although two things might agree in some particulars, we were not, therefore, justified in inferring their mutual dependence. But Louisa took pleasure in believing the connection of these two circumstances, particularly as she had received intelligence that her intended was quite well; and as to the rest of the company, they gave full scope to the flights of their imagination.

Charles inquired of the Clergyman whether he knew a fairy tale. "The imagination," he observed, "is a divine gift, but I do not like to see it employed about the actualities of life. The airy forms to which it gives birth are delightful to contemplate, if we view them as beings of a peculiar order, but connected with truth, they become prodigies, and are disapproved by our reason and judgment. The imagination," he continued, "should not deal in facts, nor be employed to establish facts. Its proper province is art, and there its influence should operate like sweet music, which awakens our emotions, and makes us forget the cause by which these emotions are awakened."

"Continue," said the old Clergyman, "and explain still further your view of the proper attributes of imaginative works. Another property is essential to their enjoyment—that the exercise of imagination should be voluntary. It can effect nothing by compulsion; it must wait for the moment of inspiration. Without design, and without any settled course, it soars aloft upon its own pinions, and as it is borne forward, leaves a trace of its wonderful and devious course.

But you must allow me to take my accustomed walk, that I may awaken in my soul the sweet fancies which, in former years, were accustomed to enchant me. I promise to relate a fairy tale this evening that will amuse you all.

They at once consented, particularly as they all hoped in the mean time to hear the news of which Frederick was the bearer.

A FAIRY TALE.

WEARIED with the labours of the day, an old Ferryman lay asleep in his hut, on the bank of a wide river, which the late heavy rains had swollen to an unprecedented height. In the middle of the night he was awakened by a loud cry,—he listened—it was the call of some travellers who wished to be ferried over.

Upon opening the door, he was surprised to see two Will-o'-the-wisps dancing round his boat, which was still secured to its moorings. Speaking with human voices, they assured him that they were in the greatest possible hurry, and wished to be carried instantly to the other side of the river. Without losing a moment, the old Ferryman pushed off and rowed across with his usual dexterity. During the passage the strangers whispered together in an unknown language, and several times burst into loud laughter, whilst they amused themselves with dancing upon the sides and seats of the boat, and cutting fantastic capers at the bottom.

" The boat reels," cried the old man, " and if you continue so restless, it may upset. Sit down, you Will-o'-the-wisps."

They burst into loud laughter at this command, ridiculed the boatman, and became more troublesome than ever. But he bore their annoyance patiently, and they soon reached the opposite bank of the river.

" Here is something for your trouble," said the passengers, shaking themselves, when a number of glittering gold pieces fell into the boat. " What are you doing?" cried the old man, " some misfortune will happen should a single piece of gold fall into the water. The river, which has a strong antipathy to gold, would become fearfully agitated and swallow both me and my boat. Who can say even what might happen to yourselves? I pray you take back your gold."

"We can take nothing back, which we have once shaken from our persons," answered one of them.

"Then I shall be compelled," replied the old boatman, as he stooped and collected the gold in his cap, "to take it to the shore and bury it."

The Will-o'-the-wisps had in the meantime leaped out of the boat, upon which the old man cried, "Pay me my fare."

"The man who refuses gold must work for nothing," answered the Will-o'-the-wisps.

"My payment must consist of fruits of the earth," rejoined the Ferryman.

"We despise them, they are not food for us," continued the Will-o'-the-wisps.

"But you shall not depart," replied the Ferryman, "till you have given me three cauliflowers, three artichokes, and three large onions."

The Will-o'-the-wisps were in the act of running away, with a laugh, when they felt themselves in some inexplicable manner fixed to the earth; they had never experienced so strange a sensation. They then promised to pay the demand without delay, upon which the Ferryman released them and instantly pushed off with his boat.

He was already far away, when they called after him, "Old man! listen, we have forgotten something important;" but he heard them not, and continued his course. When he had reached a point lower down, on the same side of the river, he came to some rocks which the water was unable to reach, and proceeded to bury the dangerous gold. Observing a deep cleft which opened between two rocks, he threw the gold into it, and returned to his dwelling. This cleft was inhabited by a beautiful green Dragon, who was awakened from her sleep by the sound of the falling money. At the very first appearance of the glittering pieces, she devoured them greedily, then searched about carefully in hopes of finding such other coins as might have fallen accidentally amongst the briers, or between the fissures of the rocks.

The Dragon immediately felt herself overpowered with the most delightful sensations, and perceived with joy that she became suddenly shining and transparent. She had been long aware that this change was possible, but entertaining some doubt whether the brilliance would continue, she felt impelled by curiosity to leave her dwelling, and ascertain, if possible, to whom she was indebted for the beautiful gold. She found no one ; but she became lost in admiration of herself, and of the brilliant light which illumined her path through the thick underwood, and shed its rays over the surrounding green. The leaves of the trees glittered like emeralds, and the flowers shone with glorious hues. In vain did she penetrate the solitary wilderness, but hope dawned when she reached the plains, and observed at a distance a light resembling her own. "Have I at last discovered my fellow ?" she exclaimed, and hastened to the spot. She found no obstacle from bog or morass ; for though the dry meadow and the high rock were her dearest habitations, and though she loved to feed upon the spicy root, and to quench her thirst with the crystal dew and with fresh water from the spring, yet for the sake of her beloved gold and of her glorious light, she was willing to encounter every privation.

Wearied and exhausted, she reached at length the confines of a wide morass, where our two Will-o'-the-wisps were amusing themselves in playing fantastic antics. She made towards them, and saluting them, expressed her delight at being able to claim relationship with such charming personages. The lights played around her, skipped from side to side, and laughed about in their own peculiar fashion. "Dear Aunt !" they exclaimed, " what does it signify, even though you are of horizontal form; we are related at least through brilliancy. But look how well a tall slender figure becomes us gentry of the vertical shape," and so saying both the lights compressed their breadth together and shut up into a thin and pointed line. "Do not be offended, dear friend," they continued, " but what family can boast of a privilege like ours. Since the first Will-o'-the-wisp was created, none of our race have ever been obliged to sit down or to take repose."

But all this time the feelings of the Dragon in the presence of her relations were anything but pleasant; for, exalt her head as high as she would, she was compelled to stoop to earth again, when she wished to advance ; and though she was proud of the brilliancy which she shed round her own dark

2 F

abode, she felt her light gradually diminish in the presence of her relatives, and she began to fear that it might finally be extinguished.

In her perplexity she hastily inquired whether the gentlemen could inform her whence the shining gold had come, which had lately fallen into the cleft of the rocks hard by, as in her opinion it was a precious shower from heaven. The Will-o'-the-wisps immediately shook themselves (at the same time laughing loudly), and a deluge of gold pieces at once flowed around. The Dragon devoured them greedily. "We hope you like them, dear Aunt," shouted the shining Will-o'-the-wisps; "we can supply you with any quantity," and they shook themselves with such copious effect, that the Dragon found it difficult to swallow the bright dainties with sufficient speed. Her brilliancy increased as the gold disappeared, till at length she shone with inconceivable radiance, while in the same proportion the Will-o'-the-wisps grew thin and tapering, without, however, losing the smallest iota of their cheerful humour.

"I am under eternal obligations to you," said the Dragon, pausing to breathe from her voracious meal; "ask of me what you please, I will give you anything you demand."

"A bargain!" answered the Will-o'-the-wisp; "tell us then where the beautiful Lily dwells, lead us to her palace and gardens without delay; we die of impatience to cast ourselves at her feet."

"You ask a favour," replied the Dragon, with a deep sigh, "which it is not in my power so quickly to bestow. The beautiful Lily lives, unfortunately, on the opposite bank of the river. We cannot cross over on this stormy night."

"Cruel river, which separates us from the object of our desires! But cannot we call back the old Ferryman?" said they.

"Your wish is vain," answered the Dragon, "for even were you to meet him on this bank, he would refuse to take you, as though he can convey passengers to this side of the stream, he can carry no one back."

"Bad news, indeed; but are there no other means of crossing the river?"

"There are, but not at this moment; I myself can take you over at mid-day."

" That is an hour," replied the Will-o'-the-wisps, " when we do not usually travel."

" Then you had better postpone your intention till evening, when you may cross in the giant's shadow."

" How is that managed ?" they inquired.

" The giant," replied the Dragon, " who lives hard by, is powerless with his body; his hands are incapable of raising even a straw, his shoulders can bear no burden, but his shadow accomplishes all for him. For this reason, he is most powerful at sunrise and at sunset. At the hour of evening, the giant will approach the river softly, and if you place yourself upon his shadow, it will carry you over. Meet me at mid-day, at the corner of the wood, where the trees hang over the river, when I myself will take you across, and introduce you to the beautiful Lily. Should you, however, shrink from the noonday heat, your only alternative is to apply to the giant, when evening casts its shadows around, and he will no doubt prove obliging."

With a graceful salutation the young gentlemen took their leave, and the Dragon rejoiced at their departure, partly that she might indulge her feelings of pleasure at her own light, and partly that she might satisfy a curiosity by which she had long been tormented.

In the clefts of the rocks where she dwelt, she had lately made a wonderful discovery ; for although she had been obliged to crawl through these chasms in darkness, she had learnt to distinguish every object by feeling. The productions of Nature, which she was accustomed everywhere to encounter, were all of an irregular kind. At one time she wound her way amongst the points of enormous crystals, at another she was for a moment impeded by the veins of solid silver, and many were the precious stones which her light discovered to her. But, to her great astonishment, she had encountered in a rock, which was securely closed on all sides, objects which betrayed the plastic hand of man. Smooth walls, which she was unable to ascend, sharp, regular angles, tapering columns, and what was even more wonderful, human figures, round which she had often entwined herself, and which appeared to her to be formed of brass or of polished marble. She was now anxious to behold all these objects with her eyes, and to confirm, by her own observation, what she had hitherto but suspected. She thought herself capable now of illumining with her own light these wonderful sub-terranean caverns, and indulged the hope of becoming thoroughly acquainted with these astonishing mysteries. She delayed not, and quickly found the opening through which she was accustomed to penetrate into the sanctuary.

Arrived at the place, she looked round with wonder, and though her brilliancy was unable to light the entire cavern, yet many of the objects were sufficiently distinct. With astonishment and awe, she raised her eyes to an illumined niche, in which stood the statue of a venerable King, of pure gold. In size the statue was colossal, but the countenance was that rather of a little than of a great man. His well-turned limbs were covered with a simple robe, and his head was encircled by an oaken garland.

Scarcely had the Dragon beheld this venerable form, than the King found utterance, and said, " How comest thou hither ? "

" Through the cleft," answered the Dragon, " in which the gold abides."

" What is nobler than gold ? " asked the King.

" Light," replied the Dragon.

" And what is more vivid than light ? " continued the Monarch.

" Speech," said the Serpent.

During this conversation, the Dragon had looked stealthily around, and observed another noble statue in an adjoining niche. A silver King sat there enthroned, of figure tall and slender ; his limbs were enveloped in an embroidered mantle ; his crown and sceptre were adorned with precious stones ; his countenance wore the serene dignity of pride, and he seemed about to speak, when a dark vein, which ran through the marble of the wall, suddenly became brilliant, and cast a soft light through the whole temple. This light discovered a third King, whose mighty form was cast in brass ; he leaned upon a massive club, his head was crowned with laurels, and his proportions resembled a rock rather than a human being.

The Dragon felt a desire to approach a fourth King, who stood before her at a distance ; but the wall suddenly opened, the illumined vein flashed like lightning, and became as sud-denly extinguished.

A man of middle stature now approached. He was clad

in the garb of a peasant; in his hand he bore a lamp, whose flame it was delightful to behold, and which lightened the entire dwelling, without leaving the trace of a shadow.

"Why dost thou come, since we have already light?" asked the Golden King.

"You know that I can shed no ray on what is dark," replied the old man.

"Will my kingdom end?" inquired the Silver Monarch.

"Late or never," answered the other.

The Brazen King then asked, with voice of thunder, "When shall I arise?"

"Soon," was the reply.

"With whom shall I be united?" continued the former.

"With thine elder brother," answered the latter.

"And what will become of the youngest?"

"He will repose."

"I am not weary," interrupted the fourth King, with a deep, but faltering voice.

During this conversation the Dragon had wound her way softly through the temple, surveyed everything which it contained, and approached the niche in which the fourth King stood. He leaned against a pillar, and his handsome countenance bore traces of melancholy. It was difficult to distinguish the metal of which the statue was composed. It resembled a mixture of the three metals of which his brothers were formed; but it seemed as if the materials had not thoroughly blended, as the veins of gold and silver crossed each other irregularly through the brazen mass, and destroyed the effect of the whole.

The Golden King now asked, "How many secrets dost thou know?"

"Three," was the reply.

"And which is the most important?" inquired the Silver King.

"The revealed," answered the old man.

"Wilt thou explain it to us?" asked the Brazen King.

"When I have learnt the fourth," was the response.

"I care not," murmured he of the strange compound.

"I know the fourth," interrupted the Dragon, approaching the old man, and whispering in his ear.

"The time is come," exclaimed the latter, with tremendous voice. The sounds echoed through the temple; the statues rang again; and in the same instant the old man disappeared towards the west, and the Dragon towards the east, and both pierced instantly through the impediments of the rock.

Every passage through which the old man bent his course became immediately filled with gold; for the lamp which he carried possessed the wonderful property of converting stones into gold, wood into silver, and dead animals into jewels. But in order to produce this effect, it was necessary that no other light should be near. In the presence of another light the lamp merely emitted a soft illumination, which, however, gave joy to every living thing.

The old man returned to his hut on the brow of the hill, and found his wife in the greatest sorrow. She was seated at the fire, her eyes filled with tears, and she refused all consolation.

" What a misfortune," she exclaimed, " that I allowed you to leave home to-day!"

" What has happened?" answered the old man, very quietly.

" You were scarcely gone," replied she with sobs, " before two rude travellers came to the door; unfortunately I admitted them, as they seemed good, worthy people. They were attired like flames, and might have passed for Will-o'-the-wisps; but they had scarcely entered the house before they commenced their flatteries, and became at length so importunate that I blush to recollect their conduct."

" Well," said the old man, smiling, " the gentlemen were only amusing themselves, and, at your age, you should have considered it as the display of ordinary politeness."

" My age!" rejoined the old woman. " Will you for ever remind me of my age; how old am I then? And ordinary politeness! But I can tell you something; look round at the walls of our hut, you will now be able to see the old stones which have been concealed for more than a hundred years. These visitors extracted all the gold more quickly than I can tell you, and they assured me that it was of capital flavour. When they had completely cleared the walls they grew cheerful, and, in a few minutes, their persons became tall, broad, and shining. They thereupon again commenced their tricks, and repeated their flatteries, calling me a queen. They shook themselves, and immediately a profusion of gold pieces fell on all sides. You may see some of them still glittering on the floor; but a calamity soon occurred. Our dog Mops swallowed some of them, and see, he lies dead in the chimney-corner. Poor animal! his death afflicts me. I did not observe it till they had departed, otherwise I should not have promised to pay the Ferryman the debt they owed him."

"How much do they owe?" inquired the old man.

"Three cauliflowers," answered his wife, "three artichokes, and three onions. I have promised to take them to the river at break of day."

"You had better oblige them," said the old man, "and they may perhaps serve us in time of need."

"I know not if they will keep their word," said she, "but they promised and vowed to serve us."

The fire had, in the meantime, died away; but the old man covered the cinders with ashes, put away the shining gold pieces, and lighted his lamp afresh. In the glorious illumination the walls became covered with gold, and Mops was transformed into the most beautiful onyx that was ever beheld. The variety of colour which glittered through the costly gem produced a splendid effect.

"Take your basket," said the old man, "and place the onyx in it. Then collect the three cauliflowers, the three artichokes, and the three onions, lay them together, and carry them to the river. The Dragon will bear you across at mid-day; then visit the beautiful Lily; her touch will give life to the onyx, as her touch gives death to every living thing; and it will be to her an affectionate friend. Tell her not to mourn; that her deliverance is nigh; that she must consider a great misfortune as her greatest blessing, for the time is come."

The old woman prepared her basket, and set forth at break of day. The rising sun shone brightly over the river, which gleamed in the far distance. The old woman journeyed slowly on, for the weight of the basket oppressed her, but it did not arise from the onyx. Nothing lifeless proved a burden, for when the basket contained dead things it rose aloft, and floated over her head. But a fresh vegetable, or the smallest living creature, induced fatigue. She had toiled along for some distance, when she started and suddenly stood still; for she had nearly placed her foot upon the shadow of the giant, which was advancing towards her from the plain. Her eye now perceived his monstrous bulk; he had just bathed in the river, and was coming out of the water. She

knew not how to avoid him.   He saw her, saluted her jestingly, and thrust the hand of his shadow into her basket.
With dexterity he stole a cauliflower, an artichoke, and an
onion, and raised them to his mouth.   He then proceeded on
his course up the stream, and left the woman alone.

She considered whether it would not be better to return,
and supply the missing vegetables from her own garden, and,
lost in these reflections, she went on her way until she
arrived at the bank of the river.   She sat down, and awaited
for a long time the arrival of the Ferryman.   He appeared at
length, having in his boat a traveller whose air was mysterious.
A handsome youth, of noble aspect, stepped on shore.

"What have you brought with you?" said the old man.

"The vegatables," replied the woman, "which the Will-o'-
the-wisps owe you," pointing to the contents of her basket.

But when he found that there were but two of each kind,
he became angry and refused to take them.

The woman implored him to relent, assuring him that she
could not then return home, as she had found her burden
heavy, and she had still a long way to go.   But he was obstinate, maintaining that the decision did not depend upon him.

"I am obliged to collect my gains for nine hours," said he,
"and I can keep nothing for myself, till I have paid a third
part to the river."

At length, after much contention, he told her there was
still a remedy.

"If you give security to the river, and acknowledge your
debt, I will take the six articles, though such a course is not
devoid of danger."

"But if I keep my word, I incur no risk," she said earnestly.

"Not the least," he replied.   "Thrust your hand into the
river, and promise that within four-and-twenty hours you will
pay the debt."

The old woman complied, but shuddered as she observed
that her hand, on drawing it out of the water, had become as
black as a coal.   She scolded angrily, exclaiming that her
hands had always been most beautiful, and that, notwithstanding her hard work, she had ever kept them white and
delicate.   She gazed at her hand with the greatest alarm, and
exclaimed, "This is still worse, it has shrunk, and is already
much smaller than the other."

" It only appears so now," said the Ferryman, " but if you break your word, it will be so in reality. Your hand will in that case grow smaller, and finally disappear, though you will still preserve the use of it."

" I would rather," she replied, " lose it altogether, and that my misfortune should be concealed. But no matter, I will keep my word, to escape this black disgrace, and avoid so much anxiety." Whereupon she took her basket, which rose aloft, and floated freely over her head. She hastened after the youth, who was walking thoughtfully along the bank. His noble figure and peculiar attire had made a deep impression upon her mind.

His breast was covered with a shining cuirass, whose transparency permitted the motions of his graceful form to be seen. From his shoulders hung a purple mantle, and his auburn locks waved in beautiful curls round his uncovered head. His noble countenance and his well-turned feet were exposed to the burning rays of the sun. Thus did he journey patiently over the hot sand, which, " true to one sorrow, he trod without feeling."

The garrulous old woman sought to engage him in conversation, but he heeded her not, or answered briefly ; until, notwithstanding his beauty, she became weary, and took leave of him, saying, " You are too slow for me, sir, and I cannot lose my time, as I am anxious to cross the river, with the assistance of the Green Dragon, and to present the beautiful Lily with my husband's handsome present." So saying she left him speedily, upon which the youth took heart and followed her without delay.

" You are going to the beautiful Lily," he exclaimed ; " if so, our way lies together. What present are you taking her?"

" Sir," answered the woman, " it is not fair that you should so earnestly inquire after my secrets, when you paid so little attention to my questions. But if you will relate your history to me, I will tell you all about my present."

They made the bargain ; the woman told her story, including the account of the dog, and allowed him to view the beautiful onyx.

He lifted the beautiful precious stone from the basket, and took Mops, who seemed to slumber softly, in his arms.

"Fortunate animal!" he exclaimed, "you will be touched by her soft hands, and restored to life, in place of flying from her contact, like all other living things, to escape an evil doom. But, alas! what words are these? Is it not a sadder and more fearful fate to be annihilated by her presence, than to die by her hand? Behold me, thus young, what a melancholy destiny is mine! This armour, which I have borne with glory in the battle-broil, this purple which I have earned by the wisdom of my government, have been converted by Fate, the one into an unceasing burden, the other into an empty honour. Crown, sceptre, and sword, are worthless. I am now as naked and destitute as every other son of clay. For such is the spell of her beautiful blue eyes, that they waste the vigour of every living creature; and those whom the contact of her hand does not destroy, are reduced to the condition of breathing shadows."

Thus he lamented long, but without satisfying the curiosity of the old woman, who sought information respecting his mental no less than his bodily sufferings. She learnt neither the name of his father nor his kingdom. He stroked the rigid Mops, to whom the beams of the sun and the caresses of the youth had imparted warmth. He inquired earnestly about the man with the lamp, about the effect of the mysterious light, and seemed to expect thence a relief from his deep sorrow.

So discoursing, they observed at a distance the majestic arch of the bridge, which stretched from one bank of the river to the other, and shone splendidly in the beams of the sun. Both were astonished at the sight, as they had never before seen it so resplendent.

"How," cried the Prince, "was it not sufficiently beautiful before, with its decorations of jasper and opal? Can we now dare to cross over it, constructed as it is of emerald and chrysolite of varied beauty?"

Neither had any idea of the change which the Dragon had undergone; for in truth it was the Dragon, whose custom it was at mid-day to arch her form across the stream, and assume the appearance of a beauteous bridge, which travellers crossed with silent reverence.

Scarcely had they reached the opposite bank, when the bridge began to sway from side to side, and gradually sank to the level of the water, when the Green Dragon assumed her accustomed shape, and followed the travellers to the shore. The latter thanked her for her condescension, in allowing them a passage across the stream, observing at the same time, that there were evidently more persons present than were actually visible. They heard a light whispering, which the Dragon answered with a similar sound. They listened, and heard the following words: "We will first make our observations unperceived, in the park of the beautiful Lily, and look for you when the shadows of evening fall, to introduce us to such perfect beauty. You will find us on the bank of the great lake."

"Agreed," answered the Dragon, and her hissing voice dissolved in the distance.

Our three travellers further consulted with what regard to precedence they should appear before the beautiful Lily; for let her visitors be ever so numerous, they must enter and depart singly, if they wished to escape bitter suffering. The woman, carrying in the basket the transformed dog, came first to the garden and sought an interview with her benefactress. She was easily found, as she was then singing to her harp. The sweet tones showed themselves first in the form of circles upon the bosom of the calm lake, and then, like a soft breeze, they imparted motion to the grass and to the tremulous leaves. She was seated in a secluded nook beneath the shade of trees, and at the very first glance she enchanted the eyes, the ear, and the heart of the old woman, who advanced towards her with rapture, and protested that since their last meeting she had become more beautiful than ever. Even from a distance she saluted the charming maiden in these words: "What joy to be in your presence! What a heaven surrounds you! What a spell proceeds from your lyre, which, encircled by your soft arms, and influenced by the pressure of your gentle bosom and slender fingers, utters such entrancing melody! Thrice happy the blessed youth who could claim so great a favour!"

So saying, she approached nearer. The beautiful Lily raised her eyes, let her hands drop, and said, "Do not distress me with your untimely praise; it makes me feel even more unhappy. And see, here is my beautiful canary dead at my feet, which used to accompany my songs so sweetly; he was accustomed to sit upon my harp, and was carefully instructed to avoid my touch. This morning, when, refreshed by sleep, I tuned a pleasant melody, the little warbler sang with increased harmony, when suddenly a hawk soared above us. My little bird sought refuge in my bosom, and at that instant I felt the last grasp of his expiring breath. It is true that the hawk, struck by my instantaneous glance, fell lifeless into the stream; but what avails this penalty to me?—my darling is dead, and his grave will but add to the number of the weeping willows in my garden."

"Take courage, beautiful Lily," interrupted the old woman, whilst at the same moment she wiped away a rising tear, which the narration of the sorrowful maiden had brought to her eye—"take courage, and learn from my experience to moderate your grief. Great misfortune is often the harbinger of intense joy. For the time approaches; but in truth," continued she, "'the web of life is of a mingled yarn.' See my hand, how black it has grown, and, in truth, it has become much diminished in size; I must be speedy, before it be reduced to nothing. Why did I promise favours to the Will-o'-the-wisps, or meet the giant, or dip my hand into the river? Can you oblige me with a cauliflower, an artichoke, or an onion? I shall take them to the river, and then my hand will become so white, that it will almost equal the lustre of your own."

"Cauliflowers and onions abound, but artichokes cannot be procured. My garden produces neither flowers nor fruit; but every twig which I plant upon the grave of anything I love, bursts into leaf at once, and grows a goodly tree. Thus, beneath my eye, alas! have grown these clustering trees and copses. These tall pines, these shadowing cypresses, these mighty oaks, these overhanging beeches, were once small twigs planted by my hand, as sad memorials in an ungenial soil."

The old woman paid but little attention to this speech, but was employed in watching her hand, which in the presence of the beautiful Lily became every instant of a darker hue, and grew gradually less. She was about to take her basket and depart, when she felt that she had forgotten the most important of her duties. She took the transformed dog in her arms, and laid him upon the grass, not far from the beautiful Lily. "My husband," she said, "sends you this present. You know that your touch can impart life to this precious stone. The good and faithful animal will be a joy to you, and my grief at losing him will be alleviated by the thought that he is yours."

The beautiful Lily looked at the pretty creature with delight, and rapture beamed from her eyes. "Many things combine together to inspire hope; but, alas! is it not a delusion of our nature, to expect that joy is near when grief is at the worst?"

> "Ah! what avail these omens all so fair?
> My sweet bird's death—my friend's hands blackly dyed,
> And Mops transformed into a jewel rare,
> Sent by the Lamp our faltering steps to guide.

> "Far from mankind and every joy I prize,
> To grief and sorrow I am still allied—
> When from the river will the Temple rise,
> Or the Bridge span it o'er from side to side?"

The old woman waited with impatience for the conclusion of the song, which the beautiful Lily had accompanied with her harp, entrancing the ears of every listener. She was about to say farewell, when the arrival of the Dragon compelled her to remain. She had heard the last words of the song, and on this account spoke words of encouragement to the beautiful Lily. "The prophecy of the bridge is fulfilled," she exclaimed; "this good woman will bear witness how splendidly the arch now appears. Formerly of untransparent jasper, which only reflected the light upon the sides, it is now converted into precious jewels of transparent hue. No beryl is so bright, and no emerald so splendid."

"I congratulate you thereupon," said the Lily, "but pardon me if I doubt whether the prediction is fulfilled. Only foot-passengers can as yet cross the arch of your bridge; and it has been foretold that horses and carriages, travellers of all descriptions, shall pass and repass in mingled multitudes. Is prediction silent with respect to the mighty pillars which are to ascend from the river?"

The old woman, whose eyes were fixed immovably upon her hand, interrupted this speech, and bade farewell.

"Wait for one moment," said the beautiful Lily, "and

take my poor canary-bird with you. Implore the Lamp to convert him into a topaz, and I will then reanimate him with my touch, and he and your good Mops will then be my greatest consolation. But make what speed you can, for with sunset decay will have commenced its withering influence, marring the beauty of its delicate form."

The old woman enveloped the little corpse in some soft young leaves, placed it in the basket, and hastened from the spot.

"Notwithstanding what you say," continued the Dragon, resuming the interrupted conversation, "the temple is built."

"But it does not yet stand upon the river," replied the beautiful Lily.

"It rests still in the bowels of the earth," continued the Dragon. "I have seen the Kings, and spoken to them."

"And when will they awake?" inquired the Lily.

The Dragon answered, "I heard the mighty voice resound through the temple, announcing that the hour was come.

A ray of joy beamed from the countenance of the beautiful Lily as she exclaimed, "Do I hear those words for the second time to-day? When will the hour arrive in which I shall hear them for the third time?"

She rose, and immediately a beautiful maiden came from the wood and relieved her of her harp. She was followed by another, who took the ivory chair upon which the beautiful Lily had been seated, folded it together, and carried it away, together with the silver-tissued cushion. The third maiden, who bore in her hand a fan inlaid with pearls, approached to tender her services if they should be needed. These three maidens were lovely beyond description, though they were compelled to acknowledge that their charms fell far short of those of their beautiful mistress.

The beautiful Lily had, in the meantime, surveyed the marvellous Mops with a look of pleasure. She leaned over him and touched him. He instantly leaped up, looked round joyously, bounded with delight, hastened to his benefactress, and caressed her tenderly. She took him in her arms, and pressed him to her bosom. "Cold though thou art," she said, "and endued with only half a life, yet art thou welcome to me. I will love thee fondly, play with thee sportively, kiss thee softly, and press thee to my heart." She let him go a little from her, called him back, chased him away again, and played with him so joyously and innocently, that no one could help sympathising in her delight and taking part in her pleasure, as they had before shared her sorrow and her woe. .

But this happiness and this pleasant pastime were interrupted by the arrival of the melancholy youth. His walk and appearance were as we have before described; but he seemed overcome by the heat of the day, and the presence of his beloved had rendered him perceptibly paler. He bore the hawk upon his wrist, where it sat with drooping wing as tranquil as a dove.

" It is not well," exclaimed the Lily,. " that you should vex my eyes with that odious bird, which has only this day murdered my little favourite."

" Blame not the luckless bird," exclaimed the youth : " rather condemn yourself and fate ; and let me find an associate in this companion of my grief."

Mops, in the meantime, was incessant in his caresses ; and the . Lily responded to his affection with the most gentle tokens of love. She clapped her hands to drive him away, and then sportively pursued to win him back. She caught him in her arms as he tried. to escape, and chased him from her when he sought to nestle in her lap. The youth looked on in silence and in sorrow ; but when at length she took him. in her arms, and pressed him to her snowy breast, and kissed him with her heavenly lips, he lost all patience, and exclaimed, in the depth of his despair, " And must I, then, whom sad destiny compels to live in your presence, and yet be separated from you, perhaps for ever,—must I, who for you have forfeited everything, even my own being,—must I look on and behold this ' defect of nature ' gain your notice, win your love, and enjoy the paradise of your embrace? Must I continue to wander and measure my solitary way along the banks of this stream ? No ! a spark of my former spirit still burns within my bosom. Oh ! that it would mount into a glorious flame. If stones may repose within your bosom, then let me be converted to a stone ; and if your touch can kill, I am content to receive my death at your hands."

· He became violently excited ; the hawk flew from his wrist ; he rushed towards the beautiful Lily ; she extended her arms to forbid his approach, and touched him undesignedly. His consciousness immediately forsook him, and with dismay she felt the beautiful burden lean for support upon her breast. She started back with a scream, and the fair youth sank lifeless from her arms to the earth.

The deed was done. The sweet Lily stood motionless, and gazed intently on the breathless corpse. Her heart ceased to beat, and her eyes were bedewed with tears. In vain did Mops seek to win her attention : the whole world had died out with her lost friend. Her dumb despair sought no help, for help was now in vain.

But the Dragon became immediately more active. Her mind seemed occupied with thoughts of rescue ; and, in truth, her mysterious movements prevented the immediate consequence of this dire misfortune. She wound her serpentine form in a wide circle round the spot where the body lay, seized the end of her tail between her teeth and remained motionless.

In a few moments one of the servants of the beautiful Lily approached, carrying the ivory chair, and with friendly entreaties compelled her mistress to be seated. Then came a second, bearing a flame-coloured veil, with which she rather adorned than covered the head of the Lily. A third maiden offered her the harp, and scarcely had she struck the chords, and awakened their delicious tones than the first maiden returned, having in her hands a circular mirror of lustrous brightness, placed herself opposite the Lily, intercepted her looks, and reflected the most enchanting countenance which nature could fashion. Her sorrow added lustre to her beauty, her veil heightened her charms, the harp lent her a new grace, and though it was impossible not to hope that her sad fate might soon undergo a change, one could almost wish that that lovely and enchanting vision might last for ever,

Silently gazing upon the mirror, she drew melting tones of music from her harp ; but her sorrow appeared to increase, and the chords responded to her melancholy mood. Once or twice she opened her sweet lips to sing, but her voice refused utterance ; whereupon her grief found refuge in tears. Her two attendants supported her in their arms, and her harp fell from her hands, but the watchful attention of her handmaid caught it and laid it aside.

" Who will fetch the man with the lamp?" whispered the Dragon in low but audible voice. The maidens looked at each other, and the Lily's tears fell faster.

At this instant the old woman with the basket returned breathless with agitation. " I am lost and crippled for life," she exclaimed. " Look! my hand is nearly withered. Neither the Ferryman nor the Giant would set me across the river, because I am indebted to the stream. In vain did I tempt them with a hundred cauliflowers and a hundred onions, they insist upon the stipulated three, and not an artichoke can be found in this neighbourhood."

" Forget your distress," said the Dragon, " and give your assistance here ; perhaps you will be relieved at the same time. Hasten, and find out the Will-o'-the-Wisps, for though you cannot see them by daylight, you may perhaps hear their laughter and their motions. If you make good speed the Giant may yet transport you across the river, and you may find the man with the lamp and send him hither."

The old woman made as much haste as possible, and the Dragon as well as the Lily evinced impatience for her return. But sad to say, the golden rays of the setting sun were shedding their last beams upon the highest tops of the trees, and lengthening the mountain shadows over lake and meadow. The motions of the Dragon showed increased impatience, and the Lily was dissolved in tears.

In this moment of distress, the Dragon looked anxiously around ; she feared every instant that the sun would set, and that decay would penetrate within the magic circle, and exert its fell influence upon the corpse of the beautiful youth. She looked into the heavens and caught sight of the purple wings and breast of the hawk, which were illumined by the last rays of the sun. Her restlessness betrayed her joy at the good omen, and she was not deceived, for instantly afterwards she saw the man with the lamp sliding across the lake as if his feet had been furnished with skates.

The Dragon did not alter her position, but the Lily rising from her seat, exclaimed, ' What good Spirit has sent you thus opportunely when you are so much longed for and required?"

" The Spirit of my Lamp impels me," replied the old man, " and the hawk conducts me hither. The former flickers

2 G

when I am needed, and I immediately look to the heavens for a sign, when some bird or meteor points the way which I should go. Be tranquil, beautiful maiden, I know not if I can help you, one alone can do but little, but he can avail who in the proper hour unites his strength with others. We must wait and hope." Then turning to the Dragon, he said, " Keep your circle closed," and seating himself upon a hillock at his side, he shed a light upon the corpse of the youth. " Now bring the little canary-bird," he continued, " and lay it also within the circle."

The maiden took the little creature from the basket and followed the directions of the old man.

The sun had set in the meantime, and as the shades of evening closed around, not only the Dragon and the Lamp cast their customary light, but the veil of the Lily was illumined with a soft brilliancy, and caused her pale cheeks and her white robe to beam like the dawn of morning, and clothed her with inexpressible grace. Her appearance gave birth to various emotions ; anxiety and sorrow were softened by hope of approaching happiness.

To the delight of all, the old woman appeared with the lively Will-o'-the-wisps, who must have led a prodigal life of late, for they looked wonderfully thin ; but, nevertheless, behaved most politely to the princess and to the other young ladies. With an air of confidence, and much force of expression, they discoursed upon ordinary topics ; and they were much struck by the charm which the shining veil shed over the beautiful Lily and her companions. The young ladies cast down their eyes with modest looks, and their beauty was heightened by the flattery which they heard. Every one was happy and contented, not excepting even the old woman. Notwithstanding the assurance of her husband that her hand would not continue to wither whilst the Lamp shone upon it, she continued to assert that if things went on thus it would disappear entirely before midnight.

The old man with the lamp had listened attentively to the speech of the Will-o'-the-wisps, and was charmed to observe that the beautiful Lily was pleased and flattered with their compliments. In very truth, midnight came before they were aware. The old man looked up to the stars, and thus spoke : " We are met at a fortunate hour : let each fulfil his office, let each discharge his duty, and a general happiness will alleviate one individual trouble, as a universal sorrow lessens particular joys."

After these observations, a mysterious murmur arose; for every one present spoke for himself, and mentioned what he had to do: the three maidens alone were silent. One had fallen asleep near the harp, the other beside the fan, and the third leaning against the ivory chair; and no one could blame them, for, in truth, it was late. The Will-o'-the-wisps, after paying some trivial compliments to the other ladies, including even the attendants, attached themselves finally to the Lily, by whose beauty they were attracted.

"Take the mirror," said the old man to the hawk, "and illumine the fair sleepers with the first beams of the sun, and rouse them from their slumbers by the light reflected from heaven."

The Dragon now began to move: she broke up the circle, and retreated with strange evolutions to the river. The Will-o'-the-wisps followed her in solemn procession, and they might have been mistaken for the most serious personages. The old woman and her husband took up the basket, the soft light from which had been hitherto scarcely observed; but it now became clearer and more brilliant. They laid the body of the youth within it, with the canary-bird reposing upon his breast, upon which the basket raised itself into the air and floated over the head of the old woman, and she followed the steps of the Will-o'-the-wisps. The beautiful Lily, taking Mops in her arms, walked after the old woman, and the man with the lamp closed the procession.

The whole neighbourhood was brilliantly illuminated with all these various lights. They all observed with astonishment, on approaching the river, that it was spanned by a majestic arch, by which means the benevolent Dragon had prepared them a lustrous passage across. The transparent jewels of which the bridge was composed were objects of no less astonishment by day than was their wondrous brilliancy by night. The clear arch above cut sharply against the dark heaven, whilst vivid rays of light beneath shone against the key-stone, revealing the firm pliability of the structure. The procession moved slowly over, and the ferryman, who witnessed the proceeding from his hut, surveyed the brilliant arch with awe, no less than the wondrous lights as they journeyed across it.

As soon as they had reached the opposite bank, the bridge began to contract as usual, and sink to the surface of the water. The Dragon made her way to the shore, and the basket descended to the ground. The Dragon now once more assumed a circular shape, and the old man bowing before her, asked what she had determined to do.

"To sacrifice myself before I am made a sacrifice ; only promise me that you will leave no stone on the land."

The old man promised, and then addressed the beautiful Lily thus : "Touch the Dragon with your left hand, and your lover with your right."

The beautiful Lily knelt down and laid her hands upon the Dragon and the corpse. In an instant, the latter became endued with life : he moved, and then sat upright. The Lily wished to embrace him, but the old man held her back, and assisted the youth whilst he led him beyond the limits of the circle.

The youth stood erect, the little canary fluttered upon his shoulder, but his mind was not yet restored. His eyes were open, but he saw, at least he appeared to look on everything with indifference. Scarcely was the wonder at this circumstance appeased, than the change which the Dragon had undergone excited attention. Her beautiful and slender form was converted into thousands and thousands of precious stones. The old woman, in the effort to seize her basket, had struck unintentionally against the Dragon, after which nothing more was seen of the figure of the latter. Only a heap of brilliant jewels lay in the grass. The old man immediately set to work to collect them into his basket, a task in which he was assisted by his wife ; they both then carried the basket to an elevated spot on the bank, when he cast the entire contents into the stream, not however without the opposition of his wife and of the beautiful Lily, who would willingly have appropriated a portion of the treasure to themselves. The jewels gleamed in the rippling waters like brilliant stars, and were carried away by the stream, and none can say whether they disappeared in the distance or sank to the bottom.

"Young gentlemen," then said the old man, respectfully, to the Will-o'-the-wisps, "I will now point out your path and lead the way, and you will render us the greatest service by opening the doors of the temple through which we must enter, and which you alone can unlock."

The Will-o'-the-wisps bowed politely, and took their post in the rear. The man with the lamp advanced first into the rocks, which opened of their own accord; the youth followed with apparent indifference; with silent uncertainty the beautiful Lily lingered slowly behind; the old woman, unwilling to be left alone, followed after, stretching out her hand that it might receive the rays of her husband's lamp; the procession was closed by the Will-o'-the-wisps, and their bright flames nodded and blended with each other as if they were engaged in active conversation. They had not gone far before they came to a large brazen gate which was fastened by a golden lock. The old man thereupon sought the assistance of the Will-o'-the-wisps, who did not want to be entreated, but at once introduced their pointed flames into the lock, when the wards yielded to their influence. The brass resounded as the doors flew wide asunder, and displayed the venerable statues of the kings illuminated by the advancing lights. Each individual in turn bowed to the reverend potentates with respect, and the Will-o'-the-wisps were prodigal of their lambent salutations.

After a short pause the Golden King asked, " Whence do you come?"

" From the world," answered the old man.

" And whither are you going?" inquired the Silver King.

" Back to the world," was the answer.

" And what do you wish with us?" asked the Brazen King.

" To accompany you," responded the old man.

The fourth king was about to speak, when the golden statue thus addressed the Will-o'-the-wisps who had advanced towards him, " Depart from me, my gold is not for you."

They then turned towards the Silver King, and his apparel assumed the golden hue of their yellow flames. " You are welcome," he said, " but I cannot feed you; satisfy yourselves elsewhere, and then bring me your light."

They departed, and stealing unobserved past the Brazen King, they attached themselves to the King composed of various metals.

" Who will rule the world ?" inquired the latter in inarti-
culate tones.

" He who stands erect," answered the old man.

" That is I," replied the King.

" Then it will be revealed," said the old man, " for the time
is come."

The beautiful Lily fell upon his neck and kissed him
tenderly. " Kind father," she said, " a thousand thanks for
allowing me to hear this comforting word for the third time,"
and so saying, she felt compelled to grasp the old man's arm,
for the earth began to tremble beneath them; the old woman
and the youth clung to each other, whilst the pliant Will-
o'-the-wisps felt not the slightest inconvenience.

It was evident that the whole temple was in motion, and
like a ship which pursues its quiet way from the harbour when
the anchor is raised, the depths of the earth seemed to open
before it, whilst it clove its way through. It encountered no
obstacle—no rock opposed its progress. Presently a very fine
rain penetrated through the cupola. The old man continued to
support the beautiful Lily, and whispered, " We are now under
the river, and shall soon attain the goal." Presently they
thought the motion ceased, but they were deceived, the temple
still moved onwards. A strange sound was now heard above
them; beams and broken rafters burst in disjointed fragments
through the opening of the cupola. The Lily and the old woman
retreated in alarm; the man with the lamp stood by the youth
and encouraged him to remain. The Ferryman's little hut
had been ploughed from the ground by the advance of the
temple, and, in its gradual fall, buried the youth and the old
man.

The women screamed in alarm, and the temple shook like a
vessel which strikes upon a hidden rock. Anxiously the
women wandered round the hut in darkness; the doors were
shut, and no one answered to their knocking. They continued
to knock more loudly, when at last the wood began to ring
with sounds; the magic power of the lamp, which was enclosed within the hut, changed it into silver, and presently its
very form was altered, for the noble metal refusing to assume
the form of planks, posts, and rafters, was converted into a
glorious building of artistic workmanship; it seemed as if a

smaller temple had grown up within the large one, or at least an altar worthy of its beauty.

The noble youth ascended a staircase in the interior, whilst the man with the lamp shed light upon his way, and another figure lent him support, clad in a short white garment, and holding in his hand a silver rudder; it was easy to recognise the Ferryman, the former inhabitant of the transformed hut.

The beautiful Lily ascended the outward steps, which led from the temple to the altar, but was compelled to remain separated from her lover. The old woman, whose hand continued to grow smaller, whilst the light of the lamp was obscured, exclaimed, " Am I still doomed to be unhappy amid so many miracles; will no miracle restore my hand?"

Her husband pointed to the open door, exclaiming, " See, the day dawns; hasten and bathe in the river."

" What advice!" she answered; " shall I not become wholly black, and dissolve into nothing, for I have not yet discharged my debt?"

" Be silent," said the old man, " and follow me; all debts are wiped away."

The old woman obeyed, and in the same instant the light of the rising sun shone upon the circle of the cupola. Then the old man, advancing between the youth and the maiden, exclaimed with a loud voice, " Three things have sway upon the earth,—Wisdom, Appearance, and Power."

At the sound of the first word the Golden King arose; at the sound of the second, the Silver King; and the Brazen King had risen at the sound of the third, when the fourth suddenly sunk awkwardly to the earth. The Will-o'-the-wisps, who had been busily employed upon him till this moment, now retreated; though paled by the light of the morning, they seemed in good condition, and sufficiently brilliant, for they had with much dexterity extracted the gold from the veins of the colossal statue with their sharp-pointed tongues. The irregular spaces which were thus displayed remained for some time exposed, and the figure preserved its previous form; but when at length the most secret veins of gold had been extracted, the statue suddenly fell with a crash, and formed a mass of shapeless ruins.

The man with the lamp conducted the youth, whose eye

was still fixed upon vacancy, from the altar towards the Brazen King. At the foot of the mighty monarch lay a sword in a brazen sheath. The youth bound it to his side. "Take the weapon in your left hand, and keep the right hand free," exclaimed the King.

They then advanced to the Silver Monarch, who bent his sceptre towards the youth; the latter seized it with his left hand, and the King addressed him in soft accents, "Feed my sheep."

When they reached the statue of the Golden King, with paternal benediction the latter pressed the oaken garland on the head of the youth, and said, "Acknowledge the highest."

The old man had, during this proceeding, watched the youth attentively. After he had girded on the sword his breast heaved, his arm was firmer, and his step more erect; and after he had touched the sceptre, his sense of power appeared to soften, and at the same time, by an inexpressible charm, to become more mighty; but when his waving locks were adorned with the oaken garland, his countenance became animated, his soul beamed from his eye, and the first word he uttered was "Lily!"

"Dear Lily," he exclaimed, as he hastened to ascend the silver stairs, for she had observed his progress from the altar where she stood—"dear Lily, what can man desire more blessed than the innocence and the sweet affection which your love brings me? Oh, my friend!" he continued, turning to the old man, and pointing to the three sacred statues, "secure and glorious is the kingdom of our fathers, but you have forgotten to enumerate that fourth power, which exercises an earlier, more universal, and certain rule over the world—the power of love."

With these words he flung his arms round the neck of the beautiful maiden; she had cast aside her veil, and her cheeks were tinged with a blush of the sweetest and most inexpressible beauty.

The old man now observed, with a smile, "Love does not rule, but controls, and that is better."

During all this delight and enchantment, no one had observed that the sun was now high in heaven, and through the open gates of the temple most unexpected objects were perceived. An empty space, of large dimensions, was surrounded by pillars, and terminated by a long and splendid bridge, whose many arches stretched across the river. On each side was a footpath, wide and convenient for passengers, of whom many thousands were busily employed in crossing over; the wide road in the centre was crowded with flocks and herds, and horsemen and carriages, and all streamed over without impeding each other's progress. All were in raptures at the union of convenience and beauty; and the new King and his spouse were as much charmed with the animation and activity of this great concourse, as they were with their own reciprocal love.

" Honour the Dragon," said the man with the lamp; " to her you are indebted for life, and your people for the bridge whereby these neighbouring shores are animated and connected. Those shining precious stones which still float by, are the remains of her self-sacrifice, and form the foundation-stones of this glorious bridge, upon which she has erected herself to subsist for ever.

The approach of four beautiful maidens, who advanced to the door of the temple, prevented any inquiry into this wonderful mystery. Three of them were recognised as the attendants of the beautiful Lily, by the harp, the fan, and the ivory chair; but the fourth, though more beautiful than the other three, was a stranger; she, however, played with the others with sisterly sportiveness, ran with them through the temple, and ascended the silver stairs.

" Thou dearest of creatures!" said the man with the lamp, addressing the beautiful Lily, " you will surely believe me for the future. Happy for thee, and every other creature who shall bathe this morning in the waters of the river!"

The old woman, who had been transformed into a beautiful young girl, and of whose former appearance no trace remained, embraced the man with the lamp with tender caresses, which he returned with affection.

" If I am too old for you," he said, with a smile, " you may to-day select another bridegroom, for no tie can henceforth be considered binding which is not this day renewed."

" But are you not aware that you also have become young?" she inquired.

" I am delighted to hear it," he replied. " If I appear to you to be a gallant youth, I take your hand anew, and hope for a thousand years of happiness to come."

The Queen welcomed her new friend, and advanced with her and the rest of her companions to the altar, whilst the King, supported by the two men, pointed to the bridge, and surveyed with wonder the crowd of passengers; but his joy was soon overshadowed by observing an object which gave him pain. The Giant, who had just awakened from his morning sleep, stumbled over the bridge, and gave rise to the greatest confusion. He was, as usual, but half awake, and had risen with the intention of bathing in the neighbouring cove, but he stumbled instead upon firm land, and found himself feeling his way upon the broad highway of the bridge. And whilst he went clumsily along in the midst of men and animals, his presence, though a matter of astonishment to all, was felt by none; but when the sun shone in his eyes, and he raised his hand to shade them, the shadow of his enormous fist fell amongst the crowd with such careless violence, that both men and animals huddled together in promiscuous confusion, and either sustained personal injury, or ran the risk of being driven into the water.

The King, observing this calamity, with an involuntary movement placed his hand upon his sword; but, upon reflection, turned his eyes upon his sceptre, and then upon the the lamp and the rudder of his companions.

" I guess your thought," said the man with the lamp, " but we are powerless against this monster; be tranquil, he injures for the last time, and happily his shadow is turned from us."

In the meantime the Giant had approached, and overpowered with astonishment at what he saw, his hands sunk down, became powerless for injury, and gazing with surprise, he entered the court-yard.

In imagination he was ascending toward heaven, when he felt himself suddenly fast bound to the earth. He stood like a colossal pillar constructed of red shining stones, and his shadow indicated the hours which were marked in a circle on the ground, not however in figures, but in noble and significant effigies.

The King was not a little delighted to see the shadow of the monster rendered harmless; and the Queen was not less astonished, as she advanced from the altar with her maidens, all adorned with the greatest magnificence, to observe the strange wonder which almost covered the whole prospect from the temple to the bridge.

In the meantime the people had crowded after the Giant, and surrounding him as he stood still, had observed his transformation with the utmost awe. They bent their steps then towards the temple, of the existence of which they now seemed to be for the first time aware, and thronged the doorways.

The hawk was now observed aloft, towering over the building, and carrying the mirror, with which he caught the light of the sun, and turned the rays upon the multifarious group which stood around the altar. The King, the Queen, and their attendants, illumined by the beam from heaven, appeared beneath the dim arches of the temple; their subjects fell prostrate before them. When they had recovered, and had risen again, the King and his attendants had descended to the altar, in order to reach his palace by a less obstructed path, and the people dispersed through the temple to satisfy their curiosity. They beheld with astonishment the three Kings, who stood erect, and they were all anxiety to know what could be concealed behind the curtain in the fourth niche; since whatever kindness might have prompted the deed, a thoughtful discretion had extended a costly covering over the ruins of the fallen King, which no eye cared to penetrate; and no profane hand dared to uplift.

There was no end to the astonishment and wonder of the people; and the dense throng would have been crushed in the temple if their attention had not been attracted once more to the court without.

To their great surprise, a shower of gold pieces fell as if from the air, resounding upon the marble pavement, and caused a contest and commotion amongst the passers-by. Several times this wonder was repeated in different places, at some distance from each other. It is not difficult to infer that this feat was the work of the retreating Will-o'-the-wisps, who having extracted the gold from the limbs of the mutilated King, dispersed it abroad in this joyous manner. The covetous crowd continued their contentions for some time longer, pressing hither and thither, and inflicting wounds upon each other, till the shower of gold pieces ceased to fall. The multitude at length dispersed gradually, each one pursuing his own course; and the bridge, to this day, continues to swarm with travellers, and the temple is the most frequented in the world.

THE GOOD WOMEN.

HENRIETTA and Armidoro had been for some time engaged in walking through the garden, in which the Summer Club was accustomed to assemble. It had long been their practice to arrive before the other members, for they entertained the warmest attachment to each other, and their pure and virtuous friendship fostered the delightful hope that they would shortly be united in the bonds of unchanging affection.

Henrietta, who was of a lively disposition, no sooner perceived her friend Amelia approach the summer-house from a distance, than she ran to welcome her. The latter was already seated at a table in the ante-chamber, where the newspapers, journals, and other recent publications, lay displayed.

It was her custom to spend occasional evenings in reading in this apartment, without paying attention to the company who came and went, or suffering herself to be disturbed by the rattling of the dice or the loud conversation which prevailed at the gaming-tables. She spoke little, except for the purpose of rational conversation. Henrietta, on the contrary, was not so sparing of her words, being of an easily satisfied disposition, and ever ready with expressions of commendation. They were soon joined by a third person, whom we shall call Sinclair. "What news do you bring," exclaimed Henrietta, addressing him as he approached.

"You will scarcely guess," replied Sinclair, as he opened a portfolio. "And even if I inform you that I have brought for your inspection the engravings intended for the Ladies' Almanack of this year, you will hardly guess the subjects they portray; but when I tell you that young ladies are represented in a series of twelve engravings——"

"Indeed!" exclaimed Henrietta, interrupting him, "you

have no intention, I perceive, of putting our ingenuity to the test. You jest, if I mistake not; for you know how I delight in riddles and charades, and in guessing my friends' enigmas. Twelve young ladies, you say;—sketches of character, I suppose; some adventures, or situations, or something else that redounds to the honour of the sex."

Sinclair smiled in silence, whilst Amelia watched him with calm composure, and then remarked, with that fine sarcastic tone which so well became her, "If I read his countenance truly, he has something to produce of which we shall not quite approve. Men are so fond of discovering something which shall have the appearance of turning us into ridicule."

Sinclair.—You are becoming serious, Amelia, and threaten to grow satirical. I shall scarcely venture to open my little packet.

Henrietta.—Oh! produce it.

Sinclair.—They are caricatures.

Henrietta.—I love them of all things.

Sinclair.—Sketches of naughty ladies.

Henrietta.—So much the better; we do not belong to that class. Their portraits would afford us as little pleasure as their society.

Sinclair.—Shall I show them?

Henrietta.—Do so at once.

So saying, she snatched the portfolio from him, took out the pictures, spread six of them upon the table, glanced over them hastily, and then shuffled them together as if they had been a pack of cards. "Capital!" she exclaimed, "they are done to the very life. This one, for instance, holding a pinch of snuff to her nose, is the very image of Madame S——, whom we shall meet this evening; and this old lady with the cat is not unlike my grand-aunt;—that figure, holding the skein of thread, resembles our old milliner. We can find an original for every one of these ugly figures; and even amongst the men, I have somewhere or other seen an old fellow bent double, just like that picture; and also a close resemblance to the figure holding the thread. They are full of fun, these engravings, and admirably executed."

Amelia, who had glanced carelessly at the pictures, and instantly withdrawn her eyes, inquired how they could look for resemblances in such things. "One deformity is like another, just as the beautiful ever resembles the beautiful. Our minds are irresistibly attracted by the latter, in the same degree as they are repelled by the former."

Sinclair.—But our fancy and our wit find more amusement in deformity than in beauty. Much can be made of the former, but nothing at all of the latter.

" But beauty exalts, whilst deformity degrades us," observed Armidoro, who, from his post at the window, had paid silent attention to all that had occurred. Without approaching the table, he then adjourned into the adjoining cabinet.

All clubs have their peculiar epochs. The interest of the various members towards each other, and their friendly harmony together, is of a fluctuating character. The Club of which we speak had now attained its zenith. The members were, for the most part, men of refinement, or at least of calm and quiet deportment; they mutually recognized each other's value, and allowed all want of merit to find its own level. Each one sought his own individual amusement, and the general conversation was often of a nature to attract attention.

At this time, a gentleman named Seyton arrived, accompanied by his wife. He was a man who had seen much of the world, first from his engagement in business, and afterwards in political affairs; he was moreover an agreeable companion, although, in mixed society, he was chiefly remarkable for his talent as a card-player. His wife was a worthy woman, kind and faithful, and enjoying the most perfect confidence and esteem of her husband. She felt happy that she could now give uncontrolled indulgence to her taste for pleasure. At home she could not exist without a companion, and she found in amusement and dissipation the only incentive to home enjoyment.

We must treat our readers as strangers, or rather as visitors to the Club, and in full confidence we must introduce them speedily to our new Society. A poet paints his characters, by describing their actions; we must adopt a shorter course, and by a hasty sketch introduce our readers rapidly to the scenes.

Seyton approached the table and looked at the pictures.

" A discussion has arisen," observed Henrietta, " with respect to caricatures. What side do you take? I am an advocate for them, and wish to know whether all caricatures do not possess something irresistibly attractive?"

Amelia.—And does not every evil calumny, provide it relate to the absent, also possess an incredible charm?

Henrietta.—But does not a sketch of this kind produce an indelible impression?

Amelia.—And that is just the reason why I condemn it. Is not the indelible impression of what is disagreeable precisely the evil which so constantly pursues us in life and destroys our greatest enjoyments?

Henrietta.—Favour us, Seyton, with your opinion.

Seyton.—I should propose a truce to the argument. Why should our pictures be better than ourselves? Our nature seems to have two sides, which cannot exist separately. Light and darkness, good and evil, height and depth, virtue and vice, and a thousand other contradictions unequally distributed, appear to constitute the component parts of human nature; and why, therefore, should I blame an artist who, whilst he paints an angel bright, brilliant and beautiful, on the other hand paints a devil black, ugly, and hateful?

Amelia.—There could be no objection to such a course, if caricaturists did not introduce within their province, subjects which belong to higher spheres.

Seyton.—So far I think you perfectly right. But artists, whose province is the Beautiful alone, also appropriate what does not precisely belong to them.

Amelia.—I have no patience, however, with caricaturists who ridicule the portraits of eminent men. In spite of my better sense, I can never consider that great man Pitt as any thing else than a snub-nosed broomstick; and Fox, who was in many respects an estimable character, anything better than a stall-fed swine.

Henrietta.—Precisely my view. Caricatures of such a nature make an indelible impression, and I cannot deny that it often affords amusement to evoke their recollection and pervert them even into worse distortions.

Sinclair.—But, ladies, allow us to revert for a moment from this discussion, to a consideration of our engravings.

Seyton.—I observe that a fancy for dogs is here delineated in no very flattering manner.

Amelia.—That I have no objection to, for I detest such animals.

Sinclair.—First an enemy to caricatures, and then unfriendly to the dog tribe.

Amelia.—And why not? What are such animals but caricatures of men?

Seyton.—You remember, probably, what a certain traveller relates of the city of Grätz, " that the place was full of dogs, and of dumb persons half idiotic." Might it not be possible that the habitual sight of so many barking, senseless animals should have produced an effect upon the human race?

Sinclair.—Our attachment to animals deteriorates our passions and affections.

Amelia.—But if our reason, according to the general expression, is sometimes capable of standing still, it may surely do so in the presence of dogs.

Sinclair.—Fortunately there is no one in our company who cares for dogs, but Madame Seyton. She is very much attached to her pretty greyhound.

Seyton.—And that same animal is particularly dear and valuable to her husband.

Madame Seyton from a distance, raised her finger to her lips in an attitude of playful threatening.

Seyton.—I know a proof that such animals detach our affections from their legitimate objects. May I not, my dear child (addressing his wife), relate our anecdote? We need not be ashamed of it.

Madame Seyton, signified her assent by a friendly nod, and he commenced his narration.

" We loved each other and had entered into an engagement to marry, before we had well considered the possibility of supporting an establishment. At length better hopes began to dawn, when I was unexpectedly compelled to set out upon a journey which threatened to last longer than I could have wished. On my departure I forgot my favourite greyhound. It had often been in the habit of accompanying me to my intended wife's house, sometimes returning with me, and occasionally remaining behind. It now became her property, was a cheerful companion, and reminded her of my return. At home the little animal afforded much amusement, and in the promenades, where we had so often walked together, it seemed constantly engaged in looking for me, and barked as if announcing me, as it sprang from among the trees. My

2 H

darling little Meta amused itself thus for a considerable time, by fancying me really present, until at length, about the time when I had hoped to return, the period of my absence being again indefinitely prolonged, the poor animal pined away and died."

Madame Seyton.—Just so, dear husband! And your narrative is sweetly interesting.

Seyton.—You are quite at liberty to interrupt me, my dear, if you think fit. My friend's house now seemed desolate, her walks had lost all their interest, her favourite dog, which had ever been at her side when she wrote to me, had grown to be an actual necessity of existence, and her letters were now discontinued. But she found, however, some consolation in the company of a handsome youth, who evinced an anxiety to fill the place of her former four-footed companion, both in the house and in the promenades. But without enlarging on this subject, and let me be ever so inimical to rash judgments, I may say that matters began to assume a rather critical appearance.

Madame Seyton.—I must let you continue. A story which is all truth and wholly free from exaggeration, is seldom worth hearing.

Seyton.—A mutual friend of ours, who was a prudent man, versed in the world, and acquainted with human nature, continued to reside near my dear friend after my departure. He paid frequent visits at her house, and observed with pain and anxiety the change which she had undergone. He formed his plan in secrecy, and called upon her one day, accompanied by a greyhound which precisely resembled mine. The cordially affectionate and appropriate address with which he accompanied his present, the unexpected appearance of a favourite, which seemed to have risen from the grave, the silent rebuke with which her susceptible heart reproached her at the sight, brought back to her mind a lively recollection of me. My young supplanter accordingly received his congé in the politest manner possible, and the new favourite was retained by the lady as her constant companion. When, upon my return, I held my beloved in my embrace, I thought the greyhound was my own, and wondered not a little that he barked at me as at a stranger. I thought that dogs of the present day had far less faithful memories than those of classical times, and observed that Ulysses had been remembered by his dog after many years' absence, whilst mine had forgotten me in an incredibly short space of time. "But yet he has taken good care of your Penelope," she replied, promising at the same time to explain her mysterious speech. This was soon done, and unbroken confidence has ever since been the characteristic of our union.

Madame Seyton.—Well now, conclude with the anecdote. If you please, I will walk for an hour, for you intend doubtless to sit down to the card-table.

He signified his assent. She took the arm of her companion and went towards the door. "Take the dog with you, my dear!" he exclaimed as she departed. The entire company smiled, as did Seyton also, when he saw the precise point of his unintentional observation, and every one else silently felt a trifling degree of malicious satisfaction.

Sinclair.—You have related an anecdote of a dog which was happily instrumental in promoting a marriage; I can tell another whose influence destroyed one. I was also once in love, and it was also my fate to set out upon a journey, and, moreover, left a dear young friend behind me. But there was this difference between the two cases, my wish to possess my treasure had been as yet undeclared. At length I returned. The many adventures in which I had engaged were imprinted strongly upon my mind. Like all travellers, I was fond of recounting them, and I hoped by this means to win the attention and sympathy of my beloved. I was anxious that she should know all the experience I had acquired and the pleasures I had enjoyed. But I found that her attention was wholly directed to a dog. Whether she so engaged herself from that spirit of opposition which so often characterises the fair sex, or whether it arose from some unlucky accident, it so happened that the amiable qualities of the dog, their amusements together, and her attachment to the little animal, were the sole topics of conversation which she could find for a lover who had long been passionately devoted to her. I wondered and felt astonished, and related a thousand circumstances to prove my affection for her. I then felt vexed at her coldness, and took my leave, but soon returned with feelings of self-reproach and became even more unhappy than before. Under these circumstances our attachment

cooled and our acquaintance was discontinued, and I felt in
my heart that I might attribute the misfortune to a dog.

Armidoro, who had once more joined the company from the
cabinet, observed, upon hearing the anecdote, " that it would
be interesting to make a collection of stories showing the influence which social animals of the lower order exercise over
mankind.   In the expectation that such a collection will be
one day made, I will relate an anecdote to show how a dog
was the cause of a very tragical occurrence."

" Ferdinand and Cardano, two young noblemen, had been
attached friends from their very earliest youth. As court pages
and as officers in the same regiment, they had shared many
adventures together, and had become thoroughly acquainted
with each other's dispositions. Cardano's attraction was the fair
sex, whilst Ferdinand had a passion for play. The former was
thoughtless and haughty, the latter suspicious and reserved.
It happened, at a time when Cardano was accidentally
obliged to break off a certain tender attachment, that he
left a beautiful little pet spaniel behind him. He soon
procured another, which he afterwards presented to a second
lady, from whom he was about to separate, and from that time,
upon taking leave of every new female friend with whom he
had become intimate, he invariably presented her with a
similar little spaniel.   Ferdinand was aware of Cardano's
peculiar habit in this respect, but he never payed much attention to the circumstance.

" The different pursuits of the two friends at length caused
a long separation between them, and when they next met,
Ferdinand had become a married man, and was leading
the life of a country gentleman.   Cardano spent some time
with him, either at his house or in the neighbourhood, where,
as he had many relations and friends, he resided for nearly
a year.

" Upon his departure Ferdinand's attention was attracted
by a very beautiful spaniel of which his wife had lately
become possessed.   He took it in his arms, admired its
beauty, stroked it, praised it, and inquired where she had
obtained so charming an animal.   She replied " from Cardano."   He was struck at once with the memory of bygone
times and events, and with a recollection of the significant
memorial with which Cardano was accustomed to mark his

insincerity ; he felt oppressed with the indignity of an injured husband, raged violently, flung the innocent little animal with fury to the earth, and ran from the apartment amid the cries of the spaniel and the supplications of his astonished wife. A fearful dispute and countless disagreeable consequences ensued, which, though they did not produce an actual divorce, ended in a mutual agreement to separate, and a ruined household was the termination of this adventure.''

The story was not quite finished when Eulalia entered the apartment. She was a young lady whose society was universally sought after, and she formed one of the most attractive ornaments of the Club—an accomplished woman and a successful authoress.

The female caricatures were laid before her with which the clever artist before alluded to, had attacked the fair sex, and she was invited to defend her good sisterhood.

" Probably," said Amelia " a collection of these charming portraits is intended for the Almanack, and possibly some celebrated author will undertake the witty task of explaining in words what the ingenious artist has represented in his pictures.''

Sinclair felt that the pictures were not worthy of utter condemnation, nor could he deny that some sort of explanation of their meaning was necessary, as a caricature which is not understood is worthless, and is in fact only valuable for its application. For however the ingenious artist may endeavour to display his wit, he cannot always succeed, and without a title or an explanation his labour is lost : words alone can give it value.

Amelia.—Then let words bestow a value upon this little picture. A young lady has fallen asleep in an armchair. having been engaged, as it appears, with some sort of writing, Another lady who stands by weeping, presents a small box, or something else, to her companion. What can it mean ?

Sinclair.—Shall I endeavour to explain it ?—notwithstanding that the ladies seem but ill disposed both to caricatures and their exposition. I am told that it is intended to represent an authoress, who was accustomed to compose at night ; she always obliged her maid to hold her inkstand, and forced the poor creature to remain in that posture even when she herself had been overcome by sleep, and the office of her maid had thus been rendered useless. She was desirous, on awaking, to resume the thread of her thoughts and of her composition, and wished to find her pen and ink ready at the same moment.

Arbon, an artist of talent who had accompanied Eulalia, declared war against the picture. He observed that to delineate the situation or circumstance above alluded to, another course should have been adopted.

Henrietta.—Let us then compose the picture afresh.

Arbon.—But let us first of all consider the subject attentively. It seems natural enough that a person employed in writing should cause the inkstand to be held, if the circumstances are such that no place can be found to set it down. So Brantome's grandmother held the inkstand for the Queen of Navarre, when the latter, reposing in her litter, composed the history which we have all read with so much pleasure. Again, that any one who writes in bed should cause his inkstand to be held, is quite conceivable. But tell us, pretty Henrietta, you who are fond so of questioning and guessing, tell us what the artist should have done to represent this subject properly.

Henrietta.—He should have put the table away, and have so arranged the sleeper, that nothing should appear at hand upon which an inkstand could be placed.

Arbon.—Quite right. I should have drawn her in a well-cushioned easy-chair, of the fashion which, if I mistake not, are called Bergères; she should have been near the fire-place, and presenting a front view to the spectator. I should suppose her to be engaged in writing upon her knee, for usually one becomes uncomfortable in exacting an inconvenience from another. The paper sinks upon her lap, the pen from her hand, and a sweet maiden stands near, holding the inkstand with a forlorn look.

Henrietta.—Quite right. But here we have an inkstand upon the table already; and what is to be done, therefore, with the inkstand in the hand of the maiden? It is not easy to conceive why she should be engaged in wiping away her tears.

Sinclair.—Here I defend the artist; he allows scope for the ingenuity of the commentator.

Arbon.—Who will probably be engaged in exercising his

wit upon the headless men that hang against the wall. This seems to me a clear proof of the inevitable confusion that arises from uniting arts between which there is no natural connection. If we were not accustomed to see engravings with explanations appended to them, the evil would cease. I have no objection that a clever artist should attempt witty representations, but they are difficult to execute, and he should at all events endeavour to make his subject independent of explanations. I could even tolerate remarks and little sentences issuing from the mouths of his figures, provided he restricted himself to being his own commentator.

Sinclair.—But if you allow such a thing as a witty picture, you must admit that it is intended only for persons of intelligence; it can possess an attraction for none but those conversant with the occurrences of the day; why then should we object to a commentator who enables us to understand the nature of the intellectual amusement prepared for us?

Arbon.—I have no objection to explanations of pictures, which fail to explain themselves. But they should be short and to the point. Wit is for the intelligent, they alone can understand a witty work, and the productions of bygone times and foreign lands are completely lost upon us. It is all well enough with the aid of such notes as we find appended to Rabelais and Hudibras, but what should we say of an author who should find it necessary to write one witty work to elucidate another? Wit, even when fresh from its fountain, is oftentimes feeble enough; it will scarcely become stronger by passing through two or three hands.

Sinclair.—How I wish that, instead of thus arguing, we could assist our friend, the owner of these pictures, who would be glad to hear the opinions that have been expressed.

Armidoro.—(Coming from the cabinet.) I perceive that the company is still engaged about these censurable pictures: had they produced a pleasant impression, they would doubtless have been laid aside long ago.

Amelia.—I propose that that be their fate now; the owner must be required to make no use of them. What! a dozen and more hateful, objectionable pictures to appear in a Ladies' Almanack! Can the man be blind to his own interest? He will ruin his speculation. What lover will present a copy to his mistress, what husband to his wife, what father to his daughter, when the first glance will display such a libel upon the sex?

Armidoro.—I have a proposal to make. These objectionable pictures are not the first of the kind which have appeared in the best almanacks. Our celebrated Chodowiecki has in his collection of monthly engravings, already represented scenes not only untrue to nature, but low and devoid of all pretensions to taste; but how did he do it? Opposite the pictures I allude to, he delineated others of a most charming character,—scenes in perfect harmony with nature, the result of a high education, of long study, and of an innate taste for the Good and Beautiful. Let us go a step beyond the editor of the proposed Almanack, and act in opposition to his project. If the intelligent artist has chosen to portray the dark side of his subject, let our author or authoress, if I may dare to express my view, choose the bright side to exercise her talents and so form a complete work. I shall not longer delay, Eulalia, to unite my own wishes to this proposal. Undertake a description of good female characters. Create the opposite to these engravings, and employ the charm of your pen, not to elucidate these pictures, but to annihilate them.

Sinclair.—Promise to comply, Eulalia. Place us under so great an obligation to you.

Eulalia.—Authors are ever apt to promise too easily, because they hope for ability to execute their wishes; but experience has rendered me cautious. And even if I could foresee the necessary leisure, within so short a space of time, I should yet hesitate to undertake the arduous duty. The praises of our sex should be spoken by a man,—a young, ardent, loving man. A degree of enthusiasm is requisite for the task, and who has enthusiasm for one's own sex?

Armidoro.—I should prefer intelligence, justice, and delicacy of taste.

Sinclair.—And who can discourse better on the character of good women than the authoress from whose fairy tale of yesterday we all derived such pleasure, and so much incomparable instruction?

Eulalia.—The fairy tale was not mine.

Sinclair.—Not yours?

Armidoro.—To that I can bear witness.

Sinclair.—But still it was a lady's?

Eulalia.—The production of a friend.

Sinclair.—Then there are two Eulalias.

Eulalia.—Many, perhaps; and better than——

Armidoro.—Will you relate to the company what you so lately confided to me? You will all hear with astonishment how this delightful production originated.

Eulalia.—A young lady, with whose great excellence I became accidentally acquainted upon a journey, found herself once in a situation of extreme perplexity, the circumstances of which it would be tedious to narrate. A gentleman to whom she was under many obligations, and who finally offered her his hand, having won her entire esteem and confidence, in a moment of weakness obtained from her the privileges of a husband, before their vows of love had been cemented by marriage. Some peculiar circumstances compelled him to travel, and, in the retirement of a country residence, she anticipated with fear and apprehension the moment when she should become a mother. She used to write to me daily, and informed me of every circumstance that happened. But there was shortly nothing more to fear—she now needed only patience, and I observed, from the tone of her letters, that she began to reflect with a disturbed mind upon all that had already occurred, and upon what was yet to take place in her regard. I determined, therefore, to address her in an earnest tone, on the duty which she owed no less to herself than to her infant, whose support, particularly at the commencement of its existence, depended so much upon her mind being free from anxiety. I sought to console and to cheer her, and for this purpose sent her several volumes of fairy tales, which I expressed a wish that she should read. Her own desire to escape from the burden of her melancholy thoughts, and the arrival of these books, formed a remarkable coincidence. She could not help reflecting frequently upon her peculiar fate, and she therefore adopted the expedient of clothing all her past sorrowful adventures, as well as her painful apprehensions for the future, in a garb of romance. The events of her past life,—her attachment, her passion, her errors, and her sweet maternal cares,—no less than her present sad condition, were all embodied by her imagination in forms vivid, though impalpable, and passed before her mind in a varied succession of strange and unearthly fancies. With pen in hand, she spent many a day and night in noting down her reflections.

Amelia.—In which occupation she must have found it difficult to hold her inkstand.

Eulalia.—Thus did I acquire the rare collection of letters which I now possess. They are all picturesque, strange, and romantic. I never received from her an account of anything actual, so that I sometimes trembled for her reason. Her own situation, the birth of her infant, her sweet affection for her offspring, her joys, her hopes, and her maternal fears, were all treated as events of another world, from which she only expected to be liberated by the arrival of her husband. Upon her nuptial day she concluded the fairy tale which you heard recited yesterday, almost in her own words, and which derives its chief interest from the unusual circumstances under which it was composed.

The company could not sufficiently express their astonishment at this statement, and Seyton, who had abandoned his place at the gaming-table to another person, now entered the apartment, and made inquiries concerning the subject of conversation. He was briefly informed that it related to a fairy tale, which, partly founded on facts, had been composed by the fantastic imagination of a mind that was diseased.

"It is a great pity," he remarked, "that private diaries are so completely out of fashion. Twenty years ago they were in general use, and many persons thought they possessed a veritable treasure in the record of their daily thoughts. I recollect a very worthy lady upon whom this custom entailed a sad misfortune. A certain governess had been accustomed from her earliest youth to keep a regular diary, and, in fact, she considered its composition to form an indispensable part of her daily duties. She continued the habit when she grew up, and did not lay it aside even when she married. Her memorandums were not looked upon by her as absolute secrets, she had no occasion for such mystery, and she frequently read passages from it for the amusement of her friends and of her husband. But the book in its entirety was entrusted to nobody. The account of her husband's attachment had been entered in her diary with the same minuteness with which she had formerly noted down the ordinary occurrences of the day; and the entire history of her own affectionate feelings had been described from their first opening hour until they had ripened into a passion, and become at length a rooted habit. Upon one occasion this diary accidentally fell in her husband's way, and the perusal afforded him a strange entertainment. He had undesignedly approached the writing-desk upon which the book lay, and, without suspicion or intention, had read through an entire page which was open before him. He took the opportunity of referring to a few previous and subsequent passages, and then retired with the comfortable assurance that it was high time to discontinue the disagreeable amusement.

Henrietta.—But, according to the wish of my friend, our conversation should be confined to good women, and already we are turning to those who can scarcely be counted amongst the best.

Seyton.—Why this constant reference to bad and good? Should we not be quite as well contented with others as with ourselves, either as we have been formed by nature, or improved by education?

Armidoro.—I think it would be at once pleasant and useful to arrange and collect a series of anecdotes such as we have heard narrated, and many of which are founded on real occurrences. Light and delicate traits, which mark the characters of men, are well worthy of our attention, even though they give birth to no extraordinary adventures. They are useless to writers of romance, being devoid of all exciting interest; and worthless to the tribe of anecdote-collectors, for they are for the most part destitute of wit and spirit, but they would always prove entertaining to a reader who, in a mood of quiet contemplation, should wish to study the general characteristics of mankind.

Sinclair.—Well said. And if we had only thought of so praiseworthy a work a little earlier, we might have assisted our friend, the editor of the Ladies' Calendar, by composing a dozen anecdotes, if not of model women, at least of well-behaved personages, to balance his catalogue of naughty ladies.

Amelia.—I should be particularly pleased with a collection of incidents to show how a woman forms the very soul and existence of a household establishment; and this because

the artist has introduced a sketch of a spendthrift and improvident wife, to the defamation of our sex.

Seyton.—I can furnish Amelia with a case precisely in
point.

Amelia.—Let us hear it. But do not imitate the usual
custom of men who undertake to defend the ladies: they
frequently begin with praise, and end with censure.

Seyton.—Upon this occasion, however, I do not fear the
perversion of my intention, through the influence of any evil
spirit. A young man once became tenant of a large hotel
which was established in a good situation. Amongst the
qualities which recommend a host, he possessed a more than
ordinary share of good temper, and as he had from his youth
been a friend to the ale-house, he was peculiarly fortunate in
selecting a pursuit in which he found it necessary to devote a
considerable portion of the day to his home duties. He was
neither careful nor negligent, and his own good temper
exercised a perceptible influence over the numerous guests
who assembled around him.

He had married a young person who was of a quiet,
passive disposition. She paid punctual attention to her
business, was attached to her household pursuits, and loved
her husband, though she often found fault with him in secret for
his carelessness in money matters. She had a great love for
ready money; she thoroughly comprehended its value, and
understood the advantage of securing a provision for herself.
Devoid of all activity of disposition, she had every tendency
to avarice. But a small share of avarice becomes a woman,
however ill extravagance may suit her. Generosity is a
manly virtue, but parsimony is becoming in a woman. This
is the rule of nature, and our judgments must be subservient
thereto.

Margaret (for such was the name of this prudent personage) was very much dissatisfied with her husband's carelessness. Upon occasions when large payments were made to
him by his customers, it was his habit to leave the money
lying for a considerable time upon the table, and then to
collect it in a basket, from which he afterwards paid it away,
without making it up into packages, and without keeping any
account of its application. His wife plainly perceived that,
even without actual extravagance, where there was such a

total want of system, considerable sums must be wasted. She was above all things anxious to make her husband change his negligent habits, and she became grieved to observe that the small savings which she collected and so carefully retained were as nothing in comparison with the money that was squandered, and she determined, therefore, to adopt a rather dangerous expedient to make her husband open his eyes. She resolved to defraud him of as much money as possible, and for this purpose had recourse to an extraordinary plan. She had observed that when he had once counted his money which he allowed to remain so long upon the table, he never reckoned it over a second time before putting it away; she therefore rubbed the bottom of a candle-stick with tallow, and then, apparently without design, she placed it near the spot where the ducats lay exposed, a species of coin for which she entertained a warm partiality. She thus gained possession of a few pieces, and subsequently of some other coins, and was soon sufficiently well satisfied with her success. She therefore repeated the operation frequently, and entertained no scruple about employing such evil means to effect so praiseworthy an object, and she tranquillized her conscience on the subject by the reflection that such a mode of abstracting her husband's money could not be termed robbery, as her hands were not employed for the purpose. Her secret treasure increased gradually, and soon became very much greater by the addition of the ready money which she herself received from the customers of the hotel, and of which she invariably retained possession.

She had carried on this practice for a whole year, and though she carefully watched her husband, she never had reason to believe that his suspicions were awakened, until at length he began to grow discontented and unhappy. She induced him to tell her the cause of his anxiety, and learned that he was grievously perplexed. After the last payment which he had made of a considerable sum of money, he had laid aside the amount of his rent, and not only this had disappeared, but he was unable to meet the demand of his landlord from any other channel; and as he had always been accustomed to keep his accounts in his head, and to write down nothing, he could not possibly understand the cause of the deficiency.

Margaret reminded him of his great carelessness, censured his thoughtless manner of receiving and paying away money, and spoke of his general imprudence. Even his generous disposition did not escape her remarks; and, in truth, he had no excuse to offer for a course of conduct the consequences of which he had so much reason to regret.

But she could not leave her husband long in this state of grievous trouble, more especially as she felt a pride in being able to render him once more happy. Accordingly, to his great astonishment, on his birthday, which she was always accustomed to celebrate by presenting him with something useful, she entered his private apartment with a basket filled with rouleaux of money. The different descriptions of coin were packed together separately, and the contents were carefully endorsed in a handwriting by no means of the best. It would be difficult to describe his astonishment at finding before him the precise sums which he had missed, or at his wife's assurance that they belonged to him. She thereupon circumstantially described the time and the manner of her abstracting them, confessed the amount which she had taken, and told also how much she had saved by her own careful attention. His despair was now changed into joy, and the result was that he abandoned to his wife all the duty of receiving and paying away money for the future. His business was carried on even more prosperously than before, although from the day of which we have spoken, not a farthing ever passed through his hands. His wife discharged the duty of banker with extraordinary credit to herself; no false money was ever taken, and the establishment of her complete authority in the house was the natural and just consequence of her activity and care; and, after the lapse of ten years, she and her husband were in a condition to purchase the hotel for themselves.

Sinclair.—And so all this truth, love, and fidelity ended in the wife becoming the veritable mistress. I should like to know how far the opinion is just that women have a tendency to acquire authority.

Amelia.—There it is again. Censure, you observe, is sure to follow in the wake of praise.

Armidoro.—Favour us with your sentiments on this subject, good Eulalia. I think I have observed in your writings no disposition to defend your sex against this imputation.

Eulalia.—In so far as it is a grievous imputation, I should wish it were removed by the conduct of our sex. But where we have a right to authority, we can need no excuse. We like authority because we are human. For what else is authority, in the sense in which we use it, than a desire for independence, and for the enjoyment of existence as much as possible. This is a privilege which all men seek with determination, but our ambition appears, perhaps, more objectionable, because nature, usage, and social regulations place restraints upon our sex, whilst they enlarge the authority of men. What men possess naturally, we have to acquire, and property obtained by a laborious struggle will always be more obstinately held than that which is inherited.

Seyton.—But women, as I think, have no reason to complain on that score. As the world goes, they inherit as much as men, if not more, and in my opinion it is a much more difficult task to become a perfect man than a perfect woman. The phrase, "He shall be thy master," is a formula characteristic of a barbarous age long since passed away. Men cannot claim a right to become educated and refined, without conceding the same privilege to women. As long as the process continues, the balance is even between them; but as women are more capable of improvement than men, experience shows that the scale soon turns in their favour.

Armidoro.—There is no doubt that in all civilized nations women in general are superior to men, for where the two sexes exert a corresponding influence over each other, man becomes effeminate, and that is a disadvantage; but when a woman acquires any masculine virtue, she is the gainer, for if she can improve her own peculiar qualities by the addition of masculine energy, she becomes an almost perfect being.

Seyton.—I have never considered the subject so deeply. But I think it is generally admitted that women do rule and must continue to do so, and therefore whenever I become acquainted with a young lady, I always inquire upon what subjects she exercises her authority, since it must be exercised somewhere.

Amelia.—And thus you establish the point with which you started?

Seyton.—And why not? Is not my reasoning as good as

that of philosophers in general, who are convinced by their experience? Active women, who are given to habits of acquisition and saving, are invariably mistresses at home; pretty women, at once graceful and superficial, rule in large societies, whilst those who possess more sound accomplishments exert their influence in smaller circles.

Amelia.—And thus we are divided into three classes.

Sinclair.—All honourable, in my opinion; and yet those three classes do not include the whole sex. There is still a fourth, to which perhaps we had better not allude, that we may escape the charge of converting our praise into censure.

Henrietta.—Then we must guess the fourth class. Let us see.

Sinclair.—Well then, the three first classes, were those whose activity was displayed at home, in large societies, or in smaller circles.

Henrietta.—What other sphere can there be where we can exercise our activity?

Sinclair.—There may be many. But I am thinking of the reverse of activity.

Henrietta.—Indolence! How could an indolent woman rule?

Sinclair.—Why not?

Henrietta.—In what manner?

Sinclair.—By opposition. Whoever adopts such a course, either from character or principle, acquires more authority than one would readily think.

Amelia.—I fear we are about to fall into the tone of censure so general to men.

Henrietta.—Do not interrupt him, Amelia. Nothing can be more harmless than these mere opinions, and we are the gainers, by learning what other persons think of us. Now then for the fourth class, what about it?

Sinclair.—I must take the liberty of speaking unreservedly. The class I allude to does not exist in our country, and does not exist in France, because the fair sex, both amongst us and our gallant neighbours, enjoys a proper degree of freedom. But in countries where women are under restraint and debarred from sharing in public amusements, the class I speak of is numerous. In a neighbouring country there is a peculiar name, by which ladies of this class are invariably designated.

Henrietta.—You must tell us the name; we can never guess names.

Sinclair.—Well I must tell you, they are called roguish.

Henrietta.—A strange appellation.

Sinclair.—Some time ago you took great interest in reading the speculations of Lavater upon physiognomy; do you remember nothing about roguish countenances in his book?

Henrietta.—It is possible, but it made no impression upon me. I may perhaps have construed the word in its ordinary sense, and read on without noticing it.

Sinclair.—It is true, that the word "roguish" in its ordinary sense is usually applied to a person who, with malicious levity, turns another into ridicule; but in its present sense it is meant to describe a young lady, who, by her indifference, coldness, and reserve—qualities which attach to her as a disease—destroys the happiness of one upon whom she is dependent. We meet with examples of this everywhere; sometimes even in our own circle. For instance, when I have praised a lady for her beauty, I have heard it said in reply—"Yes, but she is a bit of a rogue." I even remember a physician saying to a lady who complained of the anxiety she suffered about her maid-servant, " My dear madam, the girl is somewhat of a rogue, and will give a deal of trouble."

Amelia rose from her seat and left the apartment.

Henrietta.—That seems rather strange.

Sinclair.—I thought so too, and I therefore took a note of the symptoms, which seemed to mark a disease half moral and half physical, and framed an essay which I entitled, " A Chapter on Rogues," and as I meant it to form a portion of a work on general anthropological observations, I have kept it by me hitherto.

Henrietta.—But you must let us see it, and if you know any interesting anecdotes to elucidate your meaning of the word "rogue," they must find a place in our intended collection of novels.

Sinclair.—This may be all very well, but I find I have failed in the object which brought me hither. I was anxious to find some one in this intelligent assembly to undertake an explanation of these engravings, or who could recommend a talented writer for the purpose; in place of which, the engravings are abused and pronounced worthless, and I must take my leave without having attained my purpose. But if I had only made notes of our conversation and anecdotes this evening, I should almost possess an equivalent.

Armidoro.—(Coming from the cabinet, to which he had frequently retired.) Your wish is accomplished. I know the motive of our friend, the editor of the work. I have taken down the heads of our conversation upon this paper. I will arrange the draft, and if Eulalia will kindly promise to impart to the whole that spirit of charming animation which she possesses, the graceful tone of the work, and perhaps also its contents, will in some measure expiate the offence of the artist for his ungallant attack.

Henrietta.—I cannot blame your officious friendship, Armidoro, but I wish you had not taken notes of our conversation; it is setting a bad example. Our intercourse together has been quite free and unrestrained and nothing can be worse than that our unguarded conversation should be overheard and written down, perhaps even printed for the amusement of the public.

But Henrietta's scruples were silenced by a promise that nothing should meet the public eye, except the little anecdotes which had been related.

Eulalia, however, could not be persuaded to edit the notes of the short-hand writer. She had no wish to withdraw her attention from the fairy tale with which she was then occupied. The notes remained in possession of the gentlemen of the party, who, with the aid of their own memories, generously afforded their assistance, that they might thereby contribute to the general edification of all "good women."

A TALE.

THE thick fog of an early autumnal morning obscured the extensive courts which surrounded the Prince's castle, but through the mists, which gradually dispersed, a stranger might observe a cavalcade of huntsmen, consisting of horse and foot, already engaged in their early preparations for the field. The active employments of the domestics were already discernible. These latter were engaged in lengthening and shortening stirrup-leathers, preparing the rifles and ammunition, and arranging the game-bags; whilst the dogs, impatient of restraint, threatened to break away from the slips by which they were held. Then the horses became restive, from their own high mettle, or excited by the spur of the rider, who could not resist the temptation to make a vain display of his prowess, even in the obscurity by which he was surrounded. The cavalcade awaited the arrival of the Prince, who was detained a little too long by the tender endearments of his young wife.

Lately married, they thoroughly appreciated the happiness of their own congenial dispositions; both were lively and animated, and each shared with delight the pleasures and pursuits of the other. The Prince's father had already survived and enjoyed that period of life when one learns that all the members of a State should spend their time in diligent employments, and that every one should engage in some energetic occupation corresponding with his taste, and should by this means first acquire, and then enjoy, the fruits of his labour.

How far these maxims had proved successful might have been observed on this very day, for it was the anniversary of the great market in the town, a festival which might indeed be considered a species of fair. The Prince had on the previous day conducted his wife on horseback through the busy scene, and had caused her to observe what a convenient exchange was carried on between the productions of the mountainous districts and those of the plain, and he took occasion then and there to direct her attention to the industrious character of his subjects.

But whilst the Prince was entertaining himself and his courtiers almost exclusively with subjects of this nature, and was perpetually employed with his finance minister, his chief huntsman did not lose sight of his duty, and upon his representation it was impossible, during these favourable autumnal days, any longer to postpone the amusement of the chase, as the promised meeting had already been several times deferred, not only to his own mortification, but to that of many strangers who had arrived to take part in the sport.

The Princess remained, reluctantly, at home. It had been determined to hunt over the distant mountains, and to disturb the peaceful inhabitants of the forests in those districts by an unexpected declaration of hostilities.

Upon taking his departure, the Prince recommended his wife to seek amusement in equestrian exercise, under the conduct of her uncle Frederick; "and I commend you, moreover," he said, "to the care of our trusty Honorio, who will act as your esquire, and pay you every attention:" and saying this as he descended the stairs, and gave the proper instructions to a comely youth who stood at hand, the Prince quickly disappeared amid the crowd of assembled guests and followers.

The Princess, who had continued waving her handkerchief to her husband as long as he remained in the court-yard, now retired to an apartment at the back of the castle, which showed an extensive prospect over the mountain, as the castle itself was situated on the brow of the hill, from which a view at once distant and varied opened in all directions. She found the telescope in the spot where it had been left on the previous evening, when they had amused themselves in surveying the landscape, and the extent of mountain and forest, amid which the lofty ruins of their ancestral castle were situated. It was a noble relic of ancient times, and shone out gloriously in the evening illumination. A grand

but somewhat inadequate idea of its importance was con-
veyed by the large masses of light and shadow which now
fell upon it. Moreover, by the aid of the telescope, the
autumnal foliage was seen to lend an indescribable charm to
the prospect, as it waved upon trees which had grown up
amid the ruins, undisturbed and unmolested for countless
years. But the Princess soon turned the telescope in the
direction of a dry and sandy plain beneath her, across which
the hunting cavalcade was expected to bend its course. She
patiently surveyed the spot, and was at length rewarded, as
the clear magnifying power of the instrument enabled her
delighted eyes to recognize the Prince and his chief equerry.
Upon this she once more waved her handkerchief as she
observed, or rather fancied she observed, a momentary pause
in the advance of the procession.

Her uncle Frederick was now announced, and he entered
the apartment, accompanied by an artist, bearing a large
portfolio under his arm.

"Dear cousin," observed the worthy knight, addressing
her, "we have brought some sketches of the ancestral castle
for your inspection, to show how the old walls and battlements were calculated to afford defence and protection in
stormy seasons and in years gone by, though they have
tottered in some places, and in others have covered the plain
with their ruins. Our efforts have been unceasing to render
the place accessible, since few spots offer more beauty or
sublimity to the eye of the astonished traveller."

The Prince continued, as he opened the portfolio containing the different views. "Here, as you ascend the hollow
way, through the outer fortifications, you meet the principal
tower, and a rock forbids all further progress. It is the
firmest of the mountain range. A castle has been erected upon
it, so constructed that it is difficult to say where the work
of nature ceases and the aid of art begins. At a little
distance, side-walls and buttresses have been raised, the whole
forming a sort of terrace. The height is surrounded by a
wood. For upwards of a century and a half, no sound of an axe
has been heard within these precincts, and giant trunks of trees
appear on all sides. Close to the very walls spring the glossy
maple, the rough oak, and the tall pine. They oppose our
progress with their boughs and roots, and compel us to make

a circuit to secure our advance. See how admirably our artist has sketched all this upon paper; how accurately he has represented the trees as they become entwined amid the masonry of the castle, and thrust their boughs through the opening in the walls. It is a solitude which possesses the indescribable charm of displaying the traces of human power long since past away, contending with perpetual and still reviving nature."

Opening a second picture, he continued his discourse. "What say you to this representation of the castle court, which has been rendered impassable for countless years by the falling of the principal tower? We endeavoured to approach it from the side, and in order to form a convenient private road, were compelled to blow up the old walls and vaults with gunpowder. But there was no necessity for similar operations within the castle walls. Here is a flat rocky surface which has been levelled by the hand of nature, through which, however, mighty trees have here and there been able to strike their roots. They have thriven well, and thrust their branches into the very galleries where the knights of old were wont to exercise, and have forced their way through doors and windows into vaulted halls, from which they are not likely now to be expelled, and whence we, at least, shall not remove them. They have become lords of the territory, and may remain so. Concealed beneath heaps of dried leaves, we found a perfectly level floor, which probably cannot be equalled in the world.

"In ascending the steps which lead to the chief tower, it is remarkable to observe, in addition to all that we have mentioned above, how a maple-tree has taken root on high, and has grown to a great size, so that in ascending to the highest turret to enjoy the prospect, it is difficult to pass. And here you may refresh yourself beneath the shade, for even at this elevation, the tree of which we speak throws its shadows over all around.

"We feel much indebted to the talented artist who, in the course of several views, has brought thus the whole scenery as completely before us, as if we had actually witnessed the original scene. He selected the most beautiful hours of the day and the most favourable season of the year for his task, to which he devoted many weeks incessantly. A small dwelling was erected for him and his assistant in a corner of the castle; you can scarcely imagine what a splendid view of the country, of the court, and of the ruins he there enjoyed. We intend these pictures to adorn our country-house, and every one who enjoys a view of our regular parterres, of our bowers and shady walks, will doubtless feel anxious to feed his imagination and his eyes with an actual inspection of these scenes, and so enjoy at once the old and the new, the firm and the pliant, the indestructible and the young, the perishable and the eternal."

Honorio now entered and announced the arrival of the horses. The Princess thereupon addressing her uncle, expressed a wish to ride up to the ruins and examine personally the subjects which he had so graphically described. " Ever since my arrival here," she said, " this excursion has been intended, and I shall be delighted to accomplish what has been declared almost impracticable, and what the pictures show to be so difficult."

"Not yet, my dear," replied the Prince; "these pictures only portray what the place will become, but many difficulties impede a commencement of the work."

" But let us ride a little towards the mountain," she rejoined, "if only to the beginning of the ascent; I have a great desire to-day to enjoy an extensive prospect."

" Your desire shall be gratified," answered the Prince.

" But we will first direct our course through the town," continued the lady, " and across the market-place, where a countless number of booths wear the appearance of a small town, or of an encampment. It seems as if all the wants and occupations of every family in the country were brought together and supplied in this one spot ; for the attentive observer may behold here whatever man can produce or require. You would suppose that money was wholly unnecessary, and that business of every kind could be carried on by means of barter; and such in fact is the case. Since the Prince directed my attention to this view yesterday, I have felt pleasure in observing the manner in which the inhabitants of the mountain and of the valley mutually comprehend each other, and how both so plainly speak their wants and their wishes in this place. The mountaineer, for example, has cut

the timber of his forests into a thousand forms, and applied
his iron to multifarious uses, while the inhabitant of the
valley meets him with his various wares and merchandize, the
very materials and object of which it is difficult to know or to
conjecture."

" I am aware," observed the Prince, "that my nephew
devotes his attention wholly to these subjects, for at this
particular season of the year he receives more than he expends ; and this after all is the object and end of every national
financier, and indeed of the pettiest household economist.
But excuse me, my dear, I never ride with any pleasure
through the market or the fair ; obstacles impede one at every
step, and my imagination continually recurs to that dreadful
calamity which happened before my own eyes, when I witnessed the conflagration of as large a collection of merchandize as is accumulated here.   I had scarcely—"

" Let us not lose our time" said the Princess, interrupting
him, as her worthy uncle had more than once tortured her
with a literal account of the very same misfortune.   It had
happened when he was upon a journey, and had retired
fatigued to bed, in the best hotel of the town, which was
situated in the market-place.   It was the season of the fair,
and in the dead of the night he was awoke by screams and
by the columns of fire which approached the hotel.

The Princess hastened to mount her favourite palfrey, and
led the way for her unwilling companion, when she rode
through the front gate down the hill, in place of passing
through the back gate up the mountain.   But who could have
felt unwilling to ride at her side or to follow wherever she
led?   And even Honorio had gladly abandoned the pleasure of his favourite amusement, the chace, in order to
officiate as her devoted attendant.

As we have before observed, they could only ride through
the market step by step, but the amusing observations of the
Princess rendered every pause delightful.   " I must repeat
my lesson of yesterday," she remarked " for necessity will try
our patience."   And in truth the crowd pressed upon them
in such a manner, that they could only continue their progress
at a very slow pace.   The people testified unbounded joy at
beholding the young Princess, and the complete satisfaction

of many a smiling face evinced the pleasure of the people at finding that the first lady in the land was at once the most lovely and the most gracious.

Mingled together promiscuously were rude mountaineers who inhabited quiet cottages amongst bleak rocks and towering pine-trees, lowlanders from the plains and meadows, and manufacturers from the neighbouring small towns. After quietly surveying the motley crowd, the Princess remarked to her companion, that all the people she saw, seemed to take delight in using more stuff for their garments than was necessary, whether it consisted of cloth, linen, ribbon, or trimming. It seemed as if the wearers, both men and women, thought they would be the better if they looked a little larger.

"We must leave that matter to themselves," answered the uncle; "every man must dispose of his superfluity as he pleases; well for those who spend it in mere ornament."

The Princess nodded her assent.

They had now arrived at a wide open square which led to one of the suburbs; they there perceived a number of small booths and stalls, and also a large wooden building from whence a most discordant howling issued. It was the feeding hour of the wild animals which were there enclosed for exhibition. The lion roared with that fearful voice with which he was accustomed to terrify both woods and wastes. The horses trembled, and no one could avoid observing how the monarch of the deserts made himself terrible in the tranquil circles of civilized life. Approaching nearer, they remarked the tawdry colossal pictures on which the beasts were painted in the brightest colours, intended to afford irresistible temptation to the busy citizen. The grim and fearful tiger was in the act of springing upon a negro to tear him to pieces. The lion stood in solemn majesty as if he saw no worthy prey before him. Other wonderful creatures in the same group presented inferior attractions.

"Upon our return," said the Princess, "we will alight and take a nearer inspection of these rare creatures."

"Is it not extraordinary," replied the Prince, "that man takes pleasure in fearful excitements? The tiger, for instance, is lying quietly enough within his cage, and yet here the brute must be painted in the act of springing fiercely on a negro, in order that the public may believe that the same scene is to be witnessed within. Do not murder and death, fire and deso- lation, sufficiently abound, but that every mountebank must repeat such horrors? The worthy people like to be alarmed, that they may afterwards enjoy the delightful sensation of freedom and security."

But whatever feelings of terror such frightful representa- tions might have inspired, they disappeared when they reached the gate, and surveyed the cheerful prospects around. The road led down to a river, a narrow brook in truth, and only calculated to bear light skiffs, but destined after- wards, when swelled into a wider stream, to take another name, and to water distant lands. They then bent their course further through carefully cultivated fruit and pleasure gardens, in an orderly and populous neighbourhood, until first a copse and then a wood received them as guests, and delighted their eyes with a limited but charming landscape. A green valley leading to the heights above, which had been lately mowed for the second time, and wore the appearance of velvet, having been watered copiously by a rich stream, now received them with a friendly welcome. They then bent their course to a higher and more open spot, which, upon issuing from the wood, they reached after a short ascent, and whence they obtained a distant view of the old castle, the object of their pilgrimage, which shone above the groups of trees, and assumed the appearance of a well-wooded rock. Behind them (for no one ever attained this height without turn- ing to look round,) they saw through occasional openings in the lofty trees, the Prince's castle on the left, illuminated by the morning sun; the higher portion of the town obscured by a light cloudy mist, and on the right hand, the lower part through which the river flowed in many windings, with its meadows and its mills; whilst straight before them, the country ex- tended in a wide productive plain.

After they had satisfied their eyes with the landscape, or rather, as is often the case in surveying an extensive view from an eminence, when they had become desirous of a wider and less circumscribed prospect, they rode slowly along a broad and stony plain, where they saw the mighty ruin stand- ing with its coronet of green, whilst its base was clad with trees of lesser height; and proceeding onwards they encountered the steepest and most impassable side of the ascent. It was defended by enormous rocks which had endured for ages ; proof against the ravages of time, they were fast rooted in the earth and towered aloft. One part of the castle had fallen, and lay in huge fragments irregularly massed, and seemed to act as an insurmountable barrier, the mere attempt to overcome which is a delight to youth, as supple limbs ever find it a pleasure to undertake, to combat, and to conquer. The Princess seemed disposed to make the attempt ; Honorio was at hand, her princely uncle assented, unwilling to acknowledge his want of agility. The horses were directed to wait for them under the trees, and it was intended they should make for a certain point where a large rock had been rendered smooth, and from which a prospect was beheld, which, though of the nature of a bird's-eye view, was sufficiently picturesque.

It was mid-day, the sun had attained its highest altitude, and shed its clearest rays around ; the princely castle in all its parts, battlements, wings, cupolas and towers, presented a glorious appearance. The upper part of the town was seen in its full extent, the eye could even penetrate into parts of the lower town, and with the assistance of the telescope, distinguish the market-place, and even the very booths. It was Honorio's invariable custom to sling this indispensable instrument to his side. They took a view of the river, in its course and its descent, and of the sloping plain, and of the luxuriant country with its gentle undulations, and then of the numerous villages, for it had been from time immemorial a subject of contention how many could be counted from this spot.

Over the wide plain there reigned a calm stillness, such as is accustomed to rule at mid-day ; an hour when, according to classical phraseology, the god Pan sleeps, and all nature is breathless, that his repose may be undisturbed.

"It is not the first time," observed the Princess "that, standing upon an eminence which presents a wide extended view, I have thought how pure and peaceful is the look of holy Nature, and the impression comes upon me, that the world beneath must be free from strife and care ; but returning to the dwellings of man, be they the cottage or the palace, be they wide or circumscribed, we find that there is in truth ever something to subdue, to struggle with, to quiet and allay."

Honorio, in the meantime, had directed the telescope towards the town, and now exclaimed, "Look, look! the town is on fire in the market-place."

They looked and saw a column of smoke arising, but the glare of daylight eclipsed the flames. "The fire increases," they exclaimed, still looking through the instrument. The Princess saw the calamity with the naked eye; from time to time they perceived a red flame ascending amid the smoke. Her uncle at length exclaimed, "Let us return; it is calamitous. I have always feared the recurrence of such a misfortune."

They descended, and having reached the horses, the Princess thus addressed her old relative, "Ride forward, sir, hastily with your attendant, but leave Honorio with me, and we will follow."

Her uncle perceived the prudence and utility of this advice, and riding on as quickly as the nature of the ground would allow, descended to the open plain. The Princess mounted her steed, upon which Honorio addressed her thus: "I pray your Highness to ride slowly; the fire-engines are in the best order, both in the town and in the castle, there can surely be no mistake or error even in so unexpected an emergency. Here, however, the way is dangerous, and riding is insecure, from the small stones and the smooth grass, and in addition, the fire will no doubt be extinguished before we reach the town."

But the Princess indulged no such hope; she saw the smoke ascend, and thought she perceived a flash of lightning and heard a thunder-clap, and her mind was filled with the frightful pictures of the conflagration which her uncle's oft-repeated narrative had impressed upon her.

That calamity had indeed been dreadful, sudden and impressive enough to make one apprehensive for the repetition of a like misfortune. At midnight a fearful fire had broken out in the market-place, which was filled with booths and stalls, before the occupants of those temporary habitations had been roused from their deep slumber. The Prince himself, after a weary day's journey, had retired to rest, but rushing to the window, perceived with dismay the flames which raged around on every side and approached the spot where he stood. The houses of the market-place, crimsoned with the reflection, appeared already to burn, and threatened every instant to burst out into a general conflagration. The fierce element raged irresistibly, the beams and rafters crackled, whilst countless pieces of consumed linen flew aloft, and the burnt and shapeless rags sported in the air and looked like foul demons revelling in their congenial element. With loud cries of distress, each individual endeavoured to rescue what he could from the flames. Servants and assistants vied with their masters in their efforts to save the huge bales of goods already half consumed, to tear what still remained uninjured from the burning stalls, and to pack it away in chests, although they were even then compelled to abandon their labours and leave the whole to fall a prey to the conflagration. How many wished that the raging blaze would allow but a single moment's respite, and pausing to consider the possibility of such a mercy, fell victims to their brief hesitation. Many buildings burned on one side, while the other side lay in obscure darkness. A few determined, self-willed characters bent themselves obstinately to the task of saving something from the flames, and suffered for their heroism. The whole scene of misery and devastation was renewed in the mind of the beautiful Princess; her countenance was clouded, which had beamed so radiantly in the early morning; her eyes had lost their lustre, and even the beautiful woods and meadows around now looked sad and mournful.

Riding onwards she entered the sweet valley, but she felt uncheered by the refreshing coolness of the place. She had, however, not advanced far, before she observed an unusual appearance in the copse near the meadow where the sparkling brook which flowed through the adjacent country took its rise. She at once recognized a tiger couched in the attitude to spring, as she had seen him represented in the painting. The impression was fearful. "Fly! gracious lady," cried Honorio, "fly at once!" She turned her horse to mount the steep hill which she had just descended, but her young attendant drew his pistol, and approaching the monster, fired; unfortunately he missed his mark, the tiger leaped aside, the horse started, and the terrified beast pursued his course and followed the Princess. The latter urged her horse up the steep stony acclivity, forgetting for a moment that the pampered animal she rode was unused to such exertions. But urged by his impetuous rider, the spirited steed made a new effort, till at length, stumbling at an inequality of the ground, after many attempts to recover his footing, he fell exhausted to the ground. The Princess released herself from the saddle with great expertness and presence of mind, and brought her horse again to its feet. The tiger was in pursuit at a slow pace. The uneven ground and sharp stones appeared to retard his progress, though as Honorio approached, his speed and strength seemed to be renewed. They now came nearer to the spot where the Princess stood by her horse, and Honorio bending down, discharged a second pistol. This time he was successful and shot the monster through the head. The animal fell, and as he lay stretched upon the ground at full length, gave evidence of that might and terror, which was now reduced to a lifeless form. Honorio had leaped from his horse, and was now kneeling on the body of the hugh brute. He had already put an end to his struggles, with the hunting knife which gleamed within his grasp. He looked even more handsome and active than the Princess had ever seen him in list or tournament. Thus had he oftentimes driven his bullet through the head of the Turk in the riding-school, piercing his forehead under the turban, and carried onward by his rapid courser, he had oftentimes struck the Moor's head to the ground with his shining sabre. In all such knightly feats he was dexterous and successful, and here he had found an opportunity for putting his skill to the test.

" Despatch him quickly," said the Princess faintly, " I fear he may injure you with his claws."

" There is no danger," answered the youth, " he is dead enough, and I do not wish to spoil his skin—it shall ornament your sledge next winter."

" Do not jest at such a time," continued the Princess; "such a moment calls forth every feeling of devotion that can fill the heart."

" And I never felt more devout than now," added Honorio, " and therefore are my thoughts cheerful; I only consider how this creature's skin may serve your pleasure."

" It would too often remind me of this dreadful moment," she replied.

"And yet," answered the youth with burning cheek, "this triumph is more innocent than that in which the arms of the defeated are borne in proud procession before the conqueror."

"I shall never forget your courage and skill," rejoined the Princess, "and let me add that you may during your whole life command the gratitude and favour of the Prince. But rise, the monster is dead; rise, I say, and let us think what next is to be done."

"Since I find myself now kneeling before you," replied Honorio, "let me be assured of a grace, of a favour, which you can bestow upon me. I have oftentimes implored your princely husband for permission to set out upon my travels. He who dares aspire to the good fortune of becoming your guest, should have seen the world. Travellers flock hither from all quarters, and when the conversation turns on some town, or on some peculiar part of the globe, your guests are asked if they have never seen the same. No one can expect confidence who has not seen everything. We must instruct ourselves for the benefit of others."

"Rise," repeated the Princess; "I can never consent to desire or request anything contrary to the wish of my husband, but if I mistake not, the cause of your detention here has already been removed. It was the wish of your Prince to mark how your character should ripen, and prove worthy of an independent nobleman, who might one day be required to assert his honour abroad, as you have done hitherto here at Court, and I doubt not that your present deed of bravery will prove as good a passport as any youth can carry with him through the world."

The Princess had scarcely time to mark, that instead of an expression of youthful delight, a shade of grief now darkened his countenance, and he could scarcely display his emotion, before a woman approached, climbing the mountain hastily and leading a boy by the hand. Honorio had just risen from his kneeling posture and seemed lost in thought, when the woman advanced with piercing cries, and immediately flung herself upon the lifeless body of the tiger. Her conduct, no less than her gaudy and peculiar attire, bore evidence that she was the owner and attendant of the animal. The boy by whom she was accompanied was remarkable for his sparkling eyes and jet-black hair. He carried a flute in his hand, and he united his tears to those of his mother, whilst, with a more calm but deep-felt sorrow than she displayed, he knelt quietly at her side.

The violent expression of this wretched woman's grief was succeeded by a torrent of expostulations which rushed from her in broken sentences, reminding one of a mountain stream whose course is interrupted by impeding rocks. Her natural expressions, short and abrupt, were forcible and pathetic; it would be a vain task to endeavour to translate them into our idiom, we must be satisfied with their general meaning. "They have murdered thee, poor animal, murdered thee without cause. Tamely thou wouldest have lain down to await our arrival, for thy feet pained thee, and thy claws were powerless. Thou didst lack thy burning native sun to bring thee to maturity. Thou wert the most beautiful animal of thy kind. Who ever beheld a more noble royal tiger stretched out to sleep, than thou art as thou liest here never to rise again? When in the morning thou awokest at the earliest dawn of day, opening thy wide jaws and stretching out thy ruddy tongue, thou seemedst to us to smile; and even when a growl burst from thee, still didst thou ever playfully take thy food from the hand of a woman, or from the fingers of a child. Long did we accompany thee in thy travels, and long was thy society to us as indispensable as profitable. To us, in very truth, did food come from the ravenous, and sweet refreshment from the strong. But alas! alas! this can never be again!"

She had not quite finished her lamentations, when a troop of horsemen was observed riding in a body over the heights which led from the castle. They were soon recognized as the hunting cavalcade of the Prince, and he himself was at their head. Riding amongst the distant hills, they had observed the dark columns of smoke which obscured the atmosphere, and, pushing on over hill and dale, as if in the heat of the chase, they had followed the course indicated by the smoke, which served them as a guide. Rushing forwards, regardless of every obstacle, they had come by surprise upon the astonished group, who presented a remarkable appearance in the opening of the hills. The recognition of each other produced a general surprise, and after a short pause, a few words of explanation cleared up the apparent mystery. The Prince heard with astonishment the extraordinary occurrence, as he stood surrounded by the crowd of horsemen and pedestrian attendants. There seemed no doubt about the necessary course. Orders and commands were at once issued by the Prince.

A stranger now forced his way forward, and appeared within the circle. He was tall in figure, and attired as gaudily as the woman and her child. The members of the family recognized each other with mutual surprise and pain. But the man, collecting himself, stood at a respectful distance from the Prince, and addressed him thus :—

"This is not a moment for complaining. My lord and mighty master, the lion has also escaped, and is concealed somewhere here in the mountain; but spare him, I implore you; have mercy upon him, that he may not perish, like this poor animal."

"The lion escaped!" exclaimed the Prince. "Have you found his track?"

"Yes, sire. A peasant in the valley, who needlessly took refuge in a tree, pointed to the direction he had taken—this is the way, to the left; but perceiving a crowd of men and horses before me, I became curious to know the occasion of their assembling, and hastened forward to obtain help."

"Well," said the Prince, "the chase must begin in this direction. Load your rifles, go deliberately to work; no misfortune can happen, if you but drive him into the thick woods below us; but in truth, worthy man, we can scarcely spare your favourite: why were you negligent enough to let him escape?"

"The fire broke out," replied the other, "and we remained quiet and prepared; it spread quickly round, but raged at a distance from us. We were provided with water in abundance, but suddenly an explosion of gunpowder took place, and the conflagration immediately extended to us and beyond us. We were too precipitate, and are now reduced to ruin."

The Prince was still engaged in issuing his orders, and there was general silence for a moment, when a man was observed flying, rather than running, down from the castle. He was quickly recognized as the watchman of the artist's studio, whose business it was to occupy the dwelling and to take care of the workmen. Breathless he advanced, and a few words served to announce the nature of his business.

2 K

"The lion had taken refuge on the heights, and had lain down in the sunshine behind the lofty walls of the castle. He was reposing at the foot of an old tree, in perfect tranquillity. But," continued the man, in a tone of bitter complaint, "unfortunately, I took my rifle to the town yesterday, to have it repaired, or the animal had never risen again; his skin, at least, would have been mine, and I had worn it in triumph for my life."

The Prince, whose military experience had often served him in time of need—for he had frequently been in situations where unavoidable danger pressed on every side—observed, in reply to the man, "What pledge can you give, that if we spare your lion, he will do no mischief in the country?"

"My wife and child," answered the father, hastily, "will quiet him and lead him peacefully along, until I repair his shattered cage, and then we shall keep him harmless and uninjured."

The child seemed to be looking for his flute. It was that species of instrument which is sometimes called the soft, sweet flute, short in the mouthpiece, like a pipe. Those who understood the art of using it, could extract from it the most delicious tones.

In the meantime, the Prince inquired of the caretaker by which path the lion had ascended the mountain.

"Through the low road," replied the latter; "it is walled in on both sides, has long been the only passage, and shall continue so. Two footpaths originally led to the same point, but we destroyed them, that there might remain but one way to that castle of enchantment and beauty which is to be formed by the taste and talent of Prince Frederick."

After a thoughtful pause, during which the Prince stood contemplating the child, who continued playing softly on his flute, the former turned towards Honorio, and said:

"Thou hast this day rendered me an essential service; finish the task you have begun. Occupy the narrow road of which we have heard, hold your rifle ready, but do not shoot, if you think it likely that the lion may be driven back; but under any circumstances kindle a fire, that he may be afraid to descend in this direction. The man and his wife must answer for the consequences.."

Honorio proceeded without delay to execute the orders he had received.

The child still continued to play upon his flute. He produced no exact melody, as a mere succession of notes followed, without any precise order or artistic arrangement, yet, perhaps for this very reason, the effect seemed replete with enchantment. Every one was delighted with the simple music, when the father, full of a noble enthusiasm, addressed the assembled spectators thus:—

"God has bestowed the gift of wisdom upon the Prince, and the power of seeing that all Divine works are good, each after its kind. Behold how the rocks stand firm and motionless, proof against the effects of sun and storm. Their summits are crowned with ancient trees, and elated with the pride of their ornaments, they look round boldly far and wide. But should a part become detached, it no longer appears as before; it breaks into a thousand pieces, and covers the side of the declivity. But even there the pieces find no resting-place; they pursue their course downwards, till the brook receives them, and carries them onward to the river. Thence, unresisting and submissive, their sharp angles having become rounded and smooth, they are borne along with greater velocity from stream to stream, till they finally attain the ocean, in whose mighty depths giants abide and dwarfs abound.

"But who celebrates the praise of the Lord, whom the stars praise from all eternity? Why, however, should we direct our vision so far? Behold the bee, how he makes his provision in harvest time, and constructs a dwelling, rectangular and level, at once the architect and workman. Behold the ant, she knows her way, and loses it not; she builds her habitation of grass and earth and tiny twigs, builds it high and strengthens it with arches, but in vain,—the prancing steed approaches and treads it into nothing, destroying the little rafters and supports of the edifice. He snorts with impatience and with restlessness, for the Lord has formed the horse as companion to the wind, and brother to the storm, that he may carry mankind whither he will. But in the palm forest even he takes to flight. There, in the wilderness, the lion roams in proud majesty; he is monarch of the beasts, and nothing can resist his strength. But man has subdued his valour; the mightiest of animals has respect for the image of God, in which the very angels are formed, and they minister to the Lord and His servants. Daniel trembled not in the lions' den; he stood full of faith and holy confidence, and the wild roaring of the monsters did not interrupt his pious song."

This address, which was delivered with an expression of natural enthusiasm, was accompanied by the child's sweet music. But when his father had concluded, the boy commenced to sing with clear and sonorous voice, and some degree of skill. His parent in the meantime seized his flute, and in soft notes accompanied the child as he sung:

> " Hear the Prophet's song ascending
>   From the cavern's dark retreat,
> Whilst an Angel, earthward bending,
>   Cheers his soul with accents sweet.
> Fear and terror come not o'er him,
>   As the lion's angry brood
> Crouch with placid mien before him,
>   By his holy song subdued."

The father continued to accompany the verses with his flute, whilst the mother's voice was occasionally heard to intervene as second.

The effect of the whole was rendered more peculiar and impressive, by the child's frequently inverting the order of the verses. And if he did not, by this artifice, give a new sense and meaning to the whole, he at least highly excited the feelings of his audience :

> "Angels o'er us mildly bending,
>   Cheer us with their voices sweet,
> Hark! what strains enchant the ear!
>   In the cavern's dark retreat,
> Can the Prophet quake with fear?
>   Holy accents sweetly blending,
> Banish ev'ry earthly ill,
>   Whilst an Angel choir descending
> Executes the heavenly will."

Then all three joined with force and emphasis:

> "Since the Eternal eye, far-seeing,
>   Earth and sea surveys in peace,
> Lion shall with lamb agreeing
>   Live, and angry tempests cease.
> Warriors' sword no more shall lour,
>   Faith and Hope their fruit shall bear;
> Wondrous is the mighty power
>   Of Love, which pours its soul in prayer."

The music censed. Silence reigned around. Each one listened attentively to the dying tones, and now for the first time could one observe and note the general impression. Every listener was overcome, though each was affected in a different manner. The Prince looked sorrowfully at his wife, as though he had only just perceived the danger which had lately threatened him, whilst she, leaning upon his arm, did not hesitate to draw forth her embroidered handkerchief to dry the starting tear. It was delightful to relieve her youthful heart from the weight of grief with which she had for some time felt oppressed. A general silence reigned around, and the fears were forgotten which all had experienced both from the conflagration below and the appearance of the formidable lion above.

The repose of the whole company was first interrupted by the Prince, who made a signal to lead the horses nearer; he then turned to the woman and addressed her thus: "You think, then, to master the lion wherever you meet him, by the power of your song, assisted by that of the child and the tones of your flute, and believe that you can thus lead him harmless and uninjured to his cage?"

She protested and assured him that she would do so; whereupon a servant was ordered to show her the way to the castle. The Prince and a few of his attendants now took their departure hastily, whilst the Princess, accompanied by the rest, followed more slowly after. But the mother and the child, accompanied by the servant, who had armed himself with a rifle, hastened to ascend the mountain.

At the very entrance of the narrow road which led to the castle, they found the hunting attendants busily employed in piling together heaps of dry brushwood, to kindle a large fire.

"There is no necessity for such precaution," observed the woman; "all will yet turn out well."

They perceived Honorio at a little distance from them, sitting upon a fragment of the wall, with his double-barrelled rifle in his lap, prepared as it seemed for every emergency. But he paid little attention to the people who approached; he was absorbed in his own contemplations, and seemed engaged in deepest thought. The woman entreated that he would not permit the fire to be kindled, he, however, paid not the smallest attention to her request. She then raised her voice, and exclaimed with a loud cry: "Thou handsome youth, who killed my tiger, I curse thee not; but spare my lion, and I will bless thee."

But Honorio was looking upon vacancy; his eyes were bent upon the sun, which had finished its daily course and was now about to set.

"You are looking to the evening," cried the woman, "and you are right, for there is yet much to do; but hasten, delay not, and you will conquer. But first of all, conquer yourself." He seemed to smile at this observation—the woman passed on, but could not avoid looking round to observe him once more. The setting sun had cast a rosy glow upon his countenance; she thought she had never beheld so handsome a youth.

"If your child," said the attendant, "can, as you imagine, with his fluting and his singing, entice and tranquillize the lion, we shall easily succeed in mastering him; for the ferocious animal has lain down to sleep under the broken arch, through which we have secured a passage into the castle court, as the chief entrance has been long in ruins. Let the child then entice him into the interior, when we can close the gate without difficulty, and the child may, if he please, escape by a small winding staircase, which is situated in one of the corners. We may in the meantime conceal ourselves, but I shall take up a position which will enable me to assist the child at any moment with my rifle."

"These preparations are all needless; Heaven, and our own skill, bravery, and good fortune, are our best defence."

"But first let me conduct you by this steep ascent to the top of the tower, right opposite to the entrance of which I have spoken. The child may then descend into the arena, and there he can try to exercise his power over the obedient animal."

This was done. Concealed above, the attendant and the mother surveyed the proceeding. The child descended the narrow staircase, and soon appeared in the wide court-yard. He immediately entered into the narrow opening opposite, when the sweet sounds of his flute were heard, but these gradually diminished till at length they finally ceased. The pause was fearful—the solemnity of the proceeding filled the old attendant with apprehension, accustomed as he was to every sort of danger. He declared that he would rather engage the enraged animal himself. But the mother preserved her cheerful countenance, and leaning over the parapet in a listening attitude, betrayed no sign of the slightest fear.

At length the flute was heard again. The child had issued from the dark recess, his face beaming with triumph; the lion was slowly following, and seemed to walk with difficulty. Now and then the animal appeared disposed to lie down, but the child continued to lead him quietly along, bending his way through the half-leafless autumn-tinged trees, until he arrived at a spot which was illumined by the last rays of the setting sun. They were shedding their parting glory through the ruins, and in this spot he recommenced his sweet song, which we cannot refrain from repeating:

> "Hear the Prophet's song ascending
>   From the cavern's dark retreat,
> Whilst an Angel, earthward bending,
>   Cheers his soul with accents sweet.
> Fear and terror come not o'er him,
>   As the lion's angry brood
> Crouch with placid mien before him,
>   By his holy song subdued."

The lion in the mean time had lain quietly down, and raising his heavy paw, had placed it in the lap of the child. The latter stroked it gently and continued his chaunt, but soon observed that a sharp thorn had penetrated into the ball of the animal's foot. With great tenderness the child extracted the thorn, and taking his bright-coloured silk handkerchief from his neck, bound it round the foot of the huge creature, whilst the attentive mother, still joyfully leaning over the parapet with outstretched arms, would probably have testified her approbation with loud shouts and clapping of hands, if the attendant had not rudely seized her and reminded her that the danger was not yet completely over.

The child now joyfully continued his song, after he had hummed a few notes by way of prelude:

> "Since the Eternal eye, far-seeing,
>   Earth and sea surveys in peace,
> Lion shall with lamb agreeing
>   Live, and angry tempests cease.

Warriors' sword no more shall lour,
   Faith and Hope their fruit shall bear;
Wondrous is the mighty power
   Of Love, which pours its soul in prayer."

If it were possible to conceive that the features of so fierce
a monster, at once the tyrant of the forest and the despot of
the animal kingdom, could display an expression of pleasure
and grateful joy, it might have been witnessed upon this
occasion; and in very truth, the child, in the fulness of his
beauty, looked like some victorious conqueror, though it could
not be said that the lion seemed subdued, for his mighty power
was only for a time concealed; he wore the aspect of some
domesticated creature, who had been content to make a
voluntary surrender of the mighty power with which it was
endued. And thus the child continued to play and to sing,
transposing his verses or adding to them, as he felt inclined:

"Holy Angels, still untiring,
   Aid the good and virtuous child,
Every noble deed inspiring
   And restraining actions wild.
So the forest king to render
   Tame as child at parent's knee,
Still be gentle, kind, and tender,
   Use sweet love and melody."

THE END.

PRINTED BY HARRISON AND SONS,
London Gazette Office, St. Martin's Lane, and Orchard Street, Westminster.